AN EXPERIENTIAL APPROACH TO ORGANIZATION DEVELOPMENT

Third Edition

AN EXPERIENTIAL APPROACH TO ORGANIZATION DEVELOPMENT

DONALD F. HARVEY
Eastern Washington University

DONALD R. BROWN
Antelope Valley College

1982

Prentice Hall
Englewood Cliffs, New Jersey 07632

Library of Congress Cataloging-in-Publication Data

HARVEY, DONALD F.
    An experiential approach to organization development / Donald F.
Harvey, Donald R. Brown.—3rd ed.

    p.   cm.
    Includes index.
    ISBN 0-13-295122-3
    1. Organizational change.   1. Brown, Donald R.
II. Title.
HD58.8H37   1988
658.4′063-dc19   87-26207
                                                  CIP

Editorial/production supervision
 and interior design: *Sonia Meyer*
Cover design: *Wanda Lubelska Design*
Manufacturing buyer: *Ed O'Dougherty*

*Photos on chapter opening pages are used with
permission and by courtesy of: Hewlett-Packard
Company (Chapters 1, 2, 3, 5, 9, 11, 13, 16);
Rockwell International (Chapters 8, 12, 14);
Lockheed-California Company (Chapters 10, 15);
Bank of America (Chapter 7); Sperry Corporation
(Chapter 6); Xerox Information Systems Group
(Chapter 4).*

© 1988, 1982, 1976 by Prentice Hall
A Division of Simon & Schuster
Englewood Cliffs, New Jersey 07632

Printed in the United States of America
10   9   8   7   6   5   4   3   2   1

ISBN   0-13-295122-3   01

Prentice-Hall International (UK) Limited, *London*
Prentice-Hall of Australia Pty. Limited, *Sydney*
Prentice-Hall Canada Inc., *Toronto*
Prentice-Hall Hispanoamericana, S.A., *Mexico*
Prentice-Hall of India Private Limited, *New Delhi*
Prentice-Hall of Japan, Inc., *Tokyo*
Simon & Schuster Asia Pte. Ltd., *Singapore*
Editora Prentice-Hall do Brasil, Ltda., *Rio de Janeiro*

CONTENTS

PREFACE   **xi**

part **I**

AN OVERVIEW OF ORGANIZATION DEVELOPMENT

1   ORGANIZATION DEVELOPMENT: AN OVERVIEW   **1**

Objectives   1   Premeeting Preparation   1   Background Information   2

What Is Organization Development?   3
Why Organization Development?   5
The Evolution of Organization Development   9

The Organization Culture   11
The Socialization Process   12
The Psychological Contract   13
The Experiential Approach to Learning   14
An Overview of the Field of Study   16

Review Questions   18
Simulations

1.1 Auditioning for the "Johnny Carson" Guest Host Spot   19
1.2 The Psychological Contract   20

Summary   22

2   SYSTEMS, FUTURE SHOCK, AND PLANNED CHANGE   26

Objectives   26   Premeeting Preparation   27   Background
Information   27

A Dynamic Model of Change: The Systems Approach   28
The Organization as Sociotechnical System   31
Contingency Theory and OD   33
Future Shock and Change   33
Adaption to a Changing Environment   37
The Planned Change Process   40
A Model for Organization Change   42

Review Questions   49
Simulation

2.1 OD Consultant Behavior Profile I   49

Case Analysis Guidelines   56
Case: The Popular Professor   56
Summary   59

3   CHANGING THE CORPORATE CULTURE   62

Objectives   62   Premeeting Preparation   62   Background
Information   62

The Corporate Culture   63
The Goals and Values of OD   68

Review Questions   73
Simulation

3.1 RIF: A Concensus-Seeking Activity   74

Case: The Dim Lighting Co.   78
Summary   80

part **II**

THE ORGANIZATION DEVELOPMENT PROCESS

4   THE OD CONSULTANT: ROLE AND STYLE   83

*Objectives   83   Premeeting Preparation   83   Background
Information   83*

External and Internal Consultant Roles   *84*
The External-Internal Consulting Team   *88*
Types of Consultants   *89*
The Readiness of the Organization for OD   *92*
The Intervention Process   *93*
The Initial Intervention, Perception, and Assessment   *95*
Creating a Climate for Change   *101*
The Formalization of Operating Ground Rules   *104*
Red Flags in the Consultant-Client Relationship   *105*

Review Questions   106
Simulations

4.1 Consultant Style Matrix   107
4.2 Conflict Styles   116

Summary

5   THE DIAGNOSTIC PROCESS   122

*Objectives   122   Premeeting Preparation   122   Background
Information   123*

What Is Diagnosis?   *123*
The Process   *124*
Diagnostic Models   *128*
The Data Collection Process   *131*
The Implementation of the Program   *137*
The Analysis of Data   *137*
Evaluating the Effectiveness of Data Collection   *138*
Red Flags in the Diagnosis   *139*

Review Questions   141
Simulation

5.1 The Acquisition Decision   142

Case: The Old Family Bank   147
Summary   148

6   OVERCOMING RESISTANCE TO CHANGE   151

*Objectives   151   Premeeting Preparation   151   Background
Information   152*

The Life Cycle of Resistance to Change   *152*
Managing Change Forces   *154*
A Change Model   *157*
The Motivating Forces Toward Acceptance of a Change Program   *158*
The Resisting Forces Blocking Implementation of Change
    Programs   *160*
Consultant Strategies to Lessen Resistance   *163*

Review Questions   167
Simulations

6.1 The Enigma Company   168
6.2 Motivating and Resisting Forces   171

Case: Progress on Purpose   172
Summary   173

7   OD PROCESS SKILLS   176

*Objectives   176   Premeeting Preparation   176   Background
Information   177*

Process Consultation   *177*
Group Process   *178*
The Types of Process Interventions   *180*
The Results of Process Consultation   *182*
Active Listening   *182*
Purpose of Active Listening   *182*

Review Questions   184
Simulations

7.1 The STU Corporation   184
7.2 Trust Building   188
7.3 Process Consultation and Active Listening   191

Summary   194

8   OD INTERVENTION STRATEGIES   196

*Objectives   196   Premeeting Preparation   196   Background
Information   197*

Basic Approaches   *198*
The Integration of Change Strategies   *200*
Stream Analysis   *203*

Selecting an OD Intervention   *205*
The Major OD Intervention Techniques: An Overview   *206*

Review Questions   208
Simulation

8.1 The Franklin Company   208

Case: The Farm Bank   215
Summary   217

part **III**

THE INTERVENTION PROCESS

9   OD INTERPERSONAL INTERVENTIONS   220

Objectives   220   Premeeting Preparation   220   Background
Information   221

Laboratory Learning   *221*
Interpersonal Style—The Johari Window Model   *223*
Career Life Planning Interventions   *226*
Stress Management   *228*

Review Questions   233
Simulations

9.1 Johari Window   234
9.2 Career Life Planning   240

Case: The Sundale Club   240
Summary   243

10   OD TEAM DEVELOPMENT INTERVENTIONS   247

Objectives   247   Premeeting Preparation   247   Background
Information   248

The Team Approach   *248*
The Need for Team Development Techniques   *251*
Cohesiveness   *255*
The Team Development Process   *259*
Role Negotiation   *262*
Role Analysis   *263*

Review Questions   264
Simulations

10.1 Organization Task and Process   265

10.2 Team Building 271

Case: Steele Enterprises 274
Summary 278

11 OD INTERGROUP DEVELOPMENT INTERVENTIONS 280

Objectives 280   Premeeting Preparation 280   Background
Information 281

Collaboration and Conflict 281
Intergroup Operating Problems 283
Cooperation Versus Competition 286
Managing Conflict 288
Intergroup OD Techniques 289

Review Questions 293
Simulations

11.1 The Disarmament Game 294
11.2 Intergroup Building 301

Case: The Exley Chemical Company 302
Summary 305

12 OD GOAL SETTING 309

Objectives 309   Premeeting Preparation 309   Background
Information 310

Goal-Setting Theory 310
A Model for Goal Setting 312
Management by Objectives 314

Review Questions 320
Simulations

12.1 Organization Goal Setting 321
12.2 Managing by Objectives 325

Case: Western Utilities Company 328
Summary 330

13 OD PRODUCTIVITY INTERVENTIONS 333

Objectives 333   Premeeting Preparation 333   Background
Information 334

Quality of Work Life 334
Job Design 339
Quality Circles 344

Review Questions 347
Simulation

13.1 Paper House Production 347

Case: The Keyboard Company 354
Summary 358

14 OD SYSTEM-WIDE INTERVENTIONS 361

Objectives 361   Premeeting Preparation 361   Background
Information 362

The Grid® OD Program 363
Survey Research and Feedback 367
Likert's System 4 Management 369

Review Questions 372
Simulation

14.1 The Continental Manufacturing Company 373

Case: The Grayson Chemical Company 379
Summary 381

15 OD STRATEGY INTERVENTIONS 383

Objectives 383   Premeeting Preparation 383   Background
Information 384

The Corporate Culture 385
Cultural Strength 389
The Strategy-Culture Matrix 387
Strategic Change Management 391
Changing the Culture 392

Review Questions 393
Simulation

15.1 The GenTech Company 394

Case: The Space Electronics Corporation 400
Summary 403

part **IV**

THE CHALLENGE AND THE FUTURE

**16 ORGANIZATION DEVELOPMENT:
THE CHALLENGE AND THE FUTURE** 404

Objectives 404   Premeeting Preparation 404   Background
Information 405

Monitor and Stabilize Action Programs 406

Termination of the Consultant-Client Relationship   *408*
Emerging Issues   *412*
The Field of OD   *415*
Future Trends in Organization Development   *417*
The Future of OD   *418*

Review Questions   419
Simulations

16.1 Consultant Behavior Profile II   420
16.2 The OD Consultant   422
16.3 Unfinished Business   434

Summary   435

INDEX   **437**

PREFACE

This is a book about organization development: the management discipline aimed at improving organizational effectiveness by means of planned, systematic interventions.

Organization development (OD) is an emerging behavioral science discipline that provides a set of methodologies for systematically bringing about organization change and improvement. The goals of OD are to make an organization more effective and to enhance the opportunity for the individual to develop his or her potential.

OBJECTIVES

The basic objectives of this edition remain the same as those of the earlier editions. Our first objective is to provide the practicing manager with an integrated and comprehensive view of the field of organization development. We have attempted to include most of the current state-of-the-art OD techniques and whatever empirical findings exist on the results. The stages of a typical OD program are presented so as to provide a step-by-step description of the various techniques and problems involved in organization change efforts.

Our second objective is to present OD from an experiential learning approach; that is, the student not only reads the concepts but also practices and experiments by doing and using these techniques in a simulated organizational situation.

The OD concepts, techniques, and skills that make up this book were selected because of their usefulness to practitioners. To achieve this goal, we have had to integrate materials from a diverse set of approaches. Our strategy has been to try to integrate these various approaches to provide a comprehensive view of the field of OD.

OD is an organized body of knowledge, with its own concepts, techniques, and necessary skills, many of which are discussed in this book. The practice of OD concerns people in organizations; thus there is an emphasis on developing improved interpersonal skills.

Every successful change program is the result of a concerted group effort, and each OD failure is a failure for organization members. Therefore, people as agents of change, not forces or structures, determine whether the OD practitioner will manage change effectively. Because the OD practitioners' effectiveness results not only from the concepts learned but also from their managerial style and the way they influence others, our emphasis in this book is on the experiential approach to learning.

As students progress in the book, the simulations will allow them to continually utilize growing knowledge and experience, thereby building a foundation of management experience to carry forward into the managerial career. By analyzing successes and failures, students begin to develop the ability to learn from experience and to develop insights into organizational functioning that would normally take years to acquire.

NEW METHODOLOGIES

The manager of the future will probably be acting as a change agent and will be involved in initiating, designing, or implementing organization change programs. The material in the text will provide the manager with new methodologies and techniques for implementing change, as well as an opportunity for personal growth and development. The book is designed so that each one may assess his or her own behavior and begin setting some personal development goals. Also, opportunities are created for feedback on how effective the behavioral style is, which encourages greater effectiveness.

The text is designed so that the instructor may incorporate new methodologies into the learning situation, including simulations and cases. Video cases, such as movies, and Lightyear personal computer software, both commercially available, can be integrated into the text and suggestions are made through the Instructor's Manual for their use. The text is organized to present an overview of OD concepts and theories and provides behavioral simulations for each major stage and intervention of an OD program. This book may be used as an independent study guide for those wanting to learn more about organization change or as a comprehensive set of materials on how to initiate organization change for the practicing personnel or operating manager.

NEW FEATURES

This edition has many significant features.

1. Its approach is dynamic rather than static. Time is considered as a significant variable in changing organizations.

2. The individual member, the work team, and the organization culture are the basic units of study. Interpersonal behavior is presented as one of the most important factors in organization change.

3. The scope allows coverage of a broad range of organizations. How organizations can be changed to perform more effectively is examined in detail.

4. Effective change management is presented as the key to a more effective organization.

5. The book is organized into four clearly defined parts, providing a sequential view of the field of OD.

6. The examples and cases are drawn from situations that should be familiar to the student.

This book was designed to provide a variety of learning methods. Simulations are fun and involving, cases often make the concepts more understandable, and text readings provide a set of concepts to be applied and challenged. The book can be used as the primary text or as a supplemental text for courses at the junior, senior, or graduate level. We have successfully used the material with undergraduate management majors and M.B.A.s, as well as with graduate administration majors from many fields, including public administration, education administration, and health care. The material has also been used for management training and executive development program in a variety of fields with bankers, engineers, nurses, teachers, public administrators, military officers, production managers, and marketing managers; and at a variety of levels from first-line supervision to top management teams.

NEW MATERIAL IN THIS EDITION

First, corporate culture, goal setting, and productivity strategy interventions are the subjects of new chapters written for this edition (Chapters 3, 12, 13 and 15). These topics deserved more intensive treatment than they were given in previous editions. The new chapters represent the most recent theory, research, and applications available in the literature.

Second, material in existing chapters was updated. The subjects of systems theory, creativity and innovation, groupthink, organizational culture, approaches to leadership, quality of worklife, socialization, and other topics were added or expanded in appropriate chapters. In all cases, the new material complements existing material.

Third, new simulations were added in this edition. Because of positive reaction to these exercises in the last two editions, we increased the number of simulations in this edition to 27. We have also retained the most requested and popular end-of-chapter cases from the previous edition and added new ones, for a total of 13. Each case emphasizes a particular change issue or managerial technique. They cover a variety of different types and sizes of organizations and include problems of all levels of management.

Fourth, the Organization Development Applications have been enthusiastically received by students and instructors. The OD Applications report actual applications of the concepts and theories presented in the chapter and appear at the exact point in the text where the concept or theory is being discussed. Each of the chapters in this edition contains an OD application. Through the identification of actual organizational applications of text materials, the gap between the classroom and the real world can hopefully be narrowed.

Fifth, we have added a number of self-report questionnaires for the reader to complete. These questionnaires get the reader involved and let him or her take a close look at personal style, attitudes, and behavior patterns. We provide norms and averages so the reader can make comparisons.

Sixth, the supplements for the text are thorough and should be secured from the publisher. Both the student and instructor were considered in preparing these supplements, which add to the student's understanding and the instructor's ability to teach an exciting course. The Instructor's Manual, which includes a suggested lecture outline, transparency masters, a test bank, suggestions for running simulations, and additional simulations, provides excellent sources of in-class and out-of-class assignments.

Many other important changes have been incorporated into this edition.

1. The nature of open systems and contingencies has more thorough coverage.
2. Cases have been added at the end of chapters on topics directly related to the text material.

3. Approximately 75 percent of the simulations are new or extensively revised.

4. Review questions have been added at the end of each chapter.

5. The footnote references have been updated and expanded.

6. There is an opportunity to incorporate video cases and Lightyear software into the learning situation. Both the cases and software are readily available commercially and the Instructor's Manual provides suggested uses.

The book is organized into four major parts. Part I, An Overview of Organization Development, has been revised in a substantial way, primarily by the more complete explanation of the systems approach in Chapter 2. Part II, The Organization Development Process, focuses on the skills, techniques and roles of the OD practitioner and includes expanded material on consultant styles. Part III, The Intervention Process, has been revised and updated to reflect the state-of-the-art in the field of OD. Finally, Part IV, The Challenge and the Future, examines these aspects of the field.

We are grateful to the many people who contributed to this third edition. For assistance and encouragement offered throughout the development of the text, a special note of appreciation is extended to Management Chairman, Hugh Mills of Eastern Washington University. Many colleagues in the School of Business at Eastern Washington University have been helpful, but special thanks go to Professor Bill Barber, EWU, and Professor Neal Kneip, Gonzaga University, for support and review suggestions. Many students and managers have been involved in the development of the simulations and cases, but special appreciation goes to Ed Owens, Lynn Bjork, Colleen Bunnell, Joe Caldwell, Jim Sayles (IBM), Mike Miller (J. C. Penney), Kent Nealis (Times Mirror), and Donna Meyer (Antelope Valley Hospital Medical Center) for their suggestions.

Our sincere appreciation is also extended to Alison Reeves of Prentice Hall for her support and assistance and to Sonia Meyer for her valuable help as production editor.

Our thanks go also to Hewlett-Packard Company, Rockwell International, Lockheed-California Company, Bank of America, Sperry Corporation, and Xerox Information Systems Group for the photographs used in our chapter openings.

The authors would like to extend a public and personal note of thanks to family and friends. From Don Harvey of the authors' team: my wife, Becky, and sons Mikie, Scott, and Dave, have contributed in more ways than I can enumerate—not just in allowing the time for writing but in a form of involvement that can never be fully appreciated or repaid. And from Don Brown: my thanks go to my parents and to very special friends, Jan Schnorr and Kent Nealis, for their continued support.

Memo to: *The Readers*

From: *The Authors*

Subject: *Use of This Text*

Perhaps we can reflect on some of the things we tried to develop in this book to make your task easier. Since our major goal is to present knowledge (and yours, we hope, to acquire it), we thought it would be helpful to preview some of the learning tools so that you can use them as you progress.

First, there is a set of behavioral objectives at the beginning of each chapter. These are general guides to the major points in each chapter, and they are tied into the Review Questions provided at the end of each chapter.

In addition, throughout the text we have identified key terms and concepts for you to remember. There are OD terms and concepts which you should be able to use as you complete each chapter. For motivation: exams are often designed around these key concepts, so when a concept is introduced and defined, it will appear in italics in the text. Also, at the end of each chapter, key concepts will be listed with space for you to note the pages on which they are defined. In review, you can scan the text, define each concept for yourself, and—if you are unsure—move back into the text to clarify the meaning. Also, you can review the questions at the end of each chapter and then go back into the text for those you may have missed.

We hope these aids will be helpful to you. We have done our part, the rest is up to you.

Donald F. Harvey
Donald R. Brown

AN EXPERIENTIAL APPROACH TO ORGANIZATION DEVELOPMENT

1

ORGANIZATION DEVELOPMENT:
An Overview

I.
Objectives

Upon completing this chapter, you will be able to:

1. Define the concept of organization development and recognize the need for change.

2. Describe organization culture and understand its impact on the behavior of individuals in an organization.

3. Understand the expectations of the psychological contract formed on joining an organization.

II.
Premeeting
Preparation

Read the Background Information (Section III).

III.
Background
Information

Change is avalanching down upon our heads, and most people are utterly unprepared to cope with it. *Future shock*, the disorientation produced by super change, has important implications for organizations and managers, and preparing managers to cope with today's accelerating rate of change is the central concern of this book.[1] The modern manager must not only be flexible and adaptive in a changing environment but must also be able to diagnose problems and implement change programs.

Organizations are never completely static. They are in continuous interaction with external forces (see Figure 1.1). Changing consumer attitudes, new legislation, and technological breakthroughs all act on the organization to cause it to change. The degree of change may vary from one organization to another, but all face the need for adaptation to external forces. Many of these changes are forced upon the organization, whereas others are generated internally. Because change is occurring so rapidly, there is a need for new ways to manage. Organization development (OD) is a new discipline applying behavioral science to help organizations adapt to these changes. Organization development is aimed not only at improving the organization's effectiveness but also at enhancing the development of organization members.

This book introduces the practicing manager and the student to this new field of organization development. Its purpose is twofold: (1) to create an awareness of the changing environmental forces confronting the modern manager; and (2) to provide a foundation of knowledge and skills for those wishing to continue advanced studies toward the goal of functioning as an organizational practitioner within an organization or as an outside consultant.

Organizations are using OD techniques to increase their effectiveness and adaptiveness to changing conditions. In this chapter you will learn about this exciting new field: what OD is, why it has emerged, and some basic concepts about the organization change process. You will be introduced to the experiential approach to learning and will be given an overview of the field of study.

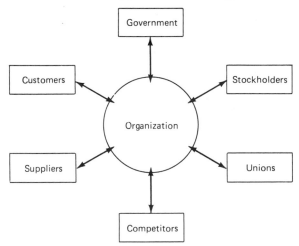

FIGURE 1.1
The Organizational Environment

WHAT IS ORGANIZATION DEVELOPMENT? ――――――――――

What makes one organization a winner, while another fails to make use of the same opportunities? In a recent study of 43 of America's best-managed companies, Thomas J. Peters and Robert H. Waterman confirm what has long been suspected: the key to survival and success lies not in the rational, quantitative approaches, but rather in a commitment to irrational, difficult-to-measure things like people, quality, and customer service.[2]

Organization development is an emerging discipline aimed at improving the effectiveness of the organization and its members by means of a systematic change program. Chester Barnard and Chris Argyris, among other management theorists, have noted that the truly effective organization is one in which both the organization and the individual can grow and develop. Such an environment may be termed a "healthy" organization, and this is what organization development is all about: making organizations healthier and more effective. These concepts apply to all types of organizations, including schools, churches, military, government, and industrial concerns.

Change is a way of life in today's organization. But organizations are also faced with maintaining a stable identity and operations in order to accomplish their primary goals. Consequently, organizations involved in managing change have found that the way in which change is handled is critical. There is a need for a systematic approach, discriminating among those features that are healthy and effective and those that are not. Erratic, short-term, unplanned, or haphazard changes may well introduce problems that did not exist before, or allow side effects of the change that may be worse than the original problem. Managers should also be aware that stability or equilibrium can contribute to a healthy state. Change just for the sake of change is not necessarily effective; in fact it may be dysfunctional.

A Definition of Organization Development ――――――――――

Organization development (OD) is defined as an attempt to achieve corporate excellence by integrating the desires of individuals for growth and development with organizational goals. According to Richard Beckhard, "organization development is an effort (1) planned, (2) organization wide, (3) managed from the top, (4) to increase organization effectiveness and health, through (5) planned interventions in the organization's processes using behavioral science knowledge."[3]

Organization development efforts, then, are planned, systematic approaches to change. They involve changes to the total organization or to relatively large segments of it. The purpose of OD efforts is to increase the effectiveness of the system, and also to develop the potential of all individual members. Finally, a series of planned behavioral science intervention activities are carried out in collaboration with organization members to help find improved ways of working together toward individual and organizational goals. Another way of understanding OD is to explain what it is not.

- *OD is not a micro approach to change.* Management development, for example, is aimed at changing individual behavior, whereas OD is focused on the macro goal of developing an organization-wide improvement in managerial style.
- *OD is more than any single technique.* Whereas OD consultants use many differing techniques, such as management training, quality circles, or job enrichment, no single technique represents the OD discipline.
- *OD does not include random or ad hoc changes.* OD is based on a systematic appraisal and diagnosis of problems, leading to specific types of change efforts.
- *OD is aimed at more than raising morale or attitudes.* OD is aimed at overall organization health and effectiveness. This may include increased participant satisfaction as one aspect of the change effort but includes other effectiveness parameters as well.

The Characteristics of Organization Development _____

To enlarge upon the definition of OD, let us examine some of the basic characteristics of OD programs (see Table 1.1). First, OD is a planned strategy to bring about organizational change. The change effort aims at specific objectives and is based on a diagnosis of problem areas.

Second, OD always involves a collaborative approach to change which includes the involvement and participation of those organization members most affected by the changes.

Third, OD programs include an emphasis on ways to improve and enhance performance.

Fourth, OD relies on a set of humanistic values about people and organizations that aims at gaining more effective organizations by opening up new opportunities for increased use of human potential.

Fifth, OD represents a systems approach concerned with the interrelationship of various divisions, departments, groups, and individuals as interdependent subsystems of the total organization. Finally, OD is based upon scientific approaches to increase organizational effectiveness.

In more general terms, organizational development is based on the notion that an organization, in order to be effective (accomplish its goal), must be more than merely efficient. It must also adapt to change.

An OD practitioner (either manager or consultant) is a person in an organization responsible for changing existing patterns to obtain more effective

TABLE 1.1 Major Characteristics of the Field of OD

Characteristics	Focal Area
1. Planned change	Change is planned by managers to achieve goals.
2. Collaborative approach	Involves collaborative approach and involvement.
3. Performance orientation	Emphasis on ways to improve and enhance performance.
4. Humanistic orientation	Emphasis upon increased opportunity and use of human potential.
5. Systems approach	Relationship among elements and excellence.
6. Scientific method	Scientific approaches supplement practical experience.

organizational performance. Organization development practitioners have come to realize that conventional training techniques are no longer sufficient for effecting the type of behavioral changes needed to create adaptive organizations. New techniques have been developed to provide participants with the competence and motivation to alter ineffective patterns of behavior.

There are many OD techniques, and any individual practitioner may rely on one or a combination of approaches. Regardless of the method selected, the objectives are to work from an overall organization perspective, thus increasing the ability of the "whole" to respond to a changing environment.

Organizations have objectives such as making profits, surviving, and growing; but individual members also have desires to achieve, unsatisfied needs to fulfill, and career goals to accomplish within the organization. OD, then, is a process for change which can benefit both the organization and the individual.

WHY ORGANIZATION DEVELOPMENT?

Why has such a fast-growing field emerged? Organizations are designed to accomplish some purpose or function and to continue doing so for as long as possible. Because of this, organizations are not necessarily intended to change.

But change can affect all types of organizations from giants like USX (formerly U.S. Steel) to the smallest business. No one can escape change. This is why managers must be skilled in organization change techniques.

There are a number of reasons why managing change is so important and necessary:

1. To change the direction of the organization in order to accelerate growth and productivity.
2. To improve the performance of weaker divisions or units.
3. To concentrate resources on priority objectives.
4. To train and develop managers to adapt to changing conditions.

At USX, for example, changing conditions are forcing the firm to become more effective in order to survive (see OD Application 1.1). In the coming decades changes in the external environment will be occurring so rapidly that organizations will need new techniques just to keep pace with the accelerated rate of innovation.

OD
Application
1.1

REMAKING USX

USX reported record losses in its 86-year history of $1.83 billion in 1986, compared to earnings of $598 million in 1985. Chairman David M. Roderick can claim to have brought USX through its most treacherous year by ending a six-month steel strike and fending off, for the time being, raider Carl C. Ichan.

Roderick is studying some of the largest U.S. companies in an effort to find acquisitions that will offset the uncertain prospects for steel. As a result of one acquisition, USX is now considered more of an oil and gas company. Roderick has announced that USX plans to convert its steel operations into a wholly owned subsidiary in order to give the company the flexibility to sell off its steel segment. But for now the major challenge is to turn its steel unit around, with its goal to earn a consistent return equal to that of the average manufacturing company.

Changes

Since becoming chairman in 1979, Roderick has imposed more change in USX than the company has ever seen. He has made three central changes:

1. *Tried to change the culture.* Roderick, who came up through the company's finance ranks, is irreverently called "the top bean counter." He has stunned production-minded managers with his "no sacred cow" edict that profitability is more important than preserving the original empird.

2. *Cut costs and inefficiencies.* Under Roderick's leadership, USX has shrunk dramatically. By 1985 he had shut down more than 150 plants and facilities, reducing steel-making capacity by more than 30 percent. He cut white-collar jobs by 54 percent. And by early 1987 he had cut capacity another 27 percent. That reduction translated into about 5,000 fewer employees, who joined the 23,000 workers already on indefinite layoff.

3. *Acquired new companies.* In one of his boldest moves, Roderick acquired Marathon Oil Co. for $5.9 billion, thus recasting the USX image into more of an oil company than a steel producer. The change in name from U.S. Steel to USX was to help alter the public and employee's perception of what the company was all about.

But for all the changes Roderick brought about, USX is still confronted by the inefficiencies, poor management, and hostile labor relations that troubled it for decades.

Corporate Culture

Roderick's central challenge is to transform one of corporate America's most hierarchical, bureaucratic managements into a lean, aggressive, market-driven team. Among his challenges include:

1. *Changes*. For his part, Roderick contends that he is on his way to creating "a new U.S. Steel." Adds J. Bruce Johnson, executive vice-president for employee relations, "We've been required to shed yesterday."

2. *Culture*. Altering a culture cast over 75 years could take a decade, if not a generation.

3. *Management style*. A "militaristic" management style has blocked change. The small amount of feedback that existed was often lost as it passed through a labyrinth of bureaucracy.

In summary, USX is faced with changing an ingrained, old-fashioned corporate culture.

Questions:
1. Do you agree with Roderick that USX needs to make changes?
2. Would organization development be appropriate in situations like this?

Sources: J. Ernest Beazley, "USX Posts Loss of $1.42 Billion for 4th Quarter," *The Wall Street Journal*, January 28, 1987, p. 3; J. Ernest Beazley, "USX to Reduce Its Steelmaking Capacity by 27%," *The Wall Street Journal*, February 5, 1987; Gregory L. Miles and Steven J. Dryden, "One More Chorus of the Steelyard Blues," *Business Week*, January 12, 1987, p. 81; Gregory L. Miles and Chuck Hawkins, "Roderick's Plan for an Encore Will Not Wow the Street," *Business Week*, February 2, 1987, p. 32; James Risen, "USX Will Close 4 Mills, Cut 3,700 More Jobs in 3 States," *Los Angeles Times*, February 5, 1987, Business Section, p. 1; and "The Toughest Job in Business," *Business Week*, February 25, 1985.

While many organizations have been able to keep pace with changes in information technology, few firms have been able to adapt to changing social and cultural conditions.

In a dynamic environment, change is unavoidable. The pace of change has become so rapid today that it is difficult to adjust or compensate for one change before another is necessary. The technological, social, and economic environment is rapidly changing, and an organization will be able to survive only if it can effectively respond to these changing demands.

Given this increasingly complex environment, it becomes even more critical for management to identify and respond to forces of social and technical change. In attempting to manage today's organizations, many executives find that insufficient consideration of the changing environment in the past is creating problems for them. For example, the Singer Corporation lost a substantial portion of the sewing machine market because it reacted too slowly to technological changes in its product line and has now been bypassed by its competitors.[4] USX, frequently criticized as "slow-moving, parochial, and autocratic," now finds itself with some of the oldest facilities in the industry and is experiencing plant shutdowns because of exorbitant operating costs.[5]

Companies must attract, motivate, and hold on to effective employees who can achieve high levels of performance. John F. Cunningham resigned as president of Wang Laboratories thus leaving a job that paid over $400,000 annually because he wanted the challenge and autonomy of a smaller high-tech firm.[6] In this case, Wang lost a valuable employee because top management had become too rigid in their structure and methods of operation. They failed to perceive the need to allow individuals to fulfill personal objectives as well as attaining company goals. The loss of key managers can greatly affect the performance of an organization and alter its ability to attract and develop new leadership.

The Emergence of OD

Organization development is one of the primary means of creating more adaptive organizations. Warren Bennis, a leading OD practitioner, has suggested three factors underlying the emergence of OD:

1. *The need for new organizational forms.* Organizations tend to adopt a form that is most appropriate to a particular time, and the current rate of change requires more adaptive forms.
2. *The focus on cultural change.* Because each organization forms a culture—a system of beliefs and values—the only real way to change is to alter this organizational culture.
3. *The increase in social awareness.* Because of the changing social climate, tomorrow's employee will no longer accept autocratic styles of management; therefore, greater social awareness is required in the organization.[7]

Today's managers exist in shifting organizational structures and can be the central force in initiating change and establishing the means for adaptation. Most organizations strive to be creative, efficient, and highly competitive, maintaining a leading edge in their respective fields rather than following trends set by others. Effective managers are vital to the continuing self-renewal and ultimate survival of the organization. The consultant (manager) must recognize when changes are occurring in the external environment and possess the necessary competence to bring about change when it is needed. The manager must also be aware of the internal system and recognize that the major element in planned change is the organizational culture: the feelings, norms, and behaviors of its members.

THE EVOLUTION OF ORGANIZATION DEVELOPMENT

It is not within the scope of this book to provide a detailed history of OD, but a brief explanation of the evolution of this field may give you a better understanding of its application today. Organization development has evolved over the past 30 years from the application of behavioral science knowledge and techniques to solving organizational problems. What has become OD started in the late 1940s at MIT and is deeply rooted in the pioneering work of applied social scientists such as Kurt Lewin, and also strongly influenced by the work of psychologists such as Carl Rogers and Abraham Maslow. The term *organization development* is widely attributed to Robert Blake and Jane Mouton (the originators of the Managerial Grid) and Herbert Shepard (a leading OD pioneer); however, Richard Beckhard (an OD consultant) claims this distinction as well. Regardless of who first coined the term, it emerged about 1957 and is generally conceded to have evolved from two basic sources: the application of laboratory methods by National Training Laboratories (NTL), and the survey research methods originated by the Survey Research Center. Both methods were pioneered by Kurt Lewin at MIT in about 1945.

NTL—Laboratory-Training Methods

In the late 1940s and early 1950s laboratory-training methods were developed and applied by a group of behavioral scientists at Bethel, Maine. Douglas McGregor (Theory X and Theory Y), working with Richard Beckhard, began applying laboratory-training methods to industry, at General Mills in 1956 and at Union Carbide in 1957. At Union Carbide, McGregor and John Paul Jones (an internal consultant) formed the first internal OD consulting group.

About this same time, Herbert Shepard and Robert Blake were initiating a series of applied behavioral science interventions at Esso, using mainly laboratory-training techniques (see Chapter 9) to improve work team processes. These early training sessions provided the basis for what Blake and Mouton later developed as an instrumented training system they called the Managerial Grid (see Chapter 14). The success of these programs led to a dissemination of such efforts to other corporations.

Survey Research and Feedback

About the same time, a group at the Survey Research Center at the University of Michigan began to apply to organizations the action research model of

Kurt Lewin. Rensis Likert and Floyd Mann administered an organization-wide survey to Detroit Edison Co., involving the systematic feedback of data to participating departments (see Chapter 14). They used what is termed an "interlocking series of conferences," feeding data back to the top management group and then down to work teams throughout the organization.

Since that time, many organizations have used the survey feedback approach. General Motors, for example, has reported success in applying Likert's survey feedback approach to organizational improvement.

In summary, the major sources of current OD practice were the pioneering work at NTL (laboratory-training techniques) and the Survey Research Center (survey feedback methods). This brief look at the past is important because OD is a new and still developing field, and you as a future OD practitioner may build upon these earlier foundations in pioneering other new approaches.

The Extent of OD Applications

From these early beginnings OD has experienced a rapid growth. A growing number of organizations worldwide are applying OD techniques and many, including most major corporations, have formed internal OD consulting groups.

The OD Network, an organization of OD practitioners, has been in existence for only a little over two decades and has grown to a membership of over 2,000 members. The National Training Laboratories, American Psychological Association, American Society for Training and Development, and Academy of Management all have professional divisions relating to organization development. The first doctoral program for training OD specialists, called the Organizational Behavior Group, was started by Shepard in 1960 at the Case Institute of Technology (now the Department of Organization and Administration at Case Western Reserve University). Shepard applied these OD techniques, in an educational setting, to the development of OD practitioners. The Organizational Behavior Group has since graduated over 100 specialists, who are involved in teaching and consulting throughout the world. Other universities with graduate programs bearing on OD include Brigham Young, Harvard, MIT, Southern Methodist, UCLA, University of Washington, Gonzaga, Pepperdine, Eastern Washington University, and Yale, with many others beginning to include OD in the curriculum.

Organization development is an exciting and rapidly growing field. OD efforts have grown into a multitude of differing approaches and are now applied in a number of organizations around the world by an expanding number of OD practitioners.

THE ORGANIZATION CULTURE

One element of an organization system which a manager needs to understand is the organization culture. The term *culture* refers to those elements of a specific civilization, society, or group that are its distinguishing characteristics. As B. F. Skinner has commented: "A culture is not the behavior of the people 'living in it'; it is the 'it' in which they live—contingencies of social reinforcement which generate and sustain their behavior."[8] The *organization culture* includes the language, dress, patterns of behavior, value system, feelings, attitudes, interactions, and group norms of the members. You may examine the patterns of behavior on your campus or in your company. How do people dress or wear their hair? What jargon or unique terms are used? (See B. C. comic strip) These are the elements that make up a culture: the accepted patterns of behavior.

Norms are the organized and shared ideas regarding what members should do and feel, how this behavior should be regulated, and what sanctions should be applied when behavior does not coincide with social expectations. The values and behaviors of each organization are also unique, as shown by Peter Gent's description of professional football in *North Dallas Forty* or Arthur Hailey's description of the Detroit automobile industry in *Wheels*.[9] Some patterns of behavior may be functional and may facilitate the accomplishment of organization goals. Other patterns of behavior or cultural norms may actually inhibit or restrict the accomplishment of organization goals.

It is helpful to look at the types of norms that exist in an organization to gain a better understanding of the culture of that organization. Norms generally are enforced only for behaviors that are viewed as most important by most group members.[10] Norms essential to accomplishing the organization's objec-

Source: B.C. by permission of Johnny Hart and Creators Syndicate, Inc.

tives are called *pivotal norms*. Norms that support and contribute to the pivotal norms but are not essential to the organization's objectives are called *peripheral norms*; for example, norms requiring a student to conform to a certain dress code are peripheral. Pivotal and peripheral norms constantly confront an individual in an organization, and he or she must decide whether or not to conform. The pressure to conform to these norms varies, allowing individuals some degree of freedom in responding to these organizational pressures depending on how they perceive the rewards or punishments. The organization also has latitude in the degree of conformity it requires of its members.

THE SOCIALIZATION PROCESS

To function effectively, a manager or a member must be aware of the norms within the organization. He or she must recognize how sharply norms are defined and how strongly enforced. The individual's initial entry into any new situation often results in some degree of anxiety or stress. The more closely an individual can relate the new situation to previous situations, the less anxiety will be felt. The less the individual can relate a situation to other situations, the greater are the feelings of anxiety and discomfort.

While the individual is experiencing a new situation, the organization may be attempting to influence the person. If a new member comes to an organization expecting to find a certain set of norms, he or she is looking for those expectations to be affirmed. If these expectations reasonably closely reflect the actual norms of that organization, the integration process for both the new member and the organization is relatively painless.

The new member often finds that the norms are unclear, confusing, and restrictive. As a result, he or she may react in several different ways when entering an organization (see Table 1.2). At one extreme the new member may choose to conform to all the norms of the organization, resulting in uniformity of behavior and complete acceptance of organization values. In an organization this conformity may result in stagnation, nonresponsiveness, and a loss of creativeness. At the other extreme the new member may choose to rebel, to reject all values, or to leave the organization altogether.

Another less obvious alternative is for the new member to accept the piv-

TABLE 1.2 The Basic Responses to Socialization

Type 1: Rebellion	Rejection of all values and norms
Type 2: Creative individualism	Acceptance only of pivotal values and norms; rejection of all others
Type 3: Conformity	Acceptance of all values and norms

Source: Edgar H. Schein, "Organization Socialization and the Profession of Management," *Industrial Management Review*, 9 (1968), p. 8.

otal norms and seriously question the peripheral norms, which Schein has termed *creative individualism*. This would be the ideal behavior for a healthy and effective organization, but it is often difficult for a newcomer to correctly determine which norms are peripheral and which are pivotal. What may be a pivotal norm in one department may be peripheral or not a norm at all in another department of the same organization. Since norms are changing and dynamic, it requires an awareness on the part of the organization member to discern the differences between pivotal and peripheral norms.

Only the more healthy organizations allow their members to challenge the norms. The aim of OD is to develop an organization climate that is appropriate to its mission and its members. In a sense, OD involves changing the culture of organizations and work groups so that a more effective means of interacting, relating, and problem solving will result. OD is involved in developing an organization to the point that it feels comfortable in allowing its members to openly examine the norms, both pivotal and peripheral, with the ultimate goal of building a more effective organization. The reaction of the individual to these norms results in the formation of an unwritten agreement with the organization.

THE PSYCHOLOGICAL CONTRACT

Psychological contract may be defined as an unwritten agreement between individuals and the organization of which they are members.[11] It describes certain expectations that the organization has of the individual and the individual's expectations of the organization. Because the two parties are growing and changing, the contract must be open-ended, so that old issues and new issues may be renegotiated.

An organization has certain expectations of its members. If it is a business organization, certain expectations of member behavior will probably be spelled out very clearly. It undoubtedly expects its members to be on the job during certain hours of the day. It is probably concerned with quality and quantity of work, loyalty, appearance, and various other things unique to the organization. For the organization to be satisfied, the individual will need to comply to some degree with the expectations. In other words, the organization has certain requirements, and the individual must do certain things to meet those requirements if there is to be a lasting and healthy relationship. In many instances, these unfulfilled expectations result in high turnover, absenteeism, sabotage, and worker alienation.[12]

Similarly, the individual has certain expectations of the organization. An individual may expect to gain work experience, security, and advancement. The individual probably expects to have an opportunity to meet people, make friends, and form social relationships; and undoubtedly expects remuneration from the organization. For the individual to be satisfied and stay, the organization will have to meet the individual's expectations.

When either the organization's or individual's expectations are not being satisfied adequately by the other party, friction and difficulties may develop. If these problems cannot be solved, they may culminate in the individual leaving the organization by either his or her own or the organization's choice. All too often, the problem is solved by not solving it: it takes too much effort to reach a real solution, so both parties just continue with a tenuous and unharmonious relationship.

In some psychological contracts between the organization and the individual, key expectations may not even be addressed. One or both of these parties may assume that the other party agrees to some unstated expectations. The phrase "it is intuitively obvious to the most casual observer" may be the underlying assumption of one or both parties. Such unstated or assumed expectations can lead to an organization manned by individuals who feel cheated or managers who feel disappointed in their subordinates. To avoid such misunderstandings, it is suggested that both parties—the members and the representatives of the organization—form a psychological contract that is continually being renegotiated.

THE EXPERIENTIAL APPROACH TO LEARNING

To learn OD techniques, a manager or student needs both the knowledge of content material and the experience of putting theory into practice. Consequently, to create a learning environment for the field of organization development at either the undergraduate or graduate level, the emphasis should be on experience.[13] In this book you will be experiencing OD techniques by means of behavioral simulations at the same time that you are learning OD theories.

You will perhaps discover a different approach to the study of organizational change. Many courses in OD approach change in a structured and traditional manner. By means of lectures and readings, useful concepts and theories are presented to the student, whose role is largely passive. This book utilizes an innovative and significantly different approach to teaching OD: the *experiential approach*. It is based on learning OD techniques by experiencing simulated organizational situations. You will actually experience situations in which you are developing a relationship with a client or diagnosing a problem rather than simply reading about them.

The Basic Concepts of Experiential Learning

Experiential learning is based upon three basic concepts:

1. You learn best when you are involved in the learning experience.

2. Concepts have to be experienced or discovered by you, the learner, if they are to change your behavior.

3. Your commitment to learning will be greatest when you are responsible for setting your own learning objectives.

In the experiential approach, the major responsibility for learning is placed upon you, the learner. You will determine your own learning objectives and influence how the class goes about achieving these objectives. You set your own goals, decide which theories you want to learn, practice the skills or techniques you want to improve, and develop the behavioral style you want to develop.

Experiential learning also involves an active rather than a passive role. Often you may sit in a class, listen, take notes, or perhaps daydream while the instructor "does his or her thing" for an hour. In this class you will be actively deciding what to do and how to do it. You will be doing, communicating, and participating in learning. You will find that you cannot learn in isolation. You are dependent upon your fellow students and they upon you for ideas, reactions, experiences, and feedback about behavior.

Learning OD Practitioner Skills _____

What is different about the experiential learning process? First, you will generate from your own experience in this class a set of concepts that will guide your behavior. These concepts will be continually modified over time and in various managerial situations to improve your effectiveness. The experiential learning process can be presented as a four-stage cycle (see Figure 1.2):

1. *Gaining conceptual knowledge and theories*—you will be reading about OD concepts and theories and doing pre-class preparation.

2. *Activity in a behavioral simulation*—you will be problem solving, making decisions, and communicating, actively practicing the concepts and theories.

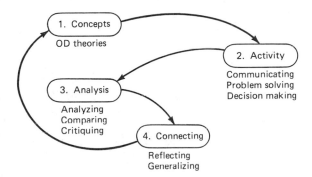

FIGURE 1.2
Schematic Diagram of Experiential Learning Cycle

3. *Analysis of activity*—you will be analyzing, critiquing, and discussing the way you solved problems, and comparing the results of different approaches.

4. *Connecting the theory and activity with prior on-the-job or life situations*—you will be writing a short analysis of each activity, a change analysis connecting your learning, reflecting upon the results, and generalizing into the future.[14]

"Student-centered" learning places the learning responsibility upon you. There will be an opportunity in the class for a high level of participation and for a challenging learning experience. Small-group learning environments will be formed wherein you may share learning with others, thus encountering feedback. Each of the learning units presents a conceptual background and a framework for a behavioral simulation. The focal point for each chapter is the action-oriented behavioral simulation.

As part of the experiential learning model in OD, feelings and emotions represent important data for learning. Open and authentic relationships in which you share your feelings with others and provide honest feedback are a necessary part of the learning situation. Each chapter is organized to help you learn concepts and skills, and each provides cases, simulations, and diagnostic instruments to help you learn more about OD. Although experiential learning can be a stimulating activity, it is important to remember that you learn from the combination of theory and experience.[14]

AN OVERVIEW OF THE FIELD OF STUDY

In this book we present the field of organization development—both theory and practice. The material has been selected to provide you with most of what is known at this time about the field of OD: the current state of the art. This includes issues, critiques, and controversy as well, for the field of OD is itself evolving and being questioned.

The book is intended to assist the participant, the manager, and the practitioner in understanding the strategies and techniques of OD and moves from the more basic elements to the more complex. The topic coverage is shown in Figure 1.3, which also identifies the chapters within which each topic area is discussed. The arrows and feedback loops show the notion of interrelationship among the various sections.

Part I, An Overview of Organization Development, introduces the concepts of planned change, future shock, and organization development. This includes what OD is, why it has emerged, and an overview of the OD process as a framework for the remainder of the book.

In Part II, The OD Process, we examine the skills and process of the OD

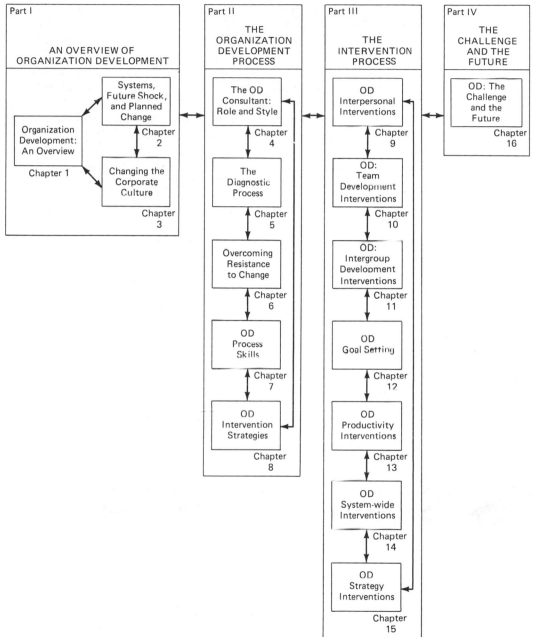

Part I

AN OVERVIEW OF
ORGANIZATION DEVELOPMENT

Organization
Development:
An Overview

Chapter 1

Systems,
Future Shock,
and Planned
Change

Chapter
2

Changing the
Corporate
Culture

Chapter
3

Part II

THE
ORGANIZATION
DEVELOPMENT
PROCESS

The OD
Consultant:
Role and Style

Chapter
4

The
Diagnostic
Process

Chapter
5

Overcoming
Resistance
to Change

Chapter
6

OD
Process
Skills

Chapter
7

OD
Intervention
Strategies

Chapter
8

Part III

THE
INTERVENTION
PROCESS

OD
Interpersonal
Interventions

Chapter
9

OD:
Team
Development
Interventions

Chapter
10

OD:
Intergroup
Development
Interventions

Chapter
11

OD
Goal Setting

Chapter
12

OD
Productivity
Interventions

Chapter
13

OD
System-wide
Interventions

Chapter
14

OD
Strategy
Interventions

Chapter
15

Part IV

THE
CHALLENGE
AND THE
FUTURE

OD: The
Challenge
and the
Future

Chapter
16

FIGURE 1.3 An Overview of this Book

practitioner. This includes the nature and role of the OD practitioner/consultant and an overall classification of OD techniques and strategies.

Part III, The Intervention Process, covers in considerable detail the OD intervention techniques and their application in OD programs, including interpersonal, team, intergroup, and system-wide interventions.

Part IV, OD: The Challenge and the Future, the concluding section, examines the end of the OD process and discusses its future prospects and problems.

We hope you find this approach interesting, and that it answers some significant questions about OD, and raises additional questions regarding this dynamic field. Basically, there is an opportunity for you to improve your consultant skills, gain an overall grasp of OD, and learn to make better predictions about the implications and consequences of any future change activities that you may undertake or be involved in.

REVIEW QUESTIONS

1. How would you define "organization development"?

2. Identify and demonstrate the uses of the psychological contract.

3. Compare and contrast planned versus unplanned change.

4. Read a book or view a video movie and identify organization culture and norms. (for example, *North Dallas Forty*, or *The Betsy*).

KEY WORDS AND CONCEPTS

Define and be able to use the following:

Disequilibrium	Peripheral norms
Organization culture	Creative individualism
Norms	Psychological contract
Pivotal norms	Organization development

**IV.
Simulations**

*SIMULATION 1.1 AUDITIONING FOR THE "JOHNNY CARSON SHOW" GUEST
HOST SPOT.*

Total time suggested: 1 hour.

The goal of this exercise is to begin building trust within the group by
sharing information about yourself with others.

A. Purpose

The purpose is to introduce your partner to the class with a focus on positive
accomplishments, yet to add some humor and demonstrate your own "guest
host" style.

B. Procedures

Step 1   Members form into dyads (pairs).
Step 2   Each dyad member (A) interviews their partner (B) to find out who
she/he is. The purpose is for you to gain enough information to introduce the
other person to the group with an emphasis on behavior. The partners then
reverse roles, with B interviewing A. The following questions are provided as a
departure point for your discussion:

1. What are strengths, past accomplishments, highlights of
    career?
2. What are likes, dislikes?
3. What is astrological sign, favorite color, music, etc.?
4. What are goals for the class?
5. What background experiences or resources can they con-
    tribute?
6. Anything not covered above?

Time suggested for Steps 1 and 2: 20 minutes.

Step 3   The total group is re-formed. Each person (A) then introduces her/
his partner. The class may ask questions to find more relevant information
about B. This proceeds around the class until each partner has been introduced.

At the end of the introductions, how many potential guest hosts did you
discover?

Step 4   Meeting with the entire class, discuss the following questions:

1. Based on the introductions, can you foresee the formation
    of any norms?
2. In the introduction process, did you learn more about the
    person being introduced or the person doing the introduc-
    tion?
3. What seems to be the type and level of participation of the
    members?

Time suggested for Steps 3 and 4: 40 minutes.

SIMULATION 1.2   THE PSYCHOLOGICAL CONTRACT

Total time suggested: 1 hour, 25 minutes.

A. Purpose

The goal of this exercise is to make explicit and share some of the major expectations and obligations between students and instructor.[15] It provides an opportunity for the instructor to find out what the class expects and for the students to learn what the instructor expects.

B. Procedures

Part A   *Instructor's Interview of Students*
Step 1   The class forms into groups of four or five persons.
Step 2   Each group elects one person as representative.
Step 3   Each group prepares its representative for the interview, and should be sure that they understand the group's position. (See the Suggested Question Guide for Instructor's Interview of Students.)
Time suggested for Steps 1 to 3: 15 minutes.
Step 4   The representatives, one from each group, meet with the instructor. The instructor interviews them about their expectations while the rest of the class observes.
Time suggested for Step 4: 20 minutes.

SUGGESTED QUESTION GUIDE FOR INSTRUCTOR'S INTERVIEW OF STUDENTS

1. What are your objectives for this course?

   a. To learn theories?
   b. To reach some desired level of knowledge?
   c. To learn new skills?
   d. To gain new behaviors?
   e. To get a good grade?
   f. To get required credit hours?

2. How can the instructor best help you to achieve your goals?

   a. By giving lectures?
   b. By assigning and discussing readings?
   c. By giving exams?
   d. By leading seminar discussions?
   e. By relating personal experiences?

   f. By letting you work on your own?

   g. By being a stern task master?

   h. By being warm and supportive?

3. How can other class members help you achieve your goals?

   a. By sharing prior experiences?

   b. By participating in group discussions?

   c. By coming to class prepared?

   d. By sharing educational background?

   e. By doing nothing?

   f. By being enthusiastic and supportive?

   g. By being critical?

   h. By being flattering?

   i. By giving honest appraisals?

4. How should class members be evaluated?

   a. By quizzes, exams, and tests?

   b. By instructor?

   c. By peers?

   d. By quantity or quality of work?

5. How should the class be motivated and how would you in reality act toward this motivation?

   a. By self-motivation?

   b. By peer pressure?

   c. By instructor pressure?

   d. By class interest?

   e. By grade pressure?

6. What is the best thing that could happen in this class?

Part B *Students' Interview of Instructor*
Step 1 The class forms into the same groups.
Step 2 Elect a different representative.
Step 3 Each group discusses any questions it would like its representative to ask the instructor. He/she should be sure to understand the group's questions and concerns. (See the Suggested Question Guide for Students' Interview of Instructor.)[16]
Time suggested for Steps 1 to 3: 15 minutes.
Step 4 The representatives, one from each group, interview the instructor to clarify the instructor's expectations of the class.
Time suggested for Step 4: 20 minutes.

It might be helpful to incorporate into Step 4 the following: The representatives and the instructor should write on the blackboard a concensus of course objectives. This will not only reaffirm and support objectives listed in the syllabus (by allowing the class to come up with the objectives), but will let the students and instructor delete or add other objectives which they feel may be important to the OD learning process.

SUGGESTED QUESTION GUIDE FOR STUDENTS' INTERVIEW OF INSTRUCTOR

You may ask the instructor *any* questions you feel are relevant to effective learning. Some areas you may want to discuss are:

1. How do people learn?
2. What are expectations about attendance?
3. What is the philosophy of evaluation? How are students evaluated?
4. What is the instructor's role in the class?
5. What stereotypes about students are held?
6. Is there anything else that you feel is important?

Part C *Identifying and Establishing Norms*
Step 1 Meeting in plenary session, do or discuss the following:

1. Identify the pivotal and peripheral norms that are being established.
2. Which of these norms are functional or dysfunctional to the class?
3. Which of these norms would you like to change?
4. Do you have any additional behaviors you would like to see become norms?

Step 2 For the norms you would like to change, make some specific plans for the changes.
Time suggested for Steps 1 and 2: 15 minutes.

**V.
SUMMARY**
This chapter has focused on several major issues. One is that organizations operate in a dynamic and changing environment and consequently must be adaptive. You have been introduced to the emerging field of organization development (OD) and the ways it is used to improve organizational effectiveness.

One of the manager's most difficult tasks is initiating organization change.

The manager must be sensitive to changes in markets, products, and competition and be aware of the need for an adaptive and flexible organization. The first step in the change process is an awareness that a problem exists.

You have had an opportunity to experience the need for organization change in this class meeting. Students frequently complain about the lack of effectiveness and learning in the classroom. In OD we call this the awareness of a problem. The university environment is changing, and today's student is not the same as the student who attended the university 10 or 20 years ago. Today's students' backgrounds, their motivation, and their expectations are different, but they face basically the same learning environment that students experienced 20 years ago.

Entering a class for the first time is very similar to the first day on the job. You may decide to rebel and reject the classroom norms, you may conform by accepting classroom norms, or you may respond with creative individualism.

In this class your role will be active. You will be an active participant, and your degree of learning and that of your fellow class members depends to a large degree upon your involvement and contributions. In this session you have become aware of the potential within other individuals and within yourself, and of the factors of organization culture and norms. We create and maintain the culture and norms, and we can change them. Frequently, organizations must change these attitudes, values, beliefs, and behaviors if they are to become more effective.

In the classroom students often feel that a course is boring, dull, and unsatisfying. Instructors often feel similarly: that students are lazy, apathetic, and immature. It is often easier to sit back passively and complain rather than attempt to change the situation. Students become accustomed to placing full responsibility for learning upon the instructor. When they are confronted with an opportunity to express expectations and to participate in setting learning goals, students may become confused, suspicious, or frustrated. Yet both students and instructor share objectives and responsibility for the learning environment.

In this class you have examined the organization culture and the norms. In the simulation you have experienced the formation of a psychological contract. As a result of the contract formation process, many underlying expectations have been brought out into the open and explained, and the interdependence and shared responsibility of student and instructor have been demonstrated.

Organization development is the discipline that applies behavioral science techniques to management problems. Since the essential task of management is to deal with change, it is the purpose of this book to better prepare managers for this task. We have found that this can best be accomplished by using the experiential approach—an approach that differs significantly from the traditional lecture-exam approach. We think you will enjoy it.

NOTES

1. See Alvin Toffler, *The Third Wave* (New York: Random House, Inc., 1980); and John Naisbitt, *Megatrends* (New York: Warnerlite Books, Inc., 1982).

2. See Thomas J. Peters and Robert H. Waterman, Jr., *In Search of Excellence* (New York: Harper & Row, Publishers, Inc., 1982).

3. Richard Beckhard, *Organizational Development: Strategies and Models* (Reading, Mass.: Addison-Wesley Publishing Co., Inc., 1969), p. 9.

4. "Behind the Snafu at Singer," *Fortune*, November 5, 1979, p. 76.

5. See James Risen, "USX Will Close 4 Mills, Cut 3,700 More Jobs in 3 States," *Los Angeles Times*, February 5, 1987, Business Section, p. 1; "Getting by without a Tin Cup," *Fortune*, December 31, 1979, p. 13; and "Getting in Trim," *The Wall Street Journal*, January 31, 1980, p. 1.

6. "Why Wang's 'American Son' Left Home," *Business Week*, August 5, 1985, p. 30.

7. Warren Bennis, *Organization Development: Its Nature, Origins and Prospects* (Reading, Mass.: Addison-Wesley Publishing Co., Inc., 1969).

8. B. F. Skinner, *Contingencies of Reinforcement* (Englewood Cliffs, N.J.: Prentice-Hall, Inc., 1969); p. 13.

9. Peter Gent, *North Dallas Forty* (New York: William Morrow & Co., Inc., 1973); and Arthur Hailey, *Wheels* (New York: Doubleday & Co., Inc., 1979).

10. Edgar H. Schein, "Coming to a New Awareness of Organizational Culture," *Sloan Management Review*, Winter 1984, pp. 3–16; Daniel C. Feldman, "The Development of Group Norms," *Academy of Management Review*, 9, no. 1 (1984), 47–53.

11. Edgar H. Schein, *Organizational Psychology* (Englewood Cliffs, N.J.: Prentice-Hall, Inc., 1970), pp. 76–79.

12. Robert W. Goddard, "The Psychological Contract," *Management World*, 13, no. 7 (August 1984), 12.

13. According to C. R. Christensen of Harvard Business School: "Our theory is that management skills are largely self-discovered," adding that Harvard students are assumed to be bright enough to absorb theory from books and apply it in practice. He likens the teaching of management to the surgeon-cadaver type of medical instruction, conducted in an atmosphere where students can make mistakes and learn without too much worry about immediate consequences. See "The Executive Needs a Catholicity of Interest," *Business Week*, May 4, 1974, p. 54.
S. P. Robbins suggested that conflict is the area where there is the most difference between what is taught as management theory and what actually exists in organizations. Therefore, power and conflict must be central topics in studying management. See "Reconciling Management Theory with Management Practice," *Business Horizons*, 20, no. 1 (February 1977), 38–47.

14. D. A. Kolb observes: "Managerial education will not be improved by eliminating theoretical analysis or relevant case problems. Improvement will come through integration of the scholarly and practical learning styles." "Management and the Learning Process," *California Management Review*, 18, no. 3 (Spring 1976), 21–31. Several management schools experimenting with ways of encouraging intuitive and creative approaches to management because of feelings that systematic and logical thinking can lead only so far. See "B-School Buzzword: Creativity," *Business Week*, August 8, 1977, p. 66.

15. This exercise is adapted from David A. Kolb, Irwin M. Rubin, and James M. McIntyre, *Organizational Psychology: An Experiential Approach*, 2nd ed. (Englewood Cliffs, N.J.: Prentice-Hall, Inc., 1974), pp. 9–17.

16. For some interesting ideas and approaches, see William P. Ferris, Russell Funelli, and Peter Hess, "Innovative Evolution Techniques," paper presented at OBTS Conference, 1982.

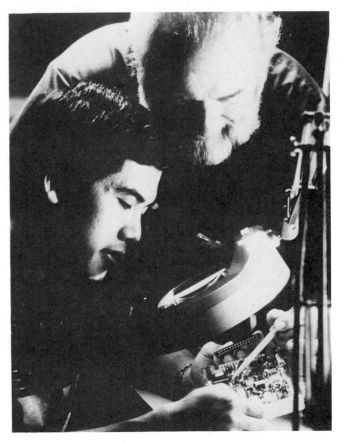

2

SYSTEMS, FUTURE SHOCK, AND PLANNED CHANGE

I.

Objectives

Upon completing this chapter, you will be able to:

1. Recognize the inevitability of change and the factors contributing to an accelerating rate of change.

2. Identify the ways in which an organization may adapt to change.

3. Determine individual and group methods of coping with change.

4. Understand and apply the systems approach to OD.

5. Describe the eight phases of the OD process model.

II.
Premeeting
Preparation

1. Read the Background Information (Section III).

2. Read the instructions for Simulation 2.1. Complete OD Consultant Profile I (Part A), and the Personal Objectives (Part B). Become familiar with material in Step 2, Part B.

3. Read and prepare analysis for Case, The Popular Professor.

III.
Background
Information

Change is the name of the game in management today. Market, product, and competitive conditions are rapidly changing. As the environment changes, organizations must adapt if they are to be successful. For example, Pan American Air Lines, once the leading international airline, reported losses of $475 million over a two-year period largely because of its failure to adapt to changing market conditions and increasing competition on overseas routes.

The job of management in the future is likely to be even more dynamic and challenging. Therefore, the focus of OD is on changing organizational systems, stressing the situational nature of problems and their system-wide impact. In solving a given problem, managers must analyze the organization, its subsystem interrelationships, and the possible effects on the inside environment as well. This approach is termed the *systems approach*, and provides a way of observing, analyzing, and solving problems in organizations. The systems approach, then, is concerned with the relationship among subsystems and the interdependencies between these elements and higher level systems.

An example of changing conditions that face organizations can be seen in the sudden decline in the sewing machine market, compared to the projected increase in the demand for personal computers. The Singer Company has had to reorganize, sell off unprofitable units, and change its marketing strategy because the number of people buying sewing machines has declined drastically. The market for personal computers, on the other hand, virtually nonexistent a few years ago, today constitutes a several-billion-dollar market.

Because of the rapid pace of technology, firms are confronted with early technological obsolescence of products. In the past, companies could grow during the long life span of a proprietary invention, but today they find their innovations are often quickly overtaken by competitors with technological improvements.

These problems are the result of an increasing rate of change and are made more difficult because of the impact of future shock on management. Managers today face risk situations unlike those of the past, and in an era of accelerating change, management's degree of excellence results from its ability to cope with these changes. Organizations either become more adaptive, flexible, and anticipative or they become rigid and stagnant, reacting to change after the fact, often when it is too late. Seldom can management decisions be based solely on the extrapolation of historical experience. Many decisions are unique, innovative, and risky, involving new products and new areas of opportunity. Putting a new product or a new process into production is a major business decision.

Because an organization exists in a changing environment, it must have the capacity to adapt. As one consultant points out: "Nobody is moving faster on the experience curve than the high technology electronic companies, and the consequences of being late are most severe in that business."[1]

In this chapter we examine the way managers react to this accelerating rate of change. The pressure of future shock results in new perspectives for management strategies and decisions. Managers must do more than just react: they must be able to anticipate the changing patterns of people, markets, products, and technology.[2] Three areas will be covered:

1. The systems approach.
2. Adaptation to a changing environment.
3. The planned change process.

A DYNAMIC MODEL OF CHANGE: THE SYSTEMS APPROACH ───────────

A *system* is a set of interrelated elements unified by design to achieve some purpose or goal. Organizations are systems. Each organization can be viewed as a number of interrelated, interdependent parts, each of which contributes to total organizational functioning and to the achievement of its goal. The systems approach is one of the most important concepts in OD because it deals with change and interrelationships in complex organizations. The notion of system interdependency is critical because a change in one part of a system has consequences in other parts of the system.

What Is a System? ─────────────────────────────────

The term *system* is used in many different contexts: for example, defense system, weapons system, solar system, and stereo system. A system has been defined as an "organized unitary whole composed of two or more interdependent parts, components or subsystems and delineated by identifiable boundaries from its environment."[3]

A system has several basic qualities:

1. A system must be designed to accomplish an objective.
2. The elements of a system must have an established arrangement.
3. Interrelationships must exist among the individual elements of a system, and these interrelationships must be synergistic in nature.

4. The basic ingredients of a process (the flows of information, energy, and materials) are more vital than the basic elements of a system.

5. Organization objectives are more important than the objectives of its elements, and thus there is a deemphasis of the parochial objectives of the elements of a system.[4]

The focus of the systems approach is the recognition of the effect of managerial functions and the interrelationship between subelements of the organization. Rather than view the organization as a static set of relationships, the organization is viewed as a set of flows of information, personnel, and material. Time and change become critical aspects. The flow of inputs and outputs is a basic starting point in the description of the system (see Figure 2.1). There are three basic elements that make up such a system:

1. *Inputs* are the resources that are applied to the processing function.

2. *Processes* are the activities and functions that are performed to transform the resources.

3. *Outputs* are the products and services that come out of the system.

A business firm takes such inputs as materials, people, and energy, and converts them into the products or services desired by consumers. The organization receives inputs from its environment, acts on those inputs by transforming them, and returns these transformed elements to the environment as products. The inputs to a hospital include money, equipment, trained staff, information, patients, and physicians; the outputs include new research, well patients, improved medicine, trained doctors and nurses, and other medical benefits.

The Organization as an Open System _____

There are two basic types of systems: open and closed. A *closed system* is one that is self-contained and isolated from its environment. In the strictest sense, closed systems exist only in theory, for all real systems interact with

Inputs	Transformation Process	Outputs
Dollars		Micro computer
Equipment	Production	Mini computer
Facilities	Marketing, etc.	Electronics, etc.
People		
Raw material		

Movement of material, energy, and information

FIGURE 2.1 The Organization as an Open System: Electronics Firm

their environment. Our emphasis is on treating organizations as open systems.

By far the most important type of system is the open system. An *open system* influences and is influenced by the environment through the process of interdependency, which results in a *dynamic (changing) equilibrium*. A business organization provides an excellent example of the process of reciprocity and, therefore, of an open system. The *open system* is in continual interaction with its environment and therefore achieves a steady state or *dynamic equilibrium*. The system could not continue to survive without the continuous influence of transformational outflow. As the open system interacts with its environment, it continually receives information, termed *feedback*, from its environment, which helps it adjust. The subsystems also interact with one another, because they have interacting tasks to perform. Therefore, the overall efficiency of the system depends upon the level and degree of interaction with other elements.

The Characteristics of Open Systems _____

Although there are various types of systems, there are certain characteristics that tend to occur in all open systems. The various organizational functions are not isolated elements. They are components interacting with each other and with the outside environment. The decisions of any one manager may well have repercussions upon other parts of the organization. The systems model is based on a number of characteristics, including the following.

1. *Interdependence.* A system is composed of interrelated parts or elements. Any element is dependent on the other elements, and change in any one means that some adjustment will occur in the others.

2. *Holism.* The system is a whole, not merely the sum of its parts, and its performance should be viewed as an integrated system.

3. *Input/output model.* All systems transform inputs into outputs. The system is viewed as a transformation process in dynamic interaction with its environment.

4. *Goal seeking—open system.* Open systems exchange information, energy, or material with their environment. Interaction between elements results in some final state or goal.

5. *Entropy.* Every transformation process involves the degradation or use of energy and resources. The tendency toward entropy is a movement toward disorder and eventually termination of functioning. To keep a system operating there must be an infusion of energy and resources.

6. *Steady state.* The notion that systems are goal seeking implies that they are adaptive and self-regulating. The open system seeks a state of dynamic equilibrium.

7. *Feedback.* The feedback of information regarding performance is used to adjust and control performance. Feedback is informational input which indicates that the system is deviating from goals and needs to readjust.

8. *Hierarchy.* One system contains several other systems within it and is also a part of a larger suprasystem.

9. *Differentiation.* In complex systems, units perform specialized functions. Open systems tend to move toward increased differentiation.

10. *Equifinality.* In complex systems, an initial state may result in several possible final states, and a similar final state may be achieved from many different initial states.

One of the current trends in OD is a shift toward using a more integrated, systems approach to organization improvement.[5]

THE ORGANIZATION AS A SOCIOTECHNICAL SYSTEM

Organization development may be referred to as a systems approach to change. An organization is viewed as an open *sociotechnical system* of coordinated human and technical activities. The various organizational functions and processes are not considered as isolated elements but as parts reacting to and influencing other system elements. As a result, changes in any one subsystem of the organization can have effects throughout the organization, because all subsystems are related. Therefore, by its very nature, OD seeks to consider the interrelationships among all basic elements of the system when changes are planned. The organization can be viewed as an open system in interaction with its environment and consisting of five primary components (see Figure 2.2).

The structural subsystem. This includes the formal design, policies, procedures, and so on. It is usually set forth by the organization chart and includes division of work and patterns of authority.

The technical subsystem. This includes the primary functions, activities, and operations, including the techniques, equipment, and so on, used to produce the output of the system.

The psychosocial subsystem. This includes the network of social relationships and behavioral patterns of members, such as norms, roles, and communications.

The goals subsystem. This includes the basic mission of the organization. Such goals might include profits, growth, or survival and are often taken from the larger environment.

The managerial subsystem. This subsystem spans the entire organization by directing, organizing, and coordinating all activities toward the basic mission. The managerial function is important in integrating the activities of the other subsystems.

One of the earliest applications of the sociotechnical systems concept was in British coal mining. The traditional "short wall" method utilized small, cohe-

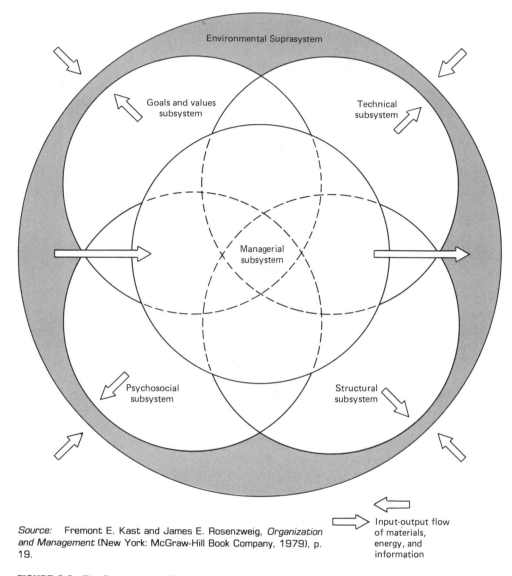

Source: Fremont E. Kast and James E. Rosenzweig, *Organization and Management* (New York: McGraw-Hill Book Company, 1979), p. 19.

FIGURE 2.2 The Sociotechnical System

sive work groups working as autonomous teams. Technological advances by engineering efficiency experts determined that the short wall method was inefficient, and introduced an improved technical system, termed the "long wall" method. Unfortunately, the long wall method resulted in lower performance and higher absenteeism. Production decreased because they had failed to consider the impact of the changes on the psychosocial system. Researchers found, as a result of reintroducing a team approach and providing team pay incentives, that productivity and morale improved substantially.

The sociotechnical systems OD approach is considered one of the most sophisticated techniques involving large-scale effort and considerable skill on the part of the OD consultant.[6]

CONTINGENCY THEORY AND OD

Systems theory provides a conceptual overview of organizational functioning, but the manager needs to know how the subsystems of a particular organization are uniquely related in that specific environment and how best to deal with its particular problems. Contingency theory recognizes that such differences do exist and that what constitutes effective management in one system may not in another setting. Contingency views tend to emphasize the characteristics of a specific organization, and suggest that to organize and manage a change program, one must consider the set of conditions in that particular setting.

The *contingency approach* suggests that there is no one best way of managing in all situations. Given certain combinations of contingencies (such as a stable external environment and a low adaptive orientation to change), one can specify general approaches to change that are likely to be more effective than others. In other words, the contingency approach identifies various types of "if-then" relationships and suggests general directions for change, depending on the situation. The contingency approach is also based on certain conceptual skills, such as diagnosing and understanding the various types of situations that are likely to confront the OD practitioner.

The contingency view suggests that managers in differing departmental units face situations that may be very different on a number of dimensions. There may be varying degrees of structure, differing motivation levels, and a diverse potential for conflict. The OD practitioner, then, must recognize that there is "no one best way" for all organizations, although some practitioners would take issue with this statement.[7] The contingency approach to OD suggests that the effectiveness of various consulting styles, intervention techniques, or strategies will vary according to the circumstances. The contingency variables that need to be considered and the relative emphasis will depend on the type of problem being considered.

FUTURE SHOCK AND CHANGE

Alvin Toffler, in *Future Shock*, suggests that most people are utterly unprepared to cope with the accelerated rate of change. "*Future shock* is a time phenomenon, a product of a greatly accelerated rate of change in society. It arises from the superimposition of a new culture on an old one."[8] Future shock, too much change in too short a time, affects managers and organizations as well.

When change occurs too rapidly, the capacity of management to react is strained, creating the danger of future shock. As a result, managers must become more adaptable and flexible than ever before. As an example, fast-changing technology has spurred growth and change in the semiconductor industry, including a bewildering array of manufacturing processes and new techniques to build more and more electronic circuitry onto a quarter-inch-square silicon chip. Yet industry leaders expect to see more changes in the next decade than have been seen in the past ten years.

Since super chips will increase the power of all computers, they will unleash almost unimaginable potential. Experts predict that within five years one chip will be able to do the work of today's mainframe computers. "If you think what we have today is amazing, just wait for Very Large-Scale Integration (VLSI)," says George H. Heilmeier, vice president of corporate research, development, and engineering at Texas Instruments. Continuing, Heilmeier says: "We must get ourselves out of the rut that says VLSI is simply going to make existing quantitative computation applications smaller, faster, and cheaper—a straight-line projection of future trends based on the past. VLSI technology is the key to . . . machine intelligence that represents not a straight-line projection but a quantum leap in opportunities."[9]

For corporate planners and top managers, the environment has never seemed as turbulent as it does today. The very uncertainties, from the cloudy economic outlook to the energy crisis, make accurate planning for the future much more difficult. In such a rapidly changing environment, some plans are out of date within 3 to 6 months.

How do we know that the rate of change is accelerating? For one thing, during the last decade the introduction of new brands has more than doubled, while the average product life expectancy has fallen from 36 months to 12 months.

The world is constantly changing in economics, social values, and technology, and these changes seem to have accelerated in recent years. These technological changes have shortened the life cycle of many products and services, and when product life cycles are shortened, organizations must become more adaptive by shortening their lead times to get into production.

There is an increasing need for new organizational forms and systems. Further, individuals within organizations are affected by change. No longer satisfied to be passive members, individuals increasingly assert their right to change the organization for their own reasons.

America's present environment is in a state of turbulent change, suggests John Naisbitt in his book *Megatrends*, because we are moving into a new era.[10] The shift in the U.S. from an industrially-based economy to a technologically-based economy is creating a state of turbulent change, both for workers and corporations. Widespread changes throughout society include the following:

1. Work increasingly relies on knowledge rather than physical effort.

2. A movement away from a production-oriented economy toward an economy relying on services.

3. Shift to a world economy from a national economy with increased competition from imports and new opportunities in foreign markets.

4. Increased emphasis on long-term strategic planning.

5. Redirection of social services offered by government and private social agencies.

6. Emphasis on decentralization in business and government.

7. More reliance on self and less dependence on government and other institutional control.

8. Shifts in population and industry from the north and east to the south and west.

These changing trends will have a significant impact on organizations. As a result managers will need to scan the environment to be aware of issues which will have major impact on their industry or organization.

Technological advancements are occurring so rapidly that most scientists' education is technically obsolete within 10 years after graduation from college. There is so much information that a professional operating in a narrow field may find it impossible to keep current on information pertinent to his or her specialty. The term *information overload*, once reserved for computer storage ability, aptly applies to managers trying to act responsibly in a changing environment.

Environmental changes affect organizational operations as well. Environmental laws add heavily to the cost of new petrochemical plants. The economics of petrochemical production demand gigantic plants, yet only four or five companies are capable of raising the capital required for such facilities. Laws dealing with pollution control, hiring of minorities, product safety, and other factors must be taken into consideration in any major decision.

During the past decade society has been placing new demands on business firms for social responsibility, and other social changes also impinge upon the organization. In the past jobs were thought of as tasks to be done, not something to be questioned or evaluated. General Motors' Lordstown, Ohio, plant, the most automated automobile plant in the world, has been plagued by sabotage and shutdowns because the workers feel "dehumanized." The traditional concept of work as a virtue and a duty is no longer applicable to younger workers. In the United States more workers earn their pay in knowledge-base jobs than in skill and nonskill jobs. For many years managers will be searching for newer, more relevant, and more effective ways of managing this increasingly intelligent and sophisticated work force.

The organization must adapt to these changing conditions. Each day brings a new set of conditions, and internal realignment is often required. Product and market strategies need to be more flexible and must depend upon raw material logistics and the ability of a company to recognize the need for change. Consequently, management will need to place an increased emphasis on human resource development. An unprecedented opportunity exists for the OD practitioner to apply specialized skills to seeking solutions for these problems of industry. In view of these factors, whether an organization can remain effective is largely dependent upon whether it is sufficiently adaptive to changing conditions, as shown at Levi Strauss in OD Application 2.1.

OD Application 2.1

FUTURE SHOCK FOR LEVI

Levi Strauss, the giant jeans maker, has been a successful company. The family-run firm built its business around three basic factors:

1. High product quality.

2. A happy family corporate culture.

3. Concentration on the jeans market.

But Levi Strauss was ill-equipped to deal with a slowdown in sales growth and a market shift toward designer jeans. In one year alone profit dropped 79 percent. In the early 1980s, Levi had problems with diversification, fashion trends, and marketing; a failure to recognize changing trends.

According to Robert D. Haas, president, chief executive officer, and great-great-grandnephew of the founder, "This company is guilty of being too rigid and too deliberative in an industry made up of entrepreneurs who hustle. And we're going to have to change."

Levi ran into problems for three reasons:

1. They lost touch with customers. People at Levi failed to see changes coming. Because of many layers of management, decision making was far removed from the customers and retailers. In an effort to counter this problem Levi is decentralizing its new units in order to get them closer to their customers.

2. Levi failed to anticipate customer shifts to new products. In retailing, fashions change rapidly and Levi could not react fast enough. Basic blue jeans, which had at one time been so popular that Levi had rationed them among retailers, lost their consumer appeal to fashion and designer jeans.

3. They failed to develop competing products to broaden the product base. Levi has tried to bring out other product lines but Levi's fashion image among consumers is so poor that some of the lines bear no Levi trademark nor suggest any link between the product and the company.

The challenge to Levi, then, is to anticipate and respond more quickly to changing market trends. "The company just didn't understand fashion," says one retailer. One question which arises: Can Levi pursue both the basic jeans and designer-fashion markets? Some have suggested that to do this, Levi must become more marketing oriented and less production oriented.

Questions:
1. Was Levi's management affected by future shock? How and why?
2. What adaptive orientation was used (see the next section of text)?
3. What should Levi be doing?

Sources: Patricia A. Bellew, "Levi Is Promoting New Fashions in a Campaign to Become More Entrepreneurial, Competitive," *The Wall Street Journal*, January 31, 1985, p. 4; and "Levi's: The Jeans's Giant Shipped as the Market Shifted," *Business Week*, November 5, 1984, p. 79.

ADAPTATION TO A CHANGING ENVIRONMENT

A major challenge facing organizations today is to manage effectively. When an organization fails to change, the cost of that failure may mean survival. Since the environment is composed of systems outside the immediate influence of the organization, the organization must attempt to adapt itself to these forces by introducing internal changes that will allow the organization to be more effective. To be successful, organizations must develop a management style that will adequately handle the challenges and opportunities which they face. A management style that was adequate under one set of conditions may become progressively less effective under changing circumstances. The OD practitioner, then, is ultimately interested in changing human behavior and organization processes to create a more adaptive and flexible organization.

Why is change so difficult? Possibly because the culture of the organization becomes a part of the people who perform the work. In changing these old patterns, people must alter not only their behavior but also their values and view of themselves. The organization structure, procedures, and relationships continue to reinforce prior patterns of behavior and to resist the new ones. As a result, organization change sometimes results in upheaval and dissatisfaction, and possibly even in resignations, dismissals, or transfers. Consequently, an organization must develop an adaptive orientation and management style which is geared to its environment. Managers in different organizations deal with situations that may be dramatically different. Some organizations exist in relatively stable environments, whereas others operate in highly dynamic settings. Each requires a different orientation to the environment.

Orientations to Stability and Adaptation

Every organization must have enough stability to continue to function satisfactorily and still prevent itself from becoming too static or stagnant to adapt to changing conditions. Both stability and adaptation are essential to continued survival and growth.

An organization that operates in a mature field with a stable product and relatively few competitors needs a different adaptive orientation than that of a firm operating in a high-growth market, among numerous competitors, and with a high degree of innovation. The former operates in an environment that is relatively stable, whereas the latter faces a more dynamic and turbulent set of conditions. A stable environment is characterized by unchanging basic products and services, a static level of competition, a low level of technological innovation, a formalized and centralized structure, and a steady, slow rate of growth. Such an environment remains relatively stable over long periods.

A dynamic environment, on the other hand, is characterized by rapidly changing product lines, an increasing and changing set of competitors, rapid and continual technological innovation, and rapid market growth. For today's organization, the idea of change is clear. A static organization can no longer survive. Yesterday's accomplishments amount to little in an environment of rapidly advancing markets, products, and life styles. To survive, organizations must devise methods of continuous self-renewal. Organizations must recognize when it is necessary to change, and they must develop the ability to implement change when needed. To meet these conditions, many companies have created specialized OD units whose primary purpose is implementing organizational changes. These units are developing new programs to help the organization improve its level of adaptation to its environment and to maintain a stable identity, so that change is not overwhelming. To achieve successful change, both of these goals must be satisfied.

A Model of Adaptive Orientation _____

A simplified model of environmental stability and adaptive orientation is shown in Figure 2.3. One dimension represents the degree of stability in the organization's environment, and the second represents the degree of adaptiveness or flexibility present in the internal orientation of the organization. Organizations can vary greatly on these dimensions, and the various combinations of these orientations can lead to differing adaptive styles. Certain types of possible orientations are described next.

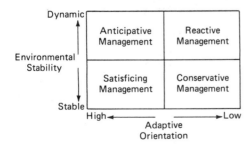

FIGURE 2.3 A Model of Environmental Adaptive Orientation in Organizations

Conservative Management (Stable Environment, Low Adaptation) ⎯⎯⎯⎯⎯

Conservative management refers to a style of management based on low risk, with formalized procedures and a high degree of structure and control. Typically, organizations that utilize conservative management have very stable goals and a highly centralized structure. They also tend to have more managerial levels, a higher ratio of superiors to subordinates, and an emphasis upon formal control systems. There may be a tendency to value tradition, to keep on doing things as they have always been done, to value seniority more than performance, and an aversion to accepting new ideas. Although this is a low-risk style of managing, it may lead to serious problems in the long run. A competitor has observed of Ray-O-Vac Corporation's declining share of the battery market: "Their technical people came up with ideas but management didn't come out with the product. They maintained the *status quo* and now they are in the follower's position."[11]

Reactive Management (Dynamic Environment, Low Adaptation) ⎯⎯⎯⎯⎯

Organizations with a low level of adaptation, but existing in a rapidly changing environment, tend to deal with problems on a short-run, crisis basis. *Reactive management* refers to a style of reacting to a stimulus after conditions in the environment have changed. It is a short-term, crisis type of adaptation, often involving replacement of key people, hasty reorganization, and drastic cutting of people and product lines. A major food corporation, for example, was feeling the pressures of changing business conditions, losing momentum, experiencing product failures, and reporting decreased earnings. The new chief executive instituted some massive changes, including a major management reorganization, a company-wide efficiency drive, cutting salaried personnel by 10 percent, and taking a very hard look at all marketing programs. The reactive approach to change implies waiting until serious problems emerge which can no longer be ignored and then taking drastic corrective measures.

Satisficing Management (Stable Environment, High Adaptation) ⎯⎯⎯⎯⎯

Satisficing management, a play off of the word satisfactory, is a management that is adequate and average. It is a style of managing that emphasizes a more centralized decision-making structure with problems being referred to the top. Because of the stable environment, there tend to be more levels of management, with coordination done by formal committees. Planning and decision making are usually concentrated at the top, with high clarity of procedures and roles. Change is accomplished at a rate that is "good enough" to keep up with the industry, but certainly well behind the state of the art. Such organizations often tend to accept strategies that are "good enough," because of the low level of pressure for change from the environment.

Anticipative Management (Dynamic Environment, High Adaptation)

Organizations with a high level of adaptation existing in a rapidly changing environment tend to utilize the anticipative management style. *Anticipative management* refers to introducing change to deal with future conditions before these conditions actually come about. Examples of anticipative management would include the innovations of corporations such as General Electric, TRW Systems, and Xerox, which have actively initiated programs of improvement before conditions became critical.

To illustrate the difference between these approaches, let us look at the Federal Aviation Administration (FAA). According to some outside authorities, the FAA has operated through much of the 1980s with fewer air traffic controllers than required and equipment that is obsolete. Only after a series of midair collisions killing hundreds of people, near misses, and congressional hearings did the FAA recognize that a problem existed and begin to formulate plans to correct it. The critics of the FAA contend, however, that the solutions will take years to implement but the problems are immediate. The reactive management approach operates on a crisis basis, waiting for a problem to reach a critical stage before making internal realignments. The anticipative approach is to recognize that changes in technology, organizations, and people will be required and initiate planned change now to deal with predicted future conditions.

These are the four basic orientations. A conservative management orientation has little ability to adapt to changes, but there is also little pressure to change because of the stable environment. A reactive management orientation has the need to respond to a rapidly changing environment but does not have the flexibility to adapt. A satisficing management orientation has the ability to respond to changing situations but finds itself in a relatively slow changing environment. An anticipative management orientation has both the ability and need to respond to a dynamic environment. It seems that most modern organizations are increasingly finding the need for the anticipative orientation.

THE PLANNED CHANGE PROCESS

Planned organizational change is a deliberate attempt to modify the functioning of the total organization or one of its major parts in order to bring about improved effectiveness.[12] The persons attempting to bring about this change will be referred to as *consultants* and the organization being changed will be referred to as the *client system*. Planned change efforts can focus on individual, group, or organization behavior.

Individual Effectiveness

An organization is made up of individual members and each member has unique values, beliefs, and motivations. The leadership style of top management and the norms, values, and beliefs of the organization's members combine to form the organization climate. Organization effectiveness can be increased by creating a climate that achieves organizational goals and at the same time satisfies members' needs.

Change efforts that focus on individual effectiveness range from informal training programs to high-powered executive development programs. These include activities that are designed to improve the skills, abilities, or motivational levels of organization members. The goals are improved technical skills or improved interpersonal competence. Such change efforts may also be directed toward improved leadership, decision making, or problem solving among organization members. The assumption underlying such efforts is that by developing better managers and employees, a more effective organization will result.

Group Effectiveness

Change efforts may also focus on group functioning as a means to improve operations. There is an emphasis on improving problem-solving processes while working through conflicts and issues surrounding ways the group can improve its effectiveness.

These activities are designed to improve the operations of work teams and may focus on *task activities*, what the group does; or they may deal with *team process*, how the group works and the quality of relationships among team members. The assumption is that work teams are the primary unit of the organization and that more effective teams will lead to improved organizations. More effective teams may increase work motivation, improve performance, and decrease turnover and absenteeism.

One technique that is often used in examining groups is called *process observation*. As we observe and analyze work groups as systems, two separate dimensions may be identified: (1) *content*—the task of the group, and (2) *process*—the way the group functions. *Group process* includes such factors as leadership, decision making, communication, and conflict. The content is *what* is being discussed; the process is *how* the group operates.

By observing the behavior of group members, one can determine the way in which a group is functioning. The observer describes group functioning in a systematic manner, such as who talks to whom, the frequency of certain behaviors, and so on. The observations are then summarized and presented to the group. The purpose is to clarify and improve team functioning. It is helpful for the OD consultant to develop skills in process observation and to learn to be a *participant-observer*; that is, to actively participate and at the same time be aware of group process. Such skills are particularly useful in developing an effective consulting team.

Organization Effectiveness _____

Another focus for planned change efforts is the organization system. The total organization may be examined by use of climate surveys; planned change programs are then designed to deal with the specific problem areas identified in the survey.

These activities aim at improving effectiveness by structural, technical, or managerial subsystem changes. The objective of such system-wide operations is to increase the effectiveness, the efficiency, and the morale of total organization functioning.

Each of these planned change efforts aims at improving the overall goal attainment of the system, but each has a specific target or focus for the change program. Organization development occurs when the change effort is focused on the total system. OD may involve individual, group, and intergroup approaches, but it becomes OD only when the total system is the target for change. In an OD program, a set of goals or purposes is identified, and a course of action is undertaken involving the commitment of organization members toward organization improvement.

As Frank Friedlander and L. Dave Brown (OD practitioners, Case Western Reserve University) have noted, attempts to change only people, only technology, or only structure meet resistance or failure.[13] In the next section we examine the sequence of stages involved in implementing a program of planned change.

A MODEL FOR ORGANIZATION CHANGE _____

OD is a continuing process of long-term organizational improvement consisting of a series of stages, as shown in Figure 2.4. At TRW Systems, one of the most imaginative and innovative major U.S. companies, managers have been willing to take big risks for a large corporation. OD techniques have been applied at TRW since the late 1960s to get organization units to operate more efficiently.[14] In an OD program the emphasis is placed on individual, group, and organization relationships.

The primary difference between OD and other behavioral science tech-

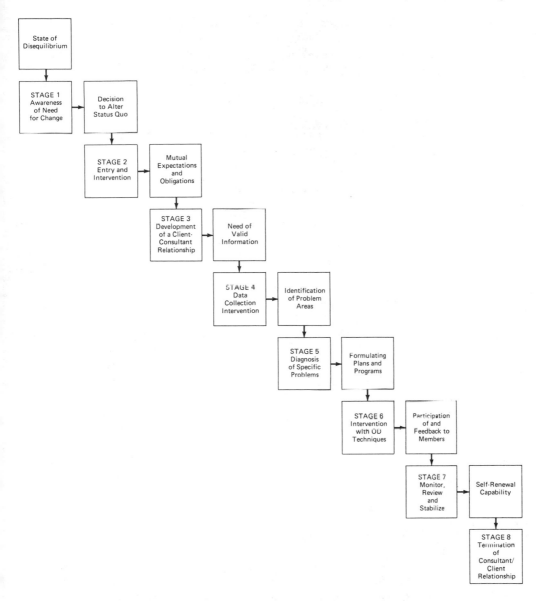

FIGURE 2.4 Overview Flow Chart of Organization Development Stages

niques is an emphasis upon viewing the organization as a total system of interacting and interrelated elements. Organization development is the application
of a *systems approach* to the functional, structural, technical, and personal relationships in organizations. OD programs are based upon a systematic analysis of
problems and a top management actively committed to the change effort. The
purpose of such a program is to increase organization effectiveness by the appli-

cation of OD techniques. Many organization development programs use the *action research model*. Action research involves collecting information about the organization, feeding this information back to the client system, and developing and implementing action programs to improve system performance. The manager also needs to be aware of the processes that should be considered when attempting to create change. In this section an eight-stage model of the total organization change process is presented. Each stage is dependent on the prior one and successful change is more probable when each of these stages is considered in logical sequence.

Stage One: The Awareness of a Need for Change

Before a program of change can be implemented, the organization must perceive the need for change. The first step is the manager's perception that the organization is somehow in a state of disequilibrium or needs improvement. This state of disequilibrium may result from growth or decline or from competitive, technological, legal, or social changes in the external environment. There must be a felt need, since only felt needs convince individuals to adopt new ways.

At USX (formerly U.S. Steel) a reorganization was implemented to revitalize the company. The stimulus for this change was an awareness by organization members that "U.S. Steel was too slow to make decisions, too slow to respond to changing conditions, and too slow to make thrusts into profitable new markets." At the root of USX's problems was a long-standing resistance to change. As the economic and political circumstances facing the steel industry altered over the past 20 years, USX had failed to accommodate to them.[15] To counter these problems, USX embarked on a change program to give managers more operating authority and responsibility for profits. At Saga, an institutional food contractor, high employee turnover led to the application of OD concepts.[16]

Stage Two: The Entry and Intervention of the Consultant

The second stage in an organization development program is the entry and intervention of a consultant into the client system. (See B.C. comic strip.) The consultant must enter the ongoing organization situation if the firm is to alter the status quo. The consultant may be a manager or other member of the organization, referred to as an *internal consultant*; or an outside expert, referred to as an *external consultant*.

The consultant must decide at what point to enter the system and what his or her role should be. For instance, the consultant may intervene with the sanction and approval of top management and either with or without the sanction and support of members in the lower levels of the organization. At Saga,

B.C. by permission of Johnny Hart and Creators Syndicate, Inc.

for example, OD started at the vice-presidential level and gradually expanded to include line managers and workers, while at TRW Systems an outside consultant from a university was invited in by the organization's industrial relations group to initiate the OD program. An example of what might be termed an "illegitimate" intervention, but not an OD program, is the union organizer who has support from the lower levels of the organization, but not the support of top management.

Stage Three: Developing the Consultant-Client Relationship

After an organization recognizes a need for change and a consultant contacts the system, a relationship begins to develop between the consultant and the client system. The development of this relationship is an important determinant of the probable success or failure of an OD program. As with many interpersonal relationships, the exchange of expectations and obligations (the formation of a psychological contract) depends to a high degree upon a good first impression or match between consultant and client system.

The consultant attempts to establish a pattern of open communication, a relationship of trust, and an atmosphere of shared responsibility. Issues dealing with responsibility, rewards, and objectives must be clarified, defined, or worked through at this point.

For example, the Diamond Shamrock Corporation was afflicted with autocratic management and intergroup rivalries. However, a new top manager took charge and began totally overhauling the corporate personality. A management consulting group was contacted and the company embarked on a change program aimed at role negotiation and improving intergroup cooperation.[17]

Stage Four: The Information-Collecting Phase _____

After the consultant has intervened and developed a working relationship with the client, the consultant and the client begin to gather data about the system. The collection of data is an important activity providing the organization and the consultant with a better understanding of client system disequilibrium.

Although organizations usually generate a large amount of "hard" or operational data, still the data may present an incomplete picture of the state of the organization. The consultant and client, then, may agree to increase the range or depth of the available data by interview or questionnaire as a basis for further action programs. Saga, for instance, was having problems of high employee turnover. In such a case the consultant would probably investigate the high turnover rate by means of interview or questionnaire to determine why this problem existed, and from these data an OD program would be designed to correct the problems. Saga's employees felt that it had become a bureaucratic organization clogged with red tape, causing high turnover. OD programs have since reduced employee turnover to 19 percent, compared with 34 percent for the industry.[18]

Stage Five: The Diagnostic Phase _____

One rule or *modus operandi* for the OD consultant is to question the client's diagnosis of the problem, because the client may well be biased in its perspective. After acquiring information relevant to the situation perceived to be in disequilibrium, the consultant and client together analyze the data to identify problem areas and causal relationships. A weak, inaccurate, or faulty diagnosis can lead to a costly and ineffective change program. The diagnostic phase, then, is used to determine the exact problem that needs solution, to identify the causal forces in the situation, and to provide a basis for selecting effective change strategies and techniques.

TRW Systems, for example, uses a matrix form of organization. This results in project teams that cut across departmental and even divisional lines, so that employees may be members of several teams at once and report to a number of bosses. "The project office and departmental support group are fundamentally at cross purposes," says D. R. McKell, an industrial relations staffer. "The chief skill needed for matrix is conflict management."[19] From a systematic diagnosis of this situation, TRW initiated an OD program focusing on team building and intergroup team building interventions.

At Pillsbury, a new executive vice president needed to move quickly to improve the division's performance. With the help of an outside consultant, data were gathered by conducting intensive interviews with top management, as well as with outsiders, to determine key problem areas. Then, without identifying the source of comments, the management team worked on the information in a 10-hour session until solutions to the major problems were hammered out.[20]

Stage Six: Action Plans, Strategies, and Techniques

The diagnostic phase leads to a series of interventions, activities, or programs aimed at resolving problems and increasing organization effectiveness. These programs apply such OD techniques as quality circles, Managerial Grid programs, management by objectives programs, team building, or intergroup development to the causes specified in the diagnostic phase. To initiate the OD program at TRW Systems, the director of industrial relations invited managers and their subordinates to attend laboratory training sessions. In such sessions there is no agenda, and the members themselves must wade through the process of deciding what to do and how to proceed. During a typical weekend or 2-week session, individuals focus on the basic raw material of the sessions: members' interactions. TRW Systems found, however, that there is no built-in link between the laboratory training experience, which is largely personal, and the work environment itself. Managers returned from the training eager to apply their managerial learnings only to receive a skeptical or even hostile reaction from their coworkers. TRW felt that there had to be more emphasis on changing the ongoing organization on a day-to-day basis, so they began to focus on the work group itself rather than on individual hang-ups. Team building, intergroup building, organization mirrors—all of these have proved more relevant to the job situation as the TRW Systems group evolved its own brand of management training.

Stage Seven: Monitoring, Reviewing, and Stabilizing the Action Programs

Once an action program is implemented, the next step is to monitor the results and stabilize the desired changes. This stage concerns the assessment of the effectiveness of change strategies in attaining stated objectives. Each stage of an OD program needs to be monitored to gain feedback on member reaction to the change efforts. The system members need to know the results of change efforts in order to determine whether they ought to modify, continue, or discontinue the activities. Once disequilibrium has been corrected and a change program implemented and monitored, means must be devised to make sure that the new behavior is stabilized. If this is not done, the tendency is for the system to regress to previous ineffective modes or states. The client system needs to develop the capability to maintain innovation without outside support.

The problem of stabilizing change and the possibility of managers reverting to previous, ingrained modes of behavior is a very real problem in many corporations. At USX (not an OD program), for example, "critics say the company is essentially reorganizing the same people—old, ingrown managers—and that USX still has a hard time attracting sharp managerial talent from outside.[21]

At Saga, on the other hand, chairman Price Laughlin felt that OD was successful because turnover was reduced to 19 percent and innovation was encouraged
at all levels. The costs and benefits of Saga's OD program have been measured
by Stanford University Researchers, and Laughlin claims that the economics
are very sound: "Profitability is borne out by increased productivity."[22] However, it should also be noted that, according to some practitioners and Saga employees, Saga's program has not been completely successful and has been more
sold than practiced, especially at lower levels.

Stage Eight: The Termination of an OD Program

The final stage is the termination or disengagement of the OD consultant
from the client system. For as an OD program stabilizes, the need for the consultant should decrease. If the client system moves toward independence and
evidences a self-renewal capacity, the gradual termination of the consultant-
client system relationship is easily accomplished. If the client system has become overly dependent upon the consultant, termination of the relationship
can be a difficult and awkward issue. At Diamond Shamrock, the program has
produced tangible benefits. Of 264 managers involved in the program, 93 percent reported that the program led to improved teamwork.[23]

At TRW Systems, as the external consultant phased out, the responsibility for continuing innovation shifted to internal consultants. TRW reports that
OD has paid off. Ruben F. Mettler of TRW says, "We are not using OD to play
games," and many TRW project managers request a team-building session every time a new project team is assembled. "Many at Systems contend that OD
techniques have developed more effective and productive managers. This cannot be proved. But other evidence is hard to quarrel with. The group's voluntary turnover rate, always lower than average, stood at 4.3 percent last year,
while the rate for the aerospace industry was 10 percent."[24] Saga's Laughlin also
notes, "Remember, we are primarily businessmen. We believe in management
by objectives. We take a systems-result oriented approach and OD is just another tool in our box. Business can't work on sensitivity alone."[25]

An important issue is whether or not the OD consultant is able to deal
effectively with power and the use of power. Hierarchical organizations,
whether they be industrial, governmental, or academic, rely on power. The
individuals in positions of influence generally constitute the power structure
and frequently are power-motivated people. Managers compete for promotions, and departments and divisions conflict over budget allocations. Political
infighting is a reality (and often a dysfunctional factor) in most organizations,
and the issue is whether OD consultants deal with these power issues in bringing about a change.

REVIEW QUESTIONS

1. What is the implication of future shock to today's organizations?

2. Identify the basic stages of an OD program.
   1.   5.
   2.   6.
   3.   7.
   4.   8.

3. Contrast the differences between a stable and a changing environment.

4. Compare and contrast the four types of management orientations used in relating to the environment.

KEY WORDS AND CONCEPTS

Define and be able to use the following:

System	Conservative management
Dynamic equilibrium	The contingency approach
Feedback	Internal consultant
Sociotechnical system	External consultant
Future shock	The OD process model
Reactive management	Open system
Anticipative management	Closed system
Satisficing management	Planned change

IV.
Simulations

SIMULATION 2.1   OD CONSULTANT BEHAVIOR PROFILE I

Total time suggested: 2 to 2 and ½ hours.

A. Purpose

The purpose of this profile is to help you gauge for yourself some aspects of your consulting style.[26] During this course you will be afforded additional opportunities to obtain information about yourself on how you behave in organizational situations. This feedback may provide the impetus for you to change, but the ultimate responsibility for that change is with you.

B. Procedures

Part A *Profile Survey*

Step 1 Based on the following scale, select the number to indicate the degree to which you feel each description is characteristic of you. Record your choice in the blank to the right.

1	2	3	4	5	6	7
Not at All Characteristic			Somewhat Characteristic			Very Characteristic

1. Having the ability to communicate in a clear, concise, and persuasive manner: _____
2. Being spontaneous—saying and doing things that seem natural on the spur of the moment: _____
3. Doing things "by the book"—noticing appropriate rules and procedures and following them: _____
4. Being creative—having a lot of unusual, original ideas; thinking of new approaches to problems others do not often come up with: _____
5. Being competitive—wanting to win and be the best: _____
6. Being able to listen to and understand others: _____
7. Being aware of other people's moods and feelings: _____
8. Being careful in your work—taking pains to make sure everything is "just right": _____
9. Being resourceful in coming up with possible ways of dealing with problems: _____
10. Being a leader—having other people look to you for direction; taking over when things are confused: _____
11. Having the ability to accept feedback without reacting defensively, becoming hostile, or withdrawing: _____
12. Having the ability to deal with conflict and anger: _____
13. Having written work neat and organized; making plans before starting on a difficult task; organizing details of work: _____
14. Thinking clearly and logically; attempting to deal with ambiguity, complexity, and confusion in a situation by thoughtful, logical analysis: _____
15. Having self-confidence when faced with a challenging situation: _____
16. Having the ability to level with others, to give feedback to others: _____
17. Doing new and different things; meeting new people; experimenting and trying out new ideas or activities: _____

18. Having a high level of aspiration, setting difficult goals: _____
19. Analyzing a situation carefully before acting; working out a course of action in detail before embarking on it: _____
20. Being effective at initiating projects and innovative ideas: _____
21. Seeking ideas from others; drawing others into discussion: _____
22. Having a tendency to seek close personal relationships, participating in social activities with friends; giving affection and receiving it from others: _____
23. Being dependable—staying on the job; doing what is expected: _____
24. Having the ability to work as a catalyst, to stimulate and encourage others to develop their own resources for solving their own problems: _____
25. Taking responsibility; relying on your own abilities and judgment rather than those of others: _____
26. Selling your own ideas effectively: _____
27. Being the dominant person; having a strong need for control or recognition: _____
28. Getting deeply involved in your work; being extremely committed to ideas or work you are doing: _____
29. Having the ability to evaluate possible solutions critically: _____
30. Having the ability to work in unstructured situations, with little or no support and to continue to work effectively even if faced with lack of cooperation, resistance, or hostility: _____

Step 2   Complete Table 2.1, Profile Form, by placing an X in the appropriate box relative to the behavior profile you have just completed. Note that the 30 descriptions have been reordered to fit into five categories. The profile may indicate items on which your score is less desirable than you would like. You may also find categories in which you have generally low ratings. These may suggest areas for improvement during this course.

Part B *Goal Setting—Personal Objectives for Course*
Step 1 After completing the Profile Form in Table 2.1, outside of class list some of the *specific* objectives and expectations you have for this class. These objectives should describe what you will be able to do and the time required. Refer to the Profile Form you have just completed and select some behaviors you would like to emphasize for change.

Performance Objectives   *Time Requirement*

Communicating Skills:

1. _____
2. _____
3. _____

TABLE 2.1 Profile Form

Not at all Characteristic		Somewhat Characteristic			Very Characteristic			
1	2	3	4	5	6	7	A.	Communicating Skills
								1. Communicates
								6. Listens
								11. Receives feedback
								16. Gives feedback
								21. Seeks ideas
								26. Sells ideas
							B.	Interpersonal Skills
								2. Is spontaneous
								7. Is aware
								12. Deals with conflict
								17. Experiments
								22. Seeks close relationships
								27. Is dominant
							C.	Aspiration-Achievement Levels
								3. Conforms
								8. Is careful
								13. Is organized
								18. Aspires
								23. Is dependable
								28. Is committed to ideas or work
							D.	Problem-solving Skills
								4. Is creative
								9. Is resourceful
								14. Is logical
								19. Analyzes
								24. Is a catalyst
								29. Evaluates
							E.	Leadership Skills
								5. Is competitive
								10. Is a leader
								15. Is confident
								20. Initiates
								25. Takes responsibility
								30. Can work in unstructured situations

Interpersonal Skills:

    1. _____

    _____

    2. _____

    _____

    3. _____

    _____

Aspiration-Achievement Levels:

    1. _____

    _____

    2. _____

    _____

    3. _____

    _____

Problem-Solving Skills:

    1. _____

    _____

    2. _____

    _____

    3. _____

    _____

Leadership Skills:

    1. _____

    _____

    2. _____

    _____

    3. _____

    _____

Other:

    1. _____

    _____

    2. _____

    _____

    3. _____

    _____

Try referring to the preceding objectives often and at least before coming to class for the remainder of this course. Do not hesitate to experiment with the new behaviors you would like to cultivate. You will be referring to these objectives again later in the book.

Step 2   Form into trios, with one person acting as the client, a second as the consultant, and the third as observer (see the Profile Form and Observer Recording Form). Refer to the end of this simulation for "Instructions for Developing Consultant/Client Roles and Skills." The consultant will review the client's Profile Form and Performance Objectives for the following:

1. Are they a complete and challenging set of goals?
2. Are they realistic and feasible?
3. Are they specific and measurable?
4. Are they things the client can do and demonstrate by the end of the course?

Time for Step 2: 15–20 minutes per person, rotating roles.

Step 3   At the end of each interview, the observer gives observations providing feedback to the consultant using the Observer Recording Form, then rotates roles so that each person is in each of the three roles.
Time suggested for Step 3: 15–20 minutes per person, rotating roles.

Step 4   *Meeting with the entire class, discuss:*

1. Ways in which performance can be improved.
2. Goal setting and feedback. Helpful? Waste of time?
3. Role of consultant. Helpful? Dysfunctional? Ways to improve?

Time suggested for Step 4: 15 minutes.

OBSERVER RECORDING FORM

Your role during this part of the simulation is important because your goal is to give individuals feedback on their strategies of change. In giving feedback during the discussion, try to focus on the dimensions listed below.

Following are listed eight criteria of helping relationships. Rate the consultant by circling the appropriate number.

NOTES:
Words,
behaviors

1. Level of involvement:
   Cautious   Low 1 : 2 : 3 : 4 : 5 : 6 : 7 : 8 : 9 : 10 High   Interested   _____

2. Level of communication:
   Doesn't
   listen   Low 1 : 2 : 3 : 4 : 5 : 6 : 7 : 8 : 9 : 10 High   Listens   _____

3. Level of openness, trust:
   Shy,   Warm,
   uncertain   Low 1 : 2 : 3 : 4 : 5 : 6 : 7 : 8 : 9 : 10 High   friendly   _____

4. Level of collaboration:
   Authori-   Seeks
   tative   Low 1 : 2 : 3 : 4 : 5 : 6 : 7 : 8 : 9 : 10 High   agreement   _____

5. Level of influence:
   Gives in   Low 1 : 2 : 3 : 4 : 5 : 6 : 7 : 8 : 9 : 10 High   Convincing   _____

6. Level of supportiveness:
   Disagrees   Low 1 : 2 : 3 : 4 : 5 : 6 : 7 : 8 : 9 : 10 High   Supports   _____

7. Level of direction:
   Easygoing,   Gives
   agreeable   Low 1 : 2 : 3 : 4 : 5 : 6 : 7 : 8 : 9 : 10 High   directions   _____

8. Level of competence:
   Unsure   Low 1 : 2 : 3 : 4 : 5 : 6 : 7 : 8 : 9 : 10 High   Competent   _____

9. Other:
                    Low 1 : 2 : 3 : 4 : 5 : 6 : 7 : 8 : 9 : 10 High   _____

10. Overall style:
    Ineffective   Low 1 : 2 : 3 ; 4 : 5 · 6 : 7 : 8 : 9 : 10 High   Effective   _____

INSTRUCTIONS FOR DEVELOPING CONSULTANT-CLIENT ROLES AND SKILLS

In this course there has been an opportunity to develop the interaction and communication atmosphere conducive to experiential learning. In experiential learning the interrelationship among students is as important as that between instructor and students. Some characteristics of the OD consultant role are:

1. Two-way communication and influence. Use open-ended questions.

2. Openness of expression of views, feelings, and emotions. Being able to tell it like it is!

3. Supportiveness. When you are in agreement with your clients, give them your support. Learn to express differences without offending. Often two people in confrontation are 90 percent in agreement on the issues, but they focus only on their differences.

4. Awareness that conflict can be creative when differences are expressed appropriately.

5. Recognition of individual differences.

6. Confrontation of client.

   a. The courage to express your own convictions.

   b. Can you give and take feedback?

   c. Are you worried about being shot down?

   d. Are you willing to attempt risk-taking behavior?

   e. Are you overusing your share of the air time?

7. You may try to reflect the feelings of the client ("You seem to feel very strongly about this").

8. You may wish to disclose something about yourself ("This is a problem for me, also").

9. You may wish to use silence or nonresponse; just let the client talk.

10. Indicate nonverbally that you hear what is said (example: eye contact, nod of head).

Case Analysis Guidelines

WHY USE CASES?

Case studies allow a learning-by-doing approach. The material in the case provides the data for analysis and decision making. Cases require you to diagnose and make decisions about the situation and to defend those decisions to your peers.

OBJECTIVES OF THE CASE METHOD

1. Helping you to acquire the skills of putting textbook knowledge about management into practice.

2. Getting you out of the habit of being a receiver of facts, concepts, and techniques and into the habit of diagnosing problems, analyzing and evaluating alternatives, and formulating workable plans of action.

3. Training you to work out answers and solutions for yourself, as opposed to relying upon the authoritative crutch of the professor or a textbook.

4. Providing you with exposure to a range of firms and managerial situations (which might take a lifetime to experience personally), thus offering you a basis for comparison when you begin your own management career.

HOW TO PREPARE A CASE

1. Begin your analysis by reading the case once for familiarity.

2. On the second reading, attempt to gain full command of the facts, organizational goals, objectives, strategies, policies, symptoms of problems, problems, basic causes of problems, unresolved issues, and roles of key individuals.

3. Arrive at a solid evaluation of the organization, based on the information in the case. Developing an ability to evaluate organizations and size up their situations is the key to case analysis.

4. Decide what you think the organization needs to do to improve its performance and to set forth a workable plan of action.

Case: The Popular Professor

Midwestern University enjoys a good reputation for a regional university. Its faculty have published in many journals, some are active in grants and research, but teaching effectiveness is widely known as the most important of several criteria for promotion.

During recent years the Sociology Department (see Exhibit 1) has become increasingly leftist in outlook and more militant and active in pressing economic, environmental, and political viewpoints. This has resulted in some criticism of the department by outside groups, local business people, and so on. Many of the older faculty (representing about half the total), who are more moderate in outlook, feel that the younger faculty are too extreme in their views and that students are given too much say in program administration.

A student representative group has become increasingly active, submitting surveys of student opinion, pushing for a grade review board, and pressing for voting representation on all departmental committees. At first the department chairman, Bill Purdy, had been willing to cooperate because he felt more student participation was desirable, but the faculty had become increasingly critical of the student requests.

One of the younger professors, Assistant Professor Bud Simpson, had actively worked for the student requests, but the situation worsened as he and Purdy sharply disagreed on many issues. They were constantly waging verbal battles—at first in faculty meetings and later in student-faculty conferences. The disagreements between the two became sharper and more polarized. Dean Frances McDonald, School of Arts and Sciences, had become concerned over charges that the faculty in the Sociology Department were growing too militant, and that standards were being overlooked.

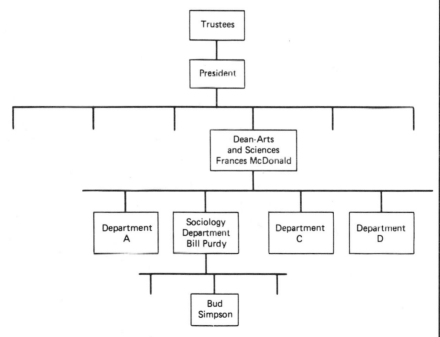

EXHIBIT 1. Organization Chart

The first incident emerged when it was announced that the administration, upon recommendation of the department, had notified Simpson that his appointment was not being renewed for the following year. The reasons given for the nonreappointment were a lack of research, no publications, little scholarly activity, and unprofessional performance. Simpson, interviewed by the school newspaper, suggested instead that it was his political viewpoints (as an avowed Marxist) and conflicts with the department chairman that had led to his dismissal. He showed student evaluation ratings which indicated outstanding teaching effectiveness, and pointed out the general low level of publishing in the department as a whole.

A week after the notification of nonreappointment, the student representatives presented a set of demands to McDonald, including:

1. The reappointment of Simpson.

2. The elimination of required courses.

3. Student representation on all committees.

4. A degree granted for any 125-hour credit program.

There were a number of other demands related to a less-structured program with increased student participation in administrative matters. A boycott of classes was threatened unless these demands were met.

CASE ANALYSIS FORM

I. Problems

  A. Macro

    1. _____

    2. _____

  B. Micro

    1. _____

    2. _____

II. Causes

    1. _____

    2. _____

    3. _____

III. Systems affected

    1. Structural _____

    2. Psychosocial _____

    3. Technical _____

    4. Managerial _____

    5. Goals _____

VI. Alternatives

    1. _____

    2. _____

    3. _____

    4. _____

    5. _____

V. Recommendations

    1. _____

    2. _____

    3. _____

V.
Summary

Change is all around us, and for managers the idea of future shock—too much change in too short a time—can be a very real problem. Managers and organizations face rapid changes in three areas: technological advancements, environmental changes, and social changes. The organization must adapt to these changing situations as each day presents a new set of conditions.

Each organization must maintain a dynamic equilibrium between stability and innovation. A systems model may be used to identify the sources of impetus for change. The environmental suprasystem has an impact on organizations through technological, economic, and cultural forces. Organizational change also comes from forces within the organizational subsystems.

Organizations may adapt to changes with four different orientations. A conservative management orientation has little ability to adapt to changes, but there is no great need because of a stable environment. A reactive management orientation has the need to respond to a rapidly changing environment but does not have the ability. A satisficing management orientation has the ability to respond to a changing environment but finds itself in a relatively stable environment. An anticipative management orientation has both the ability and the need to respond to a rapidly changing environment.

It seems that most modern organizations are increasingly finding the need for this anticipative orientation. Anticipative management predicts future conditions and makes planned changes before the conditions actually come about. For an organization to have the capacity to adapt to change and become more effective, management must initiate and create a climate that encourages creativity and innovation.

Organization development involves the long-term, system-wide application of behavioral science techniques to increase organization effectiveness. OD works on the idea that organization change involves improving the way people work together on teams and the way team activities are integrated with organization goals.

OD is a relatively new approach to change, evolving from the early work of behavioral interventionists to solve organization problems. From the early use of laboratory-training and survey feedback techniques, OD has grown to include a multitude of differing approaches, techniques, and practitioners. Many major corporations and governmental agencies have applied OD methodologies to improve organization functioning.

OD is a continuing process of organization improvement usually involving a sequence of steps, or stages. The eight stages presented here are typical of most OD programs, but they are not always exactly followed, since a change program is an unpredictable and turbulent thing. The stages may not occur in the sequence described or some of the stages may occur simultaneously, but they can be regarded as an ideal or a typical model rather than as the actual representation of every OD program. The objective of OD is a payoff in increased adaptability and productivity.

In the simulation you may have begun to sense the responsibility of being an OD consultant. What kinds of systems or individuals would you choose to help or not help? What financial criteria would you use? Would you consult with a client system even though it could not pay you? These are among the factors that a consultant must consider, and you must also be aware of your own value system: What do you believe in and stand for?

Change is the name of the game in management today, requiring rapid solving of complex problems within time constraints. In the simulation you had an opportunity to deal with these factors.

NOTES

1. "Hewlett-Packard, Where Slower Growth Is Smarter Management," *Business Week*, June 9, 1975, p. 50.

2. See Rosabeth Kanter, "Innovation—The Only Hope for Times Ahead," *Sloan Management Review*, 25, no. 4 (Summer 1984), 51–55.

3. Fremont E. Kast and James E. Rosenzweig, *Organization and Management* (New York: McGraw-Hill Book Company, 1979), p. 11.

4. See V. Luchsinger and V. Dock, *The Systems Approach: A Primer* (Dubuque, Iowa: Kendall/Hunt Publishing Company, 1976).

5. Wendy Prichard, "What's New in Organization Development," *Personnel Management*, July 1984, p. 30.

6. Marshal Sashkin and others, "OD Approaches," *Training and Development Journal*, 39, no. 2 (February 1985), 46.

7. See Robert R. Blake and Jane S. Mouton, "OD Technology for the Future," *Training and Development Journal*, November 1979, p. 55. Blake contends that there is "one best way."

8. From *Future Shock*, by Alvin Toffler. Copyright © 1970 by Alvin Toffler. Reprinted by permission of Random House, Inc. Originally appeared in *Playboy* in slightly different form. Also by permission of The Bodley Head, London. See also *The Third Wave*, 1982.

9. "Superchips: The New Frontier," *Business Week*, June 10, 1985, p. 83. See also "The Super Chip," *Wall Street Journal*, April 27, 1979, p. 1.

10. John Naisbitt, *Megatrends* (New York: Warner Books, 1982). See also John Naisbitt and Patricia Aburdene, *Re-Inventing the Corporation* (New York: Warner Books, 1985).

11. "ESB Ray-O-Vac: Decentralizing to Recharge Its Innovative Spirit," *Business Week*, March 12, 1979, p. 116.

12. Robert Chin and Kenneth D. Benne, "General Strategies for Effecting Changes in Human Systems," in *The Planning of Change*, ed. Warren G. Bennis, Kenneth D. Benne, and Robert Chin (New York: Holt, Rinehart & Winston, 1979), pp. 32–59.

13. Frank Friedlander and L. Dave Brown, "Organization Development," in *Annual Review of Psychology*, 25 (1974), 336.

14. "A Paragon Called TRW," *Forbes*, July 18, 1983, p. 102.

15. "The Toughest Job," *Business Week*, February 25, 1985, p. 50.

16. "The Humanistic Way of Managing People," *Business Week*, July 22, 1972, p. 42.

17. "They're Striking Some Strange Bargains at Diamond Shamrock," *Fortune*, January 1976, p. 142.

18. "Humanistic Way," p. 49.

19. "Team Work Through Conflict," *Business Week*, March 20, 1974, p. 45.

20. "A New Face Jolts Pillsbury," *Business Week*, May 2, 1977.

21. "The Toughest Job," *Business Week*, February 25, 1985, p. 50.

22. "Humanistic Way," p. 49.

23. "They're Striking," p. 144.

24. "Team Work Through Conflict," p. 46.

25. "Humanistic Way," p. 49.

26. This profile was adapted from a questionnaire developed by Boise Cascade Corporation. We are indebted to them for permission to include their material in this text. For information on a computerized managerial assessment system, the CMS approach, contact the authors.

3

CHANGING
THE CORPORATE CULTURE

I.
Objectives

Upon completing this chapter, you will be able to:

1. Recognize the importance of corporate culture to organizational success.

2. Identify the key factors used in assessing the corporate culture.

3. Describe the cultural and organizational factors which lead to effective organizations.

II.
Premeeting
Preparation

1. Read the Background Information (Section III).

2. Read instructions for Simulation 3.1 (Section IV). Complete Step 1.

3. Read and analyze Case: The Dim Lighting Co.

III.
Background
Information

Change, massive change, is impacting on all facets of society, creating new dimensions and great uncertainty. The issue facing us today is how to manage such change.[1]

Change is inevitable. Executives are adapting to changing market conditions and at the same time facing the need for creating an "anticipative" rather than a "reactive" managerial system. They are searching for ways to manage an increasingly complex technology and a more sophisticated work force. To accomplish these diverse goals, managers need more than piecemeal, ad hoc change programs dealing only with current crises. They need long-term efforts to prepare for future organization requirements. Richard Beckhard, an OD practitioner, notes: "Today, there is a need for longer-range, coordinated strategy to develop organization climates, ways of work, relationships, communications systems, and information systems that will be congruent with the predictable and unpredictable requirements of the years ahead."[2]

An effective organizational climate and a realistic vision of the future are both essential to future success. As R. H. Kilman has noted: "The organization itself has an invisible quality—a certain style, a character, a way of doing things—that may be more powerful than the dictates of any one person or any formal system. To understand the soul of the organization requires that we travel below the charts, rule books, machines, and buildings into the underground world of corporate cultures."[3]

The lessons of management seem to point out that companies with outstanding financial performance often have powerful corporate cultures, suggesting that "culture" is the key to an organization's success. Cultural change does not just happen in an organization, rather it is usually the result of a complex change strategy implemented by the company's management.

Given an environment of rapid change, a static organization culture can no longer be effective. Managers must be able to recognize when changes are needed and must possess the necessary skills and competence to implement these changes. The organization must try to adapt itself to a dynamic environment by introducing internal changes that will allow the organization to become more effective.

One method for bringing about such an anticipative management culture is organization development. Organization development has been described earlier as a long-range effort to introduce planned change throughout an organization.

In this chapter, we will examine the concept of corporate culture, illustrate the impact of key cultural factors, and describe the goals and values of an OD program.

THE CORPORATE CULTURE

Every organization has a culture. For example, at IBM service to the customer is a dominant value that forms a basis for action from top management down through all levels of the company.

Pepsi Cola, also, has its own culture. "Pepsi's values reflect the desire to overtake Coke. Managers engage in fierce competition against each other to acquire market share, to squeeze more profits out of their business, and to work harder. Employees who do not succeed are terminated. They must win to get ahead. A career can be made or broken on one-tenth of a point of market share. Everyone knows the corporate culture and thrives on the creative tension thus generated. The internal structure is lean and adaptable. The company picnic is characterized by intensely competitive team sports. Managers change jobs frequently and are motivated to excel. The culture is characterized by a go-go atmosphere and success at all costs."[4]

As noted in Chapter 1, a corporate culture is a system of shared values and beliefs which interact with an organization's people, structure, and systems to produce behavioral norms (the way things are done around here).

We shall use the term *corporate culture* to refer to all types of organizations; thus a university or a city government has a corporate culture, even though they are not corporations.

Management style and corporate culture are central factors in the success of a company. "One of the most critical factors in organizational strategy is management style and culture. This sets the tone for the whole organization and influences the communication, decision making, and leadership patterns of the entire system."[5] There is no basic culture that works best for all organizations. The management style and the set of norms, values, and beliefs of the organization's members combine to form the corporate culture. According to Terrence Deal and Allan Kennedy, "A shared history between members builds a distinct corporate identity or character."[6]

A corporate culture must achieve goals as well as satisfy the needs of members in order for the organization to be effective. Culture influences how managers and employees approach problems, serve customers, react to competitors and carry out activities. In comparing the style of Japanese and American automakers, Robert Waterman suggested the importance of culture:

> It has not been just strategy that led to big Japanese wins in
> the American auto market. It is a culture that inspires
> workers to excel at fits and finishes, to produce moldings
> that match and doors that won't sag.[7]

The Corporate Culture and Success _____

A corporate culture gives the whole organization a sense of how to behave, what to do, and where to place priorities in getting the job done. Culture helps members fill in the blanks between formal directives and how the work actually gets done. Because of this, culture is of critical importance in the implementation of strategy.

A great majority of outstanding companies trace their cultures back to an influential founder who personified a value system and relentlessly hammered in a few basic values which became the cultural core of the company. However, with today's rapidly changing environment, many corporate cultures fail to adapt to change and therefore fail as economic entities.

In Search of Excellence

What makes for excellence in the management of an organization? In a recent study of corporations, Tom Peters and Robert Waterman have provided some insight into developing an effective organization.[8] In their book, *In Search of Excellence* (which has sold more than 5 million copies), they studied the practices of 43 companies that are often used as examples of well-managed organizations, including IBM, McDonald's, and Hewlett-Packard and identified eight characteristics: (1) Establish a preference for doing something rather than sending an idea through endless cycles of analyses and committee reports; (2) Be customer-driven. Listen and learn customer preferences, and cater to them. (3) Encourage leaders and innovations. Break the corporation into small companies; encourage them to think independently and competitively; (4) Increase productivity by involving people. Believe in the individual employees; let them know their best efforts are essential and that they will share in the rewards of the company's success; (5) Keep executives in touch with the firm's essential business and promote a strong corporate culture; (6) Stay with the businesses the company knows best; define strengths; (7) Small plants outperform large ones; (8) Allow managers flexibility in a climate where there is dedication to the central values of the company combined with a tolerance for all employees.

The book's basic message was that U.S. organizations can regain their competitive edge by paying more attention to the culture and to people—customers and employees—and by developing those core skills and values that employees know how to do best. The book, however, has not been without its critics. Management writer Peter Drucker has termed it a "book for juveniles," and consultant Daniel T. Carroll pointed out that their sample is not truly representative and ignores the importance of such factors as proprietary technology.[9]

In Search of Excellence was a response to management's emphasis on traditional structures and values and on "number crunching" as an answer to all problems. Perhaps the most important message is that the excellent companies of today will not necessarily be the well-run companies of tomorrow: An excellent company must develop a core culture which leads to innovation and adaptation to the changing environment. At IBM, McDonald's, and Hewlett-Packard, for example, the culture and values that drive the behavior of employees are harmonious with the market-driven strategies of the companies.

Cultural Resistance to Change _____

A culture can also prevent a company from remaining competitive or adapting to a changing environment. People Express Inc. built its early success on an unusual and highly decentralized form of management in which every employee was an owner-manager. Employees were encouraged and even required to perform different functions, such as a pilot also working as a ticket agent. The result was that employees tended not to get bored and learned other aspects of the business. This type of happy disorganization worked well when the company was small but it becomes chaos and creates substantial problems for a billion-dollar-a-year company. When People was warned about their management practices being inappropriate, the company would respond with the statement: "This philosophy is what made us great. We're not going to change." The company president Donald C. Burr still held on to this culture up to the point that People, suffering from heavy losses, was forced to sell out to its arch rival, Texas Air.[10]

People Express demonstrates the importance of culture in managing a company's strategy. As a result, changing the culture to successfully implement a strategy is critical. OD Application 3.1 illustrates this difficulty at Apple Computer.

The need for devising and executing better strategies is becoming readily apparent. Recession, deregulation, technological upheavals, social factors, foreign competition, and markets that seem to emerge and vanish as quickly as they come have increased the pressure on companies to be flexible and adaptable. "The fashionable view holds that the biggest stumbling block on the path to adaptation is often an inappropriate corporate culture."[11]

Power Tools _____

Management changes to improve strategy are more likely to succeed if the factors that shape the culture can be identified and managed. In a comparison of high-innovation companies with low-innovation ones, Rosabeth Moss Kanter describes how *change masters* and *corporate entrepreneurs* are allowed to flourish in high-innovation companies.[12] Three organization "power tools" are required in the adaptive organization: information, support, and resources.

Information. The first tool is to provide people with information or an ability to gather information. People feel free to go outside of their own department to gather information and open communication patterns across departments. General Electric and Wang Laboratories have rules prohibiting closed meetings. Other organizations have information exchange meetings that cut across employee levels. "MBWA" (Management by Wandering Around) is an expression at Hewlett-Packard and is increasingly becoming a practice for managers at all levels.

OD
Application
3.1

THE CORPORATE COUNTERCULTURE AT APPLE

Apple Computer Inc. has undergone some changes in its efforts to stay abreast of the market. Back in 1985 when John Sculley, brought in by co-founder Steven Jobs to help run the company, successfully wrested control of Apple from Jobs, the company was suffering its first quarterly loss as a public corporation. Sculley introduced a massive reorganization which included laying off 20 percent of its employees. Shipments of the Macintosh, the omputer on which Apple's future was riding, were running 10,000 a month compared with an 80,000 a month capacity.

Although aware that things had to change at Apple, Sculley said, soon after he had gained control, that he did not want to lose the special culture at Apple. Jobs was primarily responsible for the informal attire of Apple's youthful staff that gave more weight to doing an important and interesting job than to the trappings of power. At that time Apple was known for Friday beer busts, parties, and occasional visits from such rock groups as The Grateful Dead. Jobs also brought to Apple a blunt style of communication and a dislike for hierarchy and rules.

But Apple has more than doubled in size since Sculley took over and pulled the company out of bad financial times. Apple is now a $2 billion plus company with 5,000 employees, and things have changed around the company.

Not everyone agrees with Sculley's success in keeping Apple's original culture intact. Some of the first people at Apple say Sculley failed. On the other hand, according to a report by Sculley at a recent annual stockholders meeting, "This is a new-product-driven industry and we have our new products on track. . . . Where Apple got in trouble in 1984 and 1985, we got behind the power curve of new products. Our goal is never to let that happen again."

Questions:
1. What happened at Apple?
2. Could you have predicted such a conflict of values?
3. How does an organization grow into a billion-dollar company, yet retain a small-company culture? And should they?

Based on the following articles: Katherine M. Hafner and Geoff Lewis, "Apple's Comeback," *Business Week*, January 19, 1987, pp. 84–89. Brenton R. Schlender, "Apple Computer Will Unveil Products that Let Macintosh Users Share Data," *The Wall Street Journal*, January 29, 1987, p. 2. Donna K. H. Walters, "Apple Goes Back to Basics at Upbeat Annual Meeting," *Los Angeles Times*, January 29, 1987, Business Section, p. 2. "Can Apple's Corporate Counterculture Survive?" *Business Week*, January 16, 1984.

Support. The second tool is to provide the corporate entrepreneur with the support and necessary "go ahead" from higher management as well as the cooperation of peers and subordinates. If the project will cut across organization lines, support and collaboration from other departments is needed. For example, interdepartment meetings and training sessions that normally bring people together can provide the opportunity to build support for projects. Organizations can remove the fear to fail and provide a climate that supports people in taking risks.

Resources.   The third tool is the resources, including funds, staff, equipment, and materials to carry out the project. One normal process of funding innovation is through budgetary channels, but traditionally this process is too time consuming to respond to the project in a timely manner. Some organizations support projects from bootlegged funds budgeted for other projects. Lockheed Aircraft is particularly known for its "skunk works" projects, and 3M normally requires a certain percent of a funded project be devoted to bootlegged projects. "Venture capital" and "innovation banks" also provide support for innovative projects. W. L. Gore and Associates, another example of a highly adaptive company, does not have employees; it has instead associates, and the company encourages people to develop their ideas into projects.

THE GOALS AND VALUES OF OD ⎯⎯⎯⎯⎯⎯⎯⎯⎯⎯⎯⎯⎯⎯⎯⎯⎯⎯⎯⎯⎯⎯

Now that a macro approach to organizational change has been described, let us examine some of the micro issues involved in change: the underlying goals, assumptions, and values basic to most OD programs.

The ultimate purpose of increasing an organization's ability to adapt to a changing environment is to make it more effective. What makes an organization effective or ineffective? Etzioni has suggested that effectiveness is the degree of goal achievement or, as he further elaborates, the amount of resources an organization needs to use in order to produce units of output.[13]

In general, OD programs are aimed at three basic organizational dimensions which affect performance. *Effectiveness* refers to the accomplishment of specific organizational goals and objectives. If organizations are using their resources to attain long-term goals, the managers are effective. The closer organizations come to achieving their strategic goals, the more effective the organization. *Efficiency* refers to the ratio of output (results) to input (resources). The higher this proportion, the more efficient the manager. When managers are able to minimize the cost of resources used to attain performance, they are managing efficiently. An organization may thus be efficient, but not effective, or vice versa. The third factor may be termed *motivational climate*, consisting of the set of employee attitudes and morale which influence the level of performance.

Warren Bennis proposes three other criteria as indicators of organizational effectiveness or health:

1.   *Adaptability*—the ability to solve problems and to react with flexibility to changing environmental demands.

2. *A sense of identity*—knowledge and insight on the part of the organization of what its goals are, and what it is to do.

3. *Capacity to test reality*—the ability to search out and accurately and correctly interpret the real properties of the environment, particularly those that have relevance for the functioning of the organization.[14]

Richard Steers raises questions of determining what effectiveness is and how it should be measured. He does not recommend specific criteria; instead, he suggests an analysis of the major processes (goal optimization, systems perspective, and emphasis on human behavior) involved in effectiveness. Steers stresses goal identification and the need for objectively determining the reality of the environment in which the organization exists.[15]

Chris Argyris has suggested that effectiveness comes from conditions that permit the integration of organization goals with individual goals. In a similar vein, Robert Blake and Jane Mouton indicate that organizational excellence is derived from the integration of concern for production with concern for people. *Organizational effectiveness* is the end result of an OD program. It is a multiple rather than a singular goal, involving all of these factors.

Organizations that are reacting to change become increasingly slow to adapt as the rate of change increases. Anticipative management results in a source of organizational flexibility, thus allowing increased adaptation to changing conditions and a more effective organization. OD seeks to improve the anticipative nature of the culture and to improve the way the organization's mission is accomplished.

Because of the impact of corporate culture, the OD practitioner must also examine the relationship between the values of OD and those of the client systems, as noted in the following.

OD Professional Values _____

There is also the question of professional values. OD is an emerging profession, and its practitioners tend to describe themselves as professionals. Even though the OD discipline may be classified as having some degree of professionalization, the individuals working in the field may vary greatly in their *professionalism*. By professionalism we refer to the internalization of a value system that is a part of the concept of the profession.

The professionalism of an individual depends on the degree to which certain values pertinent to the profession have been internalized. Although there is some disagreement, four areas appear to be important.

1. *Expertise.* The professional requires some *expertise*. This includes specialized knowledge and skills that can be obtained only through training (usually academic).

2. *Autonomy.* The professional claims *autonomy*. Professionals reserve the right to decide how their function is to be performed and to be free from restrictions.

3. *Commitment.* Professionals feel a *commitment* to the discipline. They are more likely to identify with members of their profession in other organizations than with their own organization.

4. *Code of ethics.* Finally, there is a *responsibility to society* for the maintenance of professional standards of work. They adhere to professional self-discipline and code of ethics.[16]

Value System Conflicts

One factor that differentiates an OD program from more traditional approaches concerns the set of values that the consultant brings to the situation. One of the key issues to be resolved between the OD practitioner and the client concerns the relative value orientations of each party. These include beliefs about people, the methods used to reach change goals, and the purpose of the change program.

There is a value system underlying OD approaches. These values emphasize increasing individual growth and effectiveness by creating an organizational climate that develops human potential together with achieving organizational goals. The value systems underlying OD have been derived from a number of basic ideas and approaches, including those of Chris Argyris, Warren Bennis, Abraham Maslow, Douglas MacGregor, Frederick Perls, and Carl Rogers. Wendell L. French and Cecil H. Bell, Jr. have commented:

> Organization development activities rest on a number of
> assumptions about people as individuals, in groups, and in
> total systems, about the transactional nature of organization
> improvement, and about values. These assumptions tend to
> be humanistic, developmental, and optimistic. Assumptions
> and values held by change agents need to be made explicit,
> both for enhancing working relationships with clients and for
> continuous testing through practice and research.[17]

To achieve the OD goals, the consultant has to consider certain ethical or value implications of his or her role in initiating a change program. There are a range of these ethical issues associated with an OD program; we examine next three important issues.[18]

The degree of value congruence.   The consultant brings a certain set of values to the client organization, which has its own basic values and mission. The question, then, is the degree to which the consultant's personal values are congruent with those of the client. For example, should an OD change agent help an organization doing biochemical warfare research to become more effective if his or her personal value system is opposed to the organization's methods or mission?

Many OD consultants feel that this is an initial issue to be considered prior to accepting any consulting relationship. If the client's goals are unacceptable, he or she should not try to make a system more effective. To do so, these consultants feel, would be unethical.

Others have argued that such companies are legal and follow the directions chosen by elected governmental representatives, and therefore organization development is valid in these situations. OD has been applied in defense organizations and in the military, and some practitioners believe that OD should have a value-free orientation. Just as a doctor treats both friend and foe, the OD consultant works to help organizations of all types and the individuals within these organizations to develop into a more healthy orientation.

Another issue concerns which client systems the consultant chooses to help or not to help. Some OD consultants offer their professional assistance to all potential clients regardless of financial remuneration; others limit themselves to client systems that can afford their professional fees. (See B.C. comic strip.)

Freedom to change versus imposed change. Another ethical consideration for the OD consultant is the question of choice in deciding to implement a change program. The decision to initiate an OD program is usually made by the top management group, yet it is likely to affect all members and parts of the organization. At Saga, for example, the top executives and the OD consultant decided on the OD program, which involved all members. Lower-level members may or may not have had a real choice regarding their participation in the program. If organization members do not have a choice, the consultant may tend to become an instrument for imposing change upon the rest of the organization.

One example that illustrates this issue is reported by William J. Crockett, concerning his experience in introducing change into the U.S. Department of State.

B.C. By permission of Johnny Hart and Creators Syndicate, Inc.

One of the first things that happened to me was a summons from Robert Kennedy, the Attorney General, to come to his office. There was no greeting, no small talk, and no chance for response by me except, "yes, sir," to his cryptic monologue. He said:

"First of all get your loyalties straight. No matter whom you think you work for, the President appointed you, and he is your boss. He will expect your absolute loyalty. *Second, get your job straight.* The State Department must be made to be loyal and responsive to the President. It must become more positive and proactive. It must be made to assume a leadership position in the Foreign Affairs Community. Your job is to make this happen. And thirdly, do you know how to make this happen. . .?"

While I was trying to think up an answer, he held up his hand to silence my response and added, *"You will make it happen by giving orders and firing* people who don't produce."[19]

Determining the goals of the OD program. A third issue involves which of the goals of an OD program is likely to be given precedence. As noted earlier, change programs generally are aimed at improved effectiveness, efficiency, and participant satisfaction. The question then arises: Which, or to what degree is emphasis to be placed on each goal? Are organizational or individual goals to take precedence? Although this sounds relatively simple in theory, in practice the executives who are paying for the OD program are frequently under pressures to improve efficiency and profitability, even though they also seek increased participant satisfaction and morale. The question is: How can the OD consultant help improve the productive efficiency of the organization and at the same time improve the quality of job existence for its members?

Underlying the challenges and dilemmas of OD are a set of values about the nature of human beings and their positions in an organizational context. Newton Margulies and Anthony Raia (OD practitioners) have suggested that these values include the following:

1. Providing opportunities for people to function as human beings rather than as resources in the productive process.

2. Providing opportunities for each organization member, as well as for the organization itself, to develop to his full potential.

3. Seeking to increase the effectiveness of the organization in terms of *all* of its goals.

4. Attempting to create an environment in which it is possible to find exciting and challenging work.

5. Providing opportunities for people in organizations to influence the way in which they relate to work, the organization, and the environment.

6. Treating each human being as a person with a complex set of needs, *all* of which are important in a person's work and life.[20]

In this environment of change, OD practitioners face both exciting challenges and serious dilemmas over how to fully meet the changing values and processes of change.

There has been a growing concern about the philosophical issues surrounding the field of OD. These ethical issues arise from basic inconsistencies between the values of OD practitioners and those held by client organizations.

The technology and value system of OD is itself undergoing change and revitalization: hence the feelings expressed by one OD practitioner, Jerry B. Harvey, who feels that OD consultants are becoming trapped in the rituals of their own discipline.[21]

In summary, the objectives of OD are to create organizational cultures that are more effective, more potent, more innovative, and better equipped to accomplish both organization and member goals.

REVIEW QUESTIONS

1. Describe or compare the corporate cultures of organizations written up in magazines such as *Business Week* and *Fortune*. What makes one more effective than another?

2. Compare and contrast management efficiency and effectiveness.

3. Identify the basic attributes of corporate excellence.

KEY WORDS AND CONCEPTS

Define and be able to use the following:

Corporate culture	Managerial efficiency
OD consultant	Managerial effectiveness
Excellence	OD professional values
Three power tools	

IV.
Simulations

SIMULATION 3.1   RIF: A CONSENSUS-SEEKING ACTIVITY

Total time suggested: 1 hour, 35 minutes.

A. Purpose

The purpose of the simulation is to examine the interdependence among team members and the concept of culture. The goals include:

1. To compare decisions made by individuals with those made by the group.
2. To practice effective consensus-seeking techniques.
3. To understand the concept of cultural values.

B. Procedures

Step 1   Prior to class, form into groups of five members, each group constituting an executive committee. Assign each member of your group as one of the committee members.

1. Executive vice president marketing
2. Executive vice president finance
3. Executive vice president manufacturing
4. Executive vice president personnel
5. Executive vice president research and development

Individually read the employee profiles that follow and rank-order the 10 employees on the work sheet from "1" for least likely to "10" for most likely to be expendable. Participants are to enter their ranking in column (1) on the Executive Committee Decision Work Sheet. (See page 78.)

Step 2   Executive Committee Meeting

Through group discussion, exploration, and examination, try to reach a *consensus decision* reflecting the integrated thinking and consensus of all members.

Follow these instructions for reaching consensus:

1. Avoid arguing for your individual judgments. Approach the task on the basis of logic.

2. Avoid changing your mind simply to reach agreement and to avoid conflict, but support solutions with which you are able to agree.

3. Avoid "conflict-reducing" techniques, such as majority vote, averaging, or trading in reaching your decision.

4. View differences of opinion as a help rather than a hindrance in decision making.

At this point, meet together as the Executive Committee and enter your results in column (2) on the Executive Committee Decision Work Sheet. *Time suggested for Step 2: 45 minutes.*

Step 3 Each team lists its results on the blackboard, and the instructor posts the actual performance ranking. Enter the actual performance ranking in column (3).
Time for Step 3: 10 minutes.

Step 4 Using the answers given by the instructor, score your individual and team answers by subtracting the Personal Ranking (column 1) and Committee Ranking (column 2) each from the Actual Performance Ranking (column 3). Then record the absolute difference as the Individual Score (column 4) and Team Score (column 5), respectively. By totaling the points, an individual and a team score can be calculated. Column (4) provides an indication of the individual participant's "correctness," and column (5) provides an equivalent measure of each group's performance.

Individuals and teams can be compared based on these scores. However, individuals have varying degrees of knowledge and the final score may not reflect how decisions were made during the team discussion.
Time suggested for Step 4: 10 minutes.

Step 5 The instructor leads a discussion of the activity, letting each team explain its score. Consider the following points and compare answers for the teams:

1. The consensus process within each group: assets and difficulties, whether the rules were followed, and the dynamics behind the posted scores.

2. The extent to which efficiency, effectiveness, and member satisfaction was emphasized in the meeting.

3. The culture that will likely develop as a result of the decisions made in the meeting.

4. How could an OD program help Delta and your management team?

Time for Step 5: 30 minutes.

Reduction in force: Delta Corporation

Your committee will have to make a series of recommendations for a reduction in force (layoff) of employees, all of whom are married, of the same age (28), and all with no previous experience before joining Delta.

The president has asked you to examine the personal information of the 10 employees in the company who are most expendable. They are all good employees but because of reduced sales and earnings and a declining economy, Delta needs to be prepared for a 1 percent reduction in work force (RIF). Therefore, you are meeting to rank-order from "1" for least likely, to "10" for most likely to be "riffed." There are at least 11 employees in each of the five departments. The employees other than those on the list given to you have been with the company at least 8 years, and it is not feasible to RIF them at this time.

Among the criteria you may want to consider are:

1. Education
2. Performance
3. Seniority
4. Technical ability
5. Attitude
6. Leadership
7. Effectiveness
8. Efficiency
9. Job function
10. Social Ability

EMPLOYEE PROFILES

Finance. Gwen—seniority 3½ years; 4-year college education; has performed about average on annual appraisal (75 percent); average technical abilities and leadership potential; a steady, grinding worker; works long hours; has been working on employee benefit plan for 2 years; is a nonsmoker and nondrinker; has frequently complained about working with cigarette smokers.

Hal—seniority 5½ years; 4-year college education; has been rated average and above in annual appraisals (80 percent); high technical abilities; average leadership; always in on Saturday mornings; frequently works through lunch hour; has been working on committee to computerize payroll for past 18 months; is well liked and gets along with fellow workers; is a very neat and stylish dresser.

Research and Development. Carole—PhD in engineering; seniority 2½ years; has been above-average research engineer in performance appraisal (90 percent); high technical abilities; works unusual hours (sometimes works late at night, then doesn't come in until noon the next day); developed patent on a new solid-state circuit device last year; seldom attends social events; and is said to be unfriendly and often disagrees and conflicts with fellow workers.

Dave—M.S. in engineering; seniority 3½ years; has been average to above average on performance appraisal (75 percent); average technical abilities; average leadership; works steady 8 to 5 hours; is working on several R&D projects but none yet completed; always ready for a coffee break or joke-telling session; is well liked by coworkers; and never complains about bad assignments.

Marketing. Tony—M.B.A. degree; seniority 2 years; has been rated as performing better than 95 percent on performance appraisal; high technical abilities; low leadership; works erratic hours (often comes into office at 9:30 and frequently plays golf on Wednesday afternoons); sold the highest number of product units in his product line; seldom socializes with fellow workers; and is often criticized because his desk is messy and disorganized, piled with correspondence and unanswered memos.

Ken—4-year college degree; seniority 18 months; has been rated an above-average to outstanding performer (85 percent); high technical abilities; average leadership; has been criticized for not making all his sales calls, but has a good sales record and developed advertising campaign for new product line; although a good bowler refuses to bowl on company team; and has been rumored to drink quite heavily on occasion.

Personnel. Eduardo—4-year college degree; seniority 18 months; has been rated above average as performer (85 percent); average technical abilities; high leadership; is frequently away from desk and often misses meetings; has designed and implemented a new management development program; is well liked although frequently has differences of opinion with line managers; and often takes long coffee breaks and lunch hours.

Frank—2-year college degree; seniority 4 years; has been rated average to above average as performer (70 percent); low technical abilities; above average leadership; works long hours; regularly attends all meetings; has been redesigning performance appraisal systems for past 2 years; is involved in many company activities; belongs to Toast Masters, Inc.; and is known as a friendly, easygoing guy.

Manufacturing. Irv—4-year college degree; seniority 15 months; rated an outstanding performer (90 percent); high technical abilities; low leadership; has been criticized for not attending committee meetings; designed and implemented the computerized production control process; does not socialize with fellow employees; and is known as a sloppy dresser (often wearing white or red socks with a suit).

Jackie—high school; seniority 6 years; rated an average performer (75

EXECUTIVE COMMITTEE DECISION WORK SHEET

Employee	(1) Personal Ranking	(2) Committee Ranking	(3) Actual Performance Ranking	(4) Individual Score	(5) Team Score
Gwen					
Hal					
Carole					
Dave					
Tony					
Ken					
Eduardo					
Frank					
Irv					
Jack					
Total Scores					

percent); average technical abilities; average leadership; always attends meetings; works steady 8 to 5 hours and Saturday mornings; has chaired committee to improve plant safety for past 2 years; participates in all social events; plays on company bowling and softball teams; and is known for a very neat, organized office.

**Case:
The Dim
Lighting Co.**

The Dim Lighting Company is a subsidiary of a major producer of electrical products. Each subsidiary division operates as a profit center and reports to regional, group, and product vice presidents in corporate headquarters. The Dim Lighting subsidiary produces electrical lamps, employing about 2,000 workers. The general manager is Jim West, 46, an M.B.A. from Wharton, who has been running this subsidiary successfully for the past 5 years. However, last year the division failed to realize its operating targets, as profit margins dropped by 15 percent. In developing next year's budget and profit plan, Jim West feels that he is under pressure to have a good year because 2 bad years in a row might hurt his long-term potential for advancement. (See Exhibit 1.)

DOCTOR SPINKS, DIRECTOR OF R&D

Leon Spinks, 38, director of R&D, was hired by West 3 years ago, after resigning from a major competitor. Spinks has received a number of awards from various scientific societies and his group of scientists and engineers respect his technical competence and have a high level of morale.

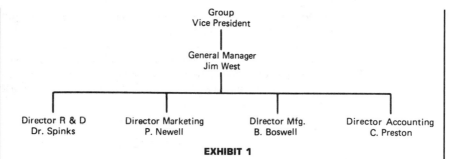

EXHIBIT 1

Although he is recognized as a talented scientist, other managers feel that Spinks is often autocratic, strong-minded, and impatient. Spinks left his former company because management lacked creativity and innovation in R&D.

THE PROPOSAL

Spinks has submitted a budget request for a major research project: the micro-miniaturization of lighting sources, to greatly reduce energy requirements. He sees this as the Lamp of the Future. The proposed budget would require $250,000 per year for 2 years, plus another $300,000 to begin production. Jim West immediately contacted corporate headquarters, and although his idea was highly praised, they were reluctant to or pand any share in the proposed project.

THE BUDGET MEETING

West called a meeting of his management group on Wednesday morning to discuss the proposed budget. Spinks presented a very rational and high-powered sales pitch for his project. He suggested that the energy crunch had long-term implications and that if they failed to move into new technologies, they would be competitively obsolete.

Carl Preston, accountant, presented a financial analysis of the proposed project, noting the high risk, the uncertain results, and the length of time before it would contribute to operating profits. "These scientists are prima donnas, who can afford to wait for long-term results. Unfortunately, if we don't do something about the bottom line right now, we may not be here to enjoy it," he noted.

Bill Boswell, production manager, agreed with Preston: "We need new machinery for our production line also, and that has a very direct payback."

Pete Newell, marketing, agreed with Spinks: "I don't feel we can put our heads in the sand. If we don't keep up competitively, how will our salespeople be able to keep selling obsolete lighting products? Besides, I'm not sure that all of Carl's figures are completely accurate in measuring the actual return on this low-energy project." A stormy debate followed, with heated arguments both for and against the project put forth, until West called the meeting to a halt.

Later in his office, thinking it over, he considered the situation. Going ahead with the micro-miniaturization project was a big gamble with high uncertainty. But if he decided against it, it was quite possible that Spinks would resign, which would shatter the R&D department he had worked so hard to assemble.

CASE ANALYSIS FORM

I. Problems

    A. Macro

        1. _____

        2. _____

    B. Micro

        1. _____

        2. _____

II. Causes

        1. _____

        2. _____

        3. _____

III. Systems affected

        1. Structural

        2. Psychosocial

        3. Technical

        4. Managerial

        5.

IV. Alternatives

        1. _____

        2. _____

        3. _____

        4. _____

        5. _____

V. Recommendations

        1. _____

        2. _____

        3. _____

V.
Summary

Change is an inevitable consequence of operating in a dynamic environment. For OD consultants and managers it is important to recognize that organization changes can be initiated by organization members (anticipative) or as a reaction to external forces (reactive). This chapter focuses on the idea that a key aspect of implementing change is the need to institutionalize the change into organizational value systems. Consequently, one important element in implementing a change program is the corporate culture.

Whether change is anticipative or reactive, it is likely to be most successful when the organization proceeds with a planned approach which takes into account the nature of the culture. In recent years, corporate culture has been recognized as a pervasive force influencing organization effectiveness. Culture has been defined as the shared values and behaviors of organizational members and represents a key factor in implementing planned change in organizations.

You have had an opportunity in the simulation to experience and observe a situation of organization change. You probably found that initiating planned change is not always as easy as it looks. You may have discovered that the functioning of a group is difficult to analyze, and gaining acceptance of change strategies presents difficulties. In reflecting upon the simulation, you may feel that the quality of your group's decision was not what it could have been. In addition to helping group members work better and more harmoniously with each other, OD programs assist employees in making more effective decisions for both the organization and its members. This simulation demonstrates many of the interpersonal and organizational factors that inhibit change. If the essential task of management is to deal with change, a manager must be able to initiate change and to implement the stages of an OD program.

Planned change efforts concentrate on problems of efficiency, effectiveness, and participant satisfaction. The focus of planned change efforts toward organization improvement include individual behavior, group and inter group relations, and overall organization problems.

OD is not a panacea, but many organizations have improved effectiveness by the application of these techniques. In the following chapters, each stage of an OD program is examined and explained in greater depth.

NOTES

1. Douglas C. Basil and Curtis W. Cook, *The Management of Change* (Great Britain: McGraw-Hill Book Company, 1984), p. 3.

2. Richard Beckhard, *Organization Development: Strategies and Models* (Reading, Mass.: Addison-Wesley Publishing Co., Inc., 1969), p. 8.

3. R. H. Kilmann, "Corporate Culture," *Psychology Today*, April 1985, p. 63.

4. P. Shrivastra, "Integrating Strategy Formulation with Organizational Culture," *Journal of Business Strategy*, Winter 1984, pp. 103–4.

5. Donald F. Harvey, *Business Policy and Strategic Management* (Columbus, Ohio: Charles E. Merrill Publishing Company, 1982), p. 44.

6. Terrence F. Deal and Allan A. Kennedy, "Culture: A New Look Through Old Lenses," *The Journal of Applied Behavioral Science*, 19, no. 4, 1983, p. 108.

7. Robert H. Waterman, Jr., "The Seven Elements of Strategic Fit," *Journal of Business Strategy*, no. 2 (1982), p. 70.

8. Thomas J. Peters and Robert H. Waterman, Jr., *In Search of Excellence* (New York: Harper & Row Publishers, Inc., 1982), pp. 13–15.

9. Daniel T. Carroll, "A Disappointing Search for Excellence," *Harvard Business Review*, November/December 1983, pp. 78–88.

10. Michael M. Miller and Patricia Bellew Gray, "Why Businesses Often Sink in 'Decisional Quicksand'," *Wall Street Journal*, December 15, 1986, p. 29.

11. Bro Uttal, "The Corporate Culture Vultures," *Fortune*, 108, no. 8 (October 17, 1983), 66.

12. Rosabeth Moss Kanter, "SMR Forum: Innovation—The Only Hope for Times Ahead?" *Sloan Management Review*, 25, no. 4 (Summer 1984), 51–55.

13. A. Etzioni, *Modern Organizations* (Englewood Cliffs, N.J.: Prentice Hall, Inc., 1964), p. 8.

14. Warren Bennis, *Organization Development, Its Nature, Origins, and Prospects* (Reading, Mass.: Addison-Wesley Publishing Co., Inc., 1969), pp. 26–32.

15. Richard Steers, "When Is an Organization Effective?" *Organizational Dynamics*, Autumn 1976, pp. 50–63.

16. George Strauss, "Professionalism and Occupational Associations," *Industrial Relations*, 2 (May 1963), 8.

17. Wendell L. French and Cecil H. Bell, Jr., *Organization Development: Behavioral Science Interventions for Organization Improvement*, 2nd ed. (Englewood Cliffs, N.J.: Prentice-Hall, Inc., 1978), p. 18.

18. Kevin C. Wooten and Louis P. White, "Ethical Problems in the Practice of Organization Development," *Training and Development Journal*, April 1983, pp. 16–23.

19. William Crockett, "Introducing Change to a Government Agency," in *Failures in Organization Development and Change*, ed. Phillip Mirvis and David Berg (New York: John Wiley & Sons, Inc., 1978), p. 113.

20. Newton Margulies and Anthony Raia, *Conceptual Foundations of Organizational Development* (New York: McGraw-Hill Book Company, 1978), p. 137.

21. Jerry B. Harvey, "Eight Myths OD Consultants Believe In . . . and Die By," *OD Practitioner*, February 1975, p. 3.

4

THE OD CONSULTANT:
Role and Style

I.
Objectives

Upon completing this chapter, you will be able to:
1. Define the role of an OD consultant-practitioner.
2. Identify your strengths and weaknesses as a potential consultant.
3. Experience and practice your own style of intervention and influence in a group.

II.
Premeeting Preparation

1. Read the Background Information (Section III).
2. Complete Steps 1 through 4 of Simulation 4.1 (Section IV).

III.
Background Information

In a turbulent and changing environment, managers are concerned not only with managing organizations as they exist at the present time, but also with changing them to meet future conditions. Change programs do not happen accidentally. Instead, they are initiated with a specific purpose and require some form of leadership to function properly. These change programs often represent a major alteration of organizational processes. Organizations consist of groups of people working together and changes alter the way the people work together, how they relate with others, and even how they see themselves. The OD practitioner initiates such changes by training, educating, and collaboratively designing new ways of functioning.

There are two types of change that may take place in an organization. The first type, termed random or haphazard change, is forced on the organization by the external environment. This type of change is not prepared for; it simply occurs and is dealt with as it happens, a practice usually called "firefighting."

The second type of change results from deliberate attempts to modify organizational operations by persons seeking to promote improvement. These changes do not automatically occur simply because someone in the organization decided an OD program would be helpful. The implementation of these steps depends largely on the consultant's abilities. Prior to the entry of the OD consultant, there must be an awareness of the need for change: usually some problem or disequilibrium causing the client system to seek help.[1]

To implement a program of planned change, the management must first identify a gap between the current situation and some desired condition. Change programs are then aimed at improving effectiveness, efficiency, and participant well-being. Too often, management will have introduced short-run, expedient change programs aimed solely at cost savings. Such programs often have unintended dysfunctional effects on participant satisfaction and the long-term goals of the organization. The OD consultant then helps the organization identify differences between where it is and where it would like to be, and then proceeds to design and implement appropriate OD interventions.

Every OD program must begin with a good working relationship between the consultant and the individual or group being helped. If this relationship is weak or superficial, the program cannot succeed. The success of almost any OD project depends to a large degree on the nature of this relationship, which must be developed in the initial stages of the change program.

This chapter focuses on the identification of the consultant and the initial intervention into the ongoing client system. We examine the major OD consultant roles and styles, and the major factors in creating a climate for change.

EXTERNAL AND INTERNAL CONSULTANT ROLES

In the past few years a growing number of major organizations, including General Electric, General Motors, TRW Systems, Union Carbide, and the U.S. Navy, have created internal OD consulting groups. Consequently, the OD consultant is also either an *external consultant* (an outside consultant called in by the client) or an *internal consultant* (an organization member acting as consultant). There are advantages and disadvantages to both roles.

The External Consultant

The external consultant is someone not previously associated with the client system. Because of coming in from the outside, the external consultant sees things from a different viewpoint and from a position of objectivity. Because the external consultant is invited into the organization, he or she has increased leverage (the degree of influence and status within the client system) and greater freedom of operation than an internal change agent. Furthermore, because external consultants are not a part of the organization, they are less in awe of the power that various members may wield. They do not depend upon the client system for raises, approval, or promotion, as an internal consultant must. Since they usually have a very broad career base and other clients to fall back on, they usually have a more independent attitude regarding risk taking and confrontations with the client system.

The disadvantages of external consultants result from these same factors. Generally, they are unfamiliar with the organization system and may be less than totally knowledgeable of its technology, such as aerospace or chemistry. They are unfamiliar with relationships, communication networks, and the formal or the informal power system. In some situations, consultants may have difficulty gathering pertinent information simply because they are outsiders.

The Internal Consultant

The internal consultant is already a member of the organization, either a top executive; a manager of personnel, human resources, or industrial relations departments; or simply an organization member who initiates change. Recently, many large organizations have established offices with the specific responsibility of helping the organization implement change programs. These internal consultants often operate out of the personnel or industrial relations area and report directly to the president of the organization. Internal consultants have certain advantages inherent in their relationship with the organization. They are familiar with the organization's culture and norms and probably accept and behave in accordance with the norms. This can save considerable time in becoming familiar with the system and becoming accepted. The internal consultant knows the power structure, who are strategic people, and how to apply leverage. He or she is already known to the employees, and has a personal interest in seeing the organization succeed.

The position of internal consultant also has disadvantages, one of the most significant of which is the lack of the specialized skills needed for organization development. Another disadvantage relates to lack of objectivity. Being a familiar person has advantages, but it can also work against the internal consultant because other employees may not understand the consultant's new role and will certainly be influenced by his or her previous work and relationships, particularly if the work and relationships have in any way been questionable. And finally, the internal consultant may lack the necessary power and authority, as it is too often the case that internal consultants are in some remote staff position and report to a midlevel manager.[2]

In an interview with *Playboy*, Admiral Elmo R. Zumwalt, Jr., past chief of naval operations, commented as follows on implementing change from within:

> I think every young generation's approach to the world is to
> generalize idealistically—dissatisfied with what they see—
> hoping for a better world. The process of maturing improves
> the society as they work to achieve their ideals. They also
> learn that the only way in which they can arrive at positions
> of influence sufficient to improve society is to make certain
> compromises. It seems to me that the essence of growth is
> to learn how to do that without giving up one's fundamental
> beliefs and aspirations. When people achieve positions of
> importance, the real test, for naval officers or petty officers
> or anybody, is whether they recall those youthful aspirations
> and measure themselves against those early ideals, modified
> by maturity, but hopefully not too much. . . .[3]

THE EXTERNAL-INTERNAL CONSULTING TEAM

A team formed of an external consultant working directly with an internal consultant to initiate and facilitate change programs is probably the most effective approach. John Lewis, for example, found that the more successful OD consultants worked upon the development of their internal counterparts.[4] Each partner brings to the consulting team complementary resources, that is, advantages and strengths that offset the disadvantages and weaknesses of the other. The external consultant brings expertise, objectivity, and new insights to organization problems. The internal consultant, on the other hand, brings detailed knowledge of organization issues and norms, a long-time acquaintance with members, and an awareness of system strengths and weaknesses.[5]

The collaborative relationship between internal and external consultants provides an integration of abilities, skills, and resources. The relationship serves as a model for the rest of the organization—a model that members can observe and see in operation, one that embodies such qualities as trust, respect, honesty, confrontation, and collaboration. The team approach allows a dividing of change program work load and a sharing of the diagnosis, plans, and strategies. The external-internal team is also less likely to accept watered-down or compromise change programs because each team member tends to provide support to the other. As an example, during the U.S. Navy's Command Development (OD) Program, the internal change agents recommended that training seminars be conducted away from the navy environment (i.e., at a resort) and that participants dress in civilian clothing to lessen authority issues. Higher authority, however, ordered the seminars to be held on naval bases and in uniform—ground rules that the internal consultants reluctantly accepted. In this situation an external consultant with greater leverage might have provided enough support and influence to have gained approval of the desired program.

Another reason for using an external-internal consulting team is to achieve greater continuity over the entire OD program. Because external consultants are involved in other outside activities, they generally are available to the organization only a few days a month, with 2- or 3-week intervals between visits. The internal consultant, on the other hand, provides a continuing point of contact for organization members at any time problems or questions arise. Since many OD programs are long-term efforts, often lasting 3 to 5 years, the external-internal team also provides continuing support for maintaining the momentum of the OD program. Most programs will hit low spots or stumbling blocks, and the external-internal combination may provide the stimulation and motivation needed to keep the change program moving during periods of resistance. The team effort is probably most effective, as it combines the advantages of both the external and internal consultants while minimizing the disadvantages.

TYPES OF CONSULTANTS

The OD consultant is the person who initiates, stimulates, or facilitates a change program, and may be an executive, a member of the organization, or an outside consultant. Change begins with the intervention of the consultant in the system to be changed. *Intervention* refers to the entrance into the client system and includes a variety of roles and activities.

Danielle B. Nees and Larry E. Greiner have identified five distinct types of consultants.[6] Table 4.1 summarizes the key features that distinguish each type. The OD consultant fits most closely into the "management-physician" category, since both types of consultants have a problem-identification approach to diagnosing general management problems with the goal of improving organizational effectiveness through leadership and organization interventions.

A number of consulting styles or approaches can be identified. Each type varies according to its underlying character—shaped by the kinds of skills and techniques consultants use, the values they bring to their clients, and the manner in which they carry out their assignments. Other research has also exam-

TABLE 4.1 Types of Consultants

	Mental Adventurer	Strategic Navigator	Management Physician	System Architect	Friendly Copilot
Knowledge base of consultants	Science	Economics	General management	Technology	Business experience
Role orientation toward client	Researcher	Planner	Diagnostician	Designer	Advisor
Approach to project	Statistical analysis	Modeling of key variables	Problem identification	Implementation of solutions	Sounding board for CEO
Focus of recommended actions	Creative answers	Future goals and objectives	Organization and leadership	Administrative procedures	Needs of CEO
Expected outcomes for client	More knowledgeable decisions	More profitable market niche	Improved organizational effectiveness	Greater efficiency	Better CEO judgment

Source: Reprinted by permission of the publisher from "Seeing Behind the Look-alike Management Consultants," by Danielle B. Nees and Larry E. Greiner, *Organizational Dynamics*, Winter 1985, p. 77. © 1985 American Management Association, New York. All rights reserved.

ined the degree of emphasis the consultant places upon two interrelated goals or dimensions of the change process. One method of classification involves the consultant's orientation to the two interrelated dimensions:

1. The degree of emphasis upon effectiveness or goal accomplishment.
2. The degree of emphasis upon relationships, morale, and participant satisfaction.

Based upon these two dimensions, five different types of consultant styles or roles may be identified (see Figure 4.1).

The agreeable style. The goal of the agreeable-style consultant is neither effectiveness nor participant satisfaction. Rather, the consultant is trying to keep from rocking the boat, and to maintain a low profile. The underlying motivation is often survival, or merely following the directives of top management. Such a role is usually found in large organizations where development programs may be part of the staff function and are not highly regarded by top management. This style is usually regarded as forced upon the individual by organi-

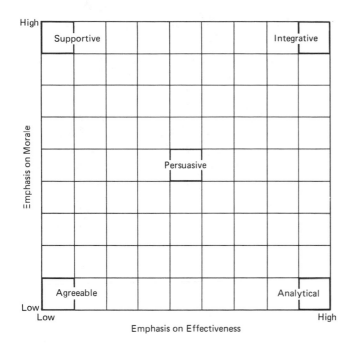

FIGURE 4.1
Consultant Styles

zation pressures, so that the individual has learned to conform and suppress internal motivations.

The supportive style The supportive style places emphasis on the satisfaction of organization members and is chiefly concerned with employee motivation and morale. The supportive consultant seeks warm working relationships and in general is more comfortable in nonconfrontative situations. Effectiveness per se is not emphasized, the assumption being that if member satisfaction is high, effectiveness will also be high. Unfortunately, there is a great deal of evidence that contradicts these assumptions. The supportive style strongly pushes for improved morale and open conflict or locking horns is avoided by attempts to smooth over differences and maintain harmony.

The analytical style. The analytical style places greatest emphasis on efficiency with little emphasis given to member satisfaction. The expert feels most comfortable with a rational assessment of problems and assumes that the facts will lead to a solution. This type of consultant may be quite confrontative, usually relying on authority to resolve conflict and on rational problem-solving processes.

The analytical consultant has a background of specialized expertise, knowledge, and experience applicable to the solution of specific problems. The client needs to have a problem solved, a service performed, or a study made, and the analytical consultant takes responsibility for providing these functions. This type of consultation is based on the belief that the client does not need to know or cannot learn the skills to solve its problems. The success of the consultant is largely dependent on the client's having properly diagnosed its problem and having called in the right kind of consultant.

The persuasive style. The persuasive style focuses on both dimensions, effectiveness and morale, yet optimizes neither. Such a style provides a relatively low risk strategy, yet avoids direct confrontation with other forces. This approach may be used when the consultant's power or leverage is low relative to other participants. This style is motivated primarily by a desire to *satisfice*; that is, to achieve something that is "good enough." A great deal of effort is applied in attempting to satisfy the differing forces, thus gaining a majority block of support for prepared changes. The resulting change program often may be watered down or weakened to the point where organization improvement is unlikely.

The integrative style. The integrative style seeks both a high degree of efficiency and high member satisfaction, believing that greater effectiveness is possible when all members are involved and problem solving is done through teamwork. There is an awareness that confrontation and conflict are often a means to a more effective organization and to more satisfied individual members. The integrative approach uses collaborative problem solving and challenges the underlying patterns of member behavior.

In a survey of about one thousand OD practitioners, it was found that the OD skills rated as most important were listening, integrity, and organizational diagnosis.[7]

The integrative consultant seeks to give the client new insights into its activities and to help the client system determine how it wishes to change and how it might go about implementing such changes. The consultant rarely informs or instructs the client system, but instead tries to discover client system problems and to challenge the underlying patterns of behavior of organization members.

The integrative consultant focuses on six types of processes essential for effective organization performance: (1) communication, (2) member roles and functions in groups, (3) group problem solving and decision making, (4) group norms and growth, (5) leadership and authority, and (6) intergroup cooperation and competition.[8]

In this section we have identified five different consultant styles. At the end of the chapter you will have an opportunity to find out where your own style fits in this classification system. Most organization problems are complex situations, however, and may not neatly fit with any one particular change approach, but will depend upon the particular consultant, the nature of the problem, and the type of organization climate that exists.

These five consulting styles are not mutually exclusive. All consultant styles can be effective and are interrelated. A consultant may use different styles at various times to meet changing client system needs and deal with diverse situations. Frequently, some combination of the types may be applied.

THE READINESS OF THE ORGANIZATION FOR OD

Upon first contacting the client system the OD practitioner begins evaluating its receptiveness for any OD program. It is a mistake to assume that because most organizations can benefit greatly from an OD program, they all must and should have one. The ironic element is that the very organizations most in need of such a program are precisely the ones least receptive. Their inflexibility and insensitivity to the need for change seem almost proverbial: "There are none so blind as those that will not see." Rather than impose organization development upon them, the consultant needs to wait until key personnel decide whether change is really needed. The motivation for any change program is then built in, not artificially contrived. To aid the consultant in gauging the preparedness of an organization for an OD program, Bennis lists four questions for which the consultant should obtain definite, precise, and positive answers before venturing further:

1. Are the learning goals of OD *appropriate*?
2. Is the cultural state of the client system *ready* for organization development?
3. Are the *key* people involved?
4. Are *members* of the client system adequately *prepared and oriented* to organization development?[9]

Once these questions have been satisfactorily answered, then and only then should the consultant proceed.

THE INTERVENTION PROCESS

The OD process involves a collaborative relationship between a consultant and a client system. OD consultants may possess differing consulting styles, philosophies, and approaches, but in general they perform a certain set of functions with regard to the client system. These functions include (1) helping the client determine its current level or state (data gathering), (2) assisting in a collaborative analysis of problem areas and planning strategies of change (diagnosis), and (3) intervening and facilitating change from the current level to some ideal or desired level. One example of this process at DuPont is shown in OD Application 4.1.

OVERHAULING A GIANT

DuPont, one of the seven largest U.S. corporations with sales of over $35 billion, has lost its competitive edge. In the first such meeting in company history, DuPont's 65 top executives gathered last July at a country club near its Wilmington, Delaware headquarters to discuss the future and draft a corporate mission statement. Chairman and chief executive Richard E. Heckert believes that every DuPont employee must be a salesman. Though insisting that "This isn't a horse race where DuPont has fallen behind the pack," he adds in the next breath: "Across the board, we simply aren't meeting our goals in terms of earnings, return on equity or share-value improvement."

DuPont's efforts to right itself resemble those of other U.S. industrial giants such as Procter & Gamble, Ford, and AT&T. All have remained profitable, but increased competition is forcing them to cut costs, reduce staff, and alter their approach to business.

Intervention Process

The changes that Mr. Heckert is attempting include changing the corporate culture. But the problem runs even deeper. Over the years, DuPont developed a highly stratified, risk-averse organization that tended to stifle the free flow of ideas. During the 1970s, for example, a plant foreman was reprimanded for going on weekend camping trips with blue-collar subordinates. Moreover, the company ignored customer needs and market changes; it assumed that it could simply invent its way to success.

When DuPont acquired Conoco, a company with a reputation as a lean fast-moving organization with few layers of bureaucracy, Constantine S. Nicandros, president of Conoco, forbade the oil company's employees to answer any questions from DuPont's headquarters until the requests had been cleared by him. "A lot of people were trying to handle us like a department of DuPont," he says. "We told them forget it. Most of the time, it was just an awful lot of people making work."

Change

Meanwhile, DuPont is attempting to adopt the business philosophy of giving employees more responsibility, a philosophy that Nicandros is widely credited with fostering. At "Japanized" DuPont plants, worker "self-management" is the buzzword. At headquarters, management layers have been reduced and responsibility pushed downward. Departments that had two vice presidents now have one or none. Plants have four levels of supervision instead of seven or eight. Newly liberated middle managers talk enthusiastically of exercising "broader spans of control."

New Strategy

The change in culture parallels a shift in strategy. DuPont is moving away from its longstanding base in fibers and plastics into an array of newer technologies, including biomedical products, specialty agricultural chemicals, and electronic products. Last year 40 percent of its sales came from high-tech specialty products rather than from bulk commodities.

Despite such strides, DuPont's transformation is far from complete.

Questions:
1. How would you describe the corporate culture at DuPont?
2. What consultant styles might work best? Why?

Based on: Christopher S. Eklund and Alison Leigh Cowan, "What's Causing the Scratches in DuPont's Teflon," *Business Week*, December 8, 1986, pp. 60–64. Alix M. Freeman and Laurie Hays, "DuPont's Woolard Named President, Operating Chief," *The Wall Street Journal*, January 29, 1987, p. 12. "Giant Overhaul," *The Wall Street Journal*, September 25, 1985, p. 1.

The Intervention

When the external or the internal consultant contacts the client system, he or she has already begun to intervene. *Intervention* refers to a coming between or among members or groups of an organization for the purpose of effecting change. More specifically, intervention refers to an array of planned activities participated in by both the consultant and the client, including shared observations of the processes occurring between members of a group or of an organization for the purpose of improving the effectiveness of the processes.[10] The intent of the intervention is to alter the status quo. Richard Beckhard suggests that a planned intervention is "moving into an existing organization and helping it, in effect, 'stop the music,' examine its present ways of work, norms, and values, and look at alternative ways of working, or relating, or rewarding."[11]

In a very broad sense, stages 2 through 8 of an OD program (explained in Chapter 2 and in the succeeding chapters of this book) describe the intervention process. During the course of an OD program there will be many interventions: interventions for gathering data, team-building activities, and so forth, but here we are concerned with the consultant's initial contact with the client system. The initial contact with the client system by the consultant is an intervention if for no other reason than it is a message to the organization members that the climate of the organization is under scrutiny and that new and more effective ways of doing things are being sought. Just this promise of a better future can effect change and therefore constitute an intervention.

The external consultant generally intervenes through either a top manager or a personnel director. As an example, when TRW Systems decided to initiate change, an external consultant was brought in by the industrial relations section. It is easier to bring about change when the intervention is made at higher levels of the client system, since greater power to influence others is concentrated there. Although change programs have been initiated at lower levels, many OD practitioners feel that if real and lasting change is to take place, it must begin at the top. Michael Beer and Edgar Huse, however, contend that change can and does begin at lower levels of an organization, but the lack of top support does increase the risk involved.[12]

The consultant must face many different types of situations when intervening in an organization. These may be categorized in terms of client system support. In the most favorable type of situation all levels of the organization recognize the need for and support change programs. In another type of situation, top management recognizes the need for change and provides support, but lower levels are nonsupportive or resistant. An example might be the Chicago Police Department where the higher authority recognized a definite need for change, but the rank and file were not in favor of reorganization.[13] Still another type of situation occurs when lower levels of the organization are supportive while top management is resistant to change.

Who Is the Client?

Finally, the consultant must determine who the client actually is. Is it the total organization? Is it certain divisions, departments, or groups? Or is it the individual who contracted for the consultant's services? This is a question that sometimes appears easy to answer at the beginning of an OD program but becomes increasingly unclear as the program develops. The client initially will be the person with whom the consultant first makes contact. But it may soon become apparent that the organization is more realistically the client. The consultant's concern may thus extend to include work groups or subsystems of the organization and even the individual members of the system. Goodstein and Boyer, for example, reported on their OD intervention with the Cincinnati Department of Health. They were originally contacted by the commissioner of health as their initial client; however, during the course of the intervention they eventually determined that the "real" client was the city council.[14]

The OD Consulting Role in the Intervention

OD consultants can be categorized into five general styles: agreeable, persuasive, analytical, supportive, and integrative. The OD consultant tends to work in the integrative style. This style is similar to that of the process consultant, which has been documented by Schein in his book *Process Consultation* and is discussed in Chapter 7 of this book. OD process consulting operates on the belief that the group is the basic building block of an organization. Therefore, group behavior is analyzed in terms of communication, roles of members, problem solving and decision making, norms and growth, leadership and power, and cooperation.

OD consultants are primarily concerned with how these six processes occur in an organization. Their role involves sharing observations of these six processes and thus helping the client improve the effectiveness of the organization. Simultaneously and equally important, the client is learning to observe and improve its own process skills and problem-solving abilities for use in the future as well as in the present. Since the client is learning to make process interventions similar to those made by the consultant, the client is also learning how to solve its own problems without having to rely on the consultant.

One basic assumption underlying the integrative consultant role is that the client needs to learn to identify problems, to participate in the diagnosis, and to be actively involved in problem solution. The consultant recognizes that either the client has useful skills and resources but does not know how to use them effectively, or the client does not have the requisite skills but has the capacity to develop the needed skills and resources. As a result, the client solves its own problems with the consultant "helping to sharpen the diagnosis and in providing alternative remedies which may not have occurred to the client."[15] The integrative consultant operates on the notion that by assisting instead of taking control, the client's problems will be solved in a more lasting manner and, furthermore, the client will have increased its skills so that it will be able to solve future problems. The process consultant teaches the client how to diagnose and solve its own problems but does not advise or suggest solutions. Initially, the client may fumble around a bit and take longer than it would with expert assistance but in the long run the client will grow and mature.

Although most writers on OD support the idea of OD process consultation, they also recognize that because clients have various needs and maturity levels, it may be necessary at times to provide expert and technical advice. The need for working in a style other than the integrative one may be more apparent at the beginning of the consulting relationship. But as a rule of thumb, the OD consultant would not encourage and perpetuate a dependent relationship. As the maturity of the client increases the consultant tends to operate more in the process consultation or integrative style.

THE INITIAL INTERVENTION, PERCEPTION, AND ASSESSMENT

One way of examining the consultant-client relationship is to view it as a system of interacting elements (see Figure 4.2). One important element is the *change agent:* the internal or external OD consultant or manager who initiates the change program aimed at improving the effectiveness of the client system. A

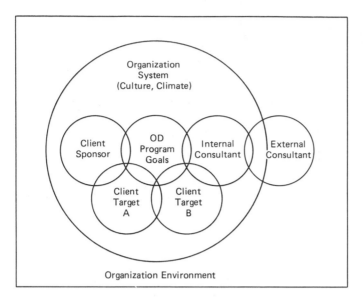

FIGURE 4.2 A Systems View of the Change Relationship

second element, within the client system, may be termed the *client contact or sponsor.* This is the person or group within the client organization who has requested the consultant's help, and who interfaces with the consultant. The third element consists of the organizational unit or units that are to be changed, and the set of behaviors and values that have been traditionally practiced. This element may be termed the *client target system:* the actual target of the OD intervention.

For example, the authors were contacted about consulting with a medium-sized manufacturing company to develop an OD program for one major division of the company. The client contact people, or sponsors, were the vice president of industrial relations and the division manager (also a vice president). The target system was to be the division, with the goal of developing a more participative management style and increasing productivity. The members of the division, however, had little voice in determining the proposed change program. It was found in preliminary discussions that some were strongly in favor of such changes, whereas others were strongly opposed or even hostile to the proposed changes. Consequently, this combination of elements needs to be considered prior to beginning any change program.

Forming the Consultant-Client Relationship ⎯⎯⎯⎯⎯⎯⎯⎯⎯

In developing the consultant-client relationship, the first stage involves an interaction between the parties which includes initial perceptions and assessments by each of the other. Such assessments involve the consultant's determination of whether or not to enter into a consulting relationship. This decision is based upon the consultant's assessment of the degree of congruence between his or her values and those of the client system. These include the attitudes of the client system toward OD and change, the ability of OD techniques to deal with the problems, and the potential of the consultant's efforts to help solve the client's problems.

The consultant's first intervention will probably be tentative. As Warren Bennis comments: "I enter a relationship on the basis that neither the client nor I know what the underlying problems are and that I need to explore and get a 'feel' for the situation before committing myself fully to the client system and before it fully entrusts itself to me."[16] This initial intervention might therefore be termed a reconnaissance on both sides. The OD practitioner is trying to evaluate the organization's readiness and commitment for change while the client system is assessing the consultant's capabilities.

Lynda McDermott and Warner Burke have suggested that power networks are important because they will influence the OD strategy that is chosen. The OD consultant has to be aware of where the power is in the organization, because that represents the major lever for change.[17]

In these exploratory interactions, first impressions are rather important in setting the climate for any future relationships. (See B.C. comic strip.) Re-

B.C. By permission of Johnny Hart and Creators Syndicate, Inc.

search by Polansky and Kounin shows that very early in the relationship, the client system makes judgments on the capabilities of the consultant.[18] *Perception* is a basic factor in understanding behavior in the consultant-client relationship because once an impression is made, regardless of its correlation with reality, that impression is difficult to change. This is because people behave on the basis of what is *perceived* versus what really *is*. A basic model of the way such perceptions are formed is shown in Figure 4.3. There are many factors involved including one's past experiences, the degree of stress in the situation, the amount of group pressure that exists, and the type of reward system involved. There are several basic factors affecting the formation of perceptions that can be identified.

Selective perception refers to the selectivity of information that is perceived. People tend to ignore information that they do not want to hear, that might be distracting or conflict with other ideas or values. However, people tend to accept information that is satisfying, pleasurable, and in agreement with their ideas and values.

Also, a similar stimulus may be interpreted differently by different indi-

FIGURE 4.3 Perception Formation and Its Effect on Relationships

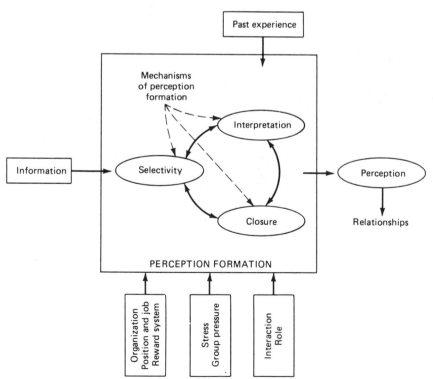

Source: Adapted from Joseph A. Litterer, *The Analysis of Organizations* (New York: John Wiley & Sons, Inc., 1965), p. 64.

viduals. Each one's *interpretation* depends upon his or her unique background and experience. Consequently, individuals tend to interpret situations in ways that reflect more favorably upon themselves.

Another process involved in perception is termed *closure*. This refers to the tendency of the individual to fill in any missing information, to complete the perception, and to give it meaning and wholeness. In this way, a person may perceive more in a given situation than is already there, adding information to make the picture seem complete. For example, if a consultant wears a certain style of dress or wears a certain hairstyle, one might perceive them as a "hippie" or a "yuppie," depending upon the stimulus perceived.

During this initial intervention each party may be selling itself to the other and trying to second-guess the other party's expectations. "Often the client system seems to be seeking assurance that the potential consultant is different enough from the client system to be a real expert and yet enough like it to be thoroughly understandable and approachable." [19] But for the consultant, the process of selling one's self has certain dangers and could possibly lead to future problems. The consultant should ideally be free of the pressure of needing the consulting work, so that one can remain neutral to judge whether the client system needs the services and whether the consultant could be helpful.

Ronald and Gordon Lippitt (OD consultants) refer to some of the elements in this assessment stage as *dilemma interactions*. Such dilemma interactions result from questions by the consultant regarding the client's definition of the problem, the awareness of the need for change, the reduction of possible client overexpectations, the client's misuse of power, and value differences between client and consultant. [20]

The issue of dependency is a real problem in many consultant-client relationships. At the beginning of any OD consulting relationship, there is bound to be some amount of dependence on the consultant by the client.

As the relationship continues, the client is likely to become more independent of the consultant and to want to reject either the help or the helper or both. This is a critical point in the relationship and the effective OD consultant must be able to let this independence flourish while maintaining the relationship. Operationally, this may mean changing roles in the problem solving and letting the client assume a greater role in the change process.

In the mature relationship, a condition of interdependence exists. In this situation the client is able to make optimum use of the resources of the consultant, knowing when to use expertise, when to take the initiative, and how to accept suggestions or ideas for consideration. The consultant feels free to give ideas and suggestions knowing that the client will use these as appropriate. One essential condition of the sound consulting relationship is a mutual confidence between the consultant and the client.

Robert Kaplan takes note of the probable gap existing between the consultant's and the client's understanding about OD and change. [21] Kaplan suggests that the consultant needs to assess the degree of this gap, since a relationship is possible only if the consultant can be flexible enough to understand where the client is and help the client to learn about the OD change process.

Developing a Trust Relationship ────────────────────────────────

One essential aspect of the OD program is the development of openness and trust between consultant and client. This is important because trust is necessary for cooperation and communication. When the trust level is low, people will tend to be dishonest, evasive, and inauthentic with one another, and communication is often inaccurate, distorted, or incomplete. In developing a trust relationship, there are several basic responses which the consultant may use in the communication process, including:

1. *Questions*—"How do you see the organization?"
2. *Applied expertise—(advising)*—"One possible intervention is team building."
3. *Reflection*—"It sounds like you would like to see a participation form of leadership."
4. *Interpretation*—"From your description, intergroup conflict could be the problem."
5. *Self-disclosure*—"I've felt discouraged myself when my ideas were rejected."
6. *Silence*—say nothing, letting the client sort out his or her thoughts.

How these basic responses are used is important in developing the consultant-client relationship. In general, the more balanced the consultant's use of these responses and the more open the range of responses, the higher the level of trust. For example, a consultant might rely almost exclusively on questions. This may tend to create a one-way flow of information but does not do any sharing or disclosing of one's own ideas or feelings. Another consultant may rely heavily on advisement responses, which may tend to develop a dependent relationship. Therefore, it is important for the consultant to be aware of the response range and to use a broad variety of responses in building toward an open, trusting relationship.

When the consultant first contacts the client system, the following types of questions may be reflected upon:

1. What is the attitude of the client system toward OD? Is there a real underlying desire for change? Or is the attitude superficial?

2. What is the nitty-gritty of the client's problem? How realistic is the client's appraisal of its own problems?

3. What are the possibilities that an OD program will alleviate the problem? Can OD solve the problem or are other change programs more appropriate?

4. What is the consultant's potential impact on the system? Based on feedback from the client, how probable is it that the consultant can bring about significant change?

Once these questions have been answered, the consultant may then decide whether to continue the change efforts or to discontinue and terminate the relationship. Some OD practitioners recommend an open confrontation with the client on these issues at an early stage.

CREATING A CLIMATE FOR CHANGE

Most OD consultants agree that an open give-and-take relationship between the consultant and the client is desirable. To some extent this depends on the ability of the consultant to form relationships of openness and trust. Good relationships do not fit into a formula or equation, but OD practitioners have noted a number of recognizable characteristics of which the potential consultant may be aware. Bennis states that "the change agent should act *congruently (authentically)*, in accordance with the values he is attempting to superimpose upon the client system's value system."[22] Or, to use an old expression, he should "practice what he preaches." The consultant must think and act in ways that will create and enhance a positive climate for participation and learning.

Value System Conflicts

There may be conflicts between the value system of the consultant and that of the client system. Michael Maccoby summarizes his findings on the type of manager who holds the leadership in large American companies. Maccoby isolated four basic types:

- The Craftsman: holds traditional values and is concerned with the *process* of making something. This person sees others in terms of whether they will help or hinder him or her in doing a craftsmanlike job.
- The Jungle Fighter: lusts for power and experiences life and work as a jungle. Others are seen as either accomplices or enemies.
- The Company Man: identity is based on being part of the organization. This person tends to sustain an atmosphere of cooperation, but lacks the daring to be innovative or competitive.

- The Gamesman: sees life in terms of options and possibilities as if playing a game. This person likes to take calculated risks and is fascinated by new technologies and methods. The main goal is to be known as a winner, the deepest fear to be labeled a loser.

The OD consultant, in a general sense, will usually find clients fitting into some of Maccoby's characteristic patterns and so must understand some of the needs, drives, and ambitions of the client system environment. The modern manager, in Maccoby's view, is molded by the requirements of the organization, presenting an emotional and spiritual underdevelopment. Consequently, Maccoby asks: "Where will we find future leaders who possess moral strength to know right from wrong and the courage to act on those convictions?"[23]

To assess the degree of difference and the likelihood of working these differences through is part of the OD practitioner's initial intervention. The consultant may desire to create a relationship of openness, authenticity, and trust. The client system managers, however, may tend not to be open, may have learned not to behave authentically, and may even feel threatened by any exploration of feelings or confrontation by the consultant. If the discrepancy between values is too great, the consultant may have reservations about the probability of a successful program. The consultant also examines the degree of conflict and collaboration between organization units and needs to be aware of this to avoid being party to any existing conflicts. "One of the most frequent forms of resistance to change," comments Lippitt, "is the perception by certain subgroups that the consultant is more closely related to other subgroups and is 'on their side' in any conflict of interests."[24]

Consultant-Client Relationship Modes

Eric H. Neilsen has identified several basic dimensions in the consultant-client relationship which can be used as indicators of the climate for change.[25] In order to collaboratively change the organization's culture: (1) members need to share their assumptions, perceptions, and feelings; and (2) members need to accept personal responsibility for their own behavior. Based upon these two dimensions, Neilsen has identified four possible modes in the consultant-client relationship (see Figure 4.4).

The apathetic mode. Members keep their true ideas about self-fulfillment and organization effectiveness to themselves. They assume that sharing this information will not make any difference, so why bother. In general, they follow established routines and avoid accepting responsibility for their actions. They simply do as they are told by others. They tend to relate to the consultant in the same manner by assuming that higher authority has sanctioned the change, but viewing it with skepticism.

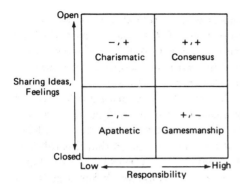

FIGURE 4.4
Four Consultant-Client Relationship Modes

Source: Adapted from Eric H. Neilsen, "Reading Clients' Values from Their Reactions to an Intervention Feedback Process," *Academy of Management Proceedings,* 1978, p. 318.

The gamesmanship mode.   Members keep their true feelings about self-fulfillment and organizational effectiveness to themselves, under the assumption that sharing information may threaten personally desired outcomes. Members make their own decisions about how to behave, thus taking responsibility for their behavior. This may include conforming outwardly to any decision-making procedure, while manipulating strategic factors to gain personal goals. Members may favor change if they can see ways in which it can serve their personal interests.

The charismatic mode.   In this mode, there is open sharing of ideas and feelings between a limited number of members and the rest, based on perceptions of leadership. The followers are looking for cues from their leaders, so that responsibility is low for most members. Members view the change process as desirable, if the leaders approve. However, they rely on the leaders to interpret the results.

The consensus mode.   Members continuously share perceptions and feelings openly, both on self-fulfillment and organizational effectiveness. Personal viewpoints are seen as relevant to organization functioning and are expressed. Decisions are made through the sharing of viewpoints and differences are worked through. This process involves both sharing of data and maintaining one's responsibility for actions. Members see the OD process as consistent with their way of operating and find the results interesting and useful.

The consultant, by his or her own attitudes and behavior, makes it possible for the client to create a climate where feelings can be freely and honestly expressed regarding the client system. The consultant also has the ability to listen effectively and to express ideas clearly and concisely. The consultant is honest with the client, as facades have no place in the relationship. By operating on the basis of power equalization, the consultant ensures that the power differential between consultant and client is not too great, or else it will become difficult to develop a collaborative relationship. This is particularly true with internal consultants, who may be in an inferior position in the organization power structure. The consultant also makes certain that all key parties in the client system are involved to some degree in the OD program. The consultant must determine to what degree the involvement of different individuals or groups is appropriate. But the outcome of ignoring key people is increased resistance and probable ineffectiveness in the change program.

These are not all the dimensions that are involved in a complex consultant-client relationship, but they are intended to provide the beginning practitioner with an awareness of some of the important dimensions that should be examined and considered. The consultant must keep in mind that this relationship is an analogue to one's impact on the total system. The practitioner's behavior will actually be a model for the organization members. When a person is attempting to create a climate of openness and collaboration between organization members and departments, one strives to develop relationships based on similar qualities. A good relationship increases the probability of a successful OD program. A tenuous or superficial relationship increases the probability that the OD program will be ineffective or unsuccessful.

THE FORMALIZATION OF OPERATING GROUND RULES

Generally, the first contact between the consultant and the client is informal, exploratory, and tentative. As many consultants (e.g., Beckhard, Bennis, and Schein) point out, successful relationships require some definition of roles and procedures. The formalization of obligations in the form of a contract is usually advisable for an external consultant. Although it is not necessary for the internal consultant to have a contract, key operating ground rules should be formalized in some manner. The contract with the external consultant will probably be incorporated in several letters transpiring between the consultant and the client. The formalization or contract normally specifies such items as:

1. The point of contact. Which person in the client system will the consultant be contacting and who will be contacting the consultant?

2. The role of the consultant. Is he or she to be an expert, a process helper, or other?

3. The fees. The amount the consultant charges for services varies, depending on the financial status of the client system and the amount of time devoted to consulting.

4. The schedule. For example, "the objectives can be accomplished over an anticipated 2-year program devoting 5 days of consulting time per month." The schedule might also include a tentative list of activities and meetings.

5. The anticipated results. The outcome should be stated as specifically as possible; however, some consultants warn

against providing any guarantee of value to the organization, as this tends to put the responsibility for change with the consultant instead of with the client. The consultant may promise to develop a valid diagnosis of organization problems, and might suggest in a very general way areas of change that would develop.

6. The operating ground rules. Such ground rules could include but are not limited to the following:

   a. The point of contact, which will usually include the top manager.

   b. The requirements of the organization members, such as being prepared for meetings.

   c. The confidentiality of consulting information.

   d. The process role, rather than having an expert coming in to define problems and implement solutions.

Although these are not all the factors involved in an agreement, they have been presented as guidelines for the beginning practitioner.

RED FLAGS IN THE CONSULTANT-CLIENT RELATIONSHIP

As previously noted, the initial meeting is a critical stage in the OD process. Consultants must decide whether or not to obligate themselves to a change project at this time. An unpromising beginning may lead to a frustrating change effort and to an OD program that is predestined to end as an unrewarding experience. Some of the critical warning signals for the consultant to consider are as follows:

The level of commitment to change.   At times the client system is not really committed to a change program. Members may verbally express commitment to the proposed OD program, but their behaviors are not congruent with their words. They may be going through the motions only to please top management.

The degree of leverage or power to influence change.   Sometimes a lower-level manager invites the consultant into the organization. This member is committed to change, but lacks any real capability to influence the system. Here the consultant must realistically assess the probability of gaining enough leverage to effectively bring about change in such a situation. If a member of the personnel department invites the consultant into the organization, the consultant may first wish to ascertain the degree of top management's receptiveness and support for any proposed change before entering into an OD program.

The client's manipulative use of the consultant. In certain situations there may be a conflict or an internal power struggle, and the client may wish to involve the consultant as a weapon against other factions or individuals within the organization system. The person in the client system requesting external assistance may want others in the organization to change their ideas or may want to use the consultant to enforce a position which is already committed. The resulting conflict would probably result in a destructive rather than constructive type of change effort, with the consultant caught in the middle. In other situations the client may intend only to use the consultant to gather information about others in the organization that would otherwise be unobtainable.

REVIEW QUESTIONS

1. Compare and contrast the five basic consultant styles.

2. What are the pros and cons of external and internal consultants? Why is the team approach a viable alternative?

3. What is the importance of an organization being ready for an OD program?

4. Compare and contrast values and goals of client versus consultant.

5. Identify the basic problems in the consultant-client relationship.

KEY WORDS AND CONCEPTS

Define and be able to use the following:

Entry	First impressions
Agreeable-style consultant	Historical resistance to change
Supportive-style consultant	The apathetic mode
Persuasive-style consultant	The gamesmanship mode
Integrative-style consultant	The charismatic mode
External consultant	The consensus mode
Internal consultant	The craftsman
External-internal consulting team	The jungle fighter
Intervention	The company man
Leverage	The gamesman
Perception	

**IV.
Simulations**

SIMULATION 4.1   CONSULTANT STYLE MATRIX

Total time suggested: 35 minutes.

A.   Purpose

At various times there are many people trying to bring about change. They probably do not operate under the guise of a "consultant" but are more commonly referred to as managers, teachers, social workers, ministers, and parents and so on. You may now be, in some aspects of your life, a consultant, and at some time in the future you will most certainly be a consultant. That is, you now are or will be trying to initiate and implement change in an individual or organization. This survey will help you gain some insights into ways you implement change.

B.   Procedures

Step 1   You will find in this survey 10 situations that call for your response. Each of the 10 situations presents five alternative ways of responding. Because you will be asked to rank-order these five responses to the situation, it is important that you read through all the responses before answering. Once you have read through all five responses, select the response that is most similar to the way you think you would actually behave or think in such a situation. Place the letter corresponding to that response (a, b, c, d, or e) somewhere on the "Most Similar" end of the 10-point scale appropriate to the intensity of your feeling. Next select the response that is least similar to the way you would actually act or think. Again place the letter corresponding to that response somewhere on the "Least Similar" end of the scale. Complete the answers by placing the remaining three responses that reflect your actions or thoughts for those responses within range of previously selected most-least points.

As an example, the answer to a situation could be:

Most Similar			c	b			e	d		a	Least Similar
	10	9	8	7	6	5	4	3	2	1	

Most Similar	d		b			c			a	e	Least Similar
	10	9	8	7	6	5	4	3	2	1	

THE CONSULTANT STYLE MATRIX

In answering these questions, think of how you would actually handle or act in the situation or how you think about change and the nature of change.

1. So that I can change another person's behavior, I will probably

   a. Counsel or help clients to work out their problems and determine needs but not tell my own preferences as to what they should do.

   b. Generally tell what is expected and then leave it up to the client to find the best alternative.

   c. Personally discuss the goals of the change and the various possibilities of handling the change and then jointly work through the alternatives to determine which one best accomplishes the change.

   d. Try to develop a friendly relationship and then suggest what in my own judgment is appropriate.

   e. Prove that my point is correct and if necessary remind the client that I am the one with authority and also the one who must ultimately take the responsibility.

Most Similar											Least Similar
	10	9	8	7	6	5	4	3	2	1	

2. In my opinion, change in another person can best be initiated when

   a. The variation of present behavior from required behavior is pointed out.

   b. The logic for the change is pointed out and penalties for noncompliance emphasized.

c. The client first has a good opinion of me and then I urge changes.

d. I help the client to gain self-confidence so the client feels capable of selecting a change program.

e. The client makes a choice for change on the basis of own needs and goals in life after being encouraged to evaluate pertinent information.

Most Similar | 10 | 9 | 8 | 7 | 6 | 5 | 4 | 3 | 2 | 1 | Least Similar

3. If I am talking with a person I am attempting to change, I usually

a. Try not to judge but be supportive by letting the client do most of the talking and thus allow the client to decide on a plan of change.

b. Try to get the upper hand in the conversation and then slowly sell the client on my methods of change.

c. Try to dominate the conversation to be sure the client understands the logic of my decision and the necessity to adopt it.

d. Share about equally in the conversation and attempt to reach a conclusion that represents an effective solution.

e. Say very little and only present my opinion when asked.

Most Similar | 10 | 9 | 8 | 7 | 6 | 5 | 4 | 3 | 2 | 1 | Least Similar

4. I think that change will be more permanent when

a. The person to be changed has been convinced that the plan for change has benefits.

b. The client and the consultant can make a choice between mutually agreed on alternatives and they jointly arrive at a final decision.

c. The change and its implementation is left up to the client.

d. The client has complete freedom to decide whether a change is needed and what course of action to take, with support given by consultant.

e. The change is decided on by the consultant, who also

checks to make sure the client follows the designated course of action.

Most Similar   10 9 8 7 6 5 4 3 2 1   Least Similar

5. If I have made a suggestion or proposal and a person reacts negatively to it, I am likely to

   a. Accept the client's position and try to reexamine my proposal, realizing that our differences are largely due to our individual ways of looking at things, rather than take reaction as a personal affront.

   b. Suggest the best course of action and make clear the results of not following that course of action.

   c. Feel upset about the disagreement but will go along with the other person's ideas and allow him or her to express ideas fully.

   d. Point out the requirements of the situation but avoid becoming involved in fruitless argument.

   e. Search for a compromise position that satisfies both points of view.

Most Similar   10 9 8 7 6 5 4 3 2 1   Least Similar

6. The person who is to change will probably be more accepting of the change if

   a. The consultant emphasizes the rewards to the client and disregards any disadvantages.

   b. The change will result in increased personal satisfaction and morale and the consultant provides help and support.

   c. The requirements of the change program are specified and then the client is made responsible for taking a course of action deemed appropriate.

   d. It is made clear that noncompliance to the proposed change will result in penalties.

   e. The client is an active participant along with the consultant in planning for the change.

Most Similar   10 9 8 7 6 5 4 3 2 1   Least Similar

7. I think change is most effective when

   a. I tell the client exactly what is expected and how to best accomplish the change.

   b. I gain the approval and friendship of the client so that the type of changes chosen will gain and keep my friendship.

   c. The client actively participates with me in setting the goals and methods for change.

   d. I point out the need for change and the repercussions if the change is not made, but leave the situation open to the client to make own decision as to whether or not to change.

   e. I allow the person to take responsibility for the change while I give personal and moral encouragement.

Most Similar											Least Similar
	10	9	8	7	6	5	4	3	2	1	

8. In determining my effectiveness as a consultant, the criterion I usually use as an indicator of the client's acceptance is

   a. The degree to which the client complies with the change as well as the amount of pushing needed to force conformance.

   b. The client's performance as measured by goals jointly set by both the client and myself.

   c. The client's evaluation of his or her performance.

   d. An adequate degree of satisfaction to ensure the client's compliance in meeting change requirements.

   e. A high level of morale in the client as well as a friendly relationship between the client and myself.

Most Similar											Least Similar
	10	9	8	7	6	5	4	3	2	1	

9. In evaluating the client's performance and efforts in bringing about a change, I tend to

   a. Look at evaluation as a mutual responsibility and we meet together to honestly appraise the accomplishment of our goals.

   b. Use a standard evaluation form to ensure objectivity and equal treatment among all persons.

    c. Present my ideas, then allow questions, but casually push for specific improvement.

    d. Compare performance with productivity standards and reports and with the output of others, and specify corrections to be made.

    e. Encourage the client to make own evaluation and then, with my moral support, make plans for improvement in areas the client thinks are necessary.

Most Similar   10 | 9 | 8 | 7 | 6 | 5 | 4 | 3 | 2 | 1   Least Similar

10. When I am trying to bring about a change in a person and there seems to be a personality conflict, I usually

    a. Try to ignore the conflict, avoid taking sides.

    b. Confront, use threats to force acceptance of my position.

    c. Try to relieve tension, smooth over differences.

    d. Try to explore differences, resolve conflict, and reach mutual goals.

    e. Try to find areas of commonality, maintain morale, and seek compromise.

Most Similar   10 | 9 | 8 | 7 | 6 | 5 | 4 | 3 | 2 | 1   Least Similar

Step 2 Scoring instructions for Table 4.2:

In Step 1 you wrote your answers (a, b, c, d, and e) above a number. Now transfer from each of the 10 situations your number values for each letter to Table 4.2. For each situation number look at the questionnaire to determine what number value you assigned to that letter and then place that number in the column headed "Your Points." The sum of each of the five columns is your score for each of the change styles. There is a further explanation of the five change styles in Step 4.

Step 3 Scoring instructions for Table 4.3:

1. Transfer the numerical sums from the score sheet in Table 4.2 to column 3 in *descending* order.

2. In column 2 write the appropriate Word Description of Approach to Change beside the score.

3. In column 4 place the numerical difference of your adjacent scores found in column 3. (The difference between the scores on the first and second lines of column 3 will be placed on the first line of column 4.) The difference between scores indicates the likelihood that a person will shift styles: a low score (1–5) suggests switching, a high score (10–20) suggests resistance to shifting.

Time suggested for Steps 2 and 3: 15 minutes.

TABLE 4.2

Analytical Style

Maximum concern for achievement of change goals.

Situation Number	Letter	Your Points
1	e	_____
2	b	_____
3	c	_____
4	e	_____
5	b	_____
6	d	_____
7	a	_____
8	a	_____
9	d	_____
10	b	_____
Total points		_____

Supportive Style

Maximum concern for individual commitment to change goals.

Situation Number	Letter	Your Points
1	a	_____
2	d	_____
3	a	_____
4	d	_____
5	c	_____
6	b	_____
7	e	_____
8	e	_____
9	e	_____
10	c	_____
Total points		_____

Agreeable Style

Minimum concern for individual commitment and for achievement of change goals.

Situation Number	Letter	Your Points
1	b	_____
2	a	_____
3	e	_____
4	c	_____
5	d	_____
6	c	_____
7	d	_____
8	c	_____
9	b	_____
10	a	_____
Total points		_____

Persuasive Style

Medium concern for individual commitment and for achievement of change goals.

Situation Number	Letter	Your Points
1	d	_____
2	c	_____
3	b	_____
4	a	_____
5	e	_____
6	a	_____
7	b	_____
8	d	_____
9	c	_____
10	e	_____
Total points		_____

(*continued*)

The Integrative Style

Maximum concern for individual commitment and for achievement of change goals

Situation Number	Letter	Your Points
1	c	_____
2	e	_____
3	d	_____
4	b	_____
5	a	_____
6	e	_____
7	c	_____
8	b	_____
9	a	_____
10	d	_____
Total points		_____

TABLE 4.3

Your Choice (col. 1)	Word Description of Approach to Change (col. 2)	Score (col. 3)	Difference between Scores of Adjacent Lines (col. 4)
1st	_____	_____	
2nd	_____	_____	_____
3rd	_____	_____	_____
4th	_____	_____	_____
5th	_____	_____	_____

Step 4 Styles of implementing change:

You have just completed and scored your consultant survey. Following is a brief explanation of the five styles.

The integrative style. The person using this style constantly strives for achievement of the change goals by other people and at the same time has maximum concern that the people involved in implementing the change are personally committed to the change.

The supportive style. This type of consulting style has medium concern for achievement of the change goals and medium concern that the people implementing the change are committed to the change goals. As a result, the consultant using this style is not consistent in behavior, and often changes the emphasis from concern for change goals to concern for the people involved in the change program. The consultant believes too rapid a change will be disruptive, and therefore attempts to implement change in small steps which allow people to become gradually accustomed to the changes.

The persuasive style. The consultant using this style has minimum concern that the stated change goals are accomplished, but does have maximum concern that the people involved in the change program are personally committed to and happy with the change. There may be as many change programs as there are people, because the persuasive-style consultant encourages members of a system to design and implement their own programs of change.

The analytical style. The person using this style has maximum concern for efficient accomplishment of the change goals and little concern that the people involved in implementing the change are personally committed to these goals. The analytical style sees people as a means to accomplish the change and believes that people must be closely guided and directed because they lack the desire or capacity to change. A person using this style tends to use an autocratic or coercive method of implementing change.

The agreeable style. This style of consultant has very minimum concern for goal accomplishment and minimum concern for the people involved. The consultant does not care to get involved and is only biding time until new orders come down. Change is viewed as a disruption of a well-ordered and secure environment.

You may now plot your style in Figure 4.5. (See page 116.)

A person does not operate using one style to the exclusion of others. The purpose of the scoring in Step 3 was to give you an indication of the importance you place on each of the five styles. The difference between your primary and backup styles indicates the strength of your preference and how quickly you will fall back on another style. Little difference between scores could indicate a tendency to vacillate between styles or vague thoughts about how to handle change. A large difference could indicate a strong reliance on the predominant change style.

This survey should be used as a point of departure for further reflection and observation concerning the way you attempt to change and influence other people. To obtain a better understanding of your change style, try to become aware in your associations with friends, peers, and working associates of how you handle change. It may also be helpful to observe other people when they try to change or influence your behavior and to become aware of how you react to their change methods.

Step 5   In plenary session, discuss the five consulting styles. Does your score for your primary and backup change style seem congruent with the way you think you operate in change situations? Share your scores with class members with whom you have been working and get their feedback. Does this feedback correlate with your scores on the matrix?

Time suggested for Steps 4 and 5: 20 minutes.

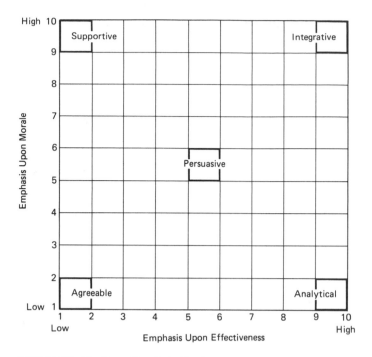

FIGURE 4.5 The Consulting Style Matrix

SIMULATION 4.2   CONFLICT STYLES

Total time suggested: 1 hour 25 minutes.

A. Purpose

This simulation is designed to allow you the opportunity to influence and change other individuals as well as to be influenced and changed by others. Although the story may seem minor, it describes a situation about which most of us have some rather strong feelings and ideas. Through diverse usage we have found it to be a means to quickly get involvement and commitment to certain issues which the participant will select. This personal involvement is necessary so that in a later part of the simulation that requires you to change others' ideas and others to change your ideas, there will be a real and prior commitment to those ideas. The goals include: (1) to identify ways of dealing with organizational or group conflict, (2) to discuss when and why different methods of resolving conflict are appropriate to different situations, and (3) to provide an experience in group decision making.

B. Procedures

Step 1   Form groups of five members each. Any extra persons may join as the sixth member of a group, but no group should have more than six or fewer than four members.

Step 2   The following is a short story you are to read. Answer the question that directly follows the story *individually*. Spaces are provided on Line A for your answer.

The Young Woman[26]

In a house is a young woman married to a man who works very hard. She feels neglected. When her husband goes off on still another trip, the young wife meets an attractive man who invites her to his house. She spends the night and at dawn she leaves, knowing her husband is coming back. Alas! The bridge is blocked by a madman who kills everyone who comes near him. The young wife follows the river and meets the ferryman, but he demands one hundred francs to take her to the other side. The young wife has no money. She runs back to her lover and asks for one hundred francs; he refuses to help. The woman remembers that a platonic friend lives close by. She runs to him and explains her plight. The friend refuses to help; she has disillusioned him by her conduct. Her only choice is to go by the bridge in spite of the danger, and the madman kills her. That is the story.

In what order do you hold the principals (woman, husband, lover, madman, ferryman, and friend) responsible for the tragedy?

Line A	1.	2.	3.	4.	5.	6.
Line B	1.	2.	3.	4.	5.	6.
Line C	1.	2.	3.	4.	5.	6.

Step 3   In your groups you are to arrive at a group consensus for the answer to the question. Most members will not have the same answer, but it is important that your group make its decision in 15 minutes. Place the group's answer on Line B.

Time suggested for Steps 1–3: 20 minutes.

Step 4   Form a class group again and focus your discussion on the following questions:

1. Was there much disagreement within your group?
2. If there was, to what could it be attributed?
3. How did your group reach its decision (consensus, voting, etc.)?
4. To what extent do you feel that other members of your group support the group's decision?

Time suggested for Step 4: 15 minutes.

Step 5   Go back to the story and on Line C answer the question again, but on an *individual* basis. Your answers may be the same as when you first responded to the story or you may alter your original position based on the team discussion.

Step 6   Meet back in your groups to observe how individuals responded on Line C. Observe to see if Line C answers are the same as those on Line B and Line A, or perhaps different from any previous answers.

Time suggested for Steps 5 and 6: 5 minutes.

Step 7   In the second column of Table 4.4 write down the word describing your perception of each of your group member's overall consulting style. Then refer again to Simulation 4.1, and for every member in your team answer questions 3 and 4 by placing in Table 4.4 the letter of the most similar behavior that represents your observations during the team decision meeting. Translate the letter to the word description (supportive, persuasive, etc.) by referring to the score sheet in Table 4.2.

Time suggested for Step 7: 10 minutes.

Step 8   In Table 4.5 transfer the information from what the other team members recorded about you in their Table 4.4. From Table 4.5 try to draw some conclusion about your style of consulting. Discuss your conclusions with the other team members.

1.   How did your survey from Simulation 4.1 compare with the information received from your team?

2.   Was there general agreement from your team on your consultant style? If there were differences, to what could they be attributed?

TABLE 4.4

Group Member's Name	Overall Approach to Change (Supportive, integrative, persuasive, agreeable, or analytical)	Question 3 from Simulation 4.1		Question 10 from Simulation 4.1	
		Letter	Word Description	Letter	Word Description

TABLE 4.5

Information Received from: (Member's Name)	Overall Approach to Change	Question 3 Word Description	Question 10 Word Description
Information from your own Simulation 4.1			

Time suggested for Step 8: 20 minutes.

Step 9 Meeting with the entire class, discuss the following questions:

1. How congruent were your scores from Simulation 4.1 with the feedback from your group members?
2. If there was any difference, to what could it be attributed?
3. What consulting styles do you feel are most effective in an OD program? Why?

Time suggested for Step 9: 15 minutes.

V. Summary

The organization is a system. The OD consultant intervenes in the system and its plans, structures, leadership, and controls for various purposes. But the overriding change goal is to develop and maintain the dynamic fit between members and tasks which is necessary to yield organization effectiveness and human satisfaction.

You have examined the various types of consulting; also their roles and their qualifications. The problems of entry into the client system were also explored. The consultant must decide at exactly what point, how, and with whom to intervene. The receptivity of the system to change must not be overlooked or taken for granted but ought to be carefully probed and realistically determined prior to further intervention.

You have had the opportunity to gain insights into your own consulting style, to assess your own strengths and weaknesses as a potential OD consultant, and to examine briefly the impact of a given style upon others. One important aspect of being a consultant is to *know yourself*. Only by being aware of your own motives, reactions, and needs can you successfully hope to influence others.

The Consultant Style Matrix provided an opportunity for you to gain some insights into how you approach change situations. It is important to recognize that your answers to the survey may reflect more the way you wish to behave—an ideal—than the way you actually do behave. Your first objective is to get a clear reading on your actual consultant style by getting feedback from your fellow participants. Their reports on how your actions affect them will enable you to move to a more effective style. You have begun this integration process here, but it should be a continuing process of feedback, reappraisal, and experimentation throughout this course and beyond.

The last simulation was intended to provide a situation where you could gain feedback on your consultant style. During the intervention in a decision situation, you have encountered the problems of developing a change strategy and observed the consequences of different styles and approaches. You have also been receiving feedback from other members of your team, which should enable you to become more proficient in handling change situations.

The OD consultant is the person who initiates, stimulates, or facilitates a change program. In this section you have experienced a situation where you have gained insights into your own style of intervention and its degree of influence in a group.

NOTES

1. Alan Carey and Glenn Varney, "Which Skills Spell Success in OD?" *Training and Development Journal*, April 1983, p. 38.

2. Philip L. Hunsaker, "Strategies for Organizational Change: The Role of the Inside Change Agent." *Personnel*, September/October 1982, pp. 10–28.

3. Excerpt from the "Playboy Interview with Admiral Elmo Zumwalt." Originally appeared in *Playboy* Magazine; copyright © 1974 by Playboy.

4. John Lewis III, "Growth of Internal Change Agents in Organization Development," doctoral dissertation, Case Western Reserve University, 1970.

5. Philip L. Hunsaker, "Strategies for Change," pp. 18–28.

6. Danielle B. Nees and Larry E. Greiner, "Seeing Behind the Look-alike Management Consultants," *Organizational Dynamics*, Winter 1985, pp. 68–79.

7. Lynda C. McDermott, "The Many Faces of the OD Professional", *Training and Development Journal*, Feb. 1984, 38, no. 2, 14–19.

8. Edgar Schein, *Process Consultation: Its Role in Organization Development* (Reading, Mass.: Addison-Wesley Publishing Co., Inc., 1969), p. 13.

9. Warren Bennis, *Organization Development: Its Nature, Origins and Prospects* (Reading, Mass.: Addison-Wesley Publishing Co., Inc., 1969), p. 48.

10. Wendell L. French and Cecil H. Bell, Jr., *Organization Development: Behavioral Science Interventions for Organization Improvement*, 2nd ed. (Englewood Cliffs, N.J.: Prentice-Hall, Inc., 1973), p. 97; and Chris Argyris, *Intervention Theory and*

Method, A Behavior Science View (Reading, Mass.: Addison-Wesley Publishing Co., Inc., 1970), p. 15.

11. Richard Beckhard, *Organization Development: Strategies and Models* (Reading, Mass.: Addison-Wesley Publishing Co., Inc., 1969), p. 13.

12. Michael Beer and Edgar Huse, "A Systems Approach to Organization Development," *Journal of Applied Behavioral Science*, 1, no. 8 (1972), 79–101.

13. Mark Starr, "Help Wanted: A Top Cop for Chicago," *The Wall Street Journal*, January 24, 1974, p. 12.

14. L. Goodstein and R. Boyer, "Crisis Intervention in a Municipal Agency: A Conceptual Case History," *Journal of Applied Behavioral Science*, May–June 1972, pp. 318–40.

15. Schein, *Process Consultation*, p. 7.

16. Bennis, *Organization Development*, p. 43.

17. Patricia Hurley, "What in the Name of OD Do We Do?" *Training and Development Journal*, April 1983, Vol. 37, no. 4, p. 44.

18. N. Polansky and J. Kounin, "Clients' Reactions to Initial Interviews: A Field Study," *Human Relations*, no. 9 (1956), 237–65.

19. Ronald Lippitt, Jeanne Watson, and Bruce Westley, *The Dynamics of Planned Change* (New York: Harcourt Brace Jovanovich, Inc., 1958), p. 66.

20. R. Lippitt and G. Lippitt, "Consulting Process in Action," *Training and Development Journal*, 29, no. 6 (June 1975).

21. R. Kaplan, "Collaborating Doesn't Grow on Trees," *Academy of Management Proceedings* 1976, p. 368.

22. Bennis, *Organization Development*, p 50.

23. Michael Maccoby, *The Gamesman: The New Corporate Leaders* (New York: Simon & Schuster, Inc., 1976).

24. Ronald Lippitt, "Dimensions of the Consultant's Job," in *The Planning of Change*, ed. W. Bennis, K. Benne, and R. Chin (New York: Holt, Rinehart & Winston, 1961), p. 160.

25. Eric H. Neilsen, "Reading Clients' Values from Their Reactions to an Intervention/Feedback Process," *Academy of Management Proceedings*, 1978, p. 318.

26. The authors of this story could not be traced.

THE DIAGNOSTIC
PROCESS

I.
Objectives

Upon completing this chapter, you will be able to:

1. Identify system parameters and recognize symptoms, problems, and causes of organization ineffectiveness.

2. Recognize the various techniques for gathering information from client systems.

3. Describe the major diagnostic models and techniques used in OD programs.

4. Apply a systematic diagnosis to organizational situations.

II.
Premeeting
Preparation

1. Read the Background Information (Section III).

2. Prepare for Simulation 5.1 (Section IV). Complete Steps 1 and 2.

3. Read and analyze Case: The Old Family Bank.

Organization diagnosis is often mentioned as the most critical element in the OD process. In a recent survey of OD practitioners, it was reported that a diagnostic phase of some type occurred in 85 percent of the projects.[1]

Organization diagnosis is aimed at providing a rigorous analysis of data on the structure, administration, interaction, procedures, interfaces, and other essential elements of the client system. The diagnosis, then, provides a basis for structural, behavioral, or technical interventions to improve organizational performance. Diagnosing a problem requires a systematic approach throughout the process. If organization change is to be effective, it must be based on a specific diagnosis of the problem.

One rule, or *modus operandi*, for the organization development consultant is to question the client's diagnosis of the problem. The client may have some preconceived ideas as to what the problem is, but these ideas should be accepted only after having been verified by research. The client is part of the system that has a problem, and this may prevent the client from taking an objective view of the situation. Also, the client will probably be operating from one part of a larger system, and it may be difficult if not impossible to see the total system. It would be appropriate for the consultant to listen to the client's definition and ideas of the problem if the client has any notions in this regard, but the consultant should openly seek permission to verify these definitions with properly conducted research.

An OD program must be based on a sound analysis of relevant data about the situation perceived to be in disequilibrium. To make a sound diagnosis, it is important to have valid information about the situation and to arrange available data into a meaningful pattern.

In this chapter, some of the important factors in the accomplishment of the diagnostic stage of an OD program are examined. This includes the major diagnostic models, data collection, and red flag situations.

WHAT IS DIAGNOSIS?

Organization development is a data-based activity. One of the characteristics of OD is the reliance on valid information about current problems and possible opportunities for improvement. Lynda McDermott, in a study of 1,000 practitioners, found that organizational diagnosis was one of the major consulting skills.[2] *The diagnosis* provides a starting point (a set of current conditions) and the change objective (an ideal or desired set of conditions). The diagnosis usually examines two broad areas. First, a diagnosis is made of the various subelements that make up the organization. These include the divisions, departments, products, and the relationships between these interacting elements. This may also include a comparison of managerial levels among the top, middle, and lower levels of the organization.

The second area of diagnosis is based on the organizational processes. These include communication networks, group problem solving, decision making, leadership and authority styles, goal setting and planning methods, and the management of conflict and competition.

Diagnosis is a systematic approach to understanding and describing the present state of the organization. The purpose of the diagnostic phase is to specify the nature of the exact problem requiring solution, to identify the underlying causal forces, and to provide a basis for selecting effective change strategies and techniques. The outcome of a weak, inaccurate, or faulty diagnosis will be a costly and ineffective OD program. Organization diagnosis, then, involves the systematic analysis of data regarding the organization structure and culture with the intention of discovering problems and areas for improvement.

THE PROCESS

Diagnosis is a cyclical process which involves data gathering, interpretation, and identification of problem areas and potential action programs, as shown in Figure 5.1. The first step is the preliminary identification of possible problem areas. Often these preliminary attempts tend to bring out symptoms as well as possible problem areas.

The second step involves gathering data based on the preliminary prob-

FIGURE 5.1 The Diagnostic Process

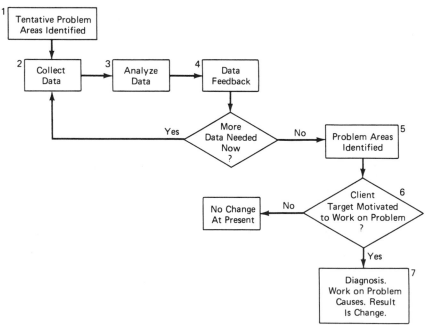

lem identification. These data are then categorized, analyzed and presented to the client in a feedback session (steps 3 and 4). This allows a collaborative diagnosis of the data as the client and consultant jointly diagnose and identify probable problem areas (step 5). Step 6 is to decide, based upon the diagnosis, what action interventions should be taken to resolve the problems. The target systems are identified and the change strategy is designed. Finally (step 7), the intervention is monitored to determine the level or degree of change that has been attained versus the desired change goals.

As noted earlier, some 85 percent of OD practitioners reported using some form of diagnostic process. One example of data collection and diagnosis occurred at Eastman Kodak and is described in OD Application 5.1. Kodak management examined its performance to identify "performance gaps"—gaps between actual and desired performance.

OD Application 5.1

DIAGNOSING CHANGES FOR KODAK

For over a decade, Eastman Kodak Chairman Colby H. Chandler had been hearing arguments for breaking up Kodak's monolithic, bureaucratic management structure into smaller groups better able to adapt to fast-paced markets. One analyst referred to Kodak as "a blue-chip company that's dead in the water." He commissioned a sweeping review of the company's management structure and practices, an intensive self-examination of the entire company.

Data Collection and Analysis

Kodak polled a widening corps of its managers and called in outside consultants. McKinsey & Co. even conducted "trap teams," where managers were invited to test out scenarios that might cause problems. Finally, Chandler reshuffled Kodak's core photo business into 17 entrepreneurial units—pretty much what he had expected to do all along.

Such a measured approach to change has been the very essence of Kodak, a company that has raised careful deliberation—some would say procrastination—to a high art. In the last decade, Kodak dragged its feet while competitors ran away with new markets such as instant photography, 35mm cameras, video recorders, and copying machines.

Today, growth is slowing in Kodak's photographic products, the mainstays of the company for 105 years. And as earnings have suffered, Chandler has resolved to push into new businesses including batteries and optical disk storage systems.

Diagnosis and Change

Chandler and his consultants saw that Kodak needed more than a "tune-up" of its existing, traditional business units. They identified "performance gaps" in several key areas.

Corporate Culture and Structure

The company's culture has changed dramatically in recent months and the old, stratified bureaucratic structure has been changed to a new, more "entrepreneurial" approach. In the past, Kodak favored caution over risk which was possible as Kodak controlled the pace of change due to a lack of competition. Now, young managers have authority over new products.

Decentralization

Decisions can now be made in a matter of days. By opting for a decentralized management, Kodak abandoned its traditional structure in which marketing and manufacturing executives each reported through a separate chain of command. Decisions would have to filter up the management ladder, often taking months or years.

New Products and Markets

One of Kodak's greatest challenges will be managing its many new ventures, something it has muffed in the past. Chandler's task is to make a big company act like a small one. Still, Kodak's diversifications are minimal so far. Industry experts believe the company needs to make even larger acquisitions to build market share in fields such as electronics and biotechnology.

Indeed, the company is moving away from consumer electronics, such as its 8mm video camera market, to focus its attention on nonconsumer applications of electronics. Kodak has failed to introduce new consumer electronic products "in an industry where you obsolete your own products every month," notes a trade newsletter.

So far, the impact of such new technologies on the bottom line has been negligible. But in 15 years, electronics could make up fully half of Kodak's business.

But will Kodak's diagnosis bring about the desired changes, and will Kodak's managers, trained in the company's staid old ways, be able to break out of its ineffective patterns?

Questions:
1. What data or information would be necessary to develop a change program?
2. What kind of performance gaps might you idenfity at Kodak?
3. Why is it so important to use diagnosis prior to implementing a change program?

Sources: "Kodak Is Trying to Break Out of Its Shell," *Business Week*, June 10, 1985; Clare Ansberry, "Analysts Speculate Kodak Is Considering Leaving 8-mm Video Camera Market," *The Wall Street Journal*, January 29, 1987, p. 8; Subrata Chakravarty, "Has the World Passed Kodak by?" *Forbes*, November 5, 1984, pp. 184-92; and Leslie Helm, "Why Kodak Is Starting to Click Again," *Business Week*, February 23, 1987, pp. 134-8.

The Performance Gap _____

One method in the diagnostic process is to determine the performance gap—the difference between what the organization could do by virtue of its opportunity in its environment and what it actually does in taking advantage of that opportunity. This leads to an approach that may be termed *gap analysis*. In this method, data are collected on the actual state of the organization on a varying set of dimensions and also on the ideal or desired state, that is, "where the organization should be." As shown in Figure 5.2, the gap or discrepancy between the actual state and the ideal forms a basis for diagnosis and the design of interventions. The gap may be characterized by ineffective performance among internal units or emerge because of other new innovations. It may also occur when the organization fails to adapt to changes in its external environment.

Competent organizational diagnosis not only provides information about the nature of the system, but it is also helpful in designing and introducing action alternatives for correcting possible problems. The diagnosis affirms the need for change and the benefits of possible changes in the client system. Many times, important problems are hidden or obscure while more conspicuous and obvious problems may be relatively unimportant. In such situations, dealing with the obvious may not be a very effective way to manage change, and points out the importance of the diagnostic stage.

The performance gap may continue for some time before it is recognized, as at Kodak. In fact, it may never be recognized. The situation must also be perceived as having significant consequences if the deviation is not narrowed or corrected.

The awareness of a performance gap may unfreeze functions within the organization that are most in need of change. When this occurs, conditions are present for altering the structure and function of the organization by introducing OD interventions.

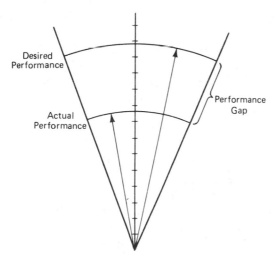

FIGURE 5.2
The Performance Gap

Sally Ver Schere suggests a self-assessment version of gap analysis where questionnaires gather information in four areas:

1. The organization's strengths.
2. What can be done to take advantage of those strengths.
3. The organization's weaknesses.
4. What can be done to alleviate those weaknesses.[3]

DIAGNOSTIC MODELS

Diagnosis is based on some understanding of how an organization functions. The conceptual framework that OD practitioners use to assess an organization are referred to as diagnostic models.[4] In a survey of 245 OD practitioners, it was found that 70 percent used a model to help diagnose the organization.[5] One method of diagnosis (presented earlier in Chapter 2) is the systems model. Diagnostic models play a critical role in an organization development program. Each of the various diagnostic models may be used to facilitate the analysis of the structure, culture, and behavior of the organization system or subsystem. Several diagnostic models will be examined in this section.

The Analytical Model

The *analytical model*, sometimes referred to as the *differentiation-integration model*, developed by Paul Lawrence and Jay Lorsch (OD consultants, Harvard), stresses the importance of a sound analytical diagnosis as the basis for planned change in organizations.[6] The model was developed to study and understand interdepartmental issues by conducting a careful diagnosis of the organization's problem areas. Most organizations are composed of departments or divisions; that is, the organization is composed of differentiated parts or units which must be integrated into a unified effort if the organization is to be effective. The various tasks that the units work on can be examined in respect to four characteristics of the organization's environment: (1) the degree of departmental structure; (2) the time orientation of members; (3) the interpersonal orientation of members toward others, and (4) organization members' orientation toward goals (see Table 5.1).

Given the differentiation between departments, the problem becomes how to achieve integration. The investigation of these four characteristics provides a basis for structural or educational interventions in the client system. When the groups in an organization tend to be highly differentiated, cooperation between them becomes difficult and it may be necessary for the organization to design methods for achieving integration.

TABLE 5.1 Typical Orientation of Functional Areas

Organization Units	Degree of Departmental Structure	Members' Orientation toward Time	Members' Orientation toward Others	Members' Goal Orientation
Research	Low	Long	Permissive	Science
Marketing	Medium	Short	Permissive	Market
Production	High	Short	Directive	Plant

Source: Adapted from Paul Lawrence and Jay Lorsch: "Organizing for Production Innovation." *Harvard Business Review*, January-February 1965, p. 113.

The Emergent-Group Behavior Model

The *emergent-group behavior model* is based primarily on the work of George Homans and provides a conceptual scheme for analyzing behavior in work groups, particularly the interdependence of groups.[7] According to this diagnostic model, a complex pattern of behavior consisting of activities, interactions, sentiments, and norms develops from the set of behaviors and relationships required to perform the work of the group. In addition, there are a complex set of behaviors that emerge in addition to those required, such as social activity. The behavior may or may not assist the group in the performance of their duties. The emergent-group behavior model helps in understanding how groups operate. This model is used to gather observations and information on these four characteristics and uses these data to diagnose problems among or within groups.

The Sociotechnical Systems Model

The *sociotechnical systems model,* developed from the work of Eric Trist and others at the Tavistock Institute, is used to analyze the organization as a sociotechnical system interacting with its external environment.[8] According to Trist and his colleagues, there exist in the organization a social system consisting of the network of interpersonal relationships and a technological system consisting of the task, activities, and tools used to accomplish the basic purpose of the organization. These two systems—the social system and the technological system—are interrelated and interdependent. The diagnosis then determines how these systems interrelate and particularly the type of feedback or lack of feedback between the various subsystems.

The Force-Field Analysis Model

The *force-field analysis model,* originated by Kurt Lewin, is a general-purpose diagnostic technique.[9] Lewin views organization behavior not as a static pattern but as a dynamic balance of forces working in opposite directions. In any organization situation there are forces that push for change as well as forces that hinder change. Those forces acting on the organization to keep it stable are called *restraining forces* and put pressure on the organization not to change. Opposite forces, called *driving forces*, put pressure on the organization to change. If the forces for change and the forces against change are equal, the result is organization equilibrium and the organization remains stable, as shown in Figure 5.3. Lewin termed this state *quasi-stationary equilibrium*. This technique assumes that at any given moment an organization is in a state of *equilibrium*; that is, it is balanced.

Change takes place when there is an imbalance between the two forces and continues until the opposing forces are brought back into equilibrium. The imbalance can be planned and specifically brought about by increasing the strength of any one of the forces, by adding a new force, by decreasing the strength of any one of the forces, or by a combination of these methods.

An example of how force-field analysis can be used might prove helpful. The manager of a hospital employing 300 workers and his immediate subordinates identified the 6 percent daily absentee rate as an area of concern. They determined that a 3 percent absentee rate would be much more acceptable. In other words, they found a "performance gap." After going over the survey results with the OD consultant, it was decided to use force-field analysis to gain an improved diagnosis of this problem. In a brainstorming session, the work team listed all of the forces tending to restrain and increase absenteeism (see Figure 5.4).

The managers made the length of the arrows proportionate to the strength of the force. The managers could then use several strategies to reduce the performance gap. They could decrease the strength of the restraining forces, increase the strength of the driving forces, or a combination of both. Generally, if those forces that put pressure on people (e.g., such as fear of los-

FIGURE 5.3

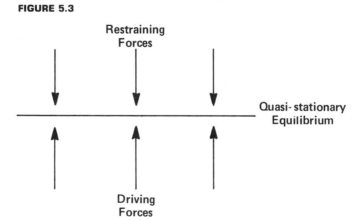

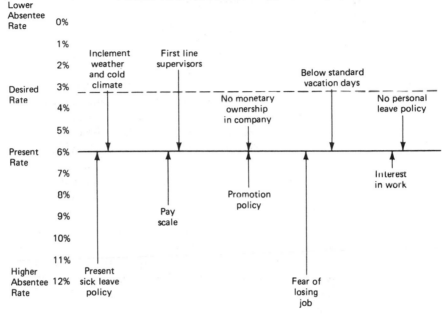

FIGURE 5.4 Example of the Use of Force-Field Analysis

ing their job) are increased, the tension within the system will also increase, bringing about possible stronger resistance and unpredictability in behavior. It is better to increase forces that do not put pressure on people (e.g., promotion policy more closely tied to an employee's absentee rate), to reduce restraining forces, or to add new driving forces.

THE DATA COLLECTION PROCESS

Organization development is a data-based change activity. The data collected are used by the members who provide the data and often lead to insights into ways of improving effectiveness. The data collection process itself involves an investigation, a body of data, and some form of processing information. For our purposes the word *data*, which is derived from the Latin verb *do, dare*, meaning "to give," is more appropriately applied to unstructured, unformed facts. It is an aggregation of all signs, signals, clues, facts, statistics, opinions, assumptions, and speculations—including accurate and inaccurate, and relevant and irrelevant items. The word *information* is derived from the Latin verb *informo*, *informare*, meaning "to give form to," and is used here to mean data that have form and structure.

The Definition Objectives

The first and most obvious step in data collection is defining the objectives of the change program. A clear understanding of these broad goals is necessary to determine what information is relevant. Unless the purpose of data collection is clearly defined, it becomes difficult to select methods and standards. The OD practitioner must first gain enough information to allow a preliminary diagnosis and then decide what further information is required to verify the problem conditions. Usually, some preliminary data gathering is needed simply to clarify the problem conditions before further large-scale data collection is undertaken.

This is usually accomplished by a session of interviews with key members of the organization, investigating possible problem areas and what an ideal organization may be like. This provides a basis for the organization and the OD practitioner to understand the way things are, versus the way members would like them to be.

Most practitioners emphasize the importance of collecting data as a significant step in the OD process. First, data gathering provides the basis for the organization to begin looking at its own processes, to focus upon *how* they are doing things and the way this affects performance. Second, data collection often begins a process of self-examination or assessment by members and work teams in the organization, leading to improved problem-solving capabilities.

The Selection of Factors

The second step in data collection is to identify the central variables involved in the situation (i.e., turnover, suboptimization, etc.). The consultant and the client decide which factors are important and what additional information is necessary to systematically diagnose the client system's problems. There is normally a considerable amount of "hard" data generated by the organization, including production reports, budgets, turnover ratio, and so forth, which may be useful as indicators of potential problems. The consultant may find, however, that it is necessary to increase the range or depth of data beyond what is readily available. (See B.C. comic strip.) The practitioner may wish to gain additional insights into other dimensions of the organization system, particularly those dealing with the quality of the transactions or relationship between individuals or groups.

This additional data gathering may examine the following dimensions:

1. What is the degree of dependence between operating groups, departments, or units?

Source: B.C. by permission of Johnny Hart and Creators Syndicate, Inc.

2. What is the quantity and quality of the exchange of information and communication between units?

3. What is the degree to which the goals and the objectives of the organization are shared and understood by members?

4. What are the norms, the attitudes, and the motivations of organization members?

5. What are the effects of the distribution of power and status within the system?

In this step, then, the consultant and client determine which factors are important and which factors can and should be investigated.

The Selection of Data-gathering Method

The third step in data collection is selecting a method of gathering data. There are many different types of data and also many different methods of tapping these data sources. There is no one best way to gather data—the selection of a method depends on the nature of the problem. The data should be acquired in a systematic manner, thus allowing quantitative or qualitative comparison between elements of the system. The task in this step is to identify certain characteristics that may be measured to help in the achievement of the OD program objectives and then to select an appropriate method to gather the required data. Some major data-collecting methods follow.

Secondary sources of data. When the OD practitioner begins the data-gathering process, it may be assumed that data are not presently available. But there are often large amounts of organization data already generated which can be used in identifying problem areas. These data may be termed secondary data or measures. Examples of secondary sources include accounting data, productivity data, and performance indicators such as employee thefts, turnover, and absentee rates. One organization used accounting data as a technique for organizational diagnosis, and found that it substantially increased their insight into planning assumptions and goals.[10]

There are certainly some limitations associated with the use of secondary data. Although the secondary data may be available, it may not be in a usable format. For example, lateness and absentee figures may not provide information by department. An additional problem involves the interpretation of the data: What are the causes underlying a given absentee rate or number of grievance reports?

Questionnaires. Questionnaires are used to gather a large number of quantitative responses. The questionnaire is particularly useful for studies of attitudes, values, and beliefs of respondents. Questionnaire data tend to be impersonal and anonymous and are often lacking in feeling and richness, but this method easily lends itself to quantitative analysis.

There are many problems involved in designing and administering an effective questionnaire. There are often problems of validity; that is: Does the questionnaire measure what it is intended to measure? There are also possible problems of the accuracy of information obtained: Did the person answer it realistically or just to make a good impression? For example, one researcher found in a follow-up study that 29 percent of questionnaire respondents admitted answering falsely to some questions.[11] To deal with these problems, there are statistical techniques available that attempt to measure the reliability of the survey responses. There are also problems of nonresponse. Those who choose to respond may be those who have strong feelings, either positive or negative, about the content of the survey but may represent only a small percentage of the total sample.

The use of the questionnaire method depends upon the depth of information desired and the purpose of the information. In some organizations survey follows survey, but without any effective change. This often leads to apathy and indifference in answering any subsequent surveys. Therefore, it is usually beneficial to inform the respondents beforehand about the purpose of the survey, how the information will be used, and how feedback of the results will be made available to them.

Surveys seem to achieve better information in terms of quantity and validity if the questionnaire shows that the researchers are familiar with key issues in the organization.[12] Such event-based questionnaires, making clear that researchers are acquainted with important aspects of the organization, are more likely to reveal information about the organization than vague, theory-based questionnaires.

Other types of instruments. Another technique for collecting data on work groups is called the *sociometric approach*. This method, developed by

Jacob Moreno, is a means of obtaining quantitative data about the network of interrelationships within groups, usually on certain given dimensions.[13] Basically, Moreno's sociometric analysis provides a means of analyzing data about the choices or preferences within a group. The sociometric instrument asks specific questions, such as "Whom do you prefer to work with?" "Whom do you communicate with?" "Who helps you the most with technical problems?" Such data enable the investigator to diagram the structure and patterns of group interaction. The results are usually presented in what is called a *sociogram* (see Figure 5.5). The highly chosen individuals are called *stars*; those with few or no choices are called *isolates*. Certain individuals will choose one another—this is known as *mutual choice*. When an individual chooses another but is not chosen in return, this designates a *one-way choice*. When three or more persons within a larger group select one another (i.e., mutual choices), this is termed a *clique*. The existence of these subgroups may indicate lack of total group cohesion and commitment.

In the sociogram each member of the group is represented by a circle, with choices designated by arrows indicating the direction of choice. The number of choices may be written in the circle under the name or code letter of the person. Sociometric techniques are useful because they provide insights into the informal structure, give some indications of group cohesiveness, and aid in pointing out possible operating problems.

Other data-collecting methods include the use of indirect questions or ambiguous stimuli to gain information. An example of this would be McClelland's use of a version of the thematic apperception test (TAT) to measure the

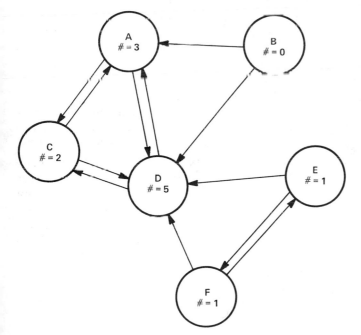

FIGURE 5.5 Sociogram

intensity of achievement, power, and affiliation motivation profiles of organization members.[14] Fordyce and Weil have also reported the use of collages and drawings made by organization members as a means of inferring organization climate.[15]

Direct observation. Another important source of data for the OD practitioner is direct observation of member behaviors and interactions. The consultant observes how people go about task performance and how they act or react in response to specific situations. The norms and attitudes expressed by members also present an important source of data. The observer looks for inconsistent or discordant behaviors: situations in which the observed actions are different from what has been previously described or expected.

It is frequently valuable to visit work sites, field locations, or assembly-line operations to compare observed with reported behavior. This is obviously of greater value if the observer has a reasonably clear idea of what to look for. Observation varies from highly systematic, structured observations to nonsystematic, random observations. The more systematic the planning, recording, and observing, the greater the likelihood that observation will yield reliable and useful data. Too often, the observers' own biases influence what they see.

Interviews. A study of 246 OD practitioners found that interviewing is one of the most widely used data-gathering techniques in OD programs.[16] It has the advantage of being more direct, personal, and flexible than a survey and is particularly well suited for studies of interaction and behavior. Interviewing usually begins with the initial intervention and is best administered in a systematic manner by a trained interviewer. Data-gathering interviews usually last at least one hour, and the purpose is to get the interviewee to talk freely about things that are important to him or her and to share these perceptions in an honest and straightforward manner.

The advantage of the interview method is that it provides data that are virtually unobtainable through other methods. Subjective data, such as norms, attitudes, and values, which are largely inaccessible through observation, may be readily inferred from effective interviews. The disadvantages to the interview are the amount of time involved, the training and skill required of the interviewer, the biases and resistances of the respondent, and the difficulty of ensuring comparability of data across respondents.

The interview itself may take on several different formats. The interview can be directed or nondirected. In the *directed interview*, certain kinds of data are desired. Therefore, specific questions are asked. Usually, the questions are formulated in advance to ensure uniformity of responses. The questions themselves may be open-ended or closed. *Open-ended questions* allow the respondent to be free and unconstrained in the answers, such as "How would you describe the work atmosphere of this organization?" The responses may be very enlightening, but may also be difficult to record and quantify. *Closed questions,* which can be answered by either a yes, no, or some other similarly abbreviated response, are easily recorded and are readily quantifiable.

In the *nondirected interview* the interview direction is chosen by the respondent and is given little guidance or direction by the interviewer. If questions are used in the nondirected interview, open-ended questions will be more appropriate than closed questions. A nondirected interview could begin with the interviewer saying, "Tell me about your job here." Possibly followed by, "You seem to be excited about your work." The data can be very detailed and significant, but because the interview is unstructured, the analysis of the data can be difficult.

THE IMPLEMENTATION OF THE PROGRAM

First, one decides from whom in the organization data will be obtained and from how many. The use of interviews may limit the number of possible respondents, whereas the use of a questionnaire may expand the number. Data should be collected from several levels and departments in the organization, but different questions may be needed for varying levels or departments. The results of a survey of OD practitioners concerning the types of methods used to gather data is reported by Burke, Clark, and Koopman.[17] The one-to-one interview is the most common type of data gathering method, used by 87 percent of those responding. Other methods include observation used by 60 percent, group interviews used by 52 percent, questionnaires used by 45 percent, and existing documents used by 37 percent. The survey also shows that consultants normally rely on a variety of data gathering methods.

After an appropriate technique has been selected, the actual data collection program must be accomplished. This includes the operational aspects of designing, printing, distributing, and collecting the data collection instrument. It has been found that having an outside data collection agent is more effective than using internal personnel. The use of an outside data collection agent is recommended, as respondents apparently feel more secure and trusting that candid answers will not be used against them.

THE ANALYSIS OF DATA

Several important questions must be considered prior to the selection of a data-collecting method: How are the data to be analyzed? Are they to be analyzed statistically, and if so, what type of analysis is to be used? Will the data be processed by hand or by computer? How are they to be coded? These questions must be taken into account prior to data collection or the data may not easily lend themselves to analysis. This is particularly true when large-scale surveys or interviews are undertaken and the quantity of data makes processing a difficult task. The analysis may include comparisons between different divisions within the organization. Comparisons can also be made between management levels. To make comparisons, however, it is necessary to properly code the surveys or interviews.

Despite the advanced statistical methods available, OD practitioners in one survey reported giving the data only the simplest analysis. Specifically, in over 80 percent of the projects the data was either "eyeballed" or subjected only to simple statistics. Only 10 percent of the consultants used advanced statistics to analyze the data.[18]

EVALUATING THE EFFECTIVENESS OF DATA COLLECTION

In a systematic data collection program, some criteria for how well the data meet the objectives in quantity and quality need to be established. Obviously, a large enough sample needs to be included to enable generalization of results. The accuracy of the data, that is, the degree to which the data deviate from the truth, is also an important factor.

A number of criteria may be used to compare various data collection techniques. The OD practitioner needs to consider the trade-off between the quantity and the accuracy of information versus the cost and the amount of time involved in collecting information. The consultant must determine what is the best available information that can be generated within given cost and time constraints. The following criteria present some guidelines.

The validity of the data. Probably the most important question to ask is: Are we measuring and collecting information on the dimensions that we intend to measure? Frequently, OD programs are dealing with difficult, subjective parameters such as attitudes and values.

The time to collect data. How long will it take to gather the information using any given technique? How much time is available?

The cost of data collection. How much does the information cost? It may cost several thousand dollars to design and administer a survey. A large-scale interviewing program also costs a great deal of time and money, and the consultant and the client must determine how much money can be spent on a given OD program in the information-gathering stage. They should also consider the problem of diminishing returns: What is the minimum number of interviews needed to be a reliable measure?

The organization culture and norms. The OD practitioner should consider which techniques are best suited to a given organization culture and will yield the most valid information given these constraints. For example: Are people likely to be open and candid, or hidden and resistant? Does the climate call for open confrontation and questions or a more indirect form of data gathering?

The Hawthorne effect in data collecting. One of the most difficult factors to eliminate is the effect of the observer upon the subject, which is called the *Hawthorne effect.* The very act of investigating and observing may influence the behavior of those being investigated.

As Greiner has pointed out, one characteristic of successful change programs is the fact that some attempt to gather data about organization problems has been made prior to the change effort.[19] An effective data collection process enables the change effort to focus on specific problems rather than rely upon a generalized program. The data collection stage also presents managers and organization members with some hard data which may be compared with intuitive, subjective problem awareness.

RED FLAGS IN THE DIAGNOSIS

The change strategy and OD intervention techniques follow from the diagnosis. An inappropriate intervention can be very costly. Such programs can disrupt operations, generate resistance or even hostility among employees, and create additional problems. These improper change strategies can simply fail to produce needed changes, or create unnecessary changes at the expense of the client system. Such ineffective change programs are usually the result of an inaccurate diagnosis.

The OD practitioner needs to recognize some of the special problems that the diagnostic phase presents. Because diagnosis is one of the most important stages in the OD process, there are certain warning signals that the practitioner should be aware of.

The Overdiagnosis

At times the diagnosis may become a process that continues to the extent that it avoids any corrective programs. The diagnosis itself may become a ritual of continual analysis. The diagnosis may continue to a point where so many problems are identified that the client becomes overwhelmed by the complexity of the situation. Although it must be remembered that diagnosis is an important step, it can also be a delaying factor and prevent change programs from ever getting started.

In most every situation, there are several problems that need correction. But if managers are faced with too many alternatives, the most important ones may be obscured or overlooked.

The Crisis Diagnosis

The OD practitioner is often in danger of falling into the trap of attending only to the immediate, short-term crises which the client sees as immediate and important. Energy is often wasted on fighting symptoms or dealing with small crises as a way of avoiding the long-run change programs necessary to develop a more effective organization. Because of time pressures, a consultant may go through an organization in a few days and quickly diagnose the problems. Often, this results in dealing only with the conspicuous problems, while more important but less visible problems may be missed.

The Threatening and Overwhelming Diagnosis

As the OD practitioner interacts with the client system and begins to perceive possible problem areas, he or she may begin to confront the client on these problems. There is a danger, however, that the consultant may come across so blunt or so strong that the relationship with the client is weakened. It may be rather difficult for the client to face and accept information concerning problem areas. The client can also be inundated with so much information that there is difficulty dealing with the information in any meaningful way. If the diagnosis becomes too threatening or overwhelming, the client may resist or reject the entire change program.

The Consultant's Favorite Diagnosis

There can be a tendency for the consultant to fall victim to his or her own biases and selective perceptions. This may result in imposing a special or favorite diagnosis regardless of the nature of the problem. As an example, certain OD practitioners may always view a problem as caused by organization structure regardless of the actual organization problems. Other consultants may see every problem as arising from interpersonal behavior. The consultant has to be aware that there may be a tendency to impose a favorite diagnosis on the problem. "One danger . . . is that the academician, fortified with his technique, is likely to warp the problem so that he can find a solution. He may omit variables that don't fit in and get an elegant solution to something that is not a problem."[20]

As Lippitt, Watson, and Westley have pointed out:

> The *diagnostic orientation* of the change agent is in many ways a self-fulfilling prediction. If he looks for difficulties in communication, for instance, he will find them; and if his help is directed toward improving communication patterns, success will demonstrate to the client system that a solution

of communication problems necessarily result in a more satisfactory state of affairs. . . . The orientation of the change agent is a primary factor in determining the "facts" which the client system will discover to be true about its own situations.[21]

The Diagnosis of Symptoms

As noted earlier, there is often a tendency to focus on the symptoms rather than on the underlying problems. The OD practitioner may be unduly influenced by certain data such as high turnover rates, and identify turnover as the problem. However, this may be merely a symptom of other problems, such as poor supervision, inadequate performance appraisal, or lack of compensation. In short, the diagnostic phase is an important and critical step in the OD process.

REVIEW QUESTIONS

1. Describe the use of performance gap analysis.

2. Compare and contrast the interview and survey methods of data collection. (Find examples from *Business Week*, *The Wall Street Journal*, *Fortune*, etc.)

3. List some possible types of organization data that you might find in your own organization (or one you are familiar with) that might be used in planning an OD program.

4. Describe the difference between symptoms and causes.

5. Identify and give examples of the force-field analysis model.

KEY WORDS AND CONCEPTS

Define and be able to use the following:

Data	Diagnosis
Information	Performance gap
Sociogram	Analytical model
Directed interview	Emergent-group behavior model
Nondirected interview	Sociotechnical systems model
Open-ended questions	Force-field analysis model
Closed questions	

IV.
Simulations

SIMULATION 5.1   THE ACQUISITION DECISION

Total time suggested: 1 hour, 30 minutes.

A. Purpose

The purpose of this simulation is to experience and observe how information affects team decision making. Specifically, it is to experience interdependence and to observe:

1. How task information is shared among team members.
2. How various problem-solving strategies influence results.
3. How collaboration and competition affect group problem solving.

B. Procedures

The two parameters of group effectiveness include (1) the determination of the one best solution to the problem and (2) the completion in the shortest amount of time.

Step 1   Form groups of six members each. Each individual is to select one role from the following:

1. Vice President, Finance
2. Vice President, Marketing
3. Vice President, Personnel
4. Vice President, Production
5. Vice President, Research and Development
6. Observer–OD Consultant

Any extra persons may serve as observers. If there are fewer than six members, a member may select more than one general manager role, but each team should have at least one observer.

Step 2 Refer to the SOS Briefing Sheet, the Role Descriptions and the Acquisition Alternative Summary Sheet (Table 5.2).

READ *ONLY* YOUR ROLE.

Time suggested for Steps 1 and 2: 10 minutes.

Step 3 Executive Committee Meeting. Your team is to select the correct acquisition candidate based on the data you will receive. There is one correct solution, and decisions are to be reached independently of the other groups. The observer will not take an active part during this phase of the simulation. The observer will focus on answering the questions in Step 4.

Time suggested for Step 3: 45 minutes.

Step 4 In your teams, consider the following questions, with the Observer–OD consultant leading the discussion:

1. What behaviors seemed to help your group to successfully complete its task?
2. What factors inhibited problem solving?
3. How much time was spent on deciding *how* to solve the problem?
4. How was information shared among the group? What does the sociogram for the team look like?
5. How did issues of authority or power affect the group?
6. How did collaboration/competition influence the outcome?
7. How did you go about diagnosing the problems?

Time suggested for Step 4: 15 minutes.

Step 5 Discuss the questions in Step 4 with the entire class.

Time suggested for Step 5: 20 minutes.

SOS BRIEFING SHEET

A. Instructions to the group

1. You are a committee made up of the key managers of SOS.
2. This is the meeting to make a decision about the acquisition.

TABLE 5.2 Acquisition Alternative Summary Sheet

Company	Previous Annual Sales (millions)	Current Annual Estimated Sales (millions)	Previous Annual Earnings (millions)	Current Annual Estimated Earnings (millions)	Price (millions)	Research and Development (millions)	Expected Annual Savings (millions)	Antitrust Reaction	Availability	Wall Street Reaction
A	330	400	20	24	240	24	38	Moderate	Most likely	Good
B	185	200	9	10	120	10	35	Minimum	Moderate	Fair
C	325	350	27	30	315	21	65	High	Most likely	Poor
D	210	250	10	13	172	20	35	Low	Definite	Good
E	135	150	7	8	75	6	10	Extreme	Moderate	Fair
F	350	380	20	22	228	23	50	Absent	Low	Poor
G	460	500	16	18	157	40	23	Moderate	Moderate	Fair
H	185	220	10	14	185	14	30	Minimum	Moderate	Fantastic

3. Basically, the data you bring with you are in your head.

4. Your job is to select an acquisition from among the possible candidates.

5. You may use a calculator or a personal computer with an electronic spread sheet.

B. Assumptions that need to be made

1. Assume that there is one solution.

2. Assume that all data are correct.

3. You have 45 minutes to work the exercise.

4. There must be substantial agreement when the problem has been solved.

5. You must work the problem as a team.

ROLE DESCRIPTIONS (READ *ONLY* YOUR ROLE)

Vice President, Finance Your committee is made up of the managers of SOS Corporation, a young and growing medium-sized software company. Your mission is to locate and identify the best acquisition candidate for your firm. Your company is quick to exit businesses that don't offer high growth, high performance opportunities.

You have already examined the data on eight companies. Your first order of business is to gain a consensus on the best selection from among the candidates listed on the Acquisition Alternative Summary Sheet. You think that the sales growth rate must be greater than 10 percent over the previous year in order to fit this criteria and the P/E ratio should be 11 or less. Should you decide to consider payback (price paid divided by expected annual savings) in the acquisition decision, anything seven years or more is a low payback.

Vice President, Personnel Your committee is made up of the managers of SOS Corporation, a young and growing medium-sized software company. Your mission is to locate and identify the best acquisition candidate for your firm. Your company is quick to exit businesses that don't offer high growth, high performance opportunities.

You have already examined the data on eight companies. Your first order of business is to gain a consensus on the best selection from among the candidates listed on the Acquisition Alternative Summary Sheet. You think that the reaction of the investment community on Wall Street must be better than fair if you are to maintain performance. Also, the company should have at least a moderate chance of being available. If you decide to consider the earnings growth rate, use the previous year's earnings as the base year.

Vice President, Research and Development Your committee is made up of the managers of SOS Corporation, a young and growing medium-sized software company. Your mission is to locate and identify the best acquisition candidate for your firm. Your company is quick to exit businesses that don't offer high growth, high performance opportunities.

You have already examined the data on eight companies. Your first order of business is to gain a consensus on the best selection from among the candidates listed on the Acquisition Alternative Summary Sheet. You think that Research and Development should be at least 6 percent of sales in order to maintain technological capabilities and annual sales must be at least $225 million. Also, if you decide to consider the rate of sales growth, use the previous year's sales as the base year. The company has decided to use a modified P/E ratio of using the ratio of price paid for the company to its current earnings.

Vice President, Marketing   Your committee is made up of the managers of SOS Corporation, a young and growing medium-sized software company. Your mission is to locate and identify the best acquisition candidate for your firm. Your company is quick to exit businesses that don't offer high growth, high performance opportunities.

You have already examined the data on eight companies. Your first order of business is to gain a consensus on the best selection from among the candidates listed on the Acquisition Alternative Summary Sheet. You think that the price should be less than $300 million to fit the performance goal; and earnings growth rate should be greater than 5 percent over the previous year. Should you decide to consider an appropriate payback, anything less than 5 years is a high payback. The annual savings of the acquisition is an average projected for the next 8 years.

Vice President, Production   Your committee is made up of the managers of SOS Corporation, a young and growing medium-sized software company. Your mission is to locate and identify the best acquisition candidate for your firm. Your company is quick to exit businesses that don't offer high growth, high performance opportunities.

You have already examined the data on eight companies. Your first order of business is to gain a consensus on the best selection from among the candidates listed on the Acquisition Alternative Summary Sheet. You think that the payback should be moderate or high to gain economies of scale. You would like a favorable price-earnings (P/E) ratio but the lower the ratio the better. Antitrust reaction should be moderate or less.

OD Consultant Guidelines   You hope to accomplish several things at this meeting:

1.   To develop a consultant-client relationship.
2.   To make a preliminary diagnosis of possible problems.
3.   To help them work more effectively as a team; however, you will not become involved with solving the problem.

**Case:
The Old
Family Bank**

THE OLD FAMILY BANK

The Old Family Bank is a large bank in a southeastern city. As a part of a comprehensive internal management study, H. Day, the data processing vice president, examined the turnover, absenteeism, and productivity figures of all work groups in the organization. The results Day obtained contained no real surprises except in the case of the check-sorting and data-processing departments.

The Study

The study revealed that in general the departments displaying high turnover and absenteeism rates had low production figures, and those with low turnover and absenteeism were highly productive. When analysis began on the check-sorting and data-processing figures, Day discovered that both departments were tied for the lead for the lowest turnover and absenteeism figures. What was surprising was that the check-sorting department ranked first as the most productive unit, whereas the electronic data-processing department ranked last.

That inconsistency was further complicated by the fact that the working conditions for check-sorting employees is extremely undesirable. They work in a large open room that is hot in the summer and cold in the winter. They work alone and operate high-speed check-sorting machines requiring a high degree of accuracy and concentration. There is little chance for interaction because they all take rotating coffee breaks. The computer room is air-conditioned, with a stable temperature the year round; it has perfect lighting and is extremely quiet and comfortable. It was known that both groups are highly cohesive and that the workers function well with others in their department. This observation was reinforced by the study's finding of the low levels of turnover and absenteeism.

The Interview Data

In an effort to understand this phenomenon, vice president Day decided to interview the members of both departments. Day hoped to gain some insight into the dynamics of each group's behavior. It was discovered that the check-sorting department displayed a great deal of loyalty to the company. Most of the group are unskilled or semiskilled workers, although they have no organized union, and each person felt that the company had made special efforts to keep their wages and benefits in line with organized operations. They knew that their work required team effort and were committed to high performance.

A quite different situation existed in the data-processing department. Although the workers liked their fellow employees, there was a uniform feeling among this highly skilled group that management placed more emphasis on production than on staff units. It was their contention that pay increases had been better for operating departments and that the gap between the wage earners and salaried employees did not reflect the skill differences. Because of that, a large percentage of the group displayed little loyalty toward the company, even though they were very close among themselves.

CASE ANALYSIS FORM

Problems

A. Macro

 1. _____

 2. _____

B. Micro

 1. _____

 2. _____

II. Causes

 1. _____

 2. _____

 3. _____

III. Systems affected

 1. Structural

 2. Psychosocial

 3. Technical

 4. Managerial

 5.

IV. Alternatives

 1. _____

 2. _____

 3. _____

 4. _____

 5. _____

V. Recommendations

 1. _____

 2. _____

 3. _____

V. Summary

In this chapter some major considerations in formulating a diagnosis have been presented. The OD practitioner has to recognize the importance of this process because the diagnosis leads to problem-solving action. A weak or inaccurate diagnosis leads to an ineffective change program. A sound diagnosis enables the consultant and the client to specify the nature of the problem causing system disequilibrium by identifying underlying forces and multiple causality.

In an OD program, intervention and data gathering occur throughout the program. The decisions about what information to collect and how it should be collected are difficult and important. No data-gathering method is of itself either right or wrong; rather, each method has its own limitations as well as its strong points. The process of collecting information is an important step in an OD program because it provides a foundation for the diagnosis of problems and the selection of change strategies and techniques. What must be determined is whether a particular method is most appropriate for the specific objectives and climate of each unique situation.

In diagnosing organization problems, the consultant and the client try to specify the problems, determine the underlying causes, and identify the opportunities for change. The OD practitioner tries to sort out factual from nonfactual information and searches for multiple sources of the problem condition. The outcome is an explicit and specific diagnosis upon which to base change efforts.

The consultant needs maximum participation from members of the client system in the diagnostic process and needs to consider the impact of the diagnosis upon his or her relationship with the client. The OD practitioner may confront the client with unpleasant facts, so the more objective the data and the more the analysis includes both strengths and weaknesses, the better the resultant OD program will be. During the diagnostic phase the OD practitioner should also be alert for danger signals or red-flag conditions.

Several diagnostic models have been described, including the analytical model, the emergent-group model, the sociotechnical systems model, and the force-field model. The models may be used by the consultant to facilitate the analysis of client system problems. You have had the opportunity to practice using various methods for diagnosing problems.

In the simulation you had a chance to experience using information and diagnosing organization problems. You may have found that diagnosis is not a simple process, since it includes both the client's needs and system problems. The diagnostic process involves identifying the problems and assessing the readiness for change of the client system. It requires an understanding of the client's felt needs by attempting to see the problem from the client's viewpoint. Similarly, the OD practitioner must apply a systems approach by specifying the interrelationships of various elements of the client system. This requires organizing the available data or evidence into some meaningful patterns.

In this chapter, the important factors and models in the diagnostic process have been described, and you have had an opportunity to practice and apply these concepts. This stage provides the foundation for subsequent OD interventions.

NOTES

1. W. Warner Burke, Lawrence P. Clark, and Cheryl Koopman, "Improve Your OD Project's Chances for Success," *Training and Development Journal*, 38, no. 9 (September, 1984), 65.

2. Lynda C. McDermott, "The Many Faces of the OD Professional", *Training and Development Journal*, February 1984, pp. 14–19.

3. Sally Ver Schere, "Assessing the Strengths and Challenges of Your Group," *Fund Raising Management*, December 1984, pp. 60–61.

4. D. Nadler, "Role of Models in Organizational Assessment," in *Organizational Assessment*, eds. E. Lawler III, D. Nadler, and C. Camman (New York: John Wiley & Sons, Inc., 1980), pp. 119–31.

5. Burke, Clark, and Koopman, "Improve Your OD Project's Chances," p. 65.

6. Paul Lawrence and Jay Lorsch, *Developing Organizations: Diagnosis and Action* (Reading, Mass.: Addison-Wesley Publishing Co., Inc., 1969), pp. 11–14.

7. George Homans, *The Human Group* (New York: Harcourt Brace Jovanovich, Inc., 1950).

8. F. Emergy, *Characteristics of Sociotechnical Systems* (London: Tavistock Institute, 1959).

9. Kurt Lewin, "Frontiers in Group Dynamics, Concepts, Methods and Reality in Social Science," *Human Relations*, 1 (June 1974), 5–42.

10. See Richard J. Boland, Jr., "Sense-Making of Accounting Data," *Management Sciences*, 30, no. 7 (July 1984), 868–82.

11. L. Dean, "Interaction Reported and Observed: The Case of One Local Union," *Human Organization*, Fall 1958, pp. 36–44.

12. See Edward J. Conlon, "Survey Feedback as a Large-Scale Change Device: An Empirical Examination," *Group and Organization Studies*, September 1984, pp. 399–416; and also Clayton P. Alderfer and L. Dave Brown, "Designing an 'Empathetic Questionnaire' for Organizational Research," *Journal of Applied Psychology*, 56, no. 6 (1972), 456–60.

13. Jacob Moreno, *Who Shall Survive?* 2nd ed. (New York: Beacon House, Inc., 1953).

14. David C. McClelland, *The Achieving Society* (Princeton, N.J.: D. Van Nostrand Company, 1961).

15. Jack Fordyce and Raymond Weil, *Managing with People* (Reading, Mass.: Addison-Wesley Publishing Co., Inc., 1971), pp. 146–52.

16. Michael A. Hitt and Robert L. Mathis, "Survey Results Shed Light Upon Important Developmental Tools," *Personal Administrator*, 28, no. 2, (February 1983), 89–97.

17. Burke, Clark, and Koopman, "Improve Your OD Project's Chances," p. 65.

18. Burke, Clark, and Koopman, "Improve Your OD Project's Chances," p. 65.

19. Larry Greiner, "Patterns of Organization Change," *Harvard Business Review*, May–June 1967, pp. 119–30.

20. Tom Alexander, "Computers Can't Solve Everything," *Fortune*, October 1969, p. 128.

21. Ronald Lippitt, Jeanne Watson, and Bruce Westley, *The Dynamics of Planned Change* (New York: Harcourt Brace Jovanovich, Inc., 1958), p. 65.

OVERCOMING RESISTANCE
TO CHANGE

I. **Objectives**	Upon completing this chapter, you will be able to: 1. Identify the forces within individuals and organizations causing resistance to change programs. 2. Recognize strategies that can increase motivation to change. 3. Experience reaction to a change situation. 4. Diagnose the resistant forces in organization change.
II. **Premeeting** **Preparation**	1. Read the Background Information (Section III). 2. Prepare for Simulation 6.1 (Section IV). Read the company background and complete Step 1. 3. Read and analyze Case: Progress on Purpose.

III.
Background
Information

A major challenge facing organizations is to manage change effectively.[1] When organizations fail to change in necessary ways, the costs of that failure are often high. In a dynamic environment, organizations must have the capacity to adapt quickly in order to survive. In most cases the speed and complexity of change may severely test the capabilities of both managers and members. Unless members are emotionally prepared for change, the sheer speed with which it occurs can be overwhelming.

Solving organizational problems usually involves the introduction of change. If the required changes are small or isolated, they can usually be accomplished without major problems. However, when the changes are on a larger scale and involve many individuals and subunits, there are often significant problems. As organizational problems emerge, managers attempt to take corrective actions. Often, these corrective actions impact upon patterns of work or values, and resistance is encountered. Although many potential problems may emerge while initiating organizational change programs, the problem most likely to be encountered is associated with human resistance to changing patterns of work. Prior to the implementation of any OD strategy or technique, the OD consultant must deal with potential resistance to change. This chapter examines a more general but nevertheless relevant issue to any OD program: the motivation of the client system. What is it that makes an individual, a group, or an organization believe that a change would be beneficial? What forces interfere with and restrict the implementation of a change program? What phases of resistance does a typical change program go through? Finally, what can a manager or OD consultant do to increase the probability of acceptance of a change program?

It would obviously be helpful to answer these questions very specifically; however, specific answers can only be given when speaking of a single client system. The answers will be formulated with the purpose of developing a criterion of forces tending to increase and decrease the acceptance of a change program. Those forces pushing for and desirous of a change program will be called motivating forces, and those restraining and interfering with a change program will be called resisting forces.

Once the decision to implement a change program has been made by the organization or its key members and the OD practitioner has been brought in to work with the organization, it is the task of these parties to energize the forces favoring the change program. So that you may more fully appreciate this process, this chapter deals with motivating and resisting forces, the phases of resistance of change programs, and the actions increasing the probability of change.

THE LIFE CYCLE OF RESISTANCE TO CHANGE

Organization development action programs involve innovation and change which will probably encounter some degree of resistance. This resistance will be evident in individuals and groups in such forms as controversy, hostility, and conflict, either overtly or covertly. The change itself tends to move through a life cycle.[2]

Phase 1. In the first phase there are only a few people who see the need for change and take the reform seriously. They represent a fringe element of the organization and may be openly criticized, ridiculed, and persecuted by whatever methods the organization has at its disposal and thinks appropriate to handle the dissidents and force them to conform to established organization norms. Resistance appears massive. At this point the change program may die or it may continue to grow.

Phase 2. As the movement for change has begun to grow, the forces for the change and against the change become identifiable. The change is discussed and it is more thoroughly understood by more of the organization's members. The threat associated with the change can be lessened because of increased understanding. "When a new idea is first introduced to us, we begin to consider it from many different viewpoints. In time, its novelty and strangeness disappear. Eventually it becomes familiar. . . . When sufficient time is not allowed for such adjustment, those involved in a change could become bewildered and apprehensive and develop feelings of opposition."[3]

Phase 3. In this phase there is a direct conflict and a showdown between the forces pro and con. This phase will probably mean life or death to the change effort, as those enthusiastic about the change frequently underestimate the strength of those resistant to the change. Those in an organization who see a change as good and needed find it difficult to believe the extent to which the opposition will go to put a stop to the change.

Phase 4. If, after the decisive battles, the supporters of the change are in power, the remaining resistance is seen as stubborn and a nuisance. There is still a possibility that the resisters to the change will mobilize enough support to shift the balance of power. Wisdom is necessary in dealing with the overt opposition and with that element which, although not openly opposed, is not yet thoroughly convinced about the benefit of the change.

Phase 5. In the last phase the resisters to the change are as few and as alienated as were the advocates in the first phase.

Although these phases may give the impression that a battle is being waged between those trying to bring about change and those resisting the change (and sometimes this is the situation), the actual conflict is usually more subtle and may only surface in small verbal disagreements, questions, reluctance, and so forth. But regardless of the degree of resistance, the organization change program, if it does not die in the process, will to some extent evolve through the five phases described above, although in some change programs, some of the phases may be brief or even omitted.

MANAGING CHANGE FORCES ⸻⸻⸻⸻⸻⸻⸻⸻⸻⸻⸻⸻⸻⸻⸻

Changing an organization involves modifying existing organizational systems, structure, and culture to some different standard or level of performance. The purpose of change is to increase organizational effectiveness or even to ensure survival. Most managers agree that if an organization is to continue to be excellent, it must continually respond to significant environmental developments. According to a study by John P. Kotter and Leonard A. Schlesinger, "Most companies or divisions of major corporations find that they must undertake moderate organizational changes at least once a year and major changes every four or five."[4] Managing change is therefore not only a challenge for managers, it is necessary for survival.

In his thought-provoking books, Alvin Toffler argues that the environment is, and will continue to be, so dynamic and complex that it threatens people and organizations with "future shock" (see Chapter Two). Toffler comments,

> I think the starting point is to assume that tomorrow will be
> different, maybe radically different. That may sound
> obvious, but there are many executives who really believe
> that the future will be pretty much like today. They feel that
> if they continue doing what was successful until now, it will
> work tomorrow.[5]

In this section, we will identify the major factors involved in the change process and present a model of the change process.

Many managers consider change to be so critical to the success of the organization that they continuously search for ways to make positive organizational changes. Chairman Roger B. Smith of General Motors, for example, is trying to lead his company into new areas of opportunity (see OD Application 6.1). The way managers like Roger Smith deal with change determines how successful these changes will be.

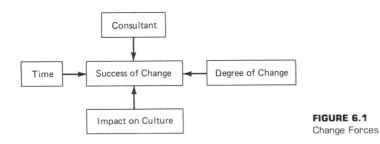

FIGURE 6.1
Change Forces

OD
Application
6.1

CHANGES AT GM

General Motors Corporation is attempting to become more competitive in a business where its market share remains below its 1978 level and profits continue to fall—26 percent in one year alone. And GM's manufacturing costs, once the lowest in the industry, are now the highest.

Restructuring GM

With these kinds of challenges, the chairman of GM, Roger B. Smith, is trying to make sure GM will be a viable competitor in the year 2000. Recent acquisitions include high-tech companies like Hughes Aircraft and Electronic Data Systems (EDS), but the big job is to mesh these sharply different cultures with GM. Within three years of the purchase of EDS, Ross Perot, the founder of EDS, left GM complaining of its entrenched bureaucracy. Perot says that trying to make GM change is like teaching an elephant to tap dance.

When Smith became chairman of GM in 1981, he saw modernizing GM's management as one of his primary tasks. A major reorganization was undertaken to reduce some of the redundancy in engineering and manufacturing. As a result Buick-Oldsmobile-Cadillac and Chevrolet-Pontiac-GM of Canada replaced a decades-old structure of competing car lines. Cutting out duplication between departments and needless paperwork could help GM reduce total car costs by as much as 30 percent, according to David Cole of the University of Michigan. However, within two years GM announced it was placing Cadillac back in its own division.

Changing the Culture

The desire is to create a streamlined GM hierarchy with decision making being pushed down into the ranks. The main obstacle is what Smith calls the "frozen middle": tens of thousands of managers made complacent by the golden days of GM. Smith may have underestimated how hard it would be to change GM into a more efficient organization.

Smith has tried to change the culture by weaning layer upon layer of cautious, by-the-book managers from their dependence on memos (there is an estimated cost of $12 every time a piece of paper changes hands at GM), committees, and reports, and by having them start thinking like entrepreneurs. This has not been an easy task, as GM car operations have over 130,000 white-collar workers in North America alone.

Culture Clash

The culture clash between the GM that Smith is trying to create and the old ways is evidenced by two types of employee behavior: passive resistance and learned helplessness. According to Smith, "Some people will think to themselves that, since they have run their departments for 30 years, if they don't like the new way of doing things, they just won't do it. So they will stand there and smile at you." Other people, having become accustomed to being told what to do, can't make independent decisions when the need arises.

Results

The changes are gradually beginning to pay off. GM has one of the oldest quality of work life programs, put in place in the early 1970s. And GM has learned that expensive robots have not paid off nearly as much as the organizing of production workers into teams. When Chevrolet marketers requested specially equipped cars to penetrate the California market, engineers were able to turn them out in less than 6 months. In the old GM culture, the program would have taken 15 months.

The problem is how deeply the signals for change reach through the company. "At the top, the vision is pretty clear," says David Ulrich, a University of Michigan professor. "The message may be down two or three levels, but they have another eight levels to go."

Questions:
1. What has been GM's response to its declining market position?
2. Could it do more to bring about faster change and should it?
3. What kind of resistance to change has there been at GM?
4. Do you think Smith's changes will be successful or are the changes too little, too late?

Sources: Dale D. Buss, "GM to Restructure Its Cadillac Division," *Wall Street Journal*, January 8, 1987, p. 3; Anne B. Fisher, "GM Is Tougher Than You Think," *Fortune*, November 10, 1986, pp. 56–64; William J. Hampton and Todd Mason, "GM Hasn't Bought Much Peace," *Business Week*, December 15, 1986, pp. 24–26; Amal Kumar Naj and John Bussey, "GM Net Fell 70% in Quarter to $382 Million," *Wall Street Journal*, February 6, 1987, p. 2; and David E. Whiteside, "Roger Smith's Campaign to Change the GM Culture," *Business Week*, April 7, 1986, pp. 84–85.

The major factors in the change process are listed next. (See also Figure 6.1 on page 154.)

1. The Consultant. Perhaps the most important factor is determining who will spearhead the change program. This may be an executive or manager (an internal consultant), or an outside consultant brought in for some specific project.

2. The Degree of Change. A second factor is the degree of change to be made. Is it a relatively minor change, such as a change in sales order forms? Or is it a major change in strategy, such as a new product line. The greater the degree of change, the more difficult it is to implement successfully.

3. The Time Frame. A third factor is the length of time chosen to implement the change program: either gradual, over several months or years; or abrupt. In general, the more gradual the change and the longer the time frame, the more chance of success.

4. The Impact on Corporate Culture. The change's impact on existing systems and culture is important (as noted earlier) because the greater the impact on existing cultural norms, the greater the amount of resistance likely to emerge, and thus the greater the difficulty in implementing the change program.

5. The Evaluation. Finally, some system of evaluating the change must be considered, so that some standards or levels of performance can be used to measure the degree of change and its impact on organization effectiveness.[6]

A CHANGE MODEL

Two major considerations in making changes in an organization are the degree of change and the impact on the culture. Evidence suggests that change is difficult to accomplish, and resistance can be expected whenever a change involves a significant impact on the traditional behavior, power, culture, and structure within an organization. The degree of change and the impact on the existing culture present four possible change situations. (See Figure 6.2.)

1. Small change, small impact. Where the change to be introduced is relatively minor, and the impact on the existing culture small, we can predict the lowest level of resistance and the highest probability of a successful change.

2. Small change, large impact. Where the change is minor but has an impact on the culture, some resistance can be expected, depending on the size of the threat, and the speed of the change.

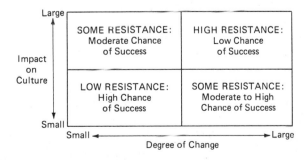

FIGURE 6.2
The Change Model

3. Large change, small impact. Here the change is major, but the impact on existing culture is minor, so while some resistance is likely, good management can probably overcome resistance.

4. Large change, large impact. When the degree of change is large and the impact on the existing culture is high, the greatest resistance can be predicted. In this situation, the probability of success is low, and change should probably not be attempted. Therefore, in managing change, experience suggests that both the level of resistance and the time it takes to implement change tend to be underestimated.

THE MOTIVATING FORCES TOWARD ACCEPTANCE OF A CHANGE PROGRAM

Motivating forces have been defined as anything that increases the inclination of the client system to implement the proposed change program. These forces vary in intensity, depending on the specifics of the individual client system and its immediate situation. Some of the forces help to create the need for and to initiate the change program: other forces develop later, as the change program progresses.

Dissatisfaction with the Present Situation

Initially, the client may feel some dissatisfaction or even pain with the present situation. The client may not know why it is dissatisfied, but it does have a desire for relief. This could be likened to a person who is sick: he does not know why or what to do to be cured, but he does want to be relieved of the pain. He may try some home remedies or seek the help of a doctor. Organizations sometimes find themselves in a similar situation: that is, they come to realize that they are unhealthy or ineffective and seek the help of a consultant. The more intense the dissatisfaction with the present situation, the greater will be the motivation to change. Members of an organization may become dissatisfied with their personal position and push for change on the belief that things cannot get much worse.

In some other situations the client system may be more cognizant of the need or desire to change. Members of the client system may perceive a difference between the present situation and the situation as they would like it to be. They may not be really dissatisfied with the situation as it now is, but perhaps after observing other organizations, they recognize a need for some improvements. The organization may have operating records that are compatible with standards for their type of organization, but they may not be satisfied with being average. They may believe that they have untapped potential but are not sure how to release their talents in a way that will further the development of their organization.

For other organizations, the need to change may be more obvious. For example, it took a nosedive in market share, sales, and earnings for top executives Bill and Joe Coors to realize that the firm was facing a fight for survival. "The Coors headquarters now is the scene of a traumatic metamorphosis for one of the nation's most unusual, conservative and controversial industrial dynasties, just now dragging its hind foot out of the 19th Century."[7] The client system may not be meeting its industry's standards on such matters as rate of return on invested capital or employee turnover. Also, internal goals, such as group production quotas, may not have been achieved. As a consequence internal pressures are brought to bear to change the present situation. There is an obvious felt need that "we had better do something, anything, and fast."

External Pressures toward Compliance

An organization does not exist in a vacuum. It is part of a larger external environment that imposes certain forces upon the organization. Sometimes various external pressures will cause the client system to change some of its present methods of operation. These pressures can vary widely from voluntary actions to involuntary legal requirements. In industry the corporation may need to adopt new technologies to remain competitive, or an organization may be required by law to make a change necessitated by environmental or civil rights legislation. A much more subtle change is occurring in the values and attitudes of the individual members of society. Education levels continue to rise and individuals are becoming more sophisticated, more knowledgeable of better ways of doing things, and more independent and assertive. There seems to be a shift in values, at least in respect to organizational life, that supports democratic principles and the worth of each person.

Momentum toward Change

When a change program has gotten under way, certain forces tend to push the program along. An OD program is built around client involvement. The client system plays a major part in directing the change, and it will probably become committed to the program. There will be forces within the client that want to see the project carried through to completion; the client will want to see "the fruits of its labor." Also, as change programs and consultants usually do not come cheap and some money has probably been spent on the program, the client may want to continue in order to get its money's worth.

Once a change program is under way in one part of an organization, it may set off a chain reaction requiring or permitting changes in other parts of the organization. This notion of change is compatible with the OD fundamental that effective change is organization-wide, or if the change is in a subpart of an organization, the subpart is reasonably well isolated.

Motivation by the Consultant

The consultant should not be overlooked as a motivating force. Words of assurance from the consultant can have a strong motivating effect on the client system. The consultant has been involved in many planned change programs, but for the client it could easily be the first major planned change program. The client system may become discouraged at the seemingly slow pace at which the change is moving. Or after having been involved in the diagnosis of problems, it may be overwhelmed by the variety and magnitude of the problems. Although the consultant should be selective in any morale building undertaken, the sharing of similar situations and past successes in other organizations can be helpful.

The consultant's own behavior can often serve as a motivating force especially if the consultant is held in high esteem by the client system. Members of the client system may be closed, untrusting, and dishonest in their relations with each other, whereas the consultant believes that effective organizations are built on openness, trust, honesty, and collaboration among the system's members. If the consultant personally behaves in this manner and is held in high regard, the client system may change its behavior.

THE RESISTING FORCES BLOCKING IMPLEMENTATION OF CHANGE PROGRAMS

Another critical factor to be considered prior to the implementation of any OD strategy or technique is the probability of resistance to change. The consultant may assume that because the goals of the program are worthwhile, members will actively support the changes, but this is not always true. Since change always alters the status quo, the consultant should anticipate some resistance among members and plan for this eventuality in the change strategy. The experience of OD practitioners indicates that one of the significant hindrances to OD is not the inadequacy of change techniques but rather the failure of management and consultants to gain acceptance of proposed changes. The success of organization development programs may depend to a great extent on the ability of the consultant doing the planning. OD practitioners can benefit from the knowledge gained by sociologists, social psychologists, and cultural anthropologists who have studied the process of change. Resistance to organization development programs is a complex rather than a simple problem; it is the cumulative effect of many factors that make up the acceptance or rejection of change.

Uncertainty Regarding Change

Organization members may have a psychological resistance to change because they seek to avoid uncertainty. Past ways of doing things are well known and predictable and the unwillingness to give up familiar tasks or relationships may cause resistance.

Fear of the unknown. A large part of resistance to change stems from a fear of the uncertain or unknown. People become anxious when they exchange the old and familiar for something new and uncertain. A lack of information or understanding often leaves a vacuum which is filled by rumor, speculation, and insecurity. Several years ago the Dow Chemical Company decided to reorganize and change from an American corporation to a completely international operation. This meant that the international division, involving the jobs of several hundred employees, would be dismantled. Even though the individuals recognized the logic of the change, this was of minor concern compared with the impact upon their own jobs and career goals. Because of a lack of information about the effect of the change, many valuable individuals panicked and sought jobs with other companies simply because of the uncertainty surrounding their future careers.

Disruption of routine. Proposed changes that disturb habitual routines or patterns are likely to encounter resistance because a person's behavior is governed largely by habit and routine. When a person first successfully copes with a situation, he or she will usually continue to operate in a similar manner. The familiar is preferred, and this is especially true when the established behavior has resulted in past successes. There is little incentive to change when the old way of behaving has been tried and is successful. Once these habits and attitudes have been firmly established, a person responds to his or her environment and to new ideas through this framework. Even situations that are in conflict with these old attitudes are sometimes altered and perceived in a way that is congruent with those attitudes. The old adage "We hear what we want to hear" has some degree of truth. People may conveniently forget some learning that is in conflict with their present behavior. This notion of selective perception means that people will successfully resist and negate the possible influence of new information upon their earlier attitudes and behavior.

Loss of Existing Benefits

When the change causes employees to feel pressured, they may interpret change as a loss of individual security. There may be an emotional loss associated with the change, a loss of the prior "comfort zone."

Any proposed change is more readily accepted if it promises to benefit those affected by it; however, the motivation of top management to change may not be shared at the operating level. In some cases resistance may be due to a lack of interest or practical appreciation of the reason for the change. In a similar vein, the expectations of a group toward a proposed change will influence its reception. A group that favors a change and expects to benefit will change more readily than one that starts with a negative attitude. People affected by a change tend to resist unless they see the need for it.

Lynda McDermott, an OD consultant, comments "My experience of organization change is that typically the focus is on 'what's in it for the organization,' but to counter resistance to change there has to be a focus, for some periods of time, on 'what's in it for the individual.' "[8]

Threat to Position Power

Any change that causes a manager or group to "lose face" will be resisted. Changes that threaten to lower the status or prestige of the individual (or group) will probably meet resistance. For example, a department manager who sees a change as reducing his or her sphere of authority is not likely to be in favor of such a change. Where a proposed change appears to be detrimental to the vested interest of any group, the groups will resist the change. Thus, even though a change to a matrix organization structure may benefit the organization as a whole, functional departments may view the change as a threat to their best interest and therefore resist.

Change sometimes results in a potential disadvantage to an individual employee or group, and people tend to resist changes that threaten the security of their environment. There may be concern for such vested interests as the loss of job, reduced promotional potential, change in career opportunities, reduction in wages or benefits, or an increase in job demands. There are many incidents where work groups have withheld a secretly invented tool or improved work method from management for fear the job will be retimed and people laid off or transferred. These fears induce a loss of security and result in resistance to change.

A major factor in resistance to innovation is that reorganization invariably implies a redistribution of power and influence. Individuals or groups who perceive that a change will lessen their degree of influence will strongly resist such changes. Those who have the most to lose will be most likely to disapprove of or resist proposed changes.

Generally, technical changes are more readily accepted when they do not disturb existing social networks. Friendships, social cliques, or informal teams may be threatened by changes. There is research evidence to indicate that the stronger the group ties, the greater the resistance to change.

Conformity to Norms and Culture

Norms are the organized and shared ideas of what members of an organization should do and feel. The members themselves define what the norms are, as well as enforce individual behavior to conform to the norms. The enforcement is imposed by the individual and by the group through peer pressure upon the individual. Because norms generally have strong support from the group, they cannot easily be changed. This is especially true of an individual attempting to alter a norm, for this person faces exclusion by the group. When a person is external to the group (say, an external consultant or a manager) the change process may be even more difficult because of lack of familiarity.

The organization culture includes the language, dress, patterns of behavior, value system, feelings, attitudes, interactions, and group norms of the members. Larger organizations will have subcultures formed around smaller work or social groups. If one accepts the gestalt view of organization behavior, it is difficult to change the ways of behaving in one part of the organization without influencing and being influenced by (perhaps through resistance) the other parts. Unless the consultant begins by considering the possible resistance from the organization as a whole, the ultimate acceptance of the change program is in serious question.

CONSULTANT STRATEGIES TO LESSEN RESISTANCE

If resistance to change can be minimized, the chances of a successful OD program are enhanced. Initially, two things in reducing resistance should be recognized by both the manager and the OD practitioner: (1) resistance to change can be predicted; and (2) resistance cannot be repressed effectively in the long run. The task of the manager or the consultant is to make conflict resulting from the resistance creative for organizational good. That is, as the repression of conflict is unwise and even futile, the objective is to turn the energies generated in the resistance of the change to good advantage. A manager or consultant can, however, minimize the threat that underlies resistance. Certain actions may be implemented to make resistance creative for the organization and to reduce resistance.

Resistance to the change are signals to the consultant that something is not working in the implementation of the program. These signals include delays and inefficiencies, failure to produce anticipated results, or even efforts to sabotage the change program. There are several actions for dealing with resistance to change, as summarized in Table 6.1.

Education and Communication

The uncertainty and fear of the unknown associated with change can be minimized by an effective communication program. (See B.C. comic strip.) The lack of reliable information leads to rumors and uncertainty. Information concerning the *what* and *why* involved in the change program should be provided to all organization members. The longer members speculate in the absence of

TABLE 6.1 Methods for Dealing with Resistance to Change

Approach	Commonly used when . . .	Advantages	Disadvantages
1. Education & Communication	There is a lack of information or inaccurate information and analysis.	Once persuaded, people will often help implement the change.	Can be very time consuming if many people are involved.
2. Participation & Involvement	The initiators do not have all the information they need to design the change, and others have considerable power to resist.	People who participate will be committed to implementing the change, and any relevant information they have will be integrated into the change plan.	Can be very time consuming if participators design an inappropriate change.
3. Facilitation & Support	People are resisting because of adjustment problems.	No other approach works as well with adjustment problems.	Can be time consuming, expensive, and still fail.
4. Negotiation & Agreement	Some person or group with considerable power to resist will clearly lose out in a change.	Sometimes it is a relatively easy way to avoid major resistance.	Can be too expensive if it alerts others to negotiate for compliance.
5. Manipulation & Co-optation	Other tactics will not work, or are too expensive.	It can be a relatively quick and inexpensive solution to resistance problems.	Can lead to future problems if people feel manipulated.
6. Explicit & Implicit Coercion	Speed is essential, and the change initiators possess considerable power.	It is speedy and can overcome any kind of resistance.	Can be risky if it leaves people angry with the intitiators.

Source: Reprinted by permission of the Harvard Business Review. An exhibit from "Choosing Strategies for Change," by John P. Kotter and Leonard A. Schlesinger, March/April 1979 Copyright © 1979 by the President and Fellows of Harvard College; all rights reserved.

reliable facts, the more likely it is that resistance will emerge. Most managers underestimate the amount of communication needed, so it is better to use "overkill" than to understate the situation. The advantages and rewards of the proposed changes should of course be emphasized in all communication, for opposition to change disappears as the fears it generates are explained away. Once the reasons underlying a change program are made clear, the members involved can more readily understand the impact of the change.

Participation of Members in the Change Program

One basic technique for increasing the acceptance of change is to be certain that the individuals involved are allowed to share in the decision process rather than being forced. The involvement of the individual in matters of concern increases the probability of having an acceptable program. An individual who has participated in the formation of a program has an interest and ownership in the program which is likely to lead to increased motivation and under-

Source: B.C. by permission of Johnny Hart and Creators Syndicate, Inc.

standing. A change that is self-designed has greater emotional appeal and a higher probability of being carried out than one from outside. A change program "prepared on high and cast as pearls before swine" will most certainly be destined to failure. Captain Queeg, in the following excerpt from *The Caine Mutiny*, very enthusiastically follows the policy of dictated change which later contributed to his overthrow:

> "Now, there are four ways of doing a thing aboard ship—the right way, the wrong way, the Navy way, and my way. I want things on this ship done my way. Don't worry about the other ways. Do things my way, and we'll get along— okay. Now are there any questions?" He looked around. There were no questions. He nodded with smiling satisfaction.[9]

To begin, the OD program should be the result of a systematic diagnosis and a careful and logical plan of action, not a series of haphazard change efforts. The plan should provide a degree of structure and a framework for proposed change so as to reduce uncertainty among those affected by the change. It will be advisable to make a written record of the plans for change, including the various stages and dates of implementation and completion. The plans, however, must remain flexible, as numerous variables may necessitate their being altered.

If potential resistors are drawn into the planning and implementation process, then resistance to the change may be reduced or even eliminated.

Facilitation and Support

Reinforcing the change process and providing support for those involved is another way OD practitioners can deal with resistance. If the situation allows, the OD consultant can arrange promotions, monetary rewards, or public recognition for those participating in the change program. In one OD program in which the authors were involved, a well publicized promotion was arranged for a manager who had endorsed and participated in the OD program despite considerable risk of criticism by his peers and immediate superiors. The result was a dramatic acceptance of the OD program by other managers.

Negotiation and Agreement

Another technique is negotiation with potential resisters. Some examples include union agreements, increasing an employee's pension benefits in exchange for early retirement, or negotiating agreement with the heads of organization departments that would be affected by the change.

Manipulation and Co-optation

Supervisors may covertly lead individuals or groups away from resistance to change. They may manipulate employees by controlling information or by structuring the sequence of change. They may also co-opt key persons within a group by giving them a leading role in designing or carrying out the change process.

Explicit and Implicit Coercion

Often managers may force people to go along with a change by explicit or implicit threats involving loss of jobs, or loss of promotion, or raises, and so forth. In some situations, managers may also dismiss or transfer employees who refuse to change. Such methods, though not uncommon, pose risks and make it more difficult to gain support for future change programs.

Overcoming resistance to change may involve using more than one of these approaches. The OD practitioner must decide which techniques to use and how to put them into effective action.

Climate Conducive to Interfacing

Creating a climate where everyone involved in the change program feels free and not threatened to interface with others can minimize resistance in the long run. If attitudes of respect, understanding, and communication prevail, this will help to break a cycle of reciprocal threat and aggressiveness on the part of the resisters and the advocates of the change program. The consultant ensures that parties do not sit in judgment of each other but instead focuses attention on the basic issues and the relevant facts.

Power Strategies

OD programs historically have been reluctant to deal with the use of power in organizations. To some extent, power strategies are antithetical to OD values. But most organizations operate within some type of system that sanctions and uses power and the organization's members are motivated to some extent by the perceived power of the organization. It may be necessary for an OD program to use the power structure in an organization to convince its members of the worthiness of the program.

In an OD program being implemented in one of the branches of the U.S. military, it was necessary to resort to a power strategy, although it was fairly low key and nonthreatening. After over a year of trying to find a unit to participate in an OD program, a volunteer unit was finally obtained. Once the program was in progress, it was decided to arrange a visit by that branch's Chief of Operations (who reported to the President) to communicate his personal appreciation for the unit's participation in the OD program. The visit served a dual purpose: it built a high degree of enthusiasm within the client for the remaining phases of the OD program, and it convinced other units sitting on the sidelines that the OD program was to be taken seriously. This power strategy was resorted to after many months of attempts to obtain a client and heated debates by the team of OD practitioners. This was certainly not the only reason for the OD program being spread throughout that military branch, but it did give that added impetus when the future of the program was at a crucial stage. This will particularly be the case when dealing with an organization that traditionally relies upon power.

REVIEW QUESTIONS

1. What strategies might be used in gaining acceptance for an OD program?

2. What are the underlying forces resisting change? Give examples.

KEY WORDS AND CONCEPTS

Define and be able to use the following concepts.

Motivating forces	Participation
Resisting forces	Communication of proposed changes
Momentum	Power strategies

**IV.
Simulations**

SIMULATION 6.1   THE ENIGMA COMPANY

Total time suggested: 1 hour, 20 minutes.

A. Purpose

This chapter discusses how people react to possible changes. In this simulation you will have an opportunity to be involved in a small-group decision on change and begin to see how different individuals may perceive a situation in differing ways. The purposes include:

1. To examine how you and others attempt to exert influence in an attempt to change another's position.
2. To understand the relationship between motivation and the acceptance or rejection of change.
3. To consider how change situations are influenced by multiple criteria, and subjective versus objective considerations.

B. Procedures

Step 1   Before coming to class, read the company situation. Each participant should then make an individual ranking of the employees from 1 (the first to be laid off) to 8 (the last to be laid off). Use the Enigma Rating Form recording your answers in column 1.

Step 2   Form groups of six members each. One person plus additional members serving as observers. Each group is to reach a consensus on the ranking. Avoid voting and trading off or bargaining. Try to reach a decision that all group members can support. Record your team decision on the Enigma Rating Form, column 2.

Time suggested for Step 2: 40 minutes.

Step 3   List each group's ranking on the blackboard, and compare and discuss differences in ranking. Also consider the following questions with the observers leading the discussion:

1. How did members differ in the criteria used to lay people off?
2. What were the reasons for the different criteria? Tangible and objective considerations? Or subjective considerations?

3. Was there any resistance among team members to changing their positions?
4. What were the strategies used to influence and change team members' positions?
5. How were the differences resolved? To what extent was the group decision really based on consensus?

Time suggested for Step 3: 30 minutes.

Step 4 Using the answers given by the instructor, score your individual and team answers. Where the actual and correct answers match, put +10 in columns (4) and (5) on the Enigma Rating Form. If the actual and correct answers do not match, put 0 in columns (4) and (5). By totaling the points, an individual and team score can be calculated. Column (4) provides an indication of the individual participant's "correctness," and column (5) provides an equivalent measure of each group's performance.

Compare the individual and team scores. Individuals come to teams with varying degrees of preparation, and the final score may not reflect how decisions were made by the team. As a class, compare the scores of the teams. *Time suggested for Step 4: 10 minutes.*

ENIGMA RATING FORM

Employee	Individual Rating Col. 1	Team Rating Col. 2	Correct Rating Col. 3	Individual Score Col. 4	Team Score Col. 5
1. A. Banks					
2. B. Brown					
3. C. Everet					
4. D. Fram					
5. P. Peters					
6. R. Alfredo					
7. F. Green					
8. G. Jones					
Total Scores					

COMPANY SITUATION: ENIGMA ENGINEERING COMPANY

The Enigma Engineering Company is a medium-sized manufacturing company located in the suburbs of Spokane, Washington. The company is nonunionized and has attempted during the past 2 years to incorporate an objective performance review system that has been designed purposefully to provide feedback to employees. The system is designed to be objective, time-oriented, and representative.

The loss of a contract bid to a competitor has forced the Enigma management to consider laying off one, two, or three of the poorest performers next week in the circuit board unit. This unit produces circuit boards that are sold to electronic firms. The layoff may only be temporary, but management wants to be sure that they have been fair in presenting an objectively based decision to the employees.

The people in the unit to be cut back are:

1. Albert Banks: white, age 42; married; 3 children; 2 years of high school; 14 years with the company.
2. Bob Brown: black; age 37; widower; 2 children; high school graduate; 8 years with the company.
3. Chris Everet: white; age 24; single; high school graduate; 2 years with the company.
4. Dave Fram: white; age 50; single; finished junior college while working; 15 years with the company.
5. Pat Peters: white; age 36; married; 4 children; high school graduate; 3 years with the company.
6. Ray Alfredo: hispanic; age 40; married; 1 child; high school graduate; 4 years with the company.
7. Fred Green: white; age 39; divorced; 2 children; 2 years of college; 7 years with the company.
8. George Jones: white; age 42; married; no children; 1 year of college; 9 years with the company.

The company has evaluated these unit employees on a number of factors

TABLE 6.2 Enigma Performance Review Data; Factors Evaluated by Supervisor

Employee	Average Weekly Output[a]	(%) Rejects[b]	(%) Absences[c]	Cooperating Attitude[d]	Loyalty[d]	Potential for Promotion[d]
Albert Banks	39.6	4.9	6.3	Good	Good	Fair
Bob Brown	43.4	5.3	7.9	Poor	Fair	Fair
Chris Everet	35.2	0.9	0.4	Excellent	Good	Good
Dave Fram	40.4	4.7	13.2	Excellent	Excellent	Fair
Pat Peters	40.2	9.6	9.3	Poor	Fair	Poor
Ray Alfredo	39.6	3.4	6.1	Good	Fair	Poor
Fred Green	36.2	4.8	5.0	Good	Good	Fair
George Jones	45.2	7.0	3.6	Fair	Fair	Good

[a]Higher score = more output.   [c]Lower score = fewer absences.
[b]Lower score = fewer rejects.   [d]Possible ratings: poor, fair, good, excellent.

listed in Table 6.2. The ratings shown have been averaged over the past 18 months of performance evaluation.

SIMULATION 6.2   MOTIVATING AND RESISTING FORCES

Total time suggested: 50 minutes.

A.   Purpose

This simulation draws on the change situation posed in Simulation 6.1. This simulation should help you further understand the diagnosis process and overcoming resistance to change.

B.   Procedures

Step 1   Form into the same groups as Simulation 6.1 and identify the team operating problems encountered in solving the task in Simulation 6.1. Then make two lists: one on the motivating forces and the other on the resisting forces for solving the problems. Put a star next to those forces in which you will probably play a part.

Make additional charts depending on the number of problems identified.
Time suggested for Step 1: 20 minutes.

Problem: _____

Motivating Forces	Resisting Forces

Problem: _____

Motivating Forces	Resisting Forces

Problem: _____

Motivating Forces	Resisting Forces

Problem: _____

Motivating Forces	Resisting Forces

Step 2   Meeting as a class, report on the significant problems and the motivating and resisting forces. To what extent are the problems similar and different between groups.
Time suggested for Step 2: 30 minutes.

**Case:
Progress on
Purpose**[10]

Carl Bolling is a participant in the company's training program titled Systems and Procedures Studies. The participants meet once weekly for two hours over an eight-month period. The program is staffed by a local college professor.

As part of the requirements of the program, each participant is required to undertake a work-study project of his own choosing with the idea of critically analyzing the work activities observed and suggesting improvement for them through the application of techniques and ideas learned in the program. It was stressed by the professor at the beginning of the program that the "human element" was one of the prime factors to pay attention to when undertaking such a study.

Carl Bolling has the title of Planning Engineer. In this capacity, he engages in coordinating activities between the operating, production, and engineering departments. His selected work-study project for the training program deals with the purchase and order of heavy equipment for installation in new plants being constructed by the company. It concerns specifically the control of costs associated with purchased equipment that sometimes sits crated on a new plant location for weeks before it is ready for installation. Carl Bolling had analyzed the scheduling procedures of the construction department and the purchasing procedures of the operating department plus the required specifications and design of equipment by the engineering department. It was his opinion that thousands of dollars yearly could be saved by the company if the construction and operating departments would adopt the formal planning and purchasing procedures that he proposed. He felt convinced that his analysis of the problem was sound and his analysis of potential cost savings accurate.

Upon submitting his work-study project to fellow participants in the training program, he felt pleased that the group and the professor endorsed this project as "sound" and "well done." Upon submitting his proposal to his immediate boss, the vice president of engineering, he was gratified to know that the vice president planned to propose the introduction of his new procedures at the next meeting of the executive management committee.

Two weeks later the vice president of engineering called Bolling to his office and told him his suggested planning and purchasing procedures had been presented to the executive management committee. The reaction had been violent! They resented a mere planning engineer crossing functional lines and making recommendations in areas other than his own. They disliked the implication that their activities were costing the company thousands of dollars yearly, and they told the vice president of engineering that, in the future, he (Bolling) would be considered *persona non grata* in their departments.

The vice president of engineering suggested to Bolling that maybe it would be best if he were transferred to another division in the company. At least he would not run the risk of meeting these executives personally.

Case Questions:
1. Could Bolling have avoided the problem brought about by his proposal? How?
2. How should the vice president of engineering have handled Bolling's proposal?
3. What do you think of the vice president's suggestion that Bolling should transfer to another division?
4. What do you think Bolling should do now?

V.
Summary

In this chapter we have examined some of the forces motivating individuals toward change, some factors that restrict or inhibit the likelihood of change, and some change strategies that are likely to enhance acceptance.

The process of change is complex because of the interaction of social, technical, and psychological factors. People often become satisfied with the status quo and react with insecurity or anxiety when change occurs.

An important factor to be considered prior to the implementation of any OD strategy is the motivation of the client system toward change. Some resistance to proposed changes may arise from perceived (real or unreal) threats to personal security.

Resistance to change is usually a reaction to methods used in implementing a change rather than any inherent human characteristic. People tend to resist changes that do not make sense to them or that are forced upon them against their will. Certain factors, such as loss of security or status, lead to resistance to change. There are ways to reduce this resistance, including good communication and participation in the change process.

You have had an opportunity to role play and observe a situation of change, to identify forces of resistance, and to apply change strategies to a situation. You may have found in the simulation, or from other personal experiences, that it is difficult to motivate a person. The motivation must come from within, and as psychologist Abraham Maslow has noted, a satisfied need is *not* a motivator. There must be a perceived need for change, within the client system, before change can take place.

You may have found that acceptance of change can be improved when certain conditions are present that minimize the potential threat or discomfort of a proposed change. These conditions include careful planning and thorough communication of the change to the target individual, group, or system. You may also have found that when you or others are allowed to participate in making it a self-designed change program, the degree of acceptance also increases. If you as a consultant can create a climate where people feel free to change, rather than being coerced, the probability of acceptance will also be higher.

NOTES

1. See G.L. Lippitt, P. Langseth, and T. Mossop, *Implementing Organizational Change* (San Francisco: Jossey Bass, 1985).

2. Goodwin Watson, "Resistance to Change," in *Concepts for Social Change*. Cooperative Project for Educational Development Series, Vol. 1 (Washington, D.C.: National Training Laboratories, 1966).

3. Arnold S. Juson, *A Manager's Guide to Making Changes* (New York: John Wiley & Sons, Inc., 1966), p. 80.

4. John P. Kotter and Leonard A. Schlesinger, "Choosing Strategies for Change," *Harvard Business Review*, 57, no. 2 (March–April 1979), p. 106.

5. B. Whalen, "Toffler on Marketing" (interview) *Marketing News*, 19:1, March 15, 1985.

6. See Alan W. Randolph, "Planned Organizational Change and Its Measurement," *Personnel Psychology*, 35, no. 1 (Spring 1982), p. 119.

7. "Men at Coors Beer Find the Old Ways Don't Work Anymore," *Wall Street Journal*, January 19, 1979, p. 1.

8. See "What in the Name of OD Do We Do?" *Training and Development Journal,* Vol. 37, no. 4, April 1983, p. 45.

9. *The Caine Mutiny: A Novel of World War II* (Garden City, New York: Doubleday & Co., Inc., 1951), p. 131. Copyright © 1951 by Herman Wouk.

10. From Kenneth W. Olm, F.J. Brewerton, Susan R. Whisnant, and Francis J. Bridges, *Management Decisions and Organizational Policy,* 3rd ed. Copyright © 1981 by Allyn and Bacon, Inc. Reprinted with permission.

7

OD PROCESS
SKILLS

<table>
<tr>
<td valign="top">I.
Objectives</td>
<td>Upon completing this chapter, you will be able to:
1.   Recognize several OD practitioner skills including process consultation, and active listening and determine how they may be applied.
2.   Practice using several OD practitioner skills.
3.   Identify and gain insights into your own practitioner styles.</td>
</tr>
<tr>
<td valign="top">II.
Premeeting
Preparation</td>
<td>
1.   Read the Background Information (Section III).
2.   Read the company information and role description in Simulation 7.1 (Section IV). Complete Step 1.
3.   Read and complete Step 1 of Simulation 7.2.
4.   Read and prepare for Step 1 of Simulation 7.3.</td>
</tr>
</table>

**III.
Background
Information**

The challenge of changing organizations and developing corporate excellence focuses more and more on the OD practitioner as a person whose efforts can result in performance gains or losses for the entire organization.

The OD practitioner is the person responsible for developing change programs and must bring a variety of skills to the client system. For the most part, these skills will have broad impact on future organization effectiveness. These skills include an understanding of management and business principles, problem-solving and analytical skills, and interpersonal and communication skills. The practitioner will at various times be teacher, counselor, cheerleader, coach, and advisor. This chapter will describe some of the basic OD practitioner skills, including process consultation and active listening.

Process consultation is one of the most-used OD practitioner skills. Its purpose is to help the client system become more aware of its processes, particularly those that relate to group behavior and interpersonal communications. When a work team becomes more keenly aware of how it operates, it will be able to better analyze and solve its own problems. The process consultant helps the work group learn to solve their own problems.

Active listening, an interpersonal skill that in many ways complements other practitioner skills, is a communication skill that involves the listener, (consultant) feeding back to the speaker (client) what the listener understood the speaker to say. The consultant listens for the total message: both the verbal and nonverbal portion of the message.

The skills discussed in this chapter should not be viewed as a cookbook approach for the practitioner. As the OD practitioner gains experience using these and other skills, they will become more integrated into a general way of relating to the client and can be used during many stages of the OD process.

PROCESS CONSULTATION

Process consultation (PC) is an OD practitioner skill for helping work groups become more effective. In one survey of OD practitioners, it was found that 80 percent of the practitioners used process consulting skills, more than any other practitioner skill mentioned.[1] Edgar Schein has perhaps best described PC in his book, *Process Consultation: Its Role in Organization Development*. Schein defines process consultation as a "set of activities on the part of a consultant which help the client to perceive, understand, and act upon process events which occur in the client's environment."[2] PC is aimed at helping the work group to become more aware of its own processes and to use its own problem-solving ability and resources. Process consultation is heavily dependent upon a very thorough joint diagnosis of the problems.

One of the major characteristics of PC is that the clients learn to identify problems and then initiate their own solutions. The process consultant helps the client organization learn to solve its own problems with the premise being that the results are more permanent.

GROUP PROCESS

The foundation of process consultation is the study of how groups and individuals within those groups behave.[3] While content is the *what* of a group, process is the *how* of the group. PC is only concerned with the content or the actual product of the group to the extent that the content is a function of the process.

Because process consultation often leads to the use of other OD approaches, the consultation process should start at the highest level of the client organization. This way the impact will be as far reaching as possible. The process consultant tries to help the organization solve its own problems by making it aware of organization process. The process consultant deals with five areas crucial to effective organization performance: communication, member roles and functions in groups, group problem solving and decision making, group norms and growth, and leadership and authority.[4]

Communications

The process consultant uses several techniques for analyzing the communications processes within a group. One method is to observe the frequency and length of time each member talks during a group discussion. These observations can be easily recorded on paper and referred to later when analyzing group behavior. It is also useful to keep a record of who talks to whom or to use a sociogram.

Another valuable observation concerns interruptions: Who interrupts whom? Is there a pattern to the interruptions? What are the apparent effects of the interruptions? Is there a pattern of who talks after whom?

Member Roles and Functions

New groups have several issues to resolve at the same time they are working on their group's task.[5] Members will be working on formulating the roles in which they feel comfortable. Many of these roles will probably not be explicitly stated but will evolve and include such roles as who is the technical expert, who is aggressive, who initiates the conversation, and who is the joke teller or tension reliever. The group will also resolve control, power, and influence issues.

Members of existing groups perform roles which can be categorized as task or maintenance functions. *Task functions* include member behaviors that directly help the group solve its task or problem. These behaviors include initiating and suggesting what is the goal of the group and how the group can proceed to accomplish its goal. Other behaviors include seeking opinions and information from other members and giving opinions and information. Asking questions of clarification and elaborating on information help the group to work on its goal. Summarizing occurs when a member pulls together and reviews briefly what the group has said or done thus far. A related function is when a member tests for group consensus by asking such questions as "What I seem to be hearing the group say is . . . Is this correct?" or "Are we ready to make our decision?"

Maintenance functions include behaviors that help the group grow and improve its members' interpersonal relationships. Harmonizing and compromising behavior help to reduce conflict and tension between members. Encouraging behavior helps people to more fully develop their ideas and helps the quieter members to make more contributions. Gatekeeping, another maintenance function, also tries to give everyone a chance to be heard.

Problem Solving and Decision Making

The process consultant helps members understand how the group makes decisions and the consequences of each method of decision making.

Problem solving begins with gathering the necessary information and identifying problem areas. Alternatives are then generated, along with forecasts of possible results. An alternative is chosen and a detailed plan of action is formulated. The decision is implemented and finally an evaluation of the decision is made.

Group consensus is an effective method for making group decisions. A decision made by group consensus is one that all members can support. Decision making by consensus, where all members really support the decision, is the ideal technique though it is the most difficult to obtain. This type of group decision is especially effective when the group members must implement the decision and their cooperation is required.

Group Norms and Growth

Norms have been defined as the organized and shared ideas regarding what group members should do and feel, how this behavior should be regulated, and what sanctions should be applied when behavior does not coincide within social expectations. The process consultant assists the group in understanding its own norms. As the group continues to meet, they should move forward from the acquaintance stage to an effectively functioning team.

The members will become more supportive, use member talents and resources, and understand how the group operates and improves upon their decision-making process.

Leadership and Authority

The process consultant can help the group understand the impact of leadership styles. Groups may have a formal or an informal leader. The leadership function may also be shared by group members; for example, the member who performs functions of gatekeeping, summarizing, or one of the other task or maintenance functions, is behaving in the role of a leader.

THE TYPES OF PROCESS INTERVENTIONS

The types of interventions that may be used by the process consultant are loosely classified by Schein[6] as agenda-setting interventions, feedback of observations, coaching or counseling, and structural suggestions.

Agenda-setting interventions

Agenda-setting interventions include setting aside time when process issues will be specifically discussed apart from content issues. The process consultant may ask the work team questions which direct attention to interpersonal issues. He or she may encourage the group to allocate time in its regular meetings to discuss the processes of the meeting or may suggest that the group hold a separate meeting just to deal with process issues. These issues may include how well members communicated with each other, how satisfied members were with the meeting, and how involved members were in the meeting.

Feedback of observations

Feedback to groups can occur during their meetings or to individuals after meetings. The process consultant often has a strong temptation to share some interesting observations whether or not the client is ready for this feedback. Before any feedback is given to either individuals or groups, it is crucial that there is a readiness to receive feedback.

Coaching or counseling

Once feedback has been given (to either an individual or group) the next question by the client is what behavior or action can be changed to improve group functioning. The process consultant should only answer after determining that the client really understands the feedback and has already begun to try and solve the problem. It is important for the OD practitioner to remember that the objective of PC is to help the client to be an active participant in identifying and solving his or her own problems.

Structural suggestions

The process consultant makes structural suggestions pertaining to group membership, communication patterns, allocation of work, assignment of responsibility, and lines of authority. This type of intervention requires the consultant to make suggestions on how work should be organized, who should be on what committees, and who should be working on specific projects. The process consultant helps the manager or work group determine the results of their actions or suggest alternatives. The process consultant must avoid stepping in and taking over, because the client will not learn to solve its own problems and a dependency relationship is created with the consultant. An example of process issues at Beatrice Company is presented in OD Application 7.1.

OD Application 7.1

MANAGEMENT PROCESS PROBLEMS AT BEATRICE

Beatrice Company, a $12.6 billion, multinational food and consumer goods company, ousted its former chairman James C. Dutt.

Apparently Dutt's leadership style was causing organizational problems:

1. "No More Mr. Nice Guy"

According to former executives, Dutt underwent a transformation from amiable and easy going, a "Mr. Nice Guy," to a hard-driving executive who fired dozens of executives over a 2-year period. Says one, "He [thought he] was the only one who could run the company."

2. Highly Centralized Controlling Management Systems

Dutt berated managers for not working hard enough, sent out his staff members to criticize fairly autonomous units; his staff members required that Dutt's picture be hung in the lobby of every major Beatrice facility throughout the uworld.

3. Lowered Morale

Morale was damaged by Dutt's highly autocratic and demanding management style. At management meetings he delivered tirades, publicly threatened to fire top executives, and had little tolerance for those who dared to disagree.

Though the board approved Dutt's goal for Beatrice to become the "premier world-wide marketer" of food and consumer products when they fired him, they were critical of the process and methods he used. Because of Dutt's reign, so many sharp senior managers either resigned or were fired by Dutt that Beatrice has a long way to go to rebuild its management ranks.

Question:
1. Would you suggest process consultation as a possible approach to such problems?

Source: Based on Kenneth Dreyfack, "Why Beatrice Had to Dump Dutt," *Business Week*, August 19, 1985; S. Hume, "How the Wheels Came Off for Jim Dutt," *Advertising Age*, 56:75, August 12, 1985; and A. M. Louis, "The Controversial Boss of Beatrice," *Fortune*, July 22, 1985, pp. 110–12.

THE RESULTS OF PROCESS CONSULTATION

While OD practitioners such as Argyris and Schein report improved organization health and functioning as an outcome of PC interventions, there is little empirical evidence to document such changes. The assumption is that a group that is aware of and acting upon its problems is likely to be more effective than a group that is not. Also, PC is usually a technique that is practiced as part of an OD program and it is often difficult to evaluate process consultation separately from the total OD program.

A recent evaluation of process consultation studies supports the problems of measuring performance results.[7] The survey examines published studies in three categories: (1) reports in which process intervention is the causal variable but performance is measured inadequately or not at all; (2) reports in which performance is measured but process consultation is not isolated as the independent variable (the case in many instances); and (3) research in which process consultation is isolated as the causal variable and performance is adequately measured. The findings suggest that process consultation does have positive effects on participants (according to self-reports): increases in personal involvement, higher mutual influence, group effectiveness, and similar variables. However, there is little if any research that clearly demonstrates that task effectiveness was increased. Most of the field studies either did not directly measure performance or the effect of process intervention was confounded with other variables.

ACTIVE LISTENING

One of the important skills of the OD practitioner is listening. *Active listening* is a skill that can be used in conjunction with process consultation and many other OD interventions. The most significant advocates of active listening have been Carl Rogers and Richard Farson.[8] Active listening is the process of translating the words of the speaker and feeding back this information. This feedback includes not only the content of the message but also the feeling or attitude of the speaker. (See B.C. comic strip.)

PURPOSE OF ACTIVE LISTENING

The purpose of active listening is to help clients identify and solve their own problems.

Active listening requires that the listener practice *empathy*, that is, the listener tries to see the world from the speaker's point of view. Then the lis-

Source: B.C. by permission of Johnny Hart and Creators Syndicate, Inc.

tener must convey back to the speaker how the message has been received. Most messages have two parts: one is the content and the other is the feeling of the speaker. The feeling of the speaker is rarely expressed in words but is often communicated nonverbally: tone of voice, facial expressions, hand and arm movements, body posture, eye movements, and so forth. The listener must "listen" to the entire message to get its full meaning.

It is important for the OD practitioner to constantly test for an understanding of what the client is saying. Empathizing with the client and then reflecting back what the speaker seems to be saying from both a content and feeling point of view builds positive relations with the client and is at the foundations of problem solving and change.

The Results of Active Listening

Like many of the other practitioner skills, there is little statistical evidence to support the success of active listening. It is a skill that is used during the entire OD program and it is hard to isolate and measure its success. Top managers and OD practitioners can stimulate their own learning in at least three ways: they can (1) listen to dissenting arguments; (2) convert events into learning opportunities; and (3) adopt an experimental frame of reference.

REVIEW QUESTIONS

1. Explain how process consultation can be used in an OD program.

2. Explain the purpose of active listening.

KEY WORDS AND CONCEPTS

Define and be able to use the following:

Process consultation
Process interventions
Group content, group process

Active listening
Decision making techniques
Effective feedback

IV.
Simulations

SIMULATION 7.1   THE STU CORPORATION

Total time suggested: 1 hour, 10 minutes.

A. Purpose

To identify the forces acting upon individuals as they interact with others and to practice using active listening and process consultation.

B. Procedures

Step 1   Form into groups of eight, prior to the class meeting. Additional people may act as observers. Six members each select one role on the STU Corporation Public Policy Committee. The seventh member will serve as the OD practitioner. The eighth and any additional team members will serve as observers. (See the Observer Form). Read the company information that follows and your role description, prior to the class meeting.

Step 2   The committee (including the OD practitioner) meets to decide on its recommendation.

Time suggested for Step 2: 40 minutes.

Step 3   After your decision is reached, the observer will provide feedback and guide the discussion using the Observer Form. All team members are encouraged to provide feedback.

Time suggested for Step 3: 20 minutes.

Step 4 As a class discuss the six questions in the Observer Form.
Time suggested for Step 4: 20 minutes.

COMPANY INFORMATION

STU is a large oil refinery located in California with $200 million in sales and $4 million profit. STU is currently involved with a problem of determining whether to expend a large amount of money on pollution control equipment. The refinery, located on the outskirts of a large city, has been marginally profitable for the past several years. About 10,000 people are employed at this plant and unemployment in the city has been over 10 percent for the past 2 years. Many of those employed by STU are long-term employees.

Recently, an environmental law has been passed controlling pollution. Because of existing and potential environmental problems, STU has been told by the environmental council of the state that it must have additional pollution control equipment operational within the next 3 years. According to the estimates of company engineers, the law will require a large capital expenditure, $10 million, and a 3-month shutdown during conversion.

The process involved is relatively new and untested, but it does represent the most advanced technology now available. State officials say that the equipment should meet current pollution control requirements, but they can not guarantee that these requirements will stay unchanged in the future. Some members of the board feel that the company should give full compliance to the law at any cost. Other members want to fight the law in court and delay any conversion. Legal costs would be high, but probably less than $1 million. However, company officers are afraid that company ROI (return on investment) would be so low that they might be replaced if they complied. Still other members feel that a compromise is best, to fight for a delay, but also to spend some effort on antipollution, say $2 or $3 million.

Environmentalist groups have been outspoken in support of full compliance; however, they are a small percentage of the stockholders. The Public Policy Committee has been charged with bringing a recommendation to the board.

The board decided to create an Environmental Public Policy Committee, with responsibility to coordinate all company environmental protection matters. C. Stark, an experienced chemical engineer, was named to head the committee. The board has provided an OD process consultant to assist at the meeting. The committee is charged with recommendations regarding meeting established environmental standards. In the first meeting, the committee must make recommendations to the board on three issues:

1. What course of action should be taken on conversion?
2. Should the nature of the committee be advisory to the board or have decision-making authority?
3. Should the duration of the committee be temporary or a permanent standing committee?

ROLE DESCRIPTIONS (READ *ONLY* YOUR ROLE)

Role 1—C. Stark. Executive vice president, corporate office; 32 years old. M.B.A., with rapid advancement in company. Highly competent—has reputation as an "efficiency expert." Married, no children. You feel that the social responsibility of business is to make a profit. Since this is a visible position for you, you favor a permanent and advisory committee.

Role 2—O. Johnson. Plant manager for past 7 years; 55 years old. With the company 27 years. Reputation as good practical manager. Married—very civic-minded; three children. Oldest daughter, 19, attends university and is active in Sierra Club and environmental demonstrations. You would like to see a temporary advisory committee.

Role 3—B. Sanford. State environmental representative; 42 years old. Engineering background. Married, three children. Active in civil rights and environmental movement. You feel that a group with decision-making authority is best, and prefer a temporary group. You also support full compliance.

Role 4—A. Davis. Member of city council; 29 years old. Schoolteacher at local community college; B.S. in education. Married, two children, spouse employed at STU plant. Active in aid for handicapped, civil rights, and environment. Member of Sierra Club. You strongly favor a group with the authority to make decisions and would like to be on a standing committee.

Role 5—F. Taylor. Business professor, state university, invited on committee to provide expertise; 38 years old. Has published and consulted in management; is active in plant safety programs. Married, two children. Receives significant consulting fee from STU. Spouse active in Sierra Club. Because of your other interests, you favor a temporary group that advises the board.

Role 6—W. Sweeney. Union vice president, worked for STU for many years; 45 years old. Outspoken on union rights, is against civil rights and environmentalist policies. Married, with four children—two attending university. You feel that to accomplish goals, a permanent committee that is advisory in nature is the answer. You are opposed to any concession.

Role 7—Practitioner. Use the practitioner skills discussed in this chapter to help the STU Committee reach their objective. Try to work with the Committee as a process consultant using active listening. Be careful not to take over and run the committee.

Role 8—Observer. Do not help the Committee while they are working on the task. You should only observe. Use the Observer Form and lead the discussion in Step 3.

OBSERVER FORM

Instructions: Put the names of the individuals in your group in the spaces at the top of the chart. Read over and become familiar with the behavior descriptions. Put a check in the appropriate block *each* time you observe the behavior.

Description of Behavior	Names of Individuals Observed						
Encourager—friendly and responsive to others; offers praise; accepts others' points of view.							
Harmonizer—mediates differences; relieves tension in conflict situations; gets people to explore their differences.							
Compromiser—when his own idea is involved in a conflict, he offers compromise and admits error. Tries to maintain group cohesion.							
Expresses group feelings—senses the feeling or mood of the group, others, and himself and shares this with the group.							
Gatekeeper—keeps communications open; suggests procedures for sharing information with others.							
Initiator—proposes tasks or goals; suggests ways to solve problems.							
Information or opinion seeker—asks for facts, ideas, or suggestions.							
Information or opinion giver—offers facts; states his belief or opinion.							
Clarifier—interprets ideas or suggestions; clears up confusions; gives examples							
Summarizer—pulls together related suggestions; offers conclusion for the group to accept or reject.							
Others:							

(continued on next page)

1. How was a decision reached? (By consensus, vote, etc.) ___

_____

2. What type of skills did the consultant use? Try to be specific and give examples?

   a. Process consultation? _____

   _____

   b. Active listening? _____

   _____

3. Did the consultant make the client feel at ease? How? ___

   _____

   _____

4. What did the consultant do or say that was helpful? _____

   _____

   _____

5. What consultant verbal and nonverbal communications seemed to help the meeting? _____

   _____

6. What consultant verbal and nonverbal communications seemed to hinder the meeting? _____

   _____

SIMULATION 7.2   TRUST BUILDING

Total time suggested: 30 minutes.

A. Purpose

The purpose of this simulation is to provide a comparison between your perception of trust behavior and how it is perceived by others.

B. Procedures

Step 1 Based on your group work in Simulation 7.1, complete and score the Group Behavior Questionnaire. Enter the scores in Figure 7.1 on page 191 by drawing horizontal and vertical lines at the appropriate numbers representing your score.

Time suggested for Step 1: 5 minutes.

GROUP BEHAVIOR QUESTIONNAIRE

The following are a series of questions[9] about your behavior in your class groups. Answer each question as honestly as you can. There are no right or wrong answers. It is important for you to describe your behavior as accurately as possible. Place a number in the blank to the right representing your choice based on the following scale.

Never 1 : 2 : 3 : 4 : 5 : 6 : 7 Always

1. I offer facts, give my opinions and ideas, provide suggestions and relevant information to help the group discussion. _____

2. I express my willingness to cooperate with other group members and my expectations that they will also be cooperative. _____

3. I am open and candid in my dealings with the entire group. _____

4. I give support to group members who are on the spot and struggling to express themselves intellectually or emotionally. _____

5. I keep my thoughts, ideas, feelings, and reactions to myself during group discussions. _____

6. I evaluate the contributions of other group members in terms of whether their contributions are useful to me and whether they are right or wrong. _____

7. I take risks in expressing new ideas and current feelings during a group discussion. _____

8. I communicate to other group members that I am aware of, and appreciate, their abilities, talents, capabilities, skills, and resources. _____

9. I offer help and assistance to anyone in the group in order to bring up the performance of everyone. _____

10. I accept and support the openness of other group members, supporting them for taking risks, and encouraging individuality in group members. _____

11. I share any materials, books, sources of information or other resources I have with the other group members in order to promote the success of all members and the group as a whole. _____

12. I often paraphrase or summarize what other members have said before I respond or comment. _____

13. I level with other group members. _____

14. I warmly encourage all members to participate, giving them recognition for their contributions, demonstrating acceptance and openness to their ideas, and generally being friendly and responsive to them. _____

SCORING OF GROUP BEHAVIOR QUESTIONNAIRE

To score this questionnaire, add the scores in the following way, reversing the scoring on the questions that are starred. Find the average response by dividing the total scores by 7.

Openness and Sharing		Acceptance and Support	
1.	_____	2.	_____
3.	_____	4.	_____
*5.	_____	*6.	_____
7.	_____	8.	_____
9.	_____	10.	_____
11.	_____	12.	_____
13.	_____	14.	_____
Total	_____	Total	_____
Average	_____	Average	_____

*Reverse the scoring on these questions. In other words, a value of 2 would be recorded as 6.

Complete Figure 7.1 on the next page.

Step 2 After completing Simulation 7.1 each member of the group rates every other group member on two dimensions from 1 (low) to 7 (high).

Member	Openness and sharing		Acceptance and support	
	Low	High	Low	High
1 _____	1 2 3 4 5 6 7		1 2 3 4 5 6 7	
2 _____	1 2 3 4 5 6 7		1 2 3 4 5 6 7	
3 _____	1 2 3 4 5 6 7		1 2 3 4 5 6 7	
4 _____	1 2 3 4 5 6 7		1 2 3 4 5 6 7	
5 _____	1 2 3 4 5 6 7		1 2 3 4 5 6 7	
6 _____	1 2 3 4 5 6 7		1 2 3 4 5 6 7	

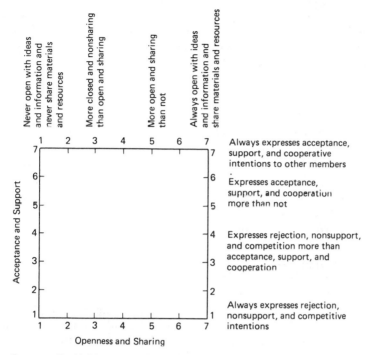

FIGURE 7.1 Trust Diagram

Source: David Johnson and Frank Johnson, *Joining Together: Group Therapy and Group Skills,* © 1975, p. 244. Adapted by permission of Prentice-Hall, Inc., Englewood Cliffs, New Jersey.

Step 3 Give each member his or her scores.
Time suggested for Steps 2 and 3: 10 minutes.

Step 4 Enter the averages of the two sets of scores received from group members by drawing dotted horizontal and vertical lines at the appropriate numbers in Figure 7.1. Each member has the results of the Group Behavior Questionnaire and the results of the feedback received from his fellow group members. Ask each group member to answer the following questions. How similar are they? Is there a close match? If not, what factors do you think contribute to the other group members' seeing your behavior differently from the way you do? How could this modify your behavior?
Time suggested for Step 4: 15 minutes.

SIMULATION 7.3 PROCESS CONSULTATION AND ACTIVE LISTENING

Total time suggested: 50 minutes.

A. Purpose

This simulation will provide you with additional practice in OD practitioner skills[10] and will give you an opportunity to practice using process consultation and active listening. You will have an opportunity to meet with a client who has a problem, and your responsibility is to help him or her clarify the problem by formulating a diagnosis. In the role play you will also experience being consulted with as a client. And you will be able, as an observer, to observe the consultant-client process.

B. Procedures

Step 1   Form into triads. There are three roles, and all members will be able to play each role. The three roles are client, consultant, and observer. Before beginning the role play, all members should read each of the following guidelines:

Client: Take a class problem or a work problem that involves you and explain this to your consultant.

Consultant: Your role is to help the client by practicing process consultation and active listening. See the Observer Form to familiarize yourself with appropriate and inappropriate helping skills.

Observer: Your job is to observe as carefully as possible both the client and the consultant. Use the Observer Form to record your observations.

Once each of you has read the roles, spend a few minutes thinking of a class problem or work situation you would like to share when it is your turn to play the client. Take about 5 to 10 minutes for each role play. At the end of *each* role play the observer will share his or her observations. Also, during this time the consultant and the client should critique each other's style. The following questions will help serve as a starting point for the critique:

1. As the client, how did you feel about responses of the consultant? Were they helpful or dysfunctional? Try to be specific.
2. As the consultant, how did you feel about the way the client behaved? Did any of his or her behaviors bother you? If so, did you share this with him or her? Try to be specific.
3. How did you feel about playing the part of the consultant or the client? Were you able to really "get into" your roles? Why?
4. Can you think of doing anything differently that might help in the next role play?
5. Any other comments or thoughts?

Step 2   Continue the simulation as described in Step 1 by switching roles until all have played each of the roles.
Time suggested for Steps 1 and 2: 40 minutes.

Step 3   In plenary session, critique the role plays. You may want to look at the questions in Step 1.
Time suggested for Step 3: 10 minutes.

OBSERVER FORM

As an observer, answer the following items. Items 1 through 6 are appropriate behaviors for process consultation and active listening; however, items 7 through 10 are inappropriate behaviors.

Remarks

1. Practiced empathy:

Low 1 : 2 : 3 : 4 : 5 : 6 : 7 High _____

2. Made eye contact:

Low 1 : 2 : 3 : 4 · 5 : 6 . 7 High _____

3. Practiced nonverbal communications:

Low 1 : 2 : 3 : 4 : 5 : 6 : 7 High _____

4. Reflected back content of message:

Low 1 : 2 : 3 : 4 : 5 : 6 : 7 High _____

5. Reflected back feeling of message:

Low 1 : 2 : 3 : 4 : 5 : 6 : 7 High _____

6. Demonstrated approval and acceptance:

Low 1 : 2 : 3 : 4 : 5 : 6 : 7 High _____

7. Sent solutions:

Low 1 : 2 : 3 : 4 : 5 : 6 : 7 High _____

8. Blamed or acted in judgment:

Low 1 : 2 : 3 : 4 : 5 : 6 : 7 High _____

9. Expressed sarcasm or humor:

Low 1 : 2 : 3 : 4 : 5 : 6 : 7 High _____

10. Participated in "small talk":

Low 1 : 2 : 3 : 4 : 5 : 6 : 7 High _____

V.
Summary

This chapter has presented an overview of several OD practitioner skills. The practitioner and the client must examine a number of factors in deciding upon an intervention. They must determine not only the depth of intervention desired but also the relative advantages and disadvantages of various possible interventions in selecting one that is best fitted to their target system. You had a chance in the simulations to experience and practice the PC skills. You may have gained some insights into your own relational style and recognized how such techniques might be used in an OD program. Often active listening and opening communication channels can be used as a means to enhance team functioning and overall performance.

NOTES

1. W. Warner Burke, Lawrence P. Clark, and Cheryl Koopman, "Improve Your OD Project's Chances for Success," *Training and Development Journal*, September 1984, p. 67.

2. Edgar Schein, *Process Consultation: Its Role in Organization Development* (Reading, Mass.: Addison-Wesley Publishing Co., Inc., 1969), p. 9.

3. For additional information on Process Consultation see: Matthew B. Miles, *Learning to Work in Groups* (New York: Teachers College Press, Teachers College, Columbia University, 1959); *Selected Readings Series One, Group Development* (Washington, D.C.: NTL Institute for Applied Behavioral Science, National Education Association, 1970); *Laboratories in Human Relations Training, Reading Book* (Washington, D.C.: NTL Institute for Applied Behavioral Science, National Education Association, 1970), p. 21–47; Edgar Schein, *Process Consultation: Its Role in Organization Development* (Reading, Mass.: Addison-Wesley Publishing Co., Inc., 1969); and Richard A. Schmuck and Patricia A. Schmuck, *Group Processes in the Classroom* (Dubuque, Iowa: Wm. C. Brown Company Publishers, 1971).

4. Schein, *Process Consultation*, p. 13.

5. Kenneth D. Benne and Paul Sheats, "Functional Roles of Group Members," *The Journal of Social Issues*, IV, no. 2 (Spring 1948), 42–47.

6. Schein, *Process Consultation*, p. 102.

7. R. Kaplan, "The Conspicuous Absence of Evidence that Process Consultation Enhances Task Performance," *Journal of Applied Behavioral Science*, 15 (1979), pp. 346–60.

8. Carl R. Rogers and Richard E. Farson, *Active Listening* (Chicago: Industrial Relations Center, The University of Chicago). A copy of the article can be found in David A. Kolb, Irwin M. Rubin, and James M. McIntyre, *Organizational Psychology, Readings on Human Behavior in Organizations* (Englewood Cliffs, N.J.: Prentice-Hall, Inc., 1984), pp. 255–278. Additional material on this subject can be found in Carl R. Rogers and F.J. Roethlisberger, "Barriers and Gateways to Communication," *Harvard Business Review*, July–August 1952, pp. 28–34; Robert R. Carkhuff, *The Art of Helping: A Guide for Developing Helping Skills for Parents, Teachers and Counselors* (Amherst, Mass.: Human Resource Development Press, 1972); Carl R. Rogers, *On Becoming a Person* (Boston: Houghton Mifflin Company, 1961); Thomas Gordon, *Leader Effectiveness Training* (New York: Peter H.

Wayden, Inc., Publisher, 1977), and Jack R. Gibb, "Defensive Communication," *Journal of Communication*, XI, No. 3 (September 1961), 141–48.

9.   David Johnson and Frank Johnson, *Joining Together: Group Theory and Group Skills*, © 1975, p. 244. Adapted by permission of Prentice-Hall, Inc., Englewood Cliffs, New Jersey.

10.   This simulation is based upon exercises in David Kolb, Irwin Rubin, and James McIntyre, *Organizational Psychology, An Experiential Approach*, 3rd ed. (Englewood Cliffs, N.J.: Prentice-Hall, Inc., 1979); and Donald Nylen, J. Robert Mitchell, and Anthony Stout, *Handbook of Staff Development and Human Relations Training: Materials Developed for Use in Africa* (Washington, D.C.: Stephenson Lithograph, Inc., 1965).

8

OD INTERVENTION STRATEGIES

Upon completing this chapter, you will be able to:

1. Identify the strategies used in the OD process.

2. Understand the change strategies.

3. Identify and understand the range of major OD intervention techniques and how they may be applied.

4. Identify the way various interpersonal, team, and intergroup techniques fit into an overall OD program.

1. Read the Background Information (Section III).

2. Read the instructions for Simulation 8.1 (Section VI). Complete Step 1.

3. Read and analyze Case: The Farm Bank.

III.
Background
Information

Managing organizational change is an important and complete action. In attempting to increase organizational and individual effectiveness, the OD practitioner must understand the nature of changes needed and the possible effects of various alternative change strategies.[1]

The starting point for implementing a change program is the definition of an overall change strategy. As we have seen earlier, the consultant role and relationship with the client, as well as the organizational climate, will influence the selection of specific intervention strategies aimed at improving organization effectiveness. Figure 8.1 presents a graphic illustration of this process.

The diagnostic phase leads to the interventions, activities, or programs aimed at resolving problems and increasing organization effectiveness. At this point, specific OD strategies are designed to improve an organization's structure and processes. After diagnosing the problem areas associated with current performance, the opportunities for improvement are identified and a strategy to apply techniques and technologies for change is selected. *Strategy* involves the planning and direction of OD projects or programs; *intervention techniques* are the specific means by which change goals can be attained.

Before OD techniques can be implemented, the consultant and the client need to develop a set of strategies to guide future actions. Earlier several basic change strategies were described. OD is based primarily upon a collaborative change strategy: the client is actively involved in defining problems and selecting the means for improvement. Within this basic approach to change, an OD change strategy is developed to meet the needs of a specific client system.

This chapter describes the major OD strategies for setting up a program of change. These strategies represent the major types of change programs. In deciding whether a change program involves an OD strategy, the general determining factor is the process used to arrive at and implement the program.

FIGURE 8.1 The OD Process

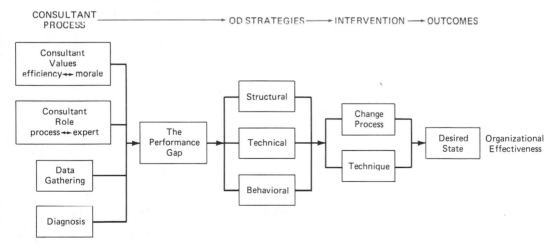

BASIC APPROACHES

Leavitt identifies three basic approaches to organization change: structural, technical, and behavioral.[2] Organization structure is important, since it provides the framework that relates elements of the organization to one another. A poor structure may inhibit efficiency. A study by McKinsey & Company (a management consulting firm) sparked a reorganization at General Motors that replaced a decades-old structure of seven divisions with two super groups—Buick-Oldsmobile-Cadillac and Chevrolet-Pontiac-GM of Canada.[3]

Technical processes also need to be given careful analysis, and often changes are required to bring them up to the state of the art in machinery, methods, automation, and job design. (See CROCK comic strip.)

Another approach, the behavioral, places emphasis on the utilization of human resources. In the past, much emphasis has been placed upon fully utilizing an organization's technical and mechanical capacities, but the organization often neglected a vast untapped resource: its human assets. Furthermore, people generally have higher morale, and are motivated toward organization goals when their personal resources and talents are being fully utilized. By increasing the level of morale, motivation, and commitment of members, organization performance can also be improved.

For OD strategies to be successful, the consultant must consider the interdependencies that exist among the various subelements of the organization. A change in one subsystem will have some impact upon other elements of the system. Richard J. Selfridge and Stanley L. Sokolik have suggested a more comprehensive approach, considering technical and structural variables as well as behavioral aspects of the system.[4] They propose an "iceberg" analogy to the organization, including overt elements, those which are easily observable; and covert elements, which are often obscure or hidden (see Figure 8.2). Often the diagnosis examines only the more visible and overt aspects of the organization and ignores the many powerful but hidden problem areas. It is essential in any change program to consider all possible problem areas, both overt and covert, if the strategy is to be successful.

CROCK by Rechin, Parker and Wilder © Field Enterprises, Inc. by permission of North American Syndicate, Inc.

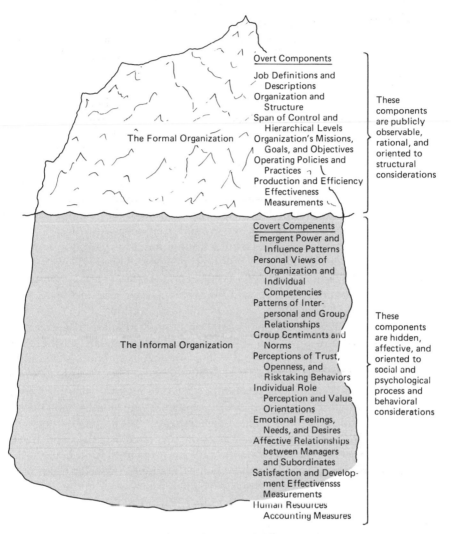

Overt Components

Job Definitions and
  Descriptions
Organization and
  Structure
Span of Control and
  Hierarchical Levels
Organization's Missions,
  Goals, and Objectives
Operating Policies and
  Practices
Production and Efficiency
  Effectiveness
  Measurements

The Formal Organization

These components are publicly observable, rational, and oriented to structural considerations

Covert Compenents

Emergent Power and
  Influence Patterns
Personal Views of
  Organization and
  Individual
  Competencies
Patterns of Inter-
  personal and Group
  Relationships
Group Sentiments and
  Norms
Perceptions of Trust,
  Openness, and
  Risktaking Behaviors
Individual Role
  Perception and Value
  Orientations
Emotional Feelings,
  Needs, and Desires
Affective Relationships
  between Managers
  and Subordinates
Satisfaction and Develop-
  ment Effectivesss
  Measurements
Human Resources
  Accounting Measures

The Informal Organization

These components are hidden, affective, and oriented to social and psychological process and behavioral considerations

Source: Adapted from Richard J. Selfridge and Stanley L. Sokolik, "A Comprehensive View of Organizational Development," *M.S.U. Business Topics*, Winter 1975, p. 47.

FIGURE 8.2 The "Organization Iceberg" Approach to OD

The importance of integrating structural, technical, and behavioral interventions is evident at Wang Laboratories, Inc., with their problems of sagging computer sales. The company's founder and president, An Wang, as well as his son, Frederick, apparently the most likely candidate for next president, understand the technology but reportedly lack the skills critical to sales and management. A former sales manager said of Frederick Wang, "He's a very bright guy in mathematics, but doesn't work very well with people."[5]

Once a diagnosis of client system problems has been made, a strategy for accomplishing the change goal needs to be determined. An OD strategy may be defined as the overall plan for relating and integrating the different organization improvement activities engaged in over a period of time to accomplish objectives. *Developing a strategy* is the planning of activities that are intended to resolve difficulties and build on strengths in order to improve the effectiveness and efficiency of the organization. Although OD is most often associated with behavioral strategies, this chapter attempts to provide a balanced description of the change process by including structural and technological strategies. It is our belief that OD techniques are an effective means for implementing many change strategies including technical and structural. Any major change effort, regardless of emphasis, must deal with the total organization system, which includes structure, technology, and people. Each of these approaches appears in most OD strategies, but they receive different emphasis. After an overall strategy has been selected, the OD practitioner and the client decide upon specific OD techniques to achieve the desired changes. These OD intervention techniques, such as the Managerial Grid, confrontation meetings, survey feedback, and team building (which are discussed in later chapters), are then implemented systematically to revitalize the organization.

The flow in developing an OD program is from the diagnosis of problems and opportunities for change (where we are now) to the setting of objectives (where we want to be), then deciding upon change strategies, and finally selecting specific intervention techniques (how we get from here to there).

The task of the OD practitioner is: (1) to help the client system generate valid information, (2) to provide free choice for the client among decision alternatives, and (3) to provide client ownership of the chosen alternatives or action plans. Intervention theory is based on the idea that data and resources are available within the client system but are prevented from being utilized. The OD practitioner-consultant then, helps the client to develop their own problem solutions. "Change," says Argyris "is not a primary task of the interventionist."[6]

THE INTEGRATION OF CHANGE STRATEGIES

Organization development has evolved during the past decade from a narrow viewpoint, with practitioners favoring one specific intervention strategy, to a more *integrated or systematic approach* to change, which attempts to deal with the total organization (see Figure 8.3).

It is increasingly evident that organizations involve complexity and contingencies. Therefore, simple cause-and-effect diagnosis and intervention strategies may overlook some critical interrelationships which influence the change effort. Consequently, it is often difficult to isolate changes to the relationship

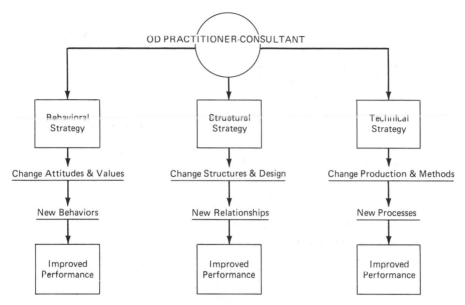

Organizational Effectiveness and Excellence

FIGURE 8.3 An Integrated Approach to Change

between any two single variables. The interrelationships between organizational variables are often complex and unclear, and the OD strategies must be comprehensive enough to provide interventions that deal with such situations.

From the organization's point of view, the purpose of an OD strategy is to become more effective or gain a position of advantage in relation to competitors. An advantage is gained by seizing opportunities in the environment that enable the organization to capitalize upon its areas of strength. For example, at an IBM board meeting, management became aware of emerging competition and a decline in their overall world market share. The IBM top management team then evolved a change strategy to meet this challenge. They selected new strategic goals and courses of action to meet potential threats and take advantage of new opportunities leading to the accomplishment of key objectives for this world market (See OD Application 8.1.)

Organization effectiveness is a function of a number of factors, including structure, technology, and people; therefore, each of the strategies can be a useful approach to change, depending on the nature of the problem. It should be remembered that the structural, technical, and behavioral change strategies are not OD change strategies per se. Often, they are highly congruent with OD programs, and the determining factor is the process used to arrive at and implement the strategies.

The problem should emerge from the diagnosis, and from these findings

IBM IS FIGHTING COMPLACENCY

Beginning in the 1970s and continuing through the 1980s, IBM fell behind the explosively expanding computer industry. In 1986 alone earnings fell 27 percent from the previous year, and 5,000 employees were cut from its work force of 237,000. Under the leadership of Chairman John F. Akers, IBM is attempting to revolutionize the way it does business.

The approach at IBM consists of five key elements:

1. Cutting costs. For the short run IBM plans to reduce payroll costs, capital spending, and miscellaneous spending for travel and consultants. However, the current policy of a virtual freeze on outside hiring has negative implications for moving ahead technologically. IBM wants to become the industry's lowest-cost pricer in an industry where its products are customarily 20 to 25 percent higher than its competition.

2. Technical advances. IBM has spent $15 billion within five years on research and development in an effort to build some of the most advanced computers. There are also plans to bring out high-performance software and continue the linking of computer systems.

3. Managerial improvement. The company's 40,000 managers are being reduced to remove layers of bureaucracy in all areas of the company, including research and production. IBM is hoping to reduce the time factor in bringing out new products in its lethargic product-planning cycle.

4. Entrepreneurial units. To explore new markets, IBM implemented entrepreneurial business units that can bypass the corporate bureaucracy. Since 1981, IBM has begun fourteen independent business units and special business units to explore opportunities beyond the company's main business. This has proved to be a low-risk way for IBM to enter emerging markets.

5. Aggressive marketing. IBM was for many years known for its strategy of not talking about computers with the customer but instead telling the customer how the computer will make him or her money. However, in the 1970s IBM focused on the competitiveness of an individual computer with a sales force attitude of "take it or leave it." IBM is now transferring people from its headquarters and putting them out in the field, creating sales offices along industry lines, and listening to consumers' needs.

The next several years will be crucial to the company as it increasingly faces stiff competition in a market it once took for granted.

Questions:
1. Can you identify the change strategies used at IBM?
2. Will they be effective in your opinion? Why? Why not?

Sources: Paul B. Carroll, "IBM Earnings Drop Is Steeper Than Expected," *Wall Street Journal*, January 21, 1987, p. 4; James Flanigan, "IBM Learned Hard Lesson in Complacency," *Los Angeles Times*, January 23, 1987, Business Section, p. 1; Marilyn A. Harris, "How IBM Is Fighting Back," *Business Week*, November 17, 1986, pp. 152–57; "IBM: More Worlds to Conquer," *Business Week*, February 18, 1985, p. 84–98; and L. Greenhalgh, R. McKersie, and R. Gilkey, "Rebalancing the Workforce at IBM: A Case Study of Redeployment and Revitalization, *Organizational Development*, Spring 1986, pp. 30–47.

the most effective strategy is then selected. This can be termed an *integrative* approach to organization change and involves combining structural, technical, and behavioral change approaches to achieve the desired goals. After the major strategy has been determined, the consultant and the client must then decide upon the specific OD techniques to be implemented in the change effort. Beer and Huse, for example, report on what they term "an eclectic approach to OD," which produced changes in task and structure as well as an individual behavior and relationships. The experience of the plant they studied showed positive results.[7]

Another factor to be considered in the selection of a change strategy is termed *second-order consequences*. This refers to the indirect or deferred consequences that result from the immediate change actions. A change in one aspect of a system to solve one problem may result in newly created problems. In summary, the change strategy selected must consider organization, individual, and work team problems. The use of an inappropriate or limited strategy of change will probably lead to ineffective results and the emergence of new problems.

STREAM ANALYSIS

Stream analysis is one method used in planning the implementation and analysis of behavioral, structural, and technical changes.[8] Stream analysis begins with the consultant and the client identifying the key organizational factors that need to be altered, either directly or indirectly, as a result of some other change. The key factors in such a program could include installing computerized control systems (technology), implementing quality circles (structure), holding team building sessions (behavioral), or a major strategy change such as the one at IBM.

Stream analysis is based on the premise that changes implemented in an organization occur over a period of time. As an example, it may be decided that team building will begin at month 0 and continue through month 5, computerized systems will be installed beginning month 3 and completed by month 5, a revised chain of command will be implemented month 4, and so on. Stream analysis presents a pictorial representation of the OD program. As shown in Figure 8.4, stream analysis charts bear some resemblance to a combination of modified PERT and Gantt planning charts.

Stream analysis is useful from several perspectives. It helps the practitioner and client diagnose and plan the interventions and keep track of their progress once the change program is underway. The client is better able to keep the organization operating as effectively as possible during the change. It may show "holes" or periods of time during which there is no activity (month 8) or periods when there is a good deal of activity (month 4). This information may be used to redesign the change program or to schedule time appropriately.

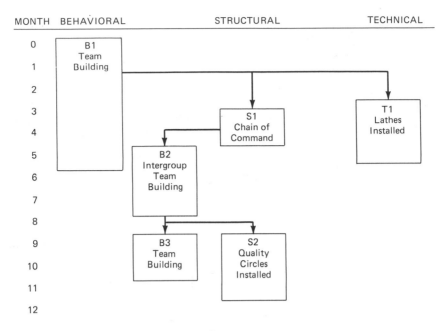

FIGURE 8.4 Completed Stream Analysis Chart

Stream analysis indicates a pattern of triggers representing one activity triggering or causing another activity to follow. For complex OD projects, it is a helpful way to pictorially represent the change program and show "where we've been and where we have to go." It can be useful to the OD practitioner if charts are made of succeeding change programs so that learning builds from one project to another.

The authors were involved in a large OD program consisting of over two dozen practitioners working with several operating divisions of a very large client system. Using stream analysis, it was possible to plan the change program and build the necessary coordination among the practitioners and the operating divisions of the client system. It was also useful to top management because they could keep track of change activities as they occurred in the field. An entire room was devoted to charts wrapping around the walls so that top managers could drop by and see that the change program was moving on schedule. An additional benefit of this approach is to give legitimacy to the OD program because top management could see that something was going on out in the field.

Once there is an awareness of a need for change and a change strategy is developed by the consultant and client, the question emerges: What specific action intervention will be most appropriate to a given organization or situation? There are a range of activities, practices, and techniques for intervening aimed at enhancing the effectiveness of the organization.

SELECTING AN OD INTERVENTION ──────────────────

There are many strategies, methods, and techniques for intervening during the action phase of an OD program. An *OD strategy* involves the overall planning and direction of change programs, whereas, *intervention techniques* deal with the operational aspects of the change—the specific means by which the OD goals are attained. An *OD intervention* refers to the range of actions designed to improve the health or functioning of the client system. An awareness of the range of diverse intervention techniques available to be applied to a given target system is important to the consultant. The major OD intervention techniques will be described in the next few chapters. All the OD interventions are aimed at changing some specific aspect of an organization: its climate, members, structure, or procedures. An organization practice is inefficient if it fails to further organization objectives; however, inefficiency may emerge slowly and become ingrained in the climate of the organization and the behaviors of the members.

When organization inefficiency emerges, there must be a shift in the values, beliefs, and behaviors of the individuals who make the system work. In general, OD intervention techniques are based upon the idea that the relationships between organization groups and organization members are one of the principal reasons for problems of inefficiency, and that certain activities do not contribute to organization objectives.

These inherent problems of inefficient practices have been summarized by C. Northcote Parkinson in *Parkinson's Laws.*[9] Parkinson proposed two principal reasons for organization inefficiency: (1) the law of multiplication of subordinates—a manager wants to increase the number of subordinates he or she directs rather than create rival organization members; and (2) the law of multiplication of work—members of the organization make work for each other. There are many similar kinds of inefficient operations that OD techniques seek to change. These intervention techniques are often used in conjunction with structural or technical strategies as a means of implementing an organization change program. In this section a checklist for selecting a technique will be discussed, together with an overview of major OD intervention techniques.

In selecting a specific OD technique the consultant and the client consider a number of factors, including the nature of the problem, the objectives of the change effort, the cultural norms of the client system, and the expected degree of resistance. Selecting a technique involves comparing and testing possible intervention techniques against some criteria. Three broad factors are of concern to the OD practitioner in selecting the appropriate intervention:

1. *The potential results of the technique*

    a. Will it solve the basic problems?

        b.   Does it have any additional positive outcomes?

        c.   Are any potentially negative consequences likely to occur?

  2. *The potential implementation of the technique*

        a.   Can the proposed technique really work in a practical application?

        b.   What are the actual dollar and human costs of this technique and the impact of cost upon the client system?

        c.   How do the estimated costs of the technique compare with the expected results (costs versus benefit)?

  3. *The potential acceptance of the technique*

        a.   Is the technique acceptable to the client system?

        b.   Is the technique adequately developed and tested?

        c.   Has the technique been adequately explained and communicated to members of the client system?

These important factors should be considered prior to making a final decision on the selection of a technique. The selection of any given technique is usually a trade-off between advantages and disadvantages because there is no precise way to answer all these questions in advance. After comparing the advantages and disadvantages, a specific technique is selected for the action phase of the OD program.

THE MAJOR OD INTERVENTION TECHNIQUES: AN OVERVIEW

This section presents an overview of the basic OD intervention techniques. Since OD is a dynamic discipline, the boundaries of "what is" and "what is not" OD are ambiguous and changing. The interventions included provide examples of the diverse techniques that exist, but they are not intended to be all-inclusive.

    These planned activities or interventions are specifically aimed at correcting inefficiencies, solving problems and developing strengths and areas of opportunity. A basic assumption underlying the intervention activity is that the client organization already contains most of the basic resources for change and the primary role of the OD practitioner is to energize these forces by assisting the client system in diagnosing and resolving its own problems.

    These interventions, then, make things happen or cause changes to occur in the client system. These OD intervention techniques include activities focusing on several organizational levels, ranging from (1) the individual or interpersonal level, (2) the team or group level, (3) the intergroup level, to (4) the total organizational system level. Certain interventions are aimed primarily at individual improvement while others are aimed at groups, but a single intervention may fit into several or all categories.

One way to categorize intervention techniques is in terms of the target system (see Table 8.1). As indicated, the consultant and the client may select a technique that is best fitted to the target system. The aspect of the organization that is being changed and the problem conditions then determine the type of intervention that is selected.

Roger Harrison differentiates intervention techniques in terms of the depth of intervention, which refers to the degree to which the change is directly related to the emotional involvement of the individual.[10] For example, management by objectives would be less individualized than personal growth laboratory learning. Harrison uses the terms *accessibility* and *individuality* to refer to the ends of the continuum. To determine the appropriate depth of intervention, Harrison suggests two criteria: "First, to intervene at a level no deeper than that required to produce enduring solutions to the problems at hand; and, second, to intervene at a level no deeper than that at which the energy and resources of the client can be committed to problem solving and to change."[11]

OD programs do not necessarily include all of these possible intervention techniques, but this grouping is representative of the range of possible activities. Usually, the specific intervention is dependent upon the nature of the target system. Certain techniques, such as Grid OD, systematically move from the individual to the total organization system.

These differing types of interventions suggest the wide range of possible interventions available to the OD practitioner. Although this discussion includes the major categories, all possible interventions are not included. There are also differences among practitioners over what is and what is not an OD technique. In the following chapters the interventions will be described, moving from techniques aimed at the individual to system-wide applications.

TABLE 8.1 OD Interventions: An Overview

Personal and Interpersonal	Team	Intergroup	Total Organization System
Job design	Team building	Intergroup development	Management by objectives
Job enrichment	Process consultation	Third-party intervention	Goal setting
Laboratory learning	Job enrichment	Organization mirror	Grid OD (phases 4, 5, and 6)
Career planning	Job design	Process consultation	Survey feedback
Goal setting	Quality circles	Grid OD (phase 3)	Action research
Managerial Grid (phase 1)	Role negotiation		Likert's System 4
Stress management	Role analysis technique		Quality of work life
Biofeedback	Grid OD (phase 2)		Decentralization

REVIEW QUESTIONS

1. Compare and contrast the basic OD strategies.

2. Identify and give examples of OD interventions for various target systems.

KEY WORDS AND CONCEPTS

Define and be able to use the following:

OD strategy

Organization structure

Technical change approach

Intervention techniques

Integrative approach

Second-order consequences

Target system

Depth of intervention

Stream analysis

IV. Simulations

SIMULATION 8.1   THE FRANKLIN COMPANY

Total time suggested: 1 hour, 35 minutes.

A. Purpose

In this simulation you will be able to plan and implement structural, technical, and behavioral strategies in an organization. You will also critique and receive feedback on the effectiveness of your strategies. The goals include:

1. To determine appropriate intervention strategy.
2. To experience diagnosing and contacting a client system.
3. To provide feedback on consulting approaches.

B. Procedures

Step 1   Everyone reads The Franklin Company Background. Prior to class, divide the class into groups of approximately 12 members in size. Five of these will serve as the Franklin Management Team. (Roles to be selected and read prior to the class meeting.) Each player should read only their role. The remainder of the group should form consulting teams of 2 members each and become familiar with the OD Consulting Guidelines and the Diagnostic Form after the role descriptions.

Step 2   The Franklin Management Team will meet with the consulting teams to decide:

1. What are the major problems?
2. Should they use an OD consultant?
3. What strategies should be used to change?

Time suggested for Step 2: 45 minutes.

Step 3 Each OD consulting-team prepares a diagnosis and OD strategy. A Diagnostic Form is provided after the roles.
Time suggested for Step 3: 20 minutes.

Step 4 Each consulting team presents their OD strategy to the Franklin team, who may ask questions. The Franklin team will then select what they consider to be the OD strategy most likely to help their organization, and present their reasoning. The class may critique the Franklin team and the consultants. Discuss problems and strategies.
Time suggested for Step 4: 30 minutes.

THE FRANKLIN COMPANY BACKGROUND

The Franklin Company, a medium-size company with about 1,800 employees, manufactures radar units for use in small aircraft and in police cars. The company is actually over 90 years old and initially manufactured wind vanes and lightning rods, but since World War II has manufactured only radar units. During the last 4 years, growth in sales has been stable and profits have decreased slightly, as contrasted to the previous 20 years of steady growth in sales and profits. Industry sales continue to show a steady growth, but new competitors have entered the field with new products and features, cutting into the firm's market share. Franklin has 12 distinct products with an average of 3 different models per product. New products have been brought on line but usually several years after the younger competitors. To make matters worse, several Franklin key managers, researchers, and sales people have joined the competition.

The current abbreviated organization chart is shown in Figure 8.5. All of the company's operations are conducted from the one site. Sales people are also physically based at the plant but they make calls throughout the U.S.

The president has called in some OD consultants to diagnose and propose solutions to the current problems.

ROLE DESCRIPTIONS (READ ONLY YOUR ROLE)

Role 1—President You have been the president of Franklin for the past 14 years and in large part its growth and success have been due to your own ability to select and motivate others. You are 48, a college graduate, and have attended many executive seminars. You have tried to apply these concepts to Franklin.

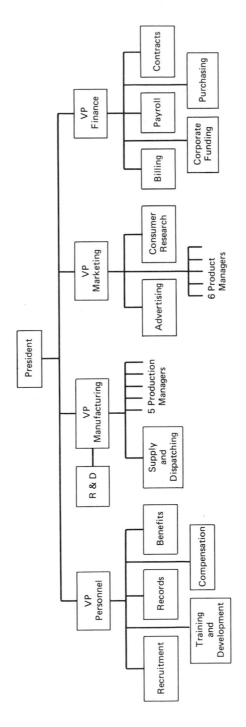

FIGURE 8.5 Franklin Organization Chart

You still maintain close contact with day-to-day operations since you believe in "management by wandering around."

Over the past few years, growth has slowed, sales and earnings have declined, and turnover problems have emerged. You feel the rapid early growth may be the cause of current problems.

You are convinced that the lack of coordination between the four operating groups is the major problem and that a more decentralized operation will help resolve this. You also think a Management Information System (MIS) will improve coordination and communication. You have asked the vice president of finance to look into MIS.

You believe that the organization needs better morale and improved bottom-line results. Your vice president of personnel has suggested that you try something new: an organization development program. The vice president has invited a team of consultants to meet with your executive committee. You believe in modern techniques, so perhaps these consultants can get the various members to find an agreeable compromise to solve the problem.

Role 2—Vice President of Personnel You are 35, with an M.B.A., and you were brought in five years ago to serve in your current position. You see the key problem as poor structure, a lack of coordination among departments, and weak managerial competence and training at all levels.

All of the other vice presidents worked their way up to their present position, and you consider their professional managerial training somewhat remiss, with the exception of the vice president of marketing who has attended many of your training sessions. This is even more of a problem at the mid- and lower-level management ranks.

You feel that the answer to the problem is a decentralized operation with increased integration and coordination between departments and a participative, team style. You have read about OD and have talked to a colleague at another company who had high praise for their OD program. You even discussed implementing an OD program with the vice president of manufacturing, but there was little response. You feel a need to get conflicts out into the open where they can be resolved rather than each unit seeking its own best interest. A unified team effort is needed.

You have attempted to initiate several training and change programs. These programs have been undercut by other managers. You got word that one vice president was openly attacking the programs, even though the president has been strongly supportive. You suggested bringing in some OD consultants in hopes of initiating some badly needed changes. Even though they might add to costs in the short run, you are sure that long-term effectiveness will be improved.

Role 3—Vice President of Manufacturing You are 52 and have been with the company for 22 years, working your way up through the ranks. You have a degree in engineering and feel that you are competent, run a tight ship, and that your department is the main reason for past success. You believe that most problems are due to rapid growth that has resulted in loose structure, lack of coordination, and lack of control.

You feel that the company has too many meddling staff managers (particularly in marketing and personnel) who do not contribute to profits and only cause problems for the line manager. Several times the vice president of personnel has tried to discuss with you management practices such as leadership and some new kind of OD program. You listened politely enough, but you got several good laughs out of it at your department meetings. The management training programs offered through the personnel division have been a waste of time and you have told your people you prefer they stay on the job instead of going to more meetings. The vice president of marketing continually wants a product modification or comes up with some goofball idea for a new product. You have made it clear that you run manufacturing and that includes R&D. You can't run a smooth operation and keep costs down if you are constantly making special modifications. You believe you manufacture enough models to allow a customer to find a suitable product or the customer can easily make some minor modifications.

You feel the solution is to move into a more highly centralized structure and appoint an executive vice president to centralize cost control (like yourself, for example) and lay off some of the deadwood.

You hear that the president has invited some OD consultants in, against your advice. You do not know much about OD, but it sounds like pouring money down a rathole to you. Besides, this OD business is a bunch of "touchie-feelie" nonsense anyway, which is the last thing you need.

Role 4—Vice President of Marketing You have been with the company for 10 years, are 40 years old. You are a college graduate with a major in psychology, but you have gained your knowledge of marketing from experience. You feel that marketing is the major factor in the company's growth, and if your product managers were given greater authority, they could turn the profit picture around.

You see the major problem as the lack of communication among departments and the failure to utilize talented managers. You have tried to get the manufacturing division to make some special modifications in radar units, but they have been willing to comply only on very large orders, and then it generally took them so long that you almost lost several of the orders from your customers. Several of your product managers have met with representatives of manufacturing to discuss new product ideas, but nothing comes of the meetings until your competitors come up with the identical product. Then it takes manufacturing a couple of years to design their own unit.

Your people are bringing back word from the field that the excellent reputation once enjoyed by Franklin is beginning to fade. It has been discouraging for you and your people to fight an uphill battle with manufacturing for new products, and the real kicker is to learn the competition comes out with your product idea.

Despite the problems with the manufacturing division, you find that if you treat your people well, they will perform for you. You have attended most of the management training sessions and have encouraged, though not mandated, your managers to attend. Your department meetings even have follow-up discussions of the training sessions.

Even though marketing has been accused of being run like a "country club," you feel your department performs well. The answer, you believe, is to decentralize the firm into major independent groups and utilize more of the "whiz kids," the young M.B.A. types, in product management by giving them more authority over product operations. You would like to see yourself as executive vice president over the product managers.

You understand that some OD consultants are coming in and see this as a great opportunity to implement your ideas.

Role 5—Vice President of Finance. You are 51 and have an M.B.A. from a major school. This and prior banking experience led to your successful 17 years at Franklin. You instituted all financial systems and made it a smooth operation.

You feel the problems are the result of too many changes in too short a time. The company has too many bright young kids and too many wasteful practices. You suggest going back to the basics by instituting a tighter centralized system of financial control and cutting about 10 percent of the deadwood. With yourself as an executive vice president (with other vice presidents reporting to you), this job could be done. You would set up some basic company rules, then force the department heads to enforce them.

You would like to see people be required to follow the chain of command. You have heard too many stories of people at lower levels cutting across the formal structure and meeting with their counterparts in another division. This may sound good on the surface, but it usually screws up the operation later on. You would like to see all communications go up through their appropriate vice president and then back down the chain of command. This type of centralized control is necessary to coordinate everything. You believe there are too many committees throughout the company, and you find it amazing that anything gets accomplished. Further, with all these committees making decisions, it's hard to figure out who to blame when something goes wrong. As far as you are concerned, a camel is a horse designed by a committee.

You avoid getting into conflicts over these issues. You like to let the facts and figures talk, and deal mainly by memo. You realize that you are not as up to date on modern computerized systems as you might be and though the president has asked you to look into a Management Information System (MIS), you consider it to be a waste of time and money. An MIS would call for a newer computer and you have heard horror stories about computers and believe your current punched-card data processing system to be excellent.

You would like to avoid changes and keep things pretty much the way they are. You hear that some OD consultants are coming and your reaction is: Why do we need them? They represent just the kind of wasteful practice you oppose.

OD Consulting Guidelines—You hope to accomplish several things at this meeting:

1. To develop a consultant/client relationship with all of the committee members.
2. To make a preliminary diagnosis of possible problems.
3. To gain support for a possible OD project and convince them of the advantages.
4. To introduce them to some of the goals of OD, by doing some process consultation during the meeting.

DIAGNOSTIC FORM

1. Who is the client?
   a. Who has the most influence in the client system? _____
      _____
      _____

   b. Who do you feel is the client? Why? _____
      _____
      _____

2. Identify major formal and informal problems of the organization. (Use Figure 8.2.)
   a. _____
      _____
   b. _____
      _____
   c. _____
      _____
   d. _____
      _____

3. What strategy(s) might you select?
   a. Structural: _____
      _____
      _____
   b. Behavioral: _____
      _____
      _____

   c. Technical: _____

_____

_____

   d. Integrated: _____

_____

_____

4. Identify possible target systems and interventions.

                         Target   Intervention

   a. _____

   b. _____

   c. _____

   d. _____

Case:
The Farm
Bank

The Farm Bank is one of the state's oldest and solidest banking institutions. Located in a regional marketing center, the bank has been active in all phases of banking, specializing in farm loans. The bank's president, Frank Swain, 72, has been with the bank for many years and is prominent in local circles.

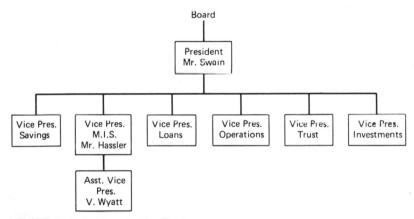

EXHIBIT 1 Partial Organization Chart

The bank is organized into five departments as shown in Exhibit 1. Each department is headed by a senior vice president. They have been with the bank for years and in general reflect a stable and conservative outlook.

THE MANAGEMENT INFORMATION SYSTEM

Two years ago, Mr. Swain felt that the bank needed to modernize its operation and with the approval of the board of directors, he decided to design and install a comprehensive management information system (MIS).

The primary goal was to improve internal operations by supplying necessary information on a more expedited basis, thereby decreasing the time necessary to service customers. The system was also to be designed to provide economic operating data for top management planning and decision making. To head up this department, he selected Al Hassler, 58, a solid operations manager, who had some knowledge and experience in the computer department.

After the system was designed and installed, Al hired a young woman, Valerie Wyatt, a young M.B.A. with a strong systems analysis background, as his assistant. She was the only woman and considerably younger than any of the other managers at this level. She was also the only M.B.A.

In the time since the system was installed, the MIS has printed thousands of pages of operating information, including reports to all vice presidents, all branch managers, and the president. The reports include weekly, monthly, and quarterly summaries and include cost of operations, projected labor costs, overhead costs, and projected earnings figures for each segment of the bank's operations.

THE MIS SURVEY

President Swain has been pleased with the system; however, he noticed little improvement in management operations. In fact, most of the older vice presidents tended to make decisions and function pretty much as they had before the MIS was installed. Swain then decided to have Valerie Wyatt conduct a survey of the users to try to evaluate the impact and benefits of the new system. Wyatt was glad to undertake the survey, since she had long felt the system was overelaborate for the bank's needs. She sent out a questionnaire to all department heads, branch managers, and so on, inquiring into the uses of the system.

As she began to assemble the survey data, a pattern began to emerge. In general, the majority of managers were strongly in favor of the system, but felt that there were a few minor modifications which could be made. As Valerie analyzed the responses several trends and important points came out: (1) 93 percent reported they did not regularly use the reports because the information was not in a useful form; (2) 76 percent reported the printouts were hard to interpret; (3) 72 percent stated they received more data than they wanted; (4) 57 percent reported finding some errors and inaccuracies; and (5) 87 percent stated they still kept manual records because they did not fully trust the MIS.

THE MEETING

Valerie Wyatt finished her report excitedly and rushed into Al Hassler's office and handed him the report. Hassler slowly scanned the report, then said, "You've done a good job here, Val. But now that we have the system operating, I don't think we should upset the apple cart, do you? Let's just keep this to ourselves for the time being and perhaps we can correct most of these problems. I'm sure Frank wouldn't want to hear this kind of stuff.

This system is his baby, so maybe we shouldn't rock the boat with this report."

Valerie returned to her office feeling uncomfortable. She wondered what to do.

CASE ANALYSIS FORM

I. Problems

   A. Macro

      1. _____

      2. _____

   B. Micro

      1. _____

      2. _____

II. Causes

      1. _____

      2. _____

      3. _____

III. Systems affected

      1. Structural

      2. Psychosocial

      3. Technical

      4. Managerial

      5.

IV. Alternatives

      1. _____

      2. _____

      3. _____

      4. _____

      5. _____

V. Recommendations

      1. _____

      2. _____

      3. _____

**V.
Summary**

This chapter examined some of the major organization development interventions.

OD is a long-term effort to introduce planned change on a system-wide basis. Therefore, the selection of specific strategies and techniques is an important action step.

The OD strategy involves the overall planning and direction of the intervention activities. A comprehensive approach involves the way the organization is managed, the way jobs are designed, and the way people are motivated. The consultant and the client determine the appropriate strategy to best attain change objectives. There are also a number of OD techniques. Based upon the change strategy, specific action interventions that will best resolve problem conditions and increase organization effectiveness are then implemented. A more detailed description of these techniques will be presented in the following chapters.

In this chapter three basic approaches to change were identified: structural, technical, and behavioral. Structure provides the framework that relates elements of the organization. These units are engaged in some task or technical accomplishment and are also bound together in an interrelated network of social and behavioral interventions.

There are also a variety of intervention strategies or approaches which may be used in organization development. Although these approaches may differ, they aim at the same basic goals: (1) to improve the functioning of the client system; (2) to increase the organization's adaptive capability toward a more anticipative system; and (3) to enhance the development and potential of the individual members of the organization.

You have had an opportunity to diagnose a problem situation and to develop a specific set of strategies and techniques for implementing an organization change program. You have probably found differing departmental objectives which must be reconciled with organization goals. You may also have experienced differing approaches to change among different individuals. One person may view the problem as calling for a structural change, although another person may view it as requiring behavioral or technical change strategies. After a change strategy has been agreed upon, specific techniques for achieving change must then be designed and implemented.

All of the major variables are interrelated, and often a change in one structure, for example, may have consequences on technical and behavioral elements. Therefore, a systems approach or integrative approach involves analyzing the way work is designed, the way the organization is managed, and the way people are motivated. The following chapters describe some specific OD interventions for changing organization conditions.

NOTES

1. See Michael McCaskey, *The Executive Challenge: Managing Change and Ambiguity*, Boston: Pitman, 1982.
2. Harold Leavitt, "Applied Organization Change in Industry: Structural, Technical and Humanistic Approaches," in *Handbook of Organizations*, ed. James March (Chicago: Rand McNally & Company, 1965).
3. David E. Whiteside, "Roger Smith's Campaign to Change the GM Culture," *Business Week*, April 7, 1986, pp. 84–85.

4. Richard J. Selfridge and Stanley L. Sokolik, "A Comprehensive View of Organizational Development," *M.S.U. Business Topics*, Winter 1975, p. 46.

5. Alex Beam, "The Revolving Door to Wang's Executive Suite," *Business Week*, April 21, 1986, p. 29.

6. Chris Argyris, *Intervention Theory and Method, A Behavioral Science View* (Reading, Mass.: Addison-Wesley Publishing Co., Inc., 1970), p. 21.

7. Michael Beer and Edgar Huse, "A Systems Approach to Organization Development," *Journal of Applied Behavioral Science*, 1, no. 8 (1972), 79–101.

8. Jerry I. Porras, Joan Harkness, and Coeleen Kiebert, "Understanding Organization Development: A Stream Approach," *Training and Development Journal*, April 1983, pp. 52–63.

9. C. Northcote Parkinson, *Parkinson's Laws* (Boston: Houghton Mifflin Company, 1957).

10. Roger Harrison, "Choosing the Depth of Organization Intervention," *Journal of Applied Behavioral Science*, April–June 1970, pp. 181–202.

11. Ibid., p. 201.

9

OD INTERPERSONAL INTERVENTIONS

I. **Objectives**	Upon completing this chapter, you will be able to:
	1. Recognize the basis for interpersonal interventions in OD programs.
	2. Experience the dynamics involved in interpersonal communication.
	3. Practice giving and receiving feedback on personal communication style.
	4. Describe career life planning and stress management as OD techniques.

II. **Premeeting** **Preparation**	1. Read the Background Information (Section III).
	2. Complete Step 1 of Simulation 9.1 (Section IV).
	3. Complete Steps 1 and 3 of Simulation 9.2.
	4. Read and analyze Case: The Sundale Club.

III.
Background
Information

Organizations are designed to use the energy and ability of individuals to perform work and achieve goals. Members bring to the organization their own values, assumptions, and behaviors. The effectiveness of the organization, then, is a function of how effectively the needs of individual members are integrated with overall objectives. People- or behavior-oriented changes are aimed at the psychosocial system functioning of the organization. These behavioral interventions may take various forms but all are intended to improve the basic skills that underlie managerial effectiveness. One essential factor in most OD programs is a greater openness of communication and improved conflict resolution, requiring the development of specialized skills among members.

There are a range of OD intervention activities aimed at enhancing the development and functioning of the individual organization member. Essentially, the underlying assumption to these approaches is: if the individual becomes more effective and more skilled, the total organization will also be improved. In a general sense, such interventions are aimed at improving the communication ability, interpersonal skill, and managerial behavior of organization members. If the interpersonal competence of managers is increased, the results should be improved organizational performance.[1]

In this chapter several interpersonal techniques are discussed that can be used to assist organization members in becoming more effective. Some of the programs include laboratory learning, the Johari Window model, career life planning, and stress management.

LABORATORY LEARNING ⎯⎯⎯⎯⎯⎯⎯⎯⎯⎯⎯⎯⎯⎯⎯⎯⎯⎯⎯

Laboratory learning programs evolved from the early group dynamics work of Kurt Lewin and the programs conducted by National Training Laboratories (NTL) in the United States and by Tavistock Institute in England.[2] Although reliable data on the extent of laboratory learning are not readily available, it grew rapidly through the mid-1970s. Recently, however, it has been used less as a training technique in OD programs (though some of the methodologies are used indirectly in other OD training techniques such as the Managerial Grid and team building).[3]

The Objectives of Laboratory Learning ⎯⎯⎯⎯⎯⎯⎯⎯⎯⎯⎯⎯⎯⎯⎯⎯

Laboratory learning has been used to increase the interpersonal skills of managers in their leadership, group, and organization situations. The basic concept involves the use of a group as a laboratory for experimenting, learning, and discovering cause-and-effect relations in interpersonal communication.

The objectives of organization laboratories include:

1. Improved insights into managerial and personal style.
2. An increased ability to assess one's impact upon others.
3. A greater awareness of the conditions that facilitate or inhibit group functioning.
4. Increased skill in analyzing and coping with change and ambiguous problem situations.

These illustrate the broad objectives of laboratory learning, but practitioners may emphasize some more than others. For example, one practitioner may emphasize group processes; another may focus on increased awareness of one's behavior. Also, the objectives are to some degree flexible and determined by the group.

The Use of Laboratory Learning in OD Programs

In 1958, Robert Blake and Herb Shepard pioneered the use of laboratory learning in company-wide programs aimed at improving organization efficiency. To date, many major corporations (e.g., TRW Systems, Texas Instruments, and Union Carbide) and the U.S. State Department have applied these techniques in organization development programs.

Results of Laboratory Learning

As already noted, some major corporations have applied laboratory learning methods as a part of management development and organization development programs. There are no clear-cut empirical studies to document their effectiveness, although a considerable amount of research has been done to determine the effect of laboratory learning performance.

There is some evidence to suggest that laboratory learning does provide increased self-insight and awareness of impact upon others and that observable changes in behavior do occur on the job.[4] David Bowers, on the other hand, found negative changes associated with laboratory training, although he states that laboratory learning may tend to be unsuccessful in organizations that are becoming more autocratic.[5] However, Procter & Gamble used laboratory learning and reported positive results.[6]

There is very little hard evidence relating laboratory learning to increased productivity or organization results. There is, however, a great deal of subjective evaluation. TRW Systems credited laboratory learning and OD with improved team and intergroup performance, and TRW's turnover rate was reportedly lower than the industry average. One problem in evaluating most OD techniques is the lack of empirical data on the results of various interventions. Frank Friedlander has noted the necessity of developing comparative studies of differing intervention processes: "We must at some point study comparative changes in the effectiveness of different work groups (or organizations) and then link these changes to the respective process interventions.[7]

INTERPERSONAL STYLE—THE JOHARI WINDOW MODEL

An organization is made up of individuals, each with a unique set of values, behaviors, and motivations. As a result of the interaction and communication between members, an organization's climate is formed as shown at Federal Express (see OD Application 9.1). If the organization uses formal communications, lines of authority, and centralized decision making, most of the communications between members may be inauthentic. People will say what they think others want to hear or expect them to say. The communication, then, is "mask to mask"; from one person's facade to another person's facade. Usually, such communication is distorted, inaccurate, and ineffective.

However, communication is a critical dimension in determining the effectiveness of most organizations. The *Johari Window Model*, by Joe Luft and Harry Ingram, is one technique for identifying interpersonal communication style.[8] In the Johari Window Model, interpersonal style is measured in terms of communication awareness. The model presents a two-dimensional, four-celled figure based on the interaction of two sources of information—the self and others. In the model (shown in Figure 9.1) each of the four cells represents a particular area of knowledge about the self, and each has an effect on the quality of the interpersonal communication process.

1. The public area. This area includes behavior, thoughts, and feelings which are known both to the person and to others. This is the area of our public image and of interaction involving mutually shared perceptions (others see us as we see ourselves). One underlying assumption of the Johari Window Model is that interpersonal effectiveness is directly related to the amount of mutually shared information—or *congruence*. The larger this area becomes, the more effective will be the communication.

2. The blind area. This area represents aspects of the self (behavior, thoughts, and feelings) not known to oneself, but readily apparent to others. These include mannerisms and habits of which a person may be unaware, but which others discover easily. The person who is red-faced and shouting "I'm not angry," or a student giving a presentation whose knees are trembling, voice is cracking, and hands are shaking, yet who says "I'm not a bit nervous" would be examples of this area. Some managers may try to be forceful and tough, rejecting any feelings of warmth as being soft, yet such feelings might be highly visible to others.

3. The closed area. This area involves behavior, thoughts, and feelings known only to oneself but not to others. For others to become aware of these areas, they must be disclosed by the person. This area includes feelings one may perceive as possibly harmful to self-image. For example, one who likes

OD
Application
9.1

"WHEN IT ABSOLUTELY, POSITIVELY HAS TO BE THERE OVERNIGHT"

Fred Smith is chairman and chief executive officer of Memphis-based Federal Express Corporation, an express delivery firm that specializes in overnight door-to-door service, using its own aircraft and vans. Some people feel that the significance of the company is that it created a $2 billion industry where none existed before and changing the way America does business. Others say the company's significance is its example of how one man, Frederick W. Smith, could see trends in the world, conceptualize a product that would capitalize on those trends, and motivate an untested work force to build a $2 billion plus empire.

In his undergraduate days at Yale, Smith reputedly wrote a paper proposing the idea of an airline system to deliver small packages from city to city. This was the blueprint for his firm, and received a low grade from his unimpressed professor. While he was not able to convince his professor of his revolutionary idea, he was able to convince the financial world.

Entrepreneurial Spirit

Frederick W. Smith may have a common last name, but he is a most uncommon man. What other modern American business leader had a revolutionary idea and converted it into a company that, starting from scratch and with heavy early losses, passed the $2 billion revenue mark and achieved high profit margins in little more than a decade?

Technological change had opened a radically new transportation market, he decided. To cut cost and time, packages from all over the country would be flown to a central point, to be sorted and flown out again to their destinations—a hub-and-spokes pattern, his company calls it today.

People Orientation

Fred Smith says,

We have had a tremendous record of esprit de corps, motivation, and innovation. . . . So our trick has been how to maintain, again, the type of motivation and interest on the part, not of a few thousand employees, but tens of thousands of employees. And what we've done is to recognize that almost every human being fits in one category or another in terms of a value system hierarchy.

I think the number one criteria, bar none, is do we think that person has the interpersonal skills and the leadership skills to be able to manage our people. And among those traits I'm speaking of, do they have the commitment to put people first?

Through all the bad times, however, Smith earned the undying loyalty of those who work for him. "He was a fantastic motivator of people," said Charles Tucker Morse, the company's first general counsel. "I have not worked since in a situation so intense and so free of politics."

Except for his persistence and willingness to bet the ranch, Frederick Smith is not an easy fit into the image of the entrepreneur. Starting an air-freight business carries with it the cash-gobbling barrier of having to operate a fleet of planes, hundreds of vehicles, scores of offices, and a vast sorting and distribution system—costs that can digest an inheritance in a hurry. At one point, Smith met part of a payroll with $27,000 he won in blackjack. Apart from personal funds, his company would require $90 million in venture capital before it went into the black in late 1975—three years after starting out. Fred Smith took a revolutionary idea, a market opportunity, and built it into a Fortune 500 company.

Questions:
1. How did interpersonal skills help Fred Smith succeed?
2. How important are the values of organization members?

Adapted from Henry Altman, "A Business Visionary," *Nation's Business*, November 1981, p. 27.

---

poetry or classical music might hide this under a guise of "macho" strength. This involves a protective facade intended to protect the ego or self-image. However, the question arises: How effective are such facades and how effective are people in using them? When one is in a new situation or with strangers, this is usually a large area because people do not know much about one another and trust is low. It is interesting that people go to great lengths to conceal this part of themselves, yet it is this element that makes each of us most human. It often takes years of knowing someone before we gain insights into this area.

4. The unknown area. Included here are behavior and feelings that are inaccessible both to oneself and to others. According to some psychologists, unconscious, deeply repressed feelings and impulses or other hidden aspects of the personality reside here. Over time, people may become aware of some of these aspects of themselves, but for our purposes this area is of less importance.

As indicated in Figure 9.1, movement along the vertical and horizontal

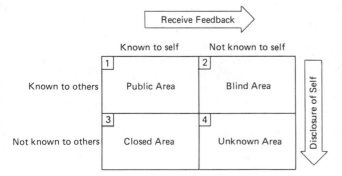

FIGURE 9.1
The Johari Window: A Model of Interpersonal Communication Processes

Source: Adapted from J. Luft, "The Johari Window," *Human Relations Training News*, 5 (1961), 6–7; *Of Human Interaction*, (Palo Alto, Calif.: National Press Books, 1961)

dimensions enables the individual to change his or her interpersonal style by increasing the amount of communication in the public or shared area. To enlarge the public area, the person may move vertically by reducing the closed area. As a person behaves in less-defensive ways and becomes more open, trusting, and risk taking, others will tend to react toward him or her with increased openness and trust. This process is termed *disclosure* and involves the open disclosure of one's feelings, thoughts, and candid feedback to others. This openness of communication leads to more open and congruent relationships.

The behavioral process used to enlarge the public area horizontally is termed *feedback* and allows one to reduce the blind area. The only way to become aware of our blind spots is for others to give us information or feedback about our behavior. The blind area can be reduced only with the help and cooperation of others, and this requires a willingness to invite and accept such feedback. Almost every organization finds that poor communication is the most important problem preventing organizational effectiveness. (see CROCK comic strip.) The Johari Window Model is one technique for examining and improving the interpersonal communication process.

CAREER LIFE PLANNING INTERVENTIONS

OD is aimed at shifting the organization climate to increase the integration of organization and individual goals, and the career development aspirations of the individual member are an important element. Managerial career development is an ongoing process of change in activities, positions, and values. People often feel caught in an "organizational trap" because their personal goals and sense of meaning become lost. Many of these individual career problems are actually symptoms of larger organization problems, such as a rigid bureaucratic structure or intergroup conflict. In Chapter 1 the concept of socialization was described; that is, the entry of the individual into a new organization. Frequently, the initial entry or socialization process is an important phase leading to eventual career development and personal goals. In the socialization process

CROCK by Rechin, Parker and Wilder © Field Enterprises, Inc. by permission of American Syndicate, Inc.

individual and organization expectations are exchanged. Consequently, as an individual develops within the organization, his or her career path reaches crisis points where the individual is faced with a choice between jobs, between professions, or between organizations. At these points there is a need for the individual to apply some form of career life planning to determine how best to achieve his or her career goals. *Career* may be defined as "a continuing process through which a person engages in a sequence of developmental tasks necessary for personal growth in occupational life.[9] The purpose of such career planning is to develop and promote high-potential employees in channels where their abilities will be utilized to the fullest.

One recent form of career development is called *career life planning*. This involves the application of laboratory-learning techniques to career development. There are a number of different approaches to career life planning, but the major one is attributed to Herb Shepard. A modification of his method has been written up by Jack Lewis, and a third approach has been designed by Kolb and Boyatzis.[10] All of these approaches try to use the idea of goal setting and achievement motivation as a means for the individual to gain greater control over his or her future career development. Career life planning is the process of choosing occupation, organization, and career path.

The Steps in Career Life Planning

Career life planning involves the following issues: (1) determining where you are now; (2) deciding where you want to be; and (3) developing a plan for getting where you want to be.

The basic intervention involves a sequence of steps, although there are a variety of ways to accomplish this. Usually workshop participants work in consulting pairs, each helping the other in the following steps:

Step 1 Prepare a set of career life goals. This consists of a list that usually includes career, professional, personal, and relational goals (list 1).

Step 2 Your consultant (partner) then goes through the list, reality testing, determining priorities, and looking for conflicting goals.

Step 3 Make a list of important past accomplishments or happenings, including peak experiences, accomplishments, things that have made you feel happy or satisfied, or times when you felt most alive or real (list 2).

Step 4 Your consultant then works through a comparison of the individual's goals (list 1) with the list of past achievements (list 2), looking for conflicts or incongruencies between the two lists. For example, one's goal might be to become an accountant or a research scientist, jobs that involve indoor activities, whereas the list of past satisfactions may indicate an emphasis upon outdoor activities. The consultant then points out the incongruencies to his or her partner.

Step 5 The outcome of Step 4 is a set of firm goals with relative priorities. Now prepare a detailed plan of action specifying how to get from where you are to where your goal indicates that you should be.

Career planning can provide employees with information to enable them to make better career decisions. Although every individual needs to continually reassess his or her life goals and assess the progress toward them, career life planning is usually done at some crisis point, where the individual is faced with possible alternative career patterns. These career goals need to be determined reasonably often because an individual's objectives and opportunities will probably change during his or her lifetime.

The Results of Career Life Planning _____

There is little evidence to indicate the outcome of career life planning interventions. There is obviously a need for such interventions because very few organizations have individualized career development programs. Career life planning, then, provides the application of a management-by-objectives type of goal setting and counseling to the individual's own life and career. The application of this method requires the help of a consultant to test and compare the individual's goals, but it may be done on an informal basis at any particular point in time. As noted, such activities are usually recommended for people at some decision point in their lives or careers. This technique can be helpful to the individual and may also aid in improving organization systems where such career concerns may be blocking job activities or inhibiting the development of individual potential. Despite the lack of data on the results of this technique, such interventions have been used in organizations and the results appear to be positive. IBM, General Electric, General Motors, TRW, and Xerox have all developed career planning to reduce turnover and improve performance.

STRESS MANAGEMENT _____

Stress is an emotional strain affecting a person's physical and mental condition. Work-related stress is not necessarily bad, and in fact some research indicates that stress may improve performance in most people.[11] But excessive stress can become an undesirable element of a job. Organizations are becoming increasingly concerned about the impact of stress upon their employees. Perhaps this motivation is caused in part by recent court decisions ruling in favor of plaintiffs seeking compensation for heart attacks allegedly caused by work stress. Similar rulings have been made in favor of plaintiffs suffering from alcoholism related to the job. In other cases, organization's motivation for helping employees manage stress is a sincere concern for their welfare. Since OD programs strive for organizational health, stress management is a possible intervention directed at both the individual and the organization.

The U.S. Department of Health and Human Services statistics reveal some of the potential costs of stress:

- Approximately 24 million people suffer from hypertension.
- Over 20 million people are alcoholic.
- About 650,000 people die annually from heart attack (almost 200,000 under 65) and 200,000 from strokes.
- Attempted annual suicides are estimated at 200,000 to 400,000, with about one in eight being successful.

Sources of Stress

Stress can be traced to on-the-job activities and to events occurring away from work. But because people cannot completely separate their work and personal lives, the way people react and handle stress is a complex issue.

One of the first major studies of stress is being carried out by Cary Cooper and Andrew Melhuish who identified 500 male senior British executives and are following them for a ten-year study.[12] The primary purpose of the study is to identify those managers who are under stress and then to determine the major causes of the stress. Though the study is not complete, it does indicate the costs of stress and some of the stress-related problems faced by managers.

In the initial research, it was found that 24 percent of the sample had one or two drinks per day, 11 percent had between three and six drinks, and almost 2 percent had more than six. The usage of drugs was just as alarming: 30 percent had taken or were taking tranquilizers and 24 percent took sleeping pills. Of those managers who said they were under stress, 57 percent said it was related to work and 45 percent said it was family problems created by work. For those indicating that work caused their stress, 34 percent indicated their relationship with their boss was the problem, 34 percent said they were frustrated over their future career, and 30 percent said the hours away from their family caused the stress.

The study thus far has indicated some significant areas of concern, particularly as they relate to the work environment. Those managers identified by the study as being candidates for a heart attack usually had four characteristics:

1. Personalities that were extremely competitive, aggressive and impatient; feelings that they were under the pressure

of time (sometimes referred to as Type A coronary-prone behavior).

2. A recent job change that placed demands on time and relationships.

3. A job with an organization with poor climate and little social support.

4. Involved in a situation where personal values were in conflict with those of the organization.[13]

The same study explored emotional and mental ill health as it related to work life. For the group of managers identified in this category it was found that the typical manager tended to be of fairly high intelligence, tense, and suspicious. Further, there is a high degree of job insecurity (such as fear of being laid off), office politics, competition, and lack of teamwork and mutual support.[14]

To summarize, potential stressful work activities include a change in policy, reorganization, unexpected changes in work schedules (overtime), conflicts with other people (subordinates, superiors, and peers) and other departments, lack of feedback, not enough time to perform expected duties, lack of participation, and ambiguity in duties expected to be performed. Stressful events occurring away from work are far-reaching but often include problems related to marriage, children, a serious illness, death of a family member or friend, finances, change in social activities, impending retirement, life and career goals, and environmental pollution (noise, traffic, and air quality). One study of more than 5,000 persons suffering from stress-related illness attempted to identify the major sources of life stress, as shown in Table 9.1[15]

Job Burnout

Job burnout refers to the negative effects of working conditions where job stress seems unavoidable and sources of satisfaction or relief seem unavailable.[16] Job burnout commonly results in a state of physical, emotional, or mental exhaustion.

Recently job burnout has come to be recognized as a major work stress problem. Burnout seems to be most common among professionals who must deal extensively with other people—clients, subordinates, customers on the job. The professionals who seem to be most vulnerable to job burnout include accountants, lawyers, managers, nurses, police officers, social workers, and teachers. While accurate statistics are not available, it has been estimated that about 20 percent of business owners, managers, professionals, and technical people in the U.S. suffer from job burnout.[17]

Those persons who experience job burnout seem to have some common characteristics which tend to be associated with a high probability of burnout. They tend to:

TABLE 9.1 The Social Readjustment Rating Scale

Life Event	Mean Value
1. Death of spouse	100
2. Divorce	73
3. Marital separation	65
4. Jail term	63
5. Death of close family member	63
6. Personal injury or illness	53
7. Marriage	50
8. Fired at work	47
9. Marital reconciliation	45
10. Retirement	45
11. Change in health of family member	44
12. Pregnancy	40
13. Sex difficulties	39
14. Gain of new family member	39
15. Business readjustment	39
16. Change in financial state	38
17. Death of close friend	37
18. Change to different line of work	36
19. Change in number of arguments with spouse	35
20. Mortgage over $10,000	31
21. Foreclosure of mortgage or loan	30
22. Change in responsibilities at work	29
23. Son or daughter leaving home	29
24. Trouble with in-laws	29
25. Outstanding personal achievement	28
26. Wife begins or stops work	26
27. Begin or end school	26
28. Change in living conditions	25
29. Revision of personal habits	24
30. Trouble with boss	23
31. Change in work hours or conditions	20
32. Change in residence	20
33. Change in schools	20
34. Change in recreation	19
35. Change in church activities	19
36. Change in social activities	18
37. Mortgage or loan less than $10,000	17
38. Change in sleeping habits	16
39. Change in number of family get-togethers	15
40. Change in eating habits	15
41. Vacation	13
42. Christmas	12
43. Minor violations of the law	11

Source: Reprinted by permission of Elsevier Science Publishing Co., Inc. from "The Social Readjustment Rating Scale," T. H. Holmes and R. H. Rahe, *Journal of Psychosomatic Medicine*, 11, 213–218. Copyright © 1967 by The American Psychosomatic Society, Inc.

- Experience a great deal of stress as a result of job-related stressors.
- Be perfectionists and/or self-motivating achievers.
- Seek unrealistic or unattainable goals.

Under the stress of burnout, the individual is no longer able to cope with the demands of the job and the willingness to try drops dramatically.

The costs of job burnout, both to organization members suffering from this syndrome and to organizations, can be high. Programs for coping with stress, which are examined in the last section of this chapter, are also useful in reducing causes and symptoms of job burnout.

Stress Management Programs _____

The programs to reduce stress are as numerous as the causes. Stress management is a concept new to most organizations and the solutions have been generally limited to individual programs. The individual response is a typical solution for organizations not involved in an OD program. An OD approach recognizes that the organization may create stressful situations. The total systems approach of OD dictates both an organizational and individual approach to reducing stress. The majority of this book deals with organizations building a healthy work climate that will reduce the amount of stress placed upon the individual. There are several methods for providing training and programs for individual stress management.

Biofeedback. A biofeedback course will usually take from several weeks to 3 or 4 months. The course takes place in a clinic with a trained technician and will normally begin with an analysis of the person's stress points: work, family, and so on. Then the person's physical reaction to stress is measured by being connected to instruments that can measure brain waves, heart activity, temperature, and muscle activity. By receiving biological feedback from the monitoring machines, the person learns to control his or her autonomic nervous system. With practice the person no longer needs the feedback from the monitoring devices and can practice "biofeedback" out of a clinic and in a work or personal activity that is stressful.

Transcendental meditation (TM). TM has become popular in dealing with stress and courses are being offered in universities, military commands, and work organizations. TM is an individual method for dealing with stress, although it has been used by entire organizations. Meditators spend two 20-minute sessions a day meditating—one in the morning and another in the late afternoon. The training usually takes as little as a couple of months and is conducted in groups. Some of the results seem to be encouraging. Meditators often report an inner peace and acceptance of themselves, higher energy and productivity levels, ability to get along better with others, lowered metabolic rates such as heart rate, and increased creativity. Meditators normally reduce their usage of alcohol and other dependent drugs. TM is so highly regarded by some companies that they have established a room for meditation. In one research project that compared employees in several companies who had been meditating for about a year with a control group, the meditators reported significant improvement in job satisfaction, performance, and relationships with supervisors and peers.[18]

Career counseling. Some cases of stress in people may need to be treated with counseling. The sessions may be in a one-to-one or group session.

Training programs in stress management. The training programs may be wide based and include instruction in time management, delegation, counseling of subordinates, self-awareness, relation techniques, and identification of stress situations and symptoms. Participation in the programs is usually organization-wide and often open to spouses as well.

Wellness program. A proper diet that is balanced and low in cholesterols and a proper exercise program can assist some people in dealing with stress. Some organizations offer wellness programs for employees to improve diet and exercise. A few companies have spent large sums of money to build gyms and elaborate training facilities.

Seminars on job burnout. Seminars to help employees understand the nature and symptoms of job problems and workshops on role clarity and analysis (see Chapter 10) have been used in a number of large companies, including Burlington Industries, Campbell Soup Company, IBM, Johnson & Johnson, and Xerox.[19]

REVIEW QUESTIONS

1. What are the advantages and disadvantages of laboratory training?

2. How can the Johari Window model be used as a tool to understand interpersonal communications?

3. How might programs identify and help reduce job burnout?

KEY WORDS AND CONCEPTS

Define and be able to use the following:

Laboratory learning   Stress management
Johari Window model   Biofeedback
Job burnout   TM
Career life planning

**IV.
Simulations**

SIMULATION 9.1   JOHARI WINDOW

Total time suggested: 45 minutes.

A. Purpose

This simulation is intended to provide you with information to compare your perceptions of your own Johari Window with perceptions of others. The survey can be a method to initiate further thought and self-exploration about your communications and interpersonal relations.

B. Procedures

Step 1   After completion of the case in this section or some other team activity, rate your team members by following the instructions in the Johari Window Survey. Additional surveys can be conducted with other team projects.
Time suggested for Step 1: 30 minutes.
Step 2   As a team, discuss the following:

1. Are the results for feedback and disclosure similar for the way I see myself and the way others see me? If they are different, to what could this be attributed?

_____
_____
_____
_____
_____

2. Do my scores seem reasonable?

_____
_____
_____
_____
_____

3. Am I as public, blind, closed, and unknown in my interpersonal styles as I thought I was?

_____
_____
_____
_____

4. If I am not satisfied with my style, what can I do to change? Anything specific?

_____
_____
_____
_____

Time suggested for Step 2: 15 minutes.

JOHARI WINDOW SURVEY

Rating Scale and Instructions

Following is the six-point values scale that you are to use in rating all your team members on the 10 Behavior Characteristics. First, become familiar with the 10 behavior characteristics and then the criteria for the six-point values scale.

Value Scale	Meaning
5	Does this consistently.
4	Does this most of the time.
3	Does this frequently.
2	Does this occasionally.
1	Does this on rare occasions only.
0	Never does this.

Then write the names of your team members along the top of the columns on the Rating Sheet. Be sure to notice that the last column is for yourself. Read over the Behavior Characteristics and determine how much each applies to the person you are rating. Select a value from 0 to 5 that reflects the degree to which this behavior is characteristic of the person.

Enter this value in the appropriate column for the person and the appropriate row for the behavior characteristic.

You may rate one person at a time on each of the 10 behavior characteristics or every person on each behavior characteristic as you go. Also feel free to use any value from the value scale as often or for as many members as you like.

Be sure to evaluate each person on all 10 Behavior Characteristics.

When you have completed your evaluations, cut the rating sheet into strips and give your team members their rating strips. You will, as well, receive a rating strip from each member of your team.

BEHAVIOR CHARACTERISTICS

1. Openly tries to influence others and control the team activities. Is not manipulative in influencing team action.

2. Interacts with the team in an open and candid manner. Is not closed and cautious in relations with others.

3. Listens to others and respects and accepts their comments. Does not dismiss or turn a deaf ear on the comments of others.

4. Says what he or she is thinking no matter how ridiculous it may be. Does not control remarks so they are in line with current ideas of others and thus be more acceptable to them.

5. If he or she feels that others are not leveling and being honest, he or she will press for additional information. Does not let the matter drop or change or allow the subject to be changed.

6. Makes sure that everyone on the team agrees and is committed to the team decisions by specifically testing or questioning them. Does not assume that members are in agreement just because they do not openly voice disagreement.

7. Takes risks in the team by exposing, when it is pertinent, highly personal information that may be both intellectual and emotional. Does not play it safe as though he or she does not trust others.

8. When others try to help him or her, no matter how critical to the point their comments may be, he or she welcomes and appreciates their efforts to help. Does not act hurt, angered, defensive, or rejective of their efforts.

9. Does things that allow others to participate, works to draw everyone into the team discussion, and is supportive of others. Does not just look out for self and leave participation up to each individual.

10. If he or she is angered or upset by others, he or she will openly confront them. Does not pretend to be unaffected or overcontrolled.

SURVEY INSTRUCTION SHEET

On each of your feedback strips you were rated on 10 Behavior Characteristics with a score of 0 to 5.

1. You have *two* types of feedback strips: you evaluating yourself and other people evaluating you. Divide the strips into these categories (notice that the word "self" identifies your self evaluation).

2. Record the data from the feedback strip labeled "self" in Table 1.

3. Add all your points from the "other" strips for each of the 10 behavior characteristics. Record the totals in Table 2, column 1. See the example below.

				Total (1)	Number (2)	Average (3)
4	5	3	2	14	4	3.5
3	0	–	6	9	3	3

4. For Table 2 determine the average for each Behavior Characteristic and record this in column 3. If you were not evaluated on every Behavior Characteristic on every list, remember to consider this in your average. See the example above.

5. Move the averages to columns 4 or 5 as indicated and total the two columns.

6. The total in column 4 represents your feedback score. This is the degree to which you actively solicit information about yourself. Compare the scores of how you think you solicit information about yourself with how others observe you soliciting information. Record both scores on the "feedback" part of the charts by drawing a vertical line at the score.

7. The total in column 5 represents your disclosure score. This is the degree to which you are open and candid of your feelings and the degree to which you share factual information that you know. Again compare your own perceptions of yourself with the perceptions of others about you. Record the scores on the "disclosure" part of the charts by drawing a horizontal line at the score.

RATING SHEET

Behavioral Characteristics

←— Team Members —→   Self

1	
2	
3	
4	
5	
6	
7	
8	
9	
10	

RATING SHEET

Behavioral Characteristics

←— Team Members —→   Self

1	
2	
3	
4	
5	
6	
7	
8	
9	
10	

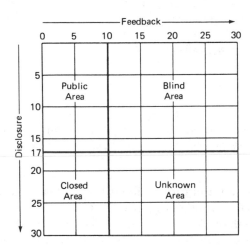

Feedback → 0 5 10 15 20 25 30 / Disclosure ↓ 5 10 15 17 20 25 30

Public Area — Blind Area
Closed Area — Unknown Area

From Self Feedback List (1)	Move Col. (1) to Col. (4) or (5) as Indicated — Feedback (4)	Disclosure (5)	Behavior Characteristics	Total from "Other" Feedback Lists (1)	Number of Times Evaluated on each Characteristic (2)	Average for each Characteristic Col. (1) = Col. (2) (3)	Move Averages in Col. (3) to Col. (4) or (5) as Indicated — Feedback (4)	Disclosure (5)
			1					
			2					
			3					
			4					
			5					
			6					
			7					
			8					
			9					
			10					
Total →						Total →		

TABLE 1 — SELF RATINGS

TABLE 2 — OTHER'S RATING OF ME

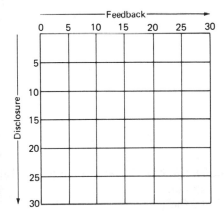

Feedback → 0 5 10 15 20 25 30 / Disclosure ↓ 5 10 15 20 25 30

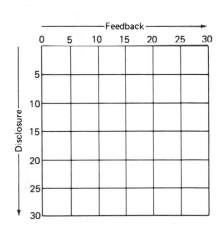

Feedback → 0 5 10 15 20 25 30 / Disclosure ↓ 5 10 15 20 25 30

SIMULATION 9.2 CAREER LIFE PLANNING

Total time suggested: 1 hour, 10 minutes.

A. Purpose

This simulation will give you experience in preparing career and life plans and in acting as a helper for someone else formulating career life plans.

B. Procedures

Step 1 Individually prepare a set of career life goals. The list could include career, professional, personal, and relational goals (list 1).

Step 2 Divide into diads with one person acting as a consultant. The consultant then goes through the list reality testing, determining priorities, and looking for conflicting goals. Revise the list as necessary. When one person has completed, trade roles.

Time suggested for Step 2: 20 minutes.

Step 3 Individually make a list of important past accomplishments or happenings, including peak experiences, accomplishments, things that have made you feel happy or satisfied, or times when you felt most alive or real (list 2).

Step 4 With each person taking a turn at being a consultant, work through a comparison of the individual's goals (list 1) with the list of past achievements (list 2); look for conflicts or incongruencies between the two lists.

Time suggested for Step 4: 20 minutes.

Step 5 The outcome of Step 4 is a set of firm goals with relative priorities. Each person now prepares a detailed plan of action specifying how to get from where he or she is to where the goal indicates he or she should be.

Time suggested for Step 5: 15 minutes.

Step 6 As a class critique the usefulness of a career life planning session. Additional questions include:

- What things did the consultants say or do that were helpful?
- What things did the consultants think they did that were helpful?
- What things did the consultants think they did that were not helpful?
- What things would the consultants not do again?

Time suggested for Step 6: 15 minutes.

**Case:
The Sundale
Club**[20]

BACKGROUND

The Sundale Club is the largest athletic-social club in the city. It has been established for many years and has a prestigious reputation. Currently, the membership is slightly under 1,000. In the past, Sundale has had a waiting list for those wishing to join. However, in the past few months the list has been exhausted and the director, Bob Watts, is considering a membership drive to fill unexpected membership vacancies.

Alice Smith had been thinking about her modeling job on her way home that evening. Today had been a dandy. Ted Ellis, the athletic director, had fired Pat Franklin, who had worked for Sundale for nearly 9 years (see Exhibit 1).

THE PROBLEM

The whole mess started 5 months ago when Ellis hired Chuck Johnson to become the men's activity manager. Shortly after Johnson arrived, rumors started that he was a homosexual. Although Johnson did not fit the stereotype of a homosexual, two of the members complained to Frank Havens, the assistant athletic director, that Johnson had made verbal passes at them.

Ted Ellis and Johnson were close friends, so Havens was reluctant to approach his boss with this problem. During the next few weeks more incidents concerning Johnson's behavior were reported by various staff members to Havens, in addition to complaints from club members.

STAFF DIRECTORY

Director · · · Bob Watts

Social Director · · · Carol Happ

Athletic Director · · · Ted Ellis

Asst. Athletic Director · · · Frank Havens

Women's Activities Manager · · · Pat Franklin

Mixed Activities Manager · · · Jim Mercer

Men's Activities Manager · · · Chuck Johnson

Women's Fitness Coordinator · · · Alice Smith

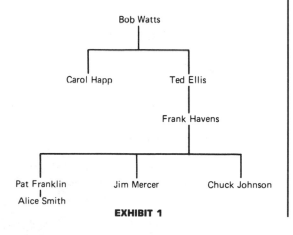

EXHIBIT 1

Havens could sense that his staff was wondering why he had not done something about the situation, and he was aware that seven of the male members had withdrawn from the club. Finally, he requested a meeting with Ted Ellis.

The Meeting

The meeting with Ellis did not go well. Ted Ellis was extremely defensive about Johnson and shouted, "Chuck Johnson has more savvy about this business in his little finger than the whole bunch of you put together."

That night, Frank decided to go over Ellis's head and talk to Bob Watts. Watts was due to retire in the next year, so he did not want to rock the boat in the final days of his tenure with Sundale. He tried to convince Frank that it was just a silly rumor.

Frank's working relationship with Ellis was very strained and he continued to receive pressure from below. That week Frank quit the organization and went to work in the same capacity for the competition. The next day, Johnson, who had been working for Sundale 5 months now, was promoted as the new assistant athletic director.

THE INCIDENT

Pat Franklin was bent! The entire athletic department, with the exception of Ellis, was shocked. Pat had been very dedicated to her job and the organization. Additionally, there was never a doubt that she would get Frank Haven's job when he moved up.

Pat Franklin burst into Ellis' office and demanded to know why she had not gotten the promotion. The next few minutes were rather ugly. Pat left Ellis' office, went to her own office, and began to cry. A knock at the door stopped the flow of tears, but after entering, Alice Smith could tell immediately something was wrong. Pat explained that she had just been fired, which started the tears again. Alice soon joined her.

On her way home, although very concerned about Pat, Alice was also concerned about her own future, and her part-time job as a model. Pat had allowed her to miss up to 8 hours from the Sundale Club each week to continue the modeling duties. Although she did not really need the modeling money, the job itself was very important to her from a personal satisfaction standpoint; she had to keep trim and well-groomed, which kept her thinking young. Also, the glamor aspects of the modeling profession satisfied her ego.

Carol Happ, the social director, was also starting to feel the effects of the internal turmoil created in the athletic department. Most of the Sundale Club's income was derived from the club's social activities. Further, Jim Mercer, the mixed activity manager, had noticed the impact of the turmoil within his own department.

Carol, acting on her own behalf, spoke privately to all the athletic department managers with the exception of Ted Ellis and Chuck Johnson. She had hoped to arrange a meeting with Bob Watts but found little support from that department because of their fear of Ted Ellis.

CASE ANALYSIS FORM

I. Problems
   A. Macro
       1. _____
       2. _____
   B. Micro
       1. _____
       2. _____

II. Causes
       1. _____
       2. _____
       3. _____

III. Systems affected
       1. Structural
       2. Psychosocial
       3. Technical
       4. Managerial
       5.

IV. Alternatives
       1. _____
       2. _____
       3. _____
       4. _____
       5. _____

V. Recommendations
       1. _____
       2. _____
       3. _____

V.
Summary

This chapter has presented an overview of several OD interpersonal interventions. The consultant and the client must examine a number of factors in deciding upon an intervention. They must determine not only the depth of intervention desired but also the relative advantages and disadvantages of various possible interventions in selecting one that is best fitted to their target system.

The Johari Window provides a way of thinking about ourselves in relation to other people. It also provides two major ways of getting to know and better understand ourselves and others: self-disclosure and feedback. The purpose of these two strategies is to enlarge our open areas as much as possible by reducing the blind and/or closed areas. To the extent that we gain clearer and more accurate perceptions of ourselves and others, we can improve our ways of communicating and working together.

Interpersonal interventions are based upon improving organization efficiency by increasing the individual's involvement, motivation, and competence. You have had a chance in the simulation to experience and practice these techniques. You may have gained some insights into your own relational style and recognized how such techniques might be used in an OD program.

One important notion regarding behavior change is the idea of *choice*. Prior to becoming aware of the consequences of certain behaviors, we often are behaving in certain ways because it has been relatively effective. However, this has been largely by habit and not by choice. As you begin receiving feedback on your "blind spots" and on the impact of your behavior on others, this opens up a choice. You can choose to continue behaving as you have and accept the consequences. Or you can choose to alter your patterns of behavior in hope of changing the consequences to more effective modes. Either way, once you have recognized the choices and take responsibility for your own actions, more authentic and effective behavior is possible.

Although research on the effectiveness of laboratory-learning programs indicates mixed results, there is evidence to suggest that this technique can influence managerial behavior. It has been used successfully in many change programs, such as the OD program at TRW Systems.

Career life planning also provides activities that assist the individual in reassessing his or her life and career goals and in redirecting his or her efforts toward new goals. You may now or at some point in the future be at a career decision point where you will want to use this technique to examine your own career or life plan.

Stress is a condition new to the twentieth century and is having an impact upon organization members. Stress management programs being implemented by organizations for their members include biofeedback, transcendental meditation, career counseling, training programs in stress management, wellness programs, and seminars on job burnout.

NOTES

1. See for example, Robert Kretiner and Fred Luthams, "A Social Learning Approach," *Organizational Dynamics*, Autumn 1984, pp. 47–65.

2. See the following for a more detailed description: L. Bradford, J. Gibb, and K. Benne, *T-Group Theory and Laboratory Method* (New York: John Wiley & Sons, Inc., 1964); and K. Back, *Beyond Words: The Story of Sensitivity Training and the Encounter Movement* (New York: Russell Sage Foundation, 1972).

3. Brian Simpson, "T-Groups, TA, NLP . . . What Should We Expect from Human Relations Training?" *Personnel Management*, November 1984, pp. 38–39.

4. See the following for a more detailed description: P. Buchanan, "Laboratory Training and Organization Development," *Administrative Science Quarterly*, 14 (1969),

466–80; and J. Campbell and M. Dunnette, "Effectiveness of T-Group Experience in Managerial Training and Development," in *Readings in Organizational Behavior and Human Performance*, eds. Larry L. Cummings and William E. Scott (Homewood, Ill.: Richard D. Irwin, Inc., 1969), p. 760.

5. David Bowers, "OD Techniques and Their Results in 23 Organizations," *Journal of Applied Behavioral Science*, October–November 1968, p. 380.

6. J. Anderson, "Giving and Receiving Feedback," in *Organizational Change and Development*, eds. G. Dalton, P. Lawrence, and L. Grener (Homewood, Ill.: Irwin-Dorsey, 1970). For discussion of these questions, see R. House, "T-Group Training: Good or Bad?" *Business Horizons*, December 1969, pp. 69–77; and W. Kearney and D. Martin, "Sensitivity Training: An Established Management Development Toll?" *Academy of Management Journal*, December 1974, pp. 755–60.

7. Frank Friedlander, "A Comparative Study of Consulting Processes and Group Development," *Journal of Applied Behavioral Science*, October–November 1968, p. 380.

8. J. Luft, *Of Human Interaction* (Palo Alto, Calif.: National Press Books, 1961); and J. Hall, "Communication Revisited," *California Management Review*, 15 (1973), p. 56–67.

9. Allen Ivey and Weston Morrill, "Career Process: A New Concept for Vocational Behavior," *Personnel and Guidance Journal*, March 1968, p. 645.

10. See John W. Lewis III, "Career/Life Planning," undated manuscript; and D. Kolb and R. Boyatzis, "Goal Setting and Self-directed Behavior Change," in *Organizational Psychology: A Book of Readings*, 4th ed., ed. D. Kolb, I. Rubin, and J. McIntyre (Englewood Cliffs, N.J.: Prentice-Hall, Inc., 1984), pp. 104–123.

11. See J.C. Quick and J.D. Quick, *Organizational Stress and Preventive Maintenance*, (New York: McGraw-Hill Book Company, 1984), pp. 2–6.

12. Cary L. Cooper and Marilyn J. Davidson, "The High Cost of Stress on Women Managers," *Organization Dynamics*, Spring 1982, p. 45. For the original study, see Cary L. Cooper and Andrew Melhuish, "Occupational Stress and Managers," *Journal of Occupational Medicine*, September 1980.

    For additional information on the management of stress see: Rabi S. Bhagat, "Effects of Stressful Life Events on Individual Performance Effectiveness and Work Adjustment Processes Within Organizational Settings: A Research Model," *Academy of Management Review*, 8, no. 4 (1983), pp. 660–71; John M. Ivancevich and Michael T. Matteson, *Stress and Work, a Managerial Perspective* (Glenview, Ill.: Scott, Foresman & Company, 1980); Arthur P. Brief, Randall S. Schuler, and Mary Van Sell, *Managing Job Stress* (Boston: Little, Brown & Company, 1981); and Karl Albrecht, *Stress and the Manager, Making it Work for You* (Englewood Cliffs, N.J.: A Spectrum Book, Prentice-Hall, Inc., 1979).

13. Cooper and Davidson, "The High Cost of Stress on Women Managers," p. 45.

14. Cooper and Davidson, "The High Cost of Stress on Women Managers," p. 46.

15. T.H. Holmes, and R.H. Rahe, "The Social Readjustment Rating Scale," *Journal of Psychomatic Medicine*, 1967, pp. 213–18.

16. L. Moss, *Management Stress*. (Reading, Mass.: Addison-Wesley Publishing Co., Inc., 1981), pp. 66.

17. D.P. Rogers, "Helping Employees Cope with Burnout," *Business*, October–December 1984, pp. 3–7.

18. David A. Frew, "Transcendental Meditation and Productivity," *Academy of Management Journal*, June 1974, pp. 362–68.

19. S.W. Hartman and J. Cozzetto, "Wellness in the Workplace," *Personnel Administration*, August 1984, pp. 108–17.

20. This case was written by Captain Pete Farmer, USAF, Fairchild AFB, and is used by permission.

OD TEAM DEVELOPMENT INTERVENTIONS

I.
Objectives

Upon completing this chapter, you will be able to:

1. Identify how team building techniques fit into an overall OD program.

2. Recognize team problems and why teams may not be operating at optimum capacity.

3. Understand and experience the concepts of team development.

II.
Premeeting
Preparation

1. Read the Background Information (Section III).

2. Complete Steps 1 and 2 of Simulation 10.1 (Section IV).

3. Read and analyze Case: Steele Enterprises.

III.
Background
Information

"All right. All right. Green right pitch twenty-nine wing T pull. On two."

My heart jumped and my mouth went dry at the call. I would have to crack back on Whitman, the outside linebacker on the righthand side. Crawford would try to get outside of my block with the help of the strongside tackle.

Whitman moved toward the sideline in a low crouch, stringing the play out and watching Andy and the leading tackle. At the last second he felt me coming back down the line at him. I dove headlong as he turned. He tried to jump the block and his knees caught me in the forehead and the side of the neck. We went down in a jumble of arms and legs, my shoulder went numb, and a hot burn shot up my neck and into the back of my head. The play gained eight yards.[1]

The excerpt above describes the team effort involved in running one football play for an 8-yard gain. Most of us have either participated in or watched games that involve teamwork. *Teamwork* may be defined as work done by a number of members, all subordinating personal prominence for the good of the team. In effective teams, members are open and honest with one another, there is support and trust, there is a high degree of cooperation and collaboration, decisions are reached by consensus, communication channels are open and well developed, and there is a strong commitment to the team goals.[2]

In this chapter we examine some reasons for using team building and discuss several work team interventions, including team development, role negotiation, and role analysis techniques.

THE TEAM APPROACH _____

Recently, organizations are beginning to emphasize teamwork and the team approach as a means of increased productivity and effectiveness. As an example, Ford Motor Company has recently begun to stress the team approach (see OD Application 10.1).

OD
Application
10.1

FORD'S SHIFT IN CULTURE

Up until a few years ago Ford was run by two of the best-known men in business, Henry Ford II and Lee A. Iacocca, and their disputes made the front pages more than once. Ford also generated losses of $3.26 billion in 3 years with products that were out of touch with the market and poorly built. Today, Ford's president, Harold Poling, and chairman and chief executive, Donald E. Petersen, work in relatively obscurity. "We don't want stars. Being part of a team is a much more productive environment," says Petersen and the company seeks to replace personality with low-profile teamwork. The efforts seem to be paying off. In 1986, Ford had a greater net income than long-time rival, General Motors—for the first time since 1924.

Team Development Programs

A radical shift is underway at Ford. The company once known for competing personalities, factionalism, and autocratic management recently established a school to teach its executives how to get along with one another: the team approach.

Mr. Petersen says that "through people we are going to have our best chance to make profits." So Ford is putting people throughout the company through an array of development programs. Ford is also putting managers (2,000 so far) through workshops where they take tests to analyze their management style and how they cope with change. Each person's results are displayed on his or her name tag. The workshops include a session at which participants confide what it is that they most admire about one another.

Cultural Change

Ford says it must change its culture because its employees must work together more effectively. Some at Ford who are more comfortable with autocratic management than they are with participative management are taking early retirement. "Guys who have lived in this environment and have succeeded in it . . . are emotionally trying to get through this," says Joseph Kordick, general manager of parts and service. "Some are making it and some are not, but most are making it."

Slow to Change

The emotional struggles may continue for some time. Of the 2,000 Ford managers given management-style tests in the company workshops, fully 76 percent were classified as noncreative types who are comfortable with strong authority. Samplings show that only 38 percent of the U.S. population would be so classified. But the test results haven't discouraged Mr. Poling. "Any time you're trying to change significantly the direction of a corporate culture," he says, "you have a basic level that you have to move from."

Questions:
1. Do you agree with Ford's team approach?
2. How would you go about implementing such a change?

Sources: Dale D. Buss, "Ford is Riding High with Smart Execution and Slashed Capacity," *Wall Street Journal*, October 7, 1986, p. 1; and Melinda Grenier Guiles and Paul Ingrassia, "A Better Idea? Ford's Leaders Push Radical Shift in Culture as Competition Grows," *Wall Street Journal*, December 3, 1985, p. 1.

The coordination of individual effort into task accomplishment is most important when members of a team are interdependent. Interdependence refers to situations where one person's performance is contingent upon how someone else performs. As an example, the success of a football running play depends upon the blocking of the linemen, the ball handling of the quarterback, and the running of the ball carrier. Although the running back carries the ball, there is a dependency upon teammates for blocking.

In an individual sport such as golf or track, on the other hand, the performance of a team is an accumulation of individual scores or performance. The team members are associates, but not interdependent. Among the three major professional sports, baseball, football, and basketball, according to Robert W. Keidel, basketball is more of a team sport than the other two.[3]

Baseball is basically a game of pooled interdependence where team member contributions are relatively independent of each other. Players are separated geographically on a large field, not all players on the field are actively involved in every play, and each player comes to bat one at a time.

Football, however, involves sequential interdependence where there is a flow of plays and first downs required in order to score. The players are closer geographically than baseball and there is a greater degree of interdependence. Players are normally grouped together functionally (i.e., offense and defense) and do not come in contact with one another. Unlike baseball, all players on the field are involved in every play.

Basketball exhibits the highest degree of interdependence. The players are closely grouped together and the team moves together on the court. Each player is likely to come in contact with any other player and the member roles or functions are less defined than football. All players are involved in offense, defense, and trying to score. Keidel suggests that organizations could use sport teams as a model for their organization. Some organizations require close teamwork similar to basketball, while other organizations require team involvement similar to baseball.

In most organizations, a large percentage of management activity is spent participating in group meetings. There is evidence to suggest that at least 94 percent of large organizations regularly use committees for problem-solving activities. Managers may complain about the excessive time spent in group meetings, but the trend seems to be toward increased use of group decision making.

One major OD technique, termed *team building* or *team development*, is used for increasing the communication, cooperation, and cohesiveness of units to make them more productive and effective. There are a number of reasons for using team development to improve organization effectiveness. First, the work group is the basic unit of the organization and thus provides a supportive change factor. Second, the operating problems of work groups are often sources of inefficiency.

Teams or work groups often have difficulty in operating effectively. Problems that inhibit effective operation include lack of clear objectives, interpersonal differences or conflicts, ineffective communication, difficulty in reaching group decisions, and inappropriate power and authority levels in the group. Consequently, team development techniques are used in change programs to increase work team effectiveness. The work team reviews and evaluates its own functioning and develops improved work and relational patterns. The emphasis is on exploring the team's functioning and processes by its own members, usually with the help of a process consultant.

THE NEED FOR TEAM DEVELOPMENT TECHNIQUES

The team or work group is the primary unit in the organization, and there is an increasing reliance on project teams, task force groups, and committees to accomplish organization goals. Work teams may be of two basic types. The first type, the *natural work team*, refers to people joining together because of related jobs or the structure of the organization design. The second type, the *temporary task team*, refers to groups meeting for limited periods of time to work on a specific project or problem, and after the solution of the problem they disband. As task teams are designated to work on organizational and technological problems, there is an increasing need for collaboration and coordination of the wide variety of resources that are brought together. Collaboration does not automatically happen, but it is possible with the use of *team development techniques*.

In deciding if team building is appropriate, Marvin R. Weisbord has described the process as being relatively straightforward.

> First, the boss calls a meeting, introduces the idea, states his or her personal goals and asks for discussion. If, as is common, a consultant has been hired, the parties need a "get-acquainted" meeting to decide whether to go forward. Often the consultant interviews team members to discover their basic concerns. Questions might include each person's objectives, the problems each faces, and the extent and kinds of help people need from each other. The consultant, then, presents a summary of interview issues to the whole team, inviting a discussion of priorities and the pros and cons of continuing the process. If the decision is made to proceed, the group schedules one or more longer meetings specifically for team building.[4]

The Use of Team Development

Some practitioners feel that team building is becoming an overused technique because "many teams agree they don't want to work together, can't work together, and have no reason to work together." As an alternative, Jerry Harvey has suggested a "team destruction" intervention, although he notes that this technique has not received overwhelming acceptance.[5]

Another OD consultant, David Casey, presents the viewpoint that team development is not appropriate for all teams.[6] He contends that the majority of work groups do not need to operate as a team. Situations which require interaction tend to fall into three categories: (1) simple situations; (2) complex situations; and (3) problem situations. The kind of task to be performed, then, determines the requirement of a team (see Figure 10.1).

The *simple situation* is one which can be solved by an individual. For example, an electronics engineer may need to consult occasionally with colleagues to obtain technical information in order to design a routine component, but the project is one which the engineer is expected to complete alone based on technical expertise. There is no need to involve others except to pass along or obtain information. The involvement of others may slow down the organization's functions. Managers operating in a simple situation focus on their own responsibilities, do not involve others in their work, and thereby avoid wasting valuable time. Good social skills are important, but team development is not needed for work groups involved with simple situations.

Teamwork and employee participation is not needed, according to Rosabeth Moss Kanter[7], when:

- There is one person who is obviously more of an expert on the subject than anyone else and those affected by the decision acknowledge and accept that expertise.

- There is an obvious correct answer.

FIGURE 10.1 Situation Determines Teamwork

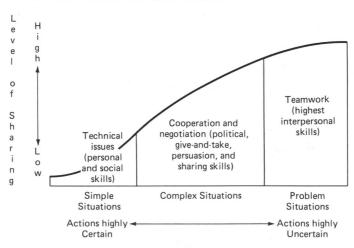

- The task or problem is part of someone's regular job assignment and it wasn't his or her idea to form the team.
- There is little or no interest in the issue.
- The involvement of others will not contribute to the issue nor would their knowledge or expertise be increased by the team experience.
- There is no time for discussion.
- Employees work more happily and productively alone.

Complex situations encompass the predominant portion of a group's work. There is a need to share information at a level that permits the work to be accomplished, since the members can not perform the task on their own. However, input is not required from all group members and the level of the input is not deeply personal. These types of activities arise constantly in most organizations and are handled by members cooperating with one another. For example, members of a finance department of a large company will need to cooperate with each other in getting out the quarterly financial statements. If acting alone, no one person will have enough information or time to complete the statements so information will be shared and members will help one another. Team development is not essential, but it is recommended because members need to cooperate and negotiate with each other and coordinate their activities. Good interpersonal skills are required including the ability to give and take, to see situations from another member's point of view, to negotiate, to persuade, to listen, and to share information.

Problem situations are atypical, consequential, unprecedented, and have an impact outside an individual's scope of influence. For example, a company that is planning to introduce a new product will have to work effectively not only within respective departments to formulate plans but also between departments to arrive at an overall strategy. The uncertainty involved with these types of problems and the need to involve others in the solutions requires a team-building approach.

Different modes of working require different processes. Kanter contends that the team approach is appropriate:

- To permit members to gain new expertise and experience and to develop and educate members.
- To allow those who know something about the subject to become involved.
- To build consensus and commitment on a controversial issue.
- To work on a problem that does not belong to any one person.
- To allow more creative discussions by pulling together people of unusual and different backgrounds and interests.

- To avoid the obvious decision and explore a variety of effects.[8]

Operating Problems of Work Teams _____

When individuals are brought together to work on some problem or goal of the organization, there is likely to emerge a rather complex pattern of behaviors, interactions, and feelings between the members. One of the primary functions will be to preserve the norms of the group and protect it from outside pressures perceived to be threats. Those people who receive rewards from and support the group norms represent a core group of "regular" members. At the other extreme are usually the "isolates," who have little to do with the others and seem to have little interest in and need for observing the group norms.

The work unit also serves three basic functions for the individual: (1) the satisfaction of social needs such as affiliation, acceptance, and status; (2) emotional support and identity for the individual; and (3) task accomplishment or assistance in attaining individual and group goals.

A survey sponsored by the American Management Association found the principal causes of organization conflict included value differences, goal disagreements, poor cooperation, authority and responsibility disputes, poor personal performance, frustration, competition for organization resources, not following policies and work rules, misunderstandings, and personality clashes.[9] The sources of work team operating problems or dysfunctional aspects, as shown in Figure 10.2, include the following:

Goals. The individual often has difficulty in defining and clarifying his or her goals, and in work teams the problem is multiplied. Often in work groups objectives become misunderstood, confused, or changed without any definite clarification. Similarly, groups tend to lose their purpose and direction, and they require testing from time to time to determine whether or not they are going full steam ahead, but in the wrong direction.

FIGURE 10.2
Sources of Work Team Problems

Member needs.   As previously noted, groups fill several needs of individuals, and frequently the satisfaction of completing the task is overemphasized at the expense of the social and personal needs of group members. There may be interpersonal differences, conflicts, or misunderstandings which hinder group effectiveness. Members may take sides and reject any compromise, or they may attack each other in subtle ways. Such interpersonal "garbage" or hang-ups need to be brought out on the table and dealt with.

Norms.   The team must develop norms about behavior patterns. Frequently, team members do not have the opportunity to communicate. Members need a chance to share problems, to discuss progress, and to touch base with one another.

Decision making.   Another frequent source of difficulty in groups is the way decisions are made. Decisions may be made by authoritarian decree, by majority vote, or by consensus, and each method has advantages and disadvantages. There is a good deal of evidence to show that decisions are implemented more effectively when the members have taken part in the decision.

Leadership.   One key issue for groups is the degree of power and control that the members have over themselves and others. As a consequence, groups sometimes suffer from a low level of participation, boredom, or apathy. Certain groups and individuals function better in a more structured, authoritarian situation, whereas others do not. For example, production units may operate better with more structure, while research groups probably do better with more independence.

Size.   A work team can consist of as few as 2 members to as many as 25 or 30, but 5 to 7 is generally considered the most effective size. Members of a small team behave differently than they would in a large team. A team of 2 or 3 generally is too small, whereas 12 members is probably the upper limit for the members to interact with every other member. With larger teams there is a greater likelihood that subteams of 5 to 7 will form to handle specific concerns.

COHESIVENESS

The term *group cohesiveness* refers to the attractiveness a group has for its members. Some groups have more closeness and team spirit among members, and such groups are more cohesive than those where members are indifferent. Cohesiveness can act to improve group performance. But as Irving Janis has pointed out, group cohesiveness can make the desire for uniformity greater than the need for high-quality decisions.

Groupthink is a term used by Janis to describe the problems of group cohesiveness. Groupthink refers to "a deterioration of mental efficiency, reality testing, and moral judgment that results from group pressures."[10] Groupthink occurs in a cohesive group when seeking agreement becomes such a dominant and overriding force that it tends to outweigh consideration of alternatives.

> The symptoms of groupthink arise when the members of
> decision-making groups become motivated to avoid being too
> harsh in their judgments of their leaders' or their colleagues'
> ideas. They adopt a soft line of criticism, even in their own
> thinking. At their meetings, all the members are amiable
> and seek complete concurrence on every important issue,
> with no bickering or conflict to spoil the cozy, "we-feeling"
> atmosphere.[11]

Janis identifies eight characteristics of groupthink and the problems tending to result from it:

1. *Illusion of invulnerability.* Most or all of the members share an illusion of invulnerability that masks obvious dangers and leads them to take extraordinary risks and causes them to fail to respond to clear warnings of danger.

2. *Rationalization.* Members construct rationalizations that allow them to discount warnings or other negative information.

3. *Illusion of morality.* Members unquestionably believe in the inherent morality of the group's position. Other groups with opposing views are thought of as evil. This type of thinking allows the group to disregard ethical or moral consequences of their actions.

4. *Shared stereotypes.* Views of opposing groups and especially their leaders are seen as evil or so stupid the opposing group could not possibly understand reasonable negotiations between differing groups.

5. *Direct pressure.* Direct pressure is applied to any other member who expresses doubts about the group's positions or who questions the validity of the arguments supporting a position.

6. *Self-censorship.* Avoidance of expressing views that differ from what appears to be a group consensus and even minimize to themselves the importance of their doubts.

7. *Illusion of unanimity.* An illusion that all group members are in agreement. It is partly based on the false assumption that individuals who remain silent are in agreement with the group.

8. *Mind guards.* Self-appointed members serve to protect the leader and other members from adverse information external to the group that might disrupt the cohesiveness of the group.

One example of groupthink is presented in the decision by President Kennedy's cabinet to invade Cuba at the Bay of Pigs. This was a classic example of illogical and inaccurate decision making, yet this group was made up of the finest minds in the nation, termed by David Halberstam as the "best and the brightest."[12] At one point Arthur Schlesinger questioned the quality of the decision, but was informed by Robert Kennedy, attorney general and brother of the president, that the president did not want to be bothered by dissenting remarks.

The consequences of such group problems are usually not clearly understood, but most managers agree that these problems influence motivation, morale, and productivity.

The Purpose of Team Development

A very broad objective of team development is integrating the goals of the individual and the group with the goals of the organization. To accomplish this, work teams need to spend some time on the process of their group interaction, that is, *how* they work together as well as what they accomplish. When a baseball team executes a difficult cutoff play, a basketball team executes a precise fast break, or a football team scores on a long pass play, it looks smooth and easy. Yet this ease and precision comes from hours and hours of practice and attention to details of *how* the play is run. For example, in *North Dallas Forty* the team examines game films:

> The meeting lasted over two hours. Tuesday was reserved
> for reviewing the films of the previous Sunday's game. The
> whir of the projector and the drone of B.A.'s voice were
> accompanied by the sound of forty stomachs churning in
> fear. It was bad enough to miscue in the heat and fury on a
> Sunday afternoon, but it was pure agony to sit alone in the
> dark on a cold steel folding chair while your mistake
> flickered forward, backward, in slow motion, and in stop
> action on a six-foot screen. Every misstep, stumble, and
> drop was carefully dissected and analyzed with a bovine
> detachment. B.A.'s dispassionate tones cut through the
> darkness to reduce the strongest men to cowards.[13]

The process of work teams in organizations is just as demanding and precise as in many sports activities, (See B.C. comic strip) but how many work teams ever examine their own performance? Not very many, and their reason: "We're too busy." Yet it is difficult to imagine any effective basketball or football team too busy to practice or review performance. This is what team development is all about. It is an intensive examination of team operation focusing upon *how* members function as a group, and how they can overcome operating problems and improve efficiency.

A *team* implies a group of individuals who depend upon one another to accomplish a common objective. Each team has its own structure, norms, and

B.C.: By permission of Johnny Hart and Creators Syndicate, Inc.

values, and members of the team tend to do things in certain ways. Often, the loyalty of members is greater to fellow team members than to the organization. Because of these characteristics, team development techniques are used to clarify goals and priorities, to examine how decision and communication are functioning, and to recognize how the relationships among team members influence output.

TRW Systems, for example, found that applying training techniques to the individual manager had limited return, so it moved into team development programs. "We learned that there had to be more emphasis on changing the ongoing organization on a day-to-day basis."[14] TRW Systems began to focus on the work group itself rather than on individual development, because team building and intergroup building seemed to be more relevant to the job situation.

The goals of team development include:

1. To identify objectives and set priorities.

2. To examine the content or task performance of the team.

3. To analyze group process; that is, how the group is functioning.

4. To improve communications and relationships among group members.

5. To improve the ability of the team in solving problems.

6. To decrease unhealthy competition and increase cooperation among the team members.

7. To work more effectively with other teams in the organization.

8. To increase the team members' respect for each other's individual differences.

It should not be inferred that conflict within a team leads to organization ineffectiveness and therefore should be avoided. Conflict in some situations may be healthy and improve the performance of a work group. Conflict is a natural social interaction and managers should be able to recognize the types of conflict and channel it in appropriate directions.[15] Conflict can be healthy when it is issue-oriented rather than personality-oriented, when it sharpens people's thought processes, when it is germane to the goals of the team, and when it does not produce winners and losers with the accompanying social stigma. The OD practitioner's responsibility is to find effective methods to deal with the conflict and resolve any unhealthy conflict.

THE TEAM DEVELOPMENT PROCESS

Organizations are becoming increasingly complex. No one person is able to possess all the knowledge necessary to satisfactorily analyze and solve such complex problems. In these instances, teams or work groups are used to bring together the expertise required for proper analysis and solution of the problem. Because of the nature of work groups, team-building interventions are probably the single most important and widely used OD activity. In at least one study of types of interventions used in OD, team-building activities were by far the most widely reported in use.[16]

The team development process, described by several practitioners,[17] recognizes two separate types of activities: (1) family group diagnostic meetings, aimed at identifying group problems; and (2) family group team-building meetings, aimed at improving the team's functioning. The following description incorporates both activities.

Team development is an educational process of continually reviewing and evaluating team functioning and identifying and establishing new and more effective ways of operating. Team development is an ongoing experience; that is, it is occurring simultaneously with the work itself.

A team development meeting has dual objectives: first, the task or work agenda of the group; and second, the processes by which members work on the task. Team development meetings, normally guided by a consultant, focus on the process of the team, including the team's working relationship and its patterns for accomplishing tasks. In the team development meetings, members learn how to look at their own ways of behaving, diagnose any operating problems, and determine new and more effective ways of functioning. It should be stressed that team development is not a one-time activity. Once a team learns how to do this, it can continue team development as an ongoing part of the group. The main purpose is to get team members involved in solving problems and in the decision-making process.

The procedure for team development training meetings generally follows a similar format, although the specific contents and activities of the meetings can differ significantly. Such a procedure includes certain basic steps.

Step 1: Initiating the Team Development Meeting

Within an organization the initiating of the team development meeting may come from several different sources. Operating problems of a group may have been identified and diagnosed through the previous stages of the OD program, and the team development meeting may be initiated by a manager higher in the organization structure who is not a member of the team. The need for a meeting may also be apparent to the consultant, or the manager of the work group may initiate the team development meeting. Although the initiating of the team development meeting may come from any of the foregoing people, the outcome of a successful meeting depends largely on the degree to which it is supported by the members of the team. The decision to proceed with a team development meeting is usually collaborative.

Step 2: Setting Objectives

After the decision to proceed, the next step is setting some broad objectives to be accomplished by the meeting. Such objectives might consist of evaluating the working processes of the team or improving their effectiveness. For an effective team development meeting, the entire team should agree on the objectives prior to the meeting.

The consultant may want to ask some pertinent questions before proceeding any further, such as: What is the purpose of this meeting? What do the participants and I want to achieve? Why this group of people at this time? How does this meeting fit into the OD program? What is the priority given to this project? Is there real interest and commitment among team members?

Step 3: Collecting Data

Data may be collected from the team members in various ways, but as much information as possible is gathered before the meeting. One source is the information that was gathered in Stage 4 of the organization change process: the collection of information (see Chapter 2). The usefulness of this information depends on the extent to which it can be identified with the problems of the team currently being worked with. Additional questionnaires may be administered to the team members, or they may be interviewed by the consultant. The consultant may have a minigroup meeting with the manager of the team and a selected number of participants. The consultant may also have a 2- to 4-hour preteam development meeting with all the members, designed especially to gather information.

Step 4: Planning the Meeting

The participants of the planning session may include any of the following: the consultant, the manager, and a few of the team members. Once the data have been analyzed, the actual planning may take place. An important point at this time is to restate the goals and objectives as specifically as possible. The goals should be specific behavior objectives so that the remaining work of planning the sequence of events of the meeting may flow more easily and logically. Going through this process will better ensure a meeting that satisfies the needs of all those involved.

Step 5: Conducting the Meeting

The meeting itself usually lasts 2 or 3 days. It is preferable that the physical setting be on "neutral territory," that is, away from the work area, such as at an isolated resort. One of the major reasons for this is that it helps to place everyone—superior and subordinate—on a more equal level, and it also lessens the opportunities for interruption. The nonwork setting can also help to create a climate for change and exploration of new ideas by the team members.

The meeting usually begins with a restatement of the objectives previously agreed upon. The data are presented to the entire team, with attention placed on problem areas or issues in which the team has expressed an interest, and then the team forms an agenda ranked in order of priority. At this point the team usually begins to work on the list of priority items. The team critiques its own performance to prevent dysfunctional actions and to improve functional activities. If the members feel that this is an opportunity for them to express open and honest feelings without fear of punishment, the superior or the leader of the team may come under attack. The premeeting interviews will have indicated this possibility and the leader should be forewarned and prepared by the consultant for this eventuality. The way the manager reacts to the situation can mean success or failure to the team development meeting. Once the interpersonal issues have been resolved, the team members can deal with task issues that need to be discussed in order that they may better solve their problems. The purpose is for the team to develop specific action plans for improving the ways or processes it uses to reach its organization goals. Before the meeting terminates, the team should make a list of action items to be dealt with, who will be responsible for each item, and a time schedule. This will allow the team meeting to officially terminate, but it also allows the team development effort to continue back in the work environment. The team further agrees on a future date to meet again to evaluate progress on the action items.

Step 6: Evaluating the Team Development Process _____

In this meeting the team examines the action items, exploring those that have been or are being implemented and those that do not seem to be working. Determination is made of how well the implemented action items have aided the team's operation and what further can be done. For those items that do not seem to be working, an evaluation is made as to their necessity, and those action items that are not needed may be discarded. Items that appear to be helpful may then be given additional attention and support.

John Zenger and Dale Miller suggest that effective teamwork is a key factor in achieving organizational goals and present their findings on the effectiveness of one team development program[18]

Donald F. Harvey and Neal Kneip, in a study of a team-building intervention in one major corporation, found that team activities resulted in a greater clarification of problems and an awareness of a need for change in the organization.[19]

ROLE NEGOTIATION _____

Role negotiation, a technique developed by Roger Harrison, is directed at the work relationships among group members. The technique basically involves a series of controlled negotiations between participants. In the course of the role negotiation, managers frankly discuss what they want from each other and explain why. The Diamond Shamrock Corporation teaches its managers the art of negotiation with one another during 3-day sessions at an off-site, resort setting. (It should be noted that before role negotiation takes place, the proper climate should be set. For example, at Diamond Shamrock, the first day and a half are used to create this climate before the actual role negotiation even begins.)

The steps of role negotiation include the following:

1. *Contract setting*: Each member prepares a list for each other member with three headings: (a) things to do more, (b) things to do less, and (c) things to do the same.

2. *Issue diagnosis*: Each member writes out a master list combining the lists written about him or her, and this list is posted on the wall. Members are then asked to clarify any items that need explanation.

3. *Role negotiation*: After the clarification, members decide which items they want most and sit down in pairs to negotiate, usually with a third party to assist in the process.

4. *Written role negotiation agreement*: The outcome of the role negotiation is a set of written agreements spelling out the agreements and concessions which each party finds satisfactory.

Role negotiation seems to be an effective way of improving team performance. At Diamond Shamrock they feel that the program has produced tangible benefits and more than 200 managers have attended such sessions.[20]

ROLE ANALYSIS

Another team-building intervention, called the *role analysis technique* (RAT), is designed to clarify role expectations.[21] Because group norms influence member behavior, members form expectations about one another's behavior patterns. The set of behaviors or attitudes associated with a particular position in a group is called a role. Several studies have pointed out discrepancies between the bosses' expectations of subordinates and subordinate's perception of what is expected of him or her.[22] *Role analysis* is used to clarify such role discrepancies, leading to improved group cohesiveness and functioning.

Role expectations are those behaviors of one member (role incumbent) expected or prescribed by other group members, while *role conception* refers to the focal person's own ideas about appropriate role behavior. *Role ambiguity* refers to the role incumbent's being unaware of or lacking sufficient knowledge of the expectations of others. In other words, he or she does not fully know what is expected by others.

When there is an incongruence or a discrepancy between the role expectations and the role conception, then *role conflict* occurs. Incongruence between formal job descriptions and actual role demands is another source of role conflict. Because the group members have a stake in each person's performance, they develop attitudes and expectations about what a member should or should not do in his or her role. Unfortunately, these expectations cannot always be in agreement, and role analysis provides a means for dealing with such problems. This intervention is based on the premise that consensual agreement about group member roles will lead to a more productive and satisfied team.

The steps of role analysis technique include the following:

1. *Role analysis.* The role incumbent sets forth the role as he or she perceives it, listing perceived duties, behaviors, and responsibilities: the role conception. Other group members add to or modify this list until all group members are satisfied with the role description.

2. *The role incumbent's expectations of others.* A listing of the role incumbent's expectations of other group members is now set forth. This list describes those expectations of others that affect the incumbent's role and impinge upon his or her performance. Once again, the whole group adds to or modifies this list until a complete listing is agreed upon.

3. *Role expectations*. The other members now list their expectations of the role incumbent. This list includes what they expect him or her to do and accomplish as it affects their role performance. This list is also modified until it is agreed upon by the entire work group.

4. *Role profile*. Upon agreement of the role definition, the role incumbent is then responsible for making a written summary called a *role profile*. A copy of the completed role profile is then distributed to each group member.

5. The preceding procedure is followed until each group member has completed a written role profile.

6. Periodically, the group reviews role expectations and role profiles, since these may change over time and group mission or members may also change.

As with other OD techniques, there are reports of increased effectiveness from role analysis techniques, but there is little empirical evidence upon which to base any conclusions. According to Dayal and Thomas, role analysis has been a useful technique for reducing role ambiguity and increasing group effectiveness.[23]

REVIEW QUESTIONS

1. Identify the characteristics of effective teams.

2. Identify and give examples of ways of increasing team effectiveness.

3. Identify the symptoms of groupthink. Explain how groupthink can be avoided through team development.

4. Identify the six steps in the team development process.

KEY WORDS AND CONCEPTS

Define and be able to use the following:

Teamwork   Role conception
Interdependence   Role ambiguity
Team building   Role conflict
Natural work team   Groupthink
Temporary task team   Group cohesiveness
Role analysis technique   Role negotiation

**IV.
Simulations**

SIMULATION 10.1   ORGANIZATION TASK AND PROCESS

Total time suggested: 1 hour, 20 minutes.

A. Purpose

The two parameters of group effectiveness include (1) the determination of the *one* best solution to the problem and (2) the completion in the shortest amount of time.

The purpose of this simulation is to experience and observe parameters of interpersonal and group issues that inhibit effective organization functioning. Specifically, it is to experience interdependence and to observe:

1. How task information is shared among team members.
2. How various problem-solving strategies influence results.
3. How collaboration and competition affect group problem solving.

B. Procedures

Step 1   Form groups of six members each. Each individual is to select one general manager role from the following:

1. General manager, United States plant
2. General manager, Japan plant
3. General manager, Germany plant
4. General manager, Nigeria plant
5. General manager, Mexico plant
6. Observer

Any extra persons will serve as observers. If there are fewer than six members, a member may select more than one general manager role, but each team should have at least one observer.

Step 2 Following the Energy International Briefing Sheet you will find Role Descriptions and the Candidate Summary Sheet. Read *only* your role.
Time suggested for Steps 1 and 2: 10 minutes.

Step 3 Your group is to select the correct candidate based upon the data you will receive. There is *one* correct solution, and decisions are to be reached independently of the other groups.

The observer will not take an active part during this phase of the simulation. The observer will focus on answering the questions in Step 4 and in the Decision Critique Form in Simulation 10.2. All groups will begin upon the signal from the instructor.
Time suggested for Step 3: 45 minutes.

ENERGY INTERNATIONAL BRIEFING SHEET[24]

A. Instructions to the group:

  1. You are a committee made up of the general managers of Energy International.

  2. You have just flown into town.

  3. This is the first meeting of the group.

  4. You have just learned that E.I. will open a new Brazilian plant, and your first job is to select a general manager from among the seven applicants.

  5. Basically, the data you bring with you are in your head.

B. Assumptions that need to be made explicit:

  1. Assume that there is one solution.

  2. Assume that all data are correct.

  3. You have 45 minutes to work the exercise.

  4. Assume that today's date is April 1, 1988.

  5. There must be substantial agreement when the problem has been solved.

  6. You must work the problem as a group.

ROLE DESCRIPTIONS (READ *ONLY* YOUR ROLE)

General Manager, United States Plant Your group is a committee made up of the general managers of Energy International, a young, medium-sized, growing organization. The prime mission of E.I. is to locate and develop mineral claims (copper, uranium, cobalt, etc.).

The company's business has grown rapidly, especially in South America, where your organization has been made welcome by the various governments.

In a recent meeting the board of directors decided to develop a new property near Fortaleza, in northeastern Brazil. This operation will include both mining and milling production.

The date is April 1, 1988. You have come from your respective plants in different locations. This is the initial session of your annual meeting. Your first order of business today is to select a new general manager for the Brazilian plant from among the candidates on the Candidate Summary Sheet.

Fortaleza has a hot climate, one railroad, a scheduled airline, a favorable balance of trade, a feudal attitude toward women, considerable unemployment, a low educational level, a low literacy rate, and a strongly nationalistic regime.

The government has ruled that the company must employ Brazilians in all posts except that of general manager. The government has also installed an official inspector who will make monthly reports to the government. This report must be signed by the company's representative, who must be a Fellow of the Institute of Mineralogy.

There are a number of schools offering degrees in mineralogy; the most recently founded is the New Mexico Institute of Earth Sciences. This institute was established under a special grant and opened in 1961.

To earn a bachelor's degree in mineralogy, this school requires geology, seismology, and paleontology, in addition to the usual courses.

General Manager, Japan Plant   Your group is a committee made up of the general managers of Energy International, a young, medium-sized, growing organization. The prime mission of E.I. is to locate and develop mineral claims (copper, uranium, cobalt, etc.).

The company's business has grown rapidly, especially in South America, where your organization has been made welcome by the various governments. In a recent meeting the board of directors decided to develop a new property near Fortaleza, in northeastern Brazil. This operation will include both mining and milling production.

The date is April 1, 1988. You have come from your respective plants in different locations. This is the initial session of your annual meeting. Your first order of business today is to select a new general manager for the Brazilian plant from among the candidates on the Candidate Summary Sheet.

Fortaleza has a hot climate, one railroad, a scheduled airline, a favorable balance of trade, a feudal attitude toward women, considerable unemployment, a low educational level, a low literacy rate, and a strongly nationalistic regime.

The government has ruled that the company must employ Brazilians in all posts except that of general manager. It has also installed an official inspector who will make a monthly report, which must be countersigned by the general manager. By law, the general manager must have had at least three years' experience as a manager in charge of a mining operation.

There are a number of schools offering a degree in mineralogy, a degree essential to qualify for general membership in the Institute of Mineralogy. The smaller universities require three, the larger four, of the following special subjects as a part of their graduation requirements: geology, geophysics, oceanography, paleontology, seismology. The smallest is a women's university.

General Manager, Germany Plant Your group is a committee made up of the general managers of Energy International, a young, medium-sized, growing organization. The prime mission of E.I. is to locate and develop mineral claims (copper, uranium, cobalt, etc.).

The company's business has grown rapidly, especially in South America, where your organization has been made welcome by the various governments. In a recent meeting the board of directors decided to develop a new property near Fortaleza, in northeastern Brazil. This operation will include both mining and milling production.

The date is April 1, 1988. You have come from your respective plants in different locations. This is the initial session of your annual meeting. Your first order of business today is to select a new general manager for the Brazilian plant from among the candidates on the Candidate Summary Sheet.

Fortaleza has a hot climate, one railroad, a scheduled airline, a favorable balance of trade, a feudal attitude toward women, considerable unemployment, a low educational level, a low literacy rate, and a strongly nationalistic regime.

The government has ruled that the company must employ Brazilians in all posts except that of general manager. It has also installed an official inspector who will make a monthly report, which must be countersigned by the company's representative. None of the government inspectors can read or write any language but his own.

There are a number of schools offering degrees in mineralogy, but a passing grade in paleontology is essential to qualify for general membership in the Institute of Mineralogy. The largest university is the New York School of Mines, which requires the following special subjects for graduation: geology, paleontology, geophysics, and seismology.

General Manager, Nigeria Plant Your group is a committee made up of the general managers of Energy International, a young, medium-sized, growing organization. The prime mission of E.I. is to locate and develop mineral claims (copper, uranium, cobalt, etc.).

The company's business has grown rapidly, especially in South America, where your organization has been made welcome by the various governments. In a recent meeting the board of directors decided to develop a new property near Fortaleza, in northeastern Brazil. This operation will include both mining and milling production.

The date is April 1, 1988. You have come from your respective plants in different locations. This is the initial session of your annual meeting. Your first order of business today is to select a new general manager for the Brazilian plant from among the candidates on the Candidate Summary Sheet.

Fortaleza has a hot climate, one railroad, a scheduled airline, a favorable balance of trade, a feudal attitude toward women, considerable unemployment, a low educational level, a low literacy rate, and a strongly nationalistic regime.

The government has ruled that the company must employ Brazilians in all posts except that of general manager. It has also installed an official inspector who will make a monthly report, which must be countersigned by the company's representative. None of the company's employees or staff can read or write any language but Portuguese.

There are a number of schools offering degrees in mineralogy, and a passing grade in seismology is essential to qualify for general membership in the Institute of Mineralogy. The Massachusetts Institute of Sciences requires the following special subjects for graduation: geology, seismology, oceanography, and paleontology.

General Manager, Mexico Plant Your group is a committee made up of the general managers of Energy International, a young, medium-sized, growing organization. The prime mission of E.I. is to locate and develop mineral claims (copper, uranium, cobalt, etc.).

The company's business has grown rapidly, especially in South America, where your organization has been made welcome by the various governments. In a recent meeting the board of directors decided to develop a new property near Fortaleza, in northeastern Brazil. This operation will include both mining and milling production.

The date is April 1, 1988. You have come from your respective plants in different locations. This is the initial session of your annual meeting. Your first order of business today is to select a new general manager for the Brazilian plant from among the candidates on the Candidate Summary Sheet.

Fortaleza has a hot climate, one railroad, a scheduled airline, a favorable balance of trade, a feudal attitude toward women, considerable unemployment, a low educational level, a low literacy rate, and a strongly nationalistic regime.

The government has ruled that the company must employ Brazilians in all posts except that of general manager. It has also installed an official inspector who will make a monthly report, which must be countersigned by the company's representative, who must be an American citizen.

Fellowship in the Institute of Mineralogy can be obtained by men over 35 years of age who have otherwise qualified for general membership in the institute. St. Francis University, which is not the smallest school, requires the following special courses for graduation: paleontology, geophysics, and oceanography.

ENERGY INTERNATIONAL CANDIDATE SUMMARY SHEE

Name: R. Illin
Date of Birth: March 2, 1953
Passport: L3452—U.S.A.
Education: New York School of Mines, degree in mineralogy, 1973
Employment: Research Assistant, New York School of Mines,
1974–1976
Lecturer, Mineralogy, University of Bonn, 1982–1986
Manager, Utah Copper Mining Co. Plant, 1986 to date
Language command: English, French, German, Portuguese

Name: S. Hule
Date of birth: May 4, 1945
Passport: H4567—U.S.A.
Education: New Mexico Institute of Earth Sciences, degree in
mineralogy, 1971
Employment: Uranium Unlimited, Management Trainee, 1971–1973
Anaconda Copper Co. (Montana area), Geology Officer,
1974–1981
Manager, Irish Mining Co. Ltd., 1981 to date
Language command: English, French, Portuguese

Name: T. Gadolin
Date of birth: June 5, 1946
Passport: L7239—U.S.A.
Education: New York School of Mines, degree in mineralogy, 1971
Employment: United Kingdom Mining Board, Management Trainee,
1971–1973
Assistant Manager, N.D.B. Cheshire Plant, 1974–1982
Manager, Idaho Cobalt Minerals, 1982 to date
Language command: English, Portuguese

Name: U. Samar
Date of birth: April 6, 1954
Passport: H6259—U.S.A.
Education: Mass. Institute of Sciences, degree in mineralogy, 1975
Employment: Jr. Engineer, W. Virginia Mining Research Station,
1975–1984
General Manager, Liberian State Mining Plant, 1984 to
date
Language command: English, German, Swahili, Portuguese

Name: V. Lute
Date of birth: August 6, 1951
Passport: K62371—U.S.A.
Education: New York School of Mines, degree in mineralogy, 1972
Employment: Jr. Development Mineralogist, Ontario Mining Constr.
Ltd., 1972–1975
Assistant Chief Mineralogy Officer, Canadian Dev.

	Board, 1976–1979
	Plant Manager, Welsh Mining Co. Ltd., 1980 to date
Language command:	English, French, Welsh, Pekingese

Name:	W. Noddy
Date of birth:	August 7, 1944
Passport:	H63241—U.S.A.
Education:	St. Francis University, degree in mineralogy, 1969
Employment:	Assistant Manager, Société Debunquant d'Algérie, 1969–1973
	Manager, Kemchatka Mining Co., 1974 to date
Language command:	English, Portuguese, Russian, Arabic

Name:	X. Lanta
Date of birth:	September 8, 1951
Passport:	Q123YB—Canada
Education:	University of Quebec, Diploma in English, 1971
	Mass. Institute of Sciences, degree in mineralogy, 1974
Employment:	Technical Officer, Sardinia Mining Corp., 1976–1984
	Manager, Moab Valley Mining Plant, 1984 to date
Language command:	Spanish, English, Portuguese

Step 4   In your groups, consider the following questions:

1. What behaviors seemed to help your group to successfully complete its task?
2. What factors inhibited problem solving?
3. How much time was spent on deciding *how* to solve the problem?
4. How was information shared among the group?
5. How did issues of authority or power affect the group?
6. How did collaboration/competition influence the outcome?

Time suggested for Step 4: 10 minutes.

Step 5   Discuss the questions in Step 4 with the entire class.
Time suggested for Step 5: 15 minutes.

SIMULATION 10.2   TEAM BUILDING

Total time estimated: 1 hour, 20 minutes.

A.   Purpose

To provide an opportunity for team members to diagnose and analyze their team functioning and to work on improving team processes.

B.   Procedures

Step 1   Form into the same teams as in Simulation 10.1. Working individually and using Simulation 10.1 as a source of information, complete the Team Development Profile and Decision Critique Form.

Step 2 Working with your team, collect data on team roles from Step 1 by summarizing and categorizing data using a blackboard or newsprint. The observer can supply information using the Decision Critique Form.
Time suggested for Steps 1 and 2: 30 minutes.

Step 3 Team members analyze and discuss team functioning. Members may practice process consultant interventions (see Suggested Process Interventions). Observers give their observations.

The analysis may include the following questions:

1. How was our problem-solving capability?
2. How was our decision making done?
3. How well did we utilize team resources?
4. How did member behavior influence effectiveness?

Time suggested for Step 3: 20 minutes.

Suggested Process Interventions

Try to focus your questions on the problem that seems to be emerging. Encourage the speakers to be specific. Be aware of who is and who is not talking; who talks to whom.

Questions about how people are feeling at the moment are appropriate. As an example, such a question to a member as "How did you feel when X said _____ to you?" might be appropriate. Explore feelings with the purpose of discovering how these are helping or hindering the problem solution. Additional questions include the following:

1. What behaviors seem to be aimed more at individual member needs than at task accomplishment?
2. What behaviors seemed to aid in task accomplishment?
3. How satisfied are members with current group functioning?

Step 4 Working in teams, develop a list of actions that will help improve group functioning for future team projects.
Time suggested for Step 4: 15 minutes.

Step 5 Each team shares its list and action plans from Step 4, and the class discusses team development process.
Time suggested for Step 5: 15 minutes.

TEAM DEVELOPMENT PROFILE

Based upon the team problem-solving simulation, select two members of the group who best fit the role described in each of the following questions.

1 Name the two group members who had the most influence on the outcome.

_____

2 Name the two group members who talked the least.

_____

3 Name the two group members who talked the most.

_____

4 Name two group members who have tried to keep the group warm, happy, and comfortable.

_____

5 Name the two group members who have competed or conflicted the most.

_____

6 Name the two group members who have avoided or smoothed-over conflicts.

_____

7 Name the two group members who influenced the decision the least.

_____

8 Name the two group members most likely to bring irrelevant topics into the conversation.

_____

9 Name the two group members you would most like to work with on another project.

_____

10 Name the two group members who have been most concerned with accomplishment of the task.

_____

DECISION CRITIQUE FORM

How would you rate the quality of your group decision?

- Outstanding?
- Above average?
- Average?
- Mediocre?
- Inadequate?

In a few words or in a brief sentence, describe your impression of each group member's role behavior, including your own.

	Name	*Role*
1.	_____	_____
2.	_____	_____
3.	_____	_____
4.	_____	_____
5.	_____	_____
6.	_____	_____

**Case:
Steele
Enterprises**[25]

THE PR DINNER

Gene Robertson, Public Relations Director, Steele Enterprises, knew there was trouble as soon as he saw the room. Instead of the bars being set up, with the shiny glasses, fine liqueurs, and impeccably dressed bartenders, there was chaos. Tables of hors d'oeuvres were there but with no semblance of order. Flowers had been delivered but were not placed. Cocktail tables and other furniture were still stacked. Thank God I'm early, he thought.

Richard Leeman (Chemical, Public Relations Chief) and Donna Olson (Mechanical, Public Relations Chief) were arguing—really going at it, in fact, while Judy Fields and Joe Maxwell stood by rather uncertainly, looks of distress on their faces. Gene hurried over to intervene. This was not the time for those two to get into it again. Not with over 50 marketing representatives and buyers, ambassadors for over 20 of the primary marketing outlets to which Steele Enterprises sold most of its goods, arriving in about an hour and a half. Still time to put this thing together, he thought wearily (see Exhibit 1 for organization chart).

"OK, what's this all about?" Gene asked as he carefully but easily slid between the two.

"God, am I glad to see you!" gasped Donna, as she tried to catch her breath. "Dick is just being unreasonable about this whole. . . ."

"Unreasonable!" yelled Dick. "If Judy and I hadn't happened by, the cost of the hors d'oeuvres alone would be more than we'd planned on for the whole works! As it is, we'll exceed the budget by nearly $400!"

"OK, calm down," Gene soothed, as he gently but firmly eased Dick a couple of more feet away from Donna. "Now, one at a time, you first, Donna. What is going on?"

Donna, still angry, was at least breathing more normally by this time. "You told us to get the best for this party," she said accusingly. "We told the catering manager to bring out his best stock and get us a classy spread of heavy hors d'oeuvres, but to stay within the $1,500 figure, with labor extra. Things were going great until Dick showed up. Then he

Alfred Gamble	Western Area Regional Manager Steele Enterprises, Inc.
JoAnn Stone	Secretary to Mr. Gamble
Gene Robertson	Public Relations Director, Western Area Regional Office
Doris Mills	Secretary to Mr. Robertson
Richard Leeman	Chief of Chemical Branch Public Relations
Virgina Jewell	Secretary for Chemical Branch P.R., responsible to Mr. Leeman
Jack Whitman Judy Fields Sharon Marino	Chemical Branch P.R. specialists
Donna Olson	Chief of Mechanical Branch Public Relations
Cheryl Pearson	Secretary for Mechanical Branch P.R., responsible to Ms. Olson
Evelyn Horton Joe Maxwell Norman Clark	Mechanical Branch P.R. specialists

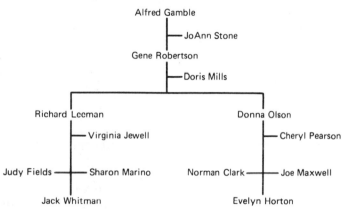

EXHIBIT 1   Steele Enterprises, Inc., Western Region, Public Relations Division

started nosing around, asking questions, giving orders, and has things all fouled up! Just look!" She waved her arms around the room, indicating the mess.

"Not true!" gritted Dick through clenched teeth. "When Judy and I got here, neither one of these two were in sight, the catering manager was trying to find out what was going on, and his cost sheet showed $2,500 instead of $1,500. I've canceled escargot, lobster tails, and the burgundy-soaked tenderloin strips, and told them to hold the liquor prices to a maximum of $15 a bottle, except for the liqueurs. Even with the cuts, food costs are going to be nearly $300 above our maximum estimate, because they've already got some oysters shelled, crab legs cracked, and shrimp peeled!"

"Hold it! Time out! Stop!" said Gene, appraising the situation. "We'll sort out who did what to whom later. Right now, we still have time to pull this thing back together and keep all our necks out of the nooses! Now, here's how we're going to handle this. . . ."

By the time the PR staff had been given their assignments (in clear, concise language, with no room for arguments), and by the time he had finished haggling with the catering manager (which cost him $50 under the table to the catering manager), getting the party cost down to within $100 of the estimated tab, *and* by the time the party was over (2:30 in the morning), Gene was really beat. It will be good to get home, he thought.

THE AFTERMATH

Gene came in about 11 o'clock the next day, and after finishing up the paperwork from the morning's mail, went to lunch. Something has to give around here, he thought. His secretary, Doris Mills, could see the consternation on his face as they sat down at the table.

"Are those two going at it again?" she asked when he finally came back to earth.

"If you mean Dick and Donna, yes," he replied. "I've just got to do something with them. I've never had two more capable people running those branches, and I don't think they've ever had a more capable staff. But this constant fighting between them just has to stop or I'm going to have to get rid of somebody, and I really wouldn't like to do that. Especially with that kind of talent. Even Mr. Gamble has kind of joked around the fact that the competition must be fierce in the PR business!" Gene looked thoughtfully at Doris. "Have you heard anything from JoAnn Stone?"

"Not about the bickering between Dick and Donna," replied Doris. "And if anything was wrong at the party, it never got passed down through the grapevine."

"Well, that's something," sighed Gene. "The fifty bucks I slipped to that jerk at the hotel to fix up the bill can at least be taken care of on the expense account. I'll call it incidental expenses or something." How lucky I am to have an efficient, competent secretary, who keeps her eyes and ears open and her mouth shut. I think she's about due for a raise, thought Gene as they ordered.

THE PROBLEM

Later that afternoon, in the privacy of his office, Gene reviewed the problems with his staff: Dick, Ginny, Judy, Jack, and Sharon in Chemical PR, and Donna, Cheryl, Norm, Ev, and Joe in Mechanical. We have the business and the budget to need that many people; the boss seems pleased with what we do; good, sharp people, every one of them, and yet a hell of a lot of fighting between the two branches. So far the staff under Dick and Donna haven't taken up the battle flags, but if I don't do something pretty soon, that could even happen, thought Gene. And the chemical-mechani-cal split suggested by Mr. Gamble, even though it's not working as it should, is out of my hands. Isn't it? worried Gene as he reviewed the backgrounds of the respective branch leaders. Something's wrong here, but what? he wondered. Maybe it's the technical breakdown, maybe we're not definite enough about which branch should work with which companies. And that fiasco last night—why did Dick come roaring in and try to take over when I thought I had made it pretty clear that Donna and her staff were to run that show? My orders *were* pretty clear, thought Gene, as he tried to assure his nagging conscience that he was doing a good job directing the PR efforts in the western region.

Good grief, I need a referee! thought Gene as he reviewed seven cases in the last 6 months in which he had had to intervene between Dick and Donna. Maybe I should try to trade one of them for Bob Lyons at the central region office at St. Louis, he mused, still feeling that he was, somehow, responsible for the conflicts.

CASE ANALYSIS FORM

I. Problems

   A. Macro

      1. _____

      2. _____

   B. Micro

      1. _____

      2. _____

II. Causes

      1. _____

      2. _____

      3. _____

III. Systems affected

      1. Structural

      2. Psychosocial

      3. Technical

      4. Managerial

      5.

IV. Alternatives

      1. _____

      2. _____

      3. _____

      4. _____

      5. _____

V. Recommendations

      1. _____

      2. _____

      3. _____

V.
Summary

One major OD intervention is termed *team development*, and it is a useful and successful vehicle for bringing about significant changes in a team. Team development includes team building, process consultation, and role analysis techniques. These techniques are used to increase the communication, cooperation, and cohesiveness of work teams, resulting in increased organization efficiency. It is important to remember that team development is only a part of an organization-wide change program that values participation, collaboration, and the maximization of the use of human resources.

Interdependence refers to situations where one person's performance is contingent upon how someone else performs. In the simulation you have had a chance to experience interdependence, since it required the combined inputs of all team members to solve the problem. You also experienced and observed differences in how problem-solving information is communicated and shared within a group. Some groups may have taken a very open and systematic approach to the problem, whereas others demonstrated the effects of closed or reactive behaviors. In the problem-solving process a great deal of time may have been spent on irrelevant topics, on going off on tangents, or on nonconstructive arguments among members, whereas very little time was spent on deciding how to best solve the problem. Some members may have talked too much when they had nothing helpful to say: others may have unintentionally withheld important information by their silence. Authority or lack of authority, and cooperation or competition, may also have influenced your group effectiveness.

In the simulation you also had an opportunity to participate in a team activity, and experience the team-building process. You have had a chance to see the influence of leader behavior and member behavior on a task outcome and to diagnose team problems and behavior. The feedback from the simulation should help you identify ways of being a more effective team member and should demonstrate how important team work and coordination are to organization efficiency.

NOTES

1. Peter Gent, *North Dallas Forty* (New York: William Morrow & Co., Inc., 1973), p. 264. Also a 1979 motion picture.
2. See David Casey, "When Is a Team Not a Team?" *Personnel Management*, January 1985, p. 26.
3. Robert W. Keidel, "Baseball, Football, and Basketball: Models for Business," *Organizational Dynamics*, Winter 1984, pp. 5–18.
4. Marvin R. Weisbord, "Team Effectiveness Theory," *Training and Development Journal*, January 1985, p. 27.
5. Jerry Harvey, "Eight Myths OD Consultants Believe In . . . and Die By," *OD Practitioner*, February 1975, p. 3.
6. Casey, "When Is a Team not a Team?" pp. 26–29.

7. Rosabeth Moss Kanter, *The Change Masters: Innovation for Productivity in the American Corporation* (New York: Simon & Schuster, 1983); and Rosabeth Moss Kanter, "Dilemmas of Managing Participation," *Organizational Dynamics*, Summer 1982, pp. 6–7.

8. Ibid.

9. K. W. Thomas and W. H. Schmidt, "A Survey of Managerial Interest with Respect to Conflict," *Academy of Management Journal*, 19 no. 2 (1976), pp. 315–18.

10. Irving L. Janis, *Victims of Group Think* (Boston: Houghton Mifflin Company, 1972), p. 9.

11. Irving L. Janis, "Groupthink," *Psychology Today*, November 1971, pp. 43–46.

12. David Halberstam, *The Best and the Brightest* (New York: Random House, Inc., 1972).

13. Gent, *North Dallas Forty*, p. 60.

14. "Team Work through Conflict," *Business Week*, March 20, 1971, p. 44.

15. Gordon Lippitt, Ronald Lippitt, and Clayton Lafferty, "Cutting Edge Trends in Organization Development," *Training and Development Journal*, July 1984, pp. 59–62.

16. W. J. Heisler, "Patterns of OD in Practice," *Business Horizons*, 18 (February 1975), pp. 77–84.

17. For a more detailed discussion, see R. Beckhard, *Organization Development: Strategies and Models* (Reading, Mass.: Addison-Wesley Publishing Co., Inc., 1969); and Jack Fordyce and Raymond Weil, *Managing with People* (Reading, Mass.: Addison-Wesley Publishing Co., Inc., 1971).

18. See J. Zenger, and D. Miller, "Building Effective Teams," *Personnel*, September 1976.

19. Donald F. Harvey and Neal Kneip, "The Results of an Integrated OD Program for Training and Team Building," a paper presented at Western Academy of Management, 1980.

20. "They're Striking Some Strange Bargains at Diamond Shamrock," *Fortune*, January 1976, p. 172.

21. Wendell L. French and Cecil H. Bell, Jr., *Organization Development: Behavioral Science Interventions for Organization Improvement* 2nd ed. (Englewood Cliffs, N.J.: Prentice-Hall, Inc., 1978).

22. Dennis C. Boyton, "Looking Out for the Best Interests of the Company," *Journal of European Industrial Training*, 6, no. 7 (1982), pp. 25–27.

23. I. Dayal and J. Thomas, "Operation KPE: Developing a New Organization," *Journal of Applied Behavioral Science*, 4, no. 4 (1968), pp. 473–506.

24. From J. William Pfeiffer and John E. Jones, eds., *The 1972 Annual Handbook for Group Facilitators* (La Jolla, Calif.: University Associates, Inc., 1972). Used by permission.

25. This case was written by Major Warren K. Funk, USAF, Fairchild AFB, and is used by permission.

11

OD INTERGROUP
DEVELOPMENT
INTERVENTIONS

I.
Objectives

Upon completing this chapter, you will be able to:

1. Identify problems of intergroup conflict and suboptimization.

2. Experience the negative effects of competition on organization effectiveness.

3. Observe and develop strategies for collaborative intergroup relations.

4. Diagnose the causes of cooperative versus competitive group relations.

II.
Premeeting
Preparation

1. Read the Background Information (Section III).

2. Prepare for Simulation 11.1 (Section IV). Read and familiarize yourself with the rules and procedures of the Disarmament Game. Complete Step 1.

3. Read and analyze Case: The Exley Chemical Company.

**III.
Background
Information**

One key area in the improvement of organization effectiveness involves the relation between operating groups or departments. Complex organizations tend to create situations of *interdependence*, where the performance of one group is contingent upon another group. Manufacturing depends upon engineering, production upon purchasing, marketing upon production, and so on. Consequently, managers must operate and function in an interdepartmental environment. Because of these contingencies, one of the most important dimensions in organization development is the interface between operating groups.[1]

Each organization is a system formed of subsystems: divisions, functions, departments, and work teams. Each work team develops its own norms, goals, and behaviors, and these forces contribute to the cohesiveness and morale of that group. When two groups are highly interdependent misunderstandings, low coordination, or conflict that can develop between the groups may be very dysfunctional for the organization. When groups are in conflict, a high degree of group effort, time, and energy is directed toward the conflict rather than toward goal accomplishment.

As a result of such problems, one set of OD interventions aims specifically at the improvement of these interdepartmental interface and intergroup operating problems. Such interventions attempt to bring to the surface underlying problems, to use joint problem solving, to correct misperceptions between groups, and to reopen channels of communication.

In this chapter, we examine some of the conditions for conflict and discuss several techniques for dealing with intergroup relations. Although the organization may have different functional or operating groups, each with specialized tasks and goals, there must be coordinated effort if it is to achieve organizational excellence.

COLLABORATION AND CONFLICT

An organization is considered to be a large system consisting of subsystems. It is clear that the subsystems have internal boundaries across which information and materials are exchanged. The points of intersection between departments are termed *interfaces*. The organization needs cooperation among its departments and divisions if it is to be effective. *Teamwork* implies that all members are contributing to an overall objective, even if it means subordinating personal prominence. In sports a group of individuals play together as a team, and usually their degree of success is a function of how well they cooperate and collaborate. The same is true of organization departments and groups. The climate of collaboration and the interface between work groups often determines organization effectiveness.

Richard Beckhard notes that "one of the major problems affecting organizational effectiveness is the amount of dysfunctional energy expended in inappropriate competition and fighting between groups that should be collaborating."[2] This competition and conflict originates in differences in objectives, values, efforts, and interests between groups. Some aspects of competition are consciously recognized and intentionally produced, whereas others are unconscious or unintentional. The interdependence of functions has been noted as one potential source of conflict.

Because of these potential group conflicts and because work teams are often interdependent, the relationship between work groups is a crucial element in organization efficiency. Within the organization there is a need for competition between these elements, but there is also a need for cooperation and collaboration. Many groups are interdependent; that is, they depend upon the exchange of resources with other elements to accomplish their own objectives. *Interdependence* is defined as a mutual dependence between groups. Often, however, these interdependencies introduce conflict into the organization system. There may be intense competition for resources, capital, or promotion between groups. For example, the personality conflict between Henry Ford II and Lee Iacocca, (then president of Ford) led to the resignation of Iacocca. Iacocca has since taken over the leadership of a major competitor, Chrysler Motor Corporation.

There is competition among divisions for all sorts of resources (financial, manpower, etc.), and often it becomes a win-lose situation. If the company decides to build a new manufacturing plant in Texas, it cannot build a new research laboratory in California. Such examples are numerous.

Conflict is increasingly perceived as inevitable. Whenever there is interdependence between units, their relationship must be worked out across boundaries. It has been reported that corporate managers spend one quarter of their time dealing with conflict, while public administrators (in schools, hospitals, cities, etc.) spend almost one-half of their time dealing with conflict. Therefore the manager's ability to manage conflict has become much more important.[3] Matrix organization is becoming increasingly common, and this design intentionally builds in controlled conflict as a means for integrating diverse activities.

Certain implications for the organization development consultant stem from this view of interdependent subsystems. First, the OD practitioner must be able to recognize the interdependence of organization units. He or she must also be aware that these interactions result in feelings and that these feelings often lead to conflicts. Finally, elements often operate without feedback, or "open loop" as it is termed. When this is the case, there is no mechanism for corrective action to take place.

One of the most important aspects of the organization is intergroup relations. Competition between groups often leads to conflict or dysfunctional behavior affecting operating efficiency. As a result, one objective of OD is to increase cooperation among organization subsystems. These intergroup interventions have been described as "the deliberate interaction of two or more complex social units which are attempting to define or redefine the terms of their interdependence."[4]

INTERGROUP OPERATING PROBLEMS

The potential for conflict (see Figure 11.1) depends on how incompatible the goals are, the extent to which required resources are scarce and shared, and the degree of interdependence of task activities. The chance of conflict is relatively low between groups that have their own resources and perform entirely different tasks directed toward completely separate goals. Electrical engineers and janitors seldom conflict because their tasks are largely separate. The potential for conflict is much higher between engineers and production managers, or between sales people and credit managers. This is true because such units tend to rely on common resources, their tasks are interdependent, and they frequently pursue incompatible goals (e.g., increasing sales versus reducing credit losses). Intergroup relationships are complex, and OD practitioners need to recognize the conditions that lead to the emergence of problems or conflicts. The conditions that are considered in this chapter are not exhaustive or mutually exclusive, but the important factors present in determining group relationships are discussed. The symptoms of such conflicts include complaints, gripes, verbal battles, inefficiency, and possibly sabotaging the other group in some way. (See CROCK comic strip.)

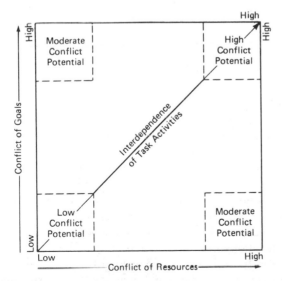

FIGURE 11.1
Factors Involved in the Potential for Conflict

CROCK by Rechin, Parker and Wilder. (c) Field Enterprises, Inc. by permission of North America Syndicate, Inc.

Suboptimization

When the goals of operating divisions are interdependent, optimization by one group may result in decreased goal attainment for other groups and the organization. As an example, engineering may design a product very quickly and inexpensively, but as a consequence the product is difficult, time consuming, and costly for the manufacturing department to produce. The financial group may cut costs by limiting hiring or overtime and may thus optimize its objectives, but other departments and the organization may lose profits or customers as a result. This is referred to as *suboptimization*. Suboptimization occurs when a group optimizes its own subgoals but loses sight of the larger goals.[5]

The objectives of OD interventions are aimed at decreasing suboptimization by increasing collaboration or integration between these interdependent groups. Paul Lawrence and Jay Lorsch studied six firms in the plastics industry and compared the level of integration with several measures of effectiveness. They found that effectiveness measures were closely related to the degree of integration.[6] From these data it may be hypothesized that suboptimization, or lack of integration, is a contributing factor to decreased organization performance.

Intergroup Competition

A second condition giving rise to intergroup problems involves groups with conflicting purposes or objectives. This condition emerges when one group desires or pursues one goal while directly opposing values that exist in another group. One example of this type of conflict would be the conflict between the Air Force and the Army over tactical air support. The Army has acquired helicopters and several fixed-wing aircraft for this function, but the Air Force feels that this function is under its jurisdiction and the result is conflict. In other types of organizations similar situations occur. Engineering may need special hand-tooled prototypes built and developed by a small manufacturing operation. Manufacturing, on the other hand, may see this as usurping its function and field of expertise. Each subsystem of the organization has its own special function or area, and these are usually jealously guarded against intrusion as almost a territorial right.

Perceived Power Imbalance between Groups

Another condition that appears to influence intergroup conflict is the differential of power between two groups. The problem emerges where there is a perceived imbalance between units or when some previously established relationship is altered. Where one group is overpowering and its views and objectives are consistently favored, a deterioration of relations with the other group is likely to result. This often forces the submissive or losing group to try manipulative tactics to revise the power balance. These may take the form of delay or rule adherence tactics.

Role Conflict, Role Ambiguity

Role conflict (as explained earlier in Chapter 10) also exists when an individual belongs to or identifies with two or more groups whose goals or values are in conflict. This is most typical in a matrix or project form of organization where an individual may belong to several work groups and report to several bosses. Where directives are vague or incompatible, intergroup conflict may result.

Role ambiguity exists when an individual or the members of a group are not clear about their functions, purposes, and goals within the organization. Staff groups such as personnel or accounting often encounter vague or unclear situations where their functions tend to interfere or conflict with line operations. Purchasing, for example, may desire to control all buying, but other departments may desire to influence such decisions. An individual or the members of a group may face a situation in which their job scope is being reduced for the good of the organization, but because of the intangible and multifaceted nature of what is good for the organization, this may result in noncompliance or conflict.

Personality Conflict

A final source of intergroup problems arises from interpersonal differences between members, usually the managers. Two individuals may be competing for promotion, rewards, or resources and may elevate this to a situation of intergroup conflict. Such conflicts may result from conflicting functions, objectives, career aspirations, or personalities. An example of this type of conflict might be the reported friction and conflict between General Motor's board member and executive H. Ross Perot and Chairman Roger B. Smith. In order to quiet Perot's criticisms regarding GM's slowness in solving its problems, GM purchased Perot's financial stake in the company for $750 million, nearly twice the current market price. In addition, GM got Perot to agree to pay fines of up to $7.5 million if he criticizes GM publicly. But as one auto analyst put it, "They spent $750 million to have quiet board meetings, but they haven't solved any of GM's problems."[7] Another observer of the auto industry commented "It was the inevitable clash of two titans."[8]

COOPERATION VERSUS COMPETITION

Competition is normally thought of in positive terms, especially in our economic system. The rationale of some managers has been to introduce competition into their organizations in order to bring about a "lean and mean" operation. Tom Peters and Robert Waterman, in *In Search of Excellence*, have suggested that competition between product innovation departments and other company groups characterize successful product innovation companies.[9] For an example of a company, Texas Instruments, that in the past has been highly successful in product innovation but more recently has encountered problems, see OD Application 11.1.

Research into the results of competition and cooperation among groups is inconclusive. It is not as simple an issue as some contend. It has been found that competitive groups are task oriented and place pressure on groups to work.[10] Members have more esteem for their groups than noncompetitive groups.[11] However, groups in competition will probably not help each other and groups losing the competition may experience a degradation in their internal cohesion.[12] There is a lack of evidence to support the position that intergroup competition will result in greater productivity than intergroup cooperation.[13]

In fact, research into group behavior indicates that cooperation promotes productivity.[14] This seems to be true when the task is more complicated and requires coordination and sharing of information.[15] In relatively simple tasks, however, competition tends to be superior to cooperation as it heightens interest and provides incentive.[16] Therefore, competition can be effective between groups who do not need to share information or resources.

Just as there are problems with competitive work groups, managers must also carefully structure cooperative groups. The task of the groups should be complicated enough to justify the group effort. The formal reward system and the norms should encourage persons and groups to help others, to share information and resources, and to work on the task together.

In a summary of the effects of competition among groups, Edgar Schein, an OD practitioner, predicts the following behavior between competing groups[17]:

MANAGEMENT PROBLEMS AT TEXAS INSTRUMENTS

Texas Instruments (TI) was one of the early entries in the home computer market. In theory, TI should have dominated the market. Instead, in 1983 TI folded its home computer business taking a $660 million operating loss. This indicated some internal weaknesses:

1. *R&D*. TI's engineers lacked expertise in consumer markets. TI cut prices to create demand for its home computer, but was unable to provide a competitive product.

2. *Marketing*. The firm was product driven rather than market driven, and failed to respond to customer needs.

3. *Management*. A byzantine management system, including matrix management, and a domineering management style lacked the flexibility to respond to changing high-tech markets.

TI is now attempting to develop an entrepreneurial culture that is more tuned to the market and to apply a strategy that builds on technological strength. The lack of intergroup cooperation was one factor in causing the inability of this firm to succeed in this high-tech industry.

Questions:
1. Is it important for different departments to work together?
2. How might TI deal with such problems?

- Each group sees the other as the enemy.
- Each group sees the best in itself and the worst in the other group.
- Communication decreases and hostility increases toward the other group.

Within a competing group:

- Each group becomes more cohesive and demands more conformity from its members.
- Concern for task accomplishment increases while concern for psychological needs of members decreases.
- Leadership styles become more autocratic and less democratic.
- Each group becomes more structured and organized.

After the task has been completed and there is a winner and a loser, the winning group:

- Becomes more cohesive.
- Releases tension, becomes complacent, and confirms their self-image of being better than the other group.
- Becomes more concerned for individual's psychological needs and less concerned for task accomplishment.

However, the losing group:

- Denies the loss if the situation is ambiguous enough or rationalizes the loss by blaming it on bad luck, unclear rules, and so forth.
- Tends to splinter and personal conflicts increase.
- Tries to find someone or something to blame.
- Expresses concern for working harder and less concern for individual's psychological needs.
- Tends to learn more about itself because its preconceived ideas about being the best group are upset. The long-term result of the loss can have positive outcomes if the group realistically accepts its loss.

MANAGING CONFLICT

Organizational conflict must not necessarily be reduced or eliminated, but managed to enhance individual, group, and organizational effectiveness.[18] One element of diagnosing conflict situations involves learning the five basic conflict styles. There are a number of styles which may be used in dealing with interpersonal or intergroup conflict. Robert Blake, Herbert Shepard, and Jane Mouton first developed a conceptual scheme for classifying conflict styles, and this scheme was reinforced by K. W. Thomas.[19] The styles are identified based on two dimensions: (1) desire to satisfy self; (2) desire to satisfy others. The five styles representing differing levels of cooperative versus assertive behaviors are:

1. *Avoiding.* This style involves a low concern for self and others; avoids conflict by withdrawing, buckpassing, or passive agreement.

2. *Obliging.* With a low concern for self, and high concern for others, this style is concerned with people satisfaction, harmony, and smoothing over differences.

3. *Dominating.* With high concern for self and low concern for others, this style attempts to accomplish personal objectives and often ignores the needs of others, forcing win-lose situations.

4. *Compromising.* This style has moderate concern for self, moderate concern for others, tending to seek out compromise between conflicting parties or elements.

5. *Integrating.* With high concern for self and others, this style is concerned

with problem solving; uses openness, sharing of information, and the examination of differences to reach a consensus solution.

Although some behavioral scientists suggest that there is one best style, most suggest an examination of styles, so that the most appropriate style for a given situation can be applied.

INTERGROUP OD TECHNIQUES

There seems to be an increasing awareness of conflict in organizations. The influx of women and minorities into the work force has resulted in new problems that cannot be resolved by old structures. The increasing popularity of decentralized structures and matrix organization, in which many organization members wind up reporting to two or more bosses, has reduced the executives' reliance on authority and increased the reliance on interpersonal conflict management skills.

Anthony Downs has suggested a law of interorganizational conflict: "Every group or organization is in partial conflict with every other group it deals with."[20] Although this may not be completely true, intergroup conflicts, including line and staff conflict, interdepartmental battles, and union-management disagreements, are very common. Dealing with such conflicts openly provides a way to manage tensions creatively, whereas unresolved conflict tends to erode away the effectiveness of an organization. To deal with intergroup conflict, the OD practitioner seeks interventions that increase interaction, negotiation, and the frequency of communication between groups.

One technique for training managers to deal with conflict is termed the egg-drop exercise (developed by Vector Management Systems). Sixteen middle-aged executives, divided into teams, race against the clock—and each other—to build a device out of assorted junk that will catch raw eggs gently enough to keep them from breaking. They get the junk from an auctioneer, who "sells" such things as metal strips and pieces of string, for which each team can bid up to $55,000. In the background a videotape machine quietly records the sights and sounds of the competition. Later, the executives watch themselves in action. To their distress, they see themselves mocking their teammates, throwing out authoritarian orders, and showing impatience. Although their goal was to beat the other teams, they discover that most of their conflicts were with persons on their side.[21]

To deal with intergroup conflicts that inhibit cooperation, the consultant seeks strategies that aim at several goals. OD intergroup techniques seek to identify areas of commonality and meta goals—the superordinate organization goals. They attempt to apply strategies that encourage interaction and negotiation and to increase frequency of communication. These techniques are aimed at avoiding the "win-lose" situations while emphasizing the "win-win" aspects of the situation.

To obtain these goals, the consultant examines group-to-group working relationships, applying joint problem-solving efforts that confront intergroup issues. The OD techniques for dealing with intergroup problems include the following.

Third-Party Consultation

One method of increasing communication and initiating intergroup problem solving is the intervention of a third party, usually an outside consultant, although the person may also be a superior, a peer, or a representative from another unit.[22] Third-party interventions, as described by Richard Walton, have the potential to solve such conflicts. One basic feature of this technique is confrontation. *Confrontation* refers to the process in which the parties directly engage each other and focus on the conflict between them. The goals of such interventions include:

1. Achieving increased understanding of the issues.
2. Accomplishing a common diagnosis.
3. Discovering alternatives for resolving the conflict.
4. Focusing on the common or meta goals—the superordinate group goals.

The third party attempts to make interventions aimed at opening communications, leveling power, and confronting the problems, including:

1. *Ensuring mutual motivation.* Each party needs some incentive for resolving the conflict.

2. *Achieving a balance in situational power.* If the situational power of the parties is not approximately equal, it is difficult to establish trust and maintain open lines of communication.

3. *Coordinating confrontation efforts.* One party's positive overtures must be coordinated with the other party's readiness to reciprocate. A failure to coordinate positive initiatives and readiness to respond can undermine future efforts to work out differences.

4. *Developing openness in communication.* The third party can help to establish norms of openness, provide reassurance and support, and decrease the risks associated with openness.

5. *Maintaining an appropriate level of tension.* If threat and tension are too low, the incentive for change or finding a solution is minimal. However, if threat and tension are too high, the parties may be unable to process information and see creative alternatives. In fact, they may begin to polarize and take rigid positions.

The third party, then, provides an objective intervention as a means of confronting or resolving issues between two disputing parties, since conflict situations are often tense and emotion-laden. Diagnostic insight is provided that is nonevaluative and a source of emotional support and skills. The third party also aids in identifying conflict factors and then helps facilitate some changes in the relationships.

Organization Mirror _____

The *organization mirror* is a technique designed to give work units feedback on how other elements of the organization view them.[23] This intervention is designed to improve relationships between groups and increase effectiveness. The work group (which could be in personnel, drafting, engineering, accounting, etc.) obtains specific information from other organization elements that it comes in contact with on a day-to-day basis. The data are usually collected by a third party and may be gathered by questionnaire, interview, or personal confrontation. The unit meets together to process the data. If possible, one or two spokespersons from each contacted group should be present to clarify the feedback if necessary.

The process of the organization mirror is as follows. An organization team that is experiencing interface problems with related work teams may initiate a feedback session by inviting key people to such a meeting. Usually, a consultant or other third party interviews these key people prior to the meeting in order to collect data and to sense the nature of the problems.

At the meeting itself, the host unit is present to process the feedback. The outside key people and the consultant discuss the data collected in an inner circle while the host group "fishbowls" and observes on the outside. Following this, the host group is allowed to ask questions of clarification (i.e., Why did you say this?) but may not argue or rebut. The host unit, with the assistance of the consultant, then discusses the data to identify problems.

Subgroups are formed of host group members and key visitors to identify specific improvements that will increase operating efficiency. Following this, the total group hears a summary report from each subgroup, and action plans are outlined and specific task assignments are made. This completes the meeting, but a follow-up meeting to assess progress is usually set up for evaluation.

The organization mirror provides a means for a work group to improve its operating relations with other groups. It allows the group to obtain feedback on what it is doing, to identify key problems, and to search for specific improvement of operating efficiency. As the TRW experience indicates, "members must listen without comment to sometimes painful evaluation of their unit's work by others."[24]

Intergroup team building _____

One intervention technique, originally developed by Robert Blake, Herb Shepard, and Jane Mouton, is termed intergroup team building or confrontation.[25] Key members of conflicting groups meet for the purpose of working on issues or interface. "An interface is any point at which contact between groups is essential to achieving a result."[26] The groups may be two interdependent organization elements, such as architects and engineers, purchasing and production, or accounting and other department heads.

Role playing is a frequently used method for gaining cross-group understanding. As in all confrontation, the third-party consultant must intervene to open communications, balance power, and shift from hostile to problem-solving confrontation. These groups have been widely used, but there is little research evidence to determine how effective they are in reducing sources of conflict.

Such intergroup team-building meetings usually take 1 or 2 days. Members are brought together to reduce misunderstanding, to open communication, and to develop mechanisms for collaboration. Most OD practitioners advise intragroup team development prior to intergroup team building. The purpose of this is to clear out any team issues or "garbage" prior to getting to work on interface problems. The intergroup confrontation meeting usually involves the following steps:

Step 1   The two work groups first separately make three lists (see Table 11.1):

1.   How do we see ourselves?
2.   How we think department B sees us?
3.   How do we see department B?

The lists are prepared on sheets of newsprint and are written in large legible print and then taped to the wall.

Step 2   The groups then meet together. A spokesperson for each group presents that group's lists. While department A, for example, is making its presen-

TABLE 11.1   Sample Intergroup Meeting Listings

1. How do we see ourselves?
   a. Agreeable
   b. Friendly
   c. Trusting
   d. Helpful
   e. Teamwork
   f. Participative
   g. Productive

2. How we think department B sees us?
   a. Aggressive
   b. Noncommunicative
   c. Defensive
   d. Naive
   e. Competitive
   f. Lacking understanding
   g. Independent

3. How do we see department B?
   a. Authoritarian
   b. Sneaky
   c. Loud
   d. Opinionated
   e. Inflexible
   f. Unrealistic

tation, department B may not defend itself, argue, or rebut; but it does have the opportunity to ask clarifying questions (i.e., What do you mean by inflexible? Could you be more specific on autocratic?)

Step 3 The groups then meet separately to discuss the discrepancies in perception and react to the feedback. The feedback allows for correcting perceptions and behaviors to a more effective mode.

Step 4 In the next phase, subgroups of five or six are formed by mixing members of groups A and B. These cross groups have the objectives of agreeing upon a diagnosis of interface problems and the development of conflict-reducing or problem-solving alternatives with action plans and follow-up activities. Together the groups develop an action plan for solving problems and assigning responsibilities for the action plan.

Step 5 Usually, a follow-up meeting is scheduled for a future date to evaluate progress and to make sure that the actions have achieved their purpose. Fordyce and Weil developed a similar procedure at TRW.[27] The two groups develop three lists:

1. A positive feedback list—what group A likes about group B.

2. A "bug" list—the things about B that bug A.

3. An "empathy" list—anticipating what B will say about A.

Although little hard evidence is available, there have been subjective reports of positive results from intergroup meetings. Blake, Shepard, and Mouton reported improved relationships in their study, and French and Bell also reported working successfully with three tribal groups.[28] Bennis also reported improved relationships between two groups of officials within the U.S. Department of State.[29] It is apparent that such interventions do aid in lessening intergroup conflicts, possibly as a result of the Hawthorne effect. The fact that a consultant and both groups are interested in resolving the issues may lead to improved relations.

REVIEW QUESTIONS

1. Identify major sources of organizational conflict.

2. Compare and contrast the effectiveness of different approaches to resolving intergroup conflict.

3. Contrast cooperation and competition between work groups.

4. Compare major conflict styles.

KEY WORDS AND CONCEPTS

Define and be able to use the following:

Interfaces	Goal conflict
Interdependence	Integrating role
Suboptimization	Superordinate group goals
Intergroup competition	Feedback
Third-party intervention	Open loop
Confrontation	Role ambiguity
Organization mirror	Intergroup team building

IV. Simulations

SIMULATION 11.1   THE DISARMAMENT GAME

Total time suggested: 1 hour, 45 minutes.

A.   Purpose

The purpose of this exercise is to simulate a situation of intergroup conflict within an organization, to observe and experience the feelings generated by such competition, and to examine strategies for developing collaboration between organization units.

B.   Procedures

Step 1   Form teams of six to nine players each. Before class, read the Disarmament Game Rules. Cut out the "play money" at the end of the simulation or, if the situation allows, use real money and play for lesser amounts (say 10 percent of the suggested amounts).

DISARMAMENT GAME RULES[30]

The Disarmament Game is played between two teams. A World Bank, which has funds, is also part of the game. Each team can win or lose money, and in this exercise your objective, as a team, is to win as much money as you can. Each team will consist of six to nine players. If there are uneven numbers of players, one person will assist the instructors, who are referees, thus making equal the number of players on each team.

The funds

1. Each player will furnish $20 to be allocated as follows (see the end of this simulation for a description of "play money"):

   a. $15 (of your $20) will be given to your team treasury to be used in the exercise. You may need to contribute more money to the treasury, depending on the performance of your team. At the end of the game the funds remaining in your team's treasury will be divided equally among members of the team.

   b. $5 will be used to supplement the funds of the World Bank, managed by the referees.

      Example: Seven players on a side.
      Allocation of funds:
      Each team—$105
      World Bank—$35 from each team

2. The World Bank will deposit, from its own funds, an amount equal to the deposit of both teams. This money can be won by the teams.

Special jobs.   You will have 15 minutes from the time the general instructions are completed until the first set begins. During this time you may read and discuss the instructions and plan team strategy. You must select persons to fill the following jobs. No person may hold more than one job at any one time. The jobs can be reassigned at any time by a majority vote of the team.

1. Two negotiators—functions stated below.

2. A team representative—to communicate group decisions to referees regarding initiation and acceptance of negotiations, moves, attacks, etc.
   a. You must elect a team representative.
   b. Referees will listen only to the team representative.

3. One recorder—to record moves of the team (on the Record of Results), specifically (a) the action taken by the team in each move, and (b) weapon status at the end of each move. He or she should also record who initiates decisions and how the team arrives at decisions.

The weapons.   Each team will be given 20 cards, or "weapons." Each card will be marked on one side with an X to designate an "armed" condition. The blank side of the card signifies that the weapon is "unarmed." To begin the game, each of the two teams will place all 20 of its weapons in an "armed" condition. During the course of the entire game, the weapons will remain in your possession and out of sight of the other team.

RECORD OF RESULTS

Move	Set 1 — Actual number of armed weapons	Set 1 — Action taken for this move (attack, not attack, negotiate)	Set 2 — Actual number of armed weapons	Set 2 — Action taken for this move (attack, not attack, negotiate)	Set 3 — Actual number of armed weapons	Set 3 — Action taken for this move (attack, not attack, negotiate)	Set 4 — Actual number of armed weapons	Set 4 — Action taken for this move (attack, not attack, negotiate)	Set 5 — Actual number of armed weapons	Set 5 — Action taken for this move (attack, not attack, negotiate)	Set 6 — Actual number of armed weapons	Set 6 — Action taken for this move (attack, not attack, negotiate)	Total of all sets
1.													
2.													
3.													
4.													
5.													
6.													
7.													
8.													
9.													
10.													
Ending no. of armed weapons of other team													
Line 1 $ paid to other team													
Line 2 $ paid to World Bank													
Line 3 $ received from other team													
Line 4 $ received from World Bank													

Total Results
(Lines 3 + 4 - 1 - 2)

The procedure

1. **The Set**

   a. As many sets as possible will be played in the allocated time (from the time the first set begins). Payments will be made after each set.

   b. Each set consists of no more than 10 moves for each team. An attack following any move ends a set. If there is no attack, the set ends after the tenth move. Each team has 2 minutes to make a move. At the end of 2 minutes, you must have moved two, one, or none of the weapons from "armed" status. If you fail to move in the allotted time, the *status quo* counts as a move. In addition, you must decide whether or not to attack and whether or not you want to negotiate (see below). Your decision must be communicated to the referee within 15 seconds after the end of a move.

   c. Each team may announce an attack on the other team following any 2-minute move period except the *third*, *sixth*, and *ninth*. You may not "attack" during negotiations.

   d. Once a set ends, begin a new set with all weapons armed. Continue with as many sets as the time allotted for the exercise will permit.

2. **The Negotiations**

   a. Between the moves you will have the opportunity to communicate with the other team through negotiations.

   b. You may call for negotiations during the 15 seconds between move periods. The other team may accept or reject your request to negotiate. Negotiations can last *no longer* than 2 minutes.

   c. When the negotiators return to their teams, the next 2-minute move period will start.

   d. Negotiators may say whatever is necessary to most benefit their team.

   e. The team is not necessarily bound by agreements made by its negotiators.

   f. Your negotiators *must* meet with those of the other team after the *third*, *sixth*, and *ninth* moves.

The payoff

1. If there is an attack, the set ends. The team with the greater number of armed weapons will win $0.50 per member for each armed weapon it has *over and above* the number of armed weapons of the other team. This is paid directly from the treasury of

the losing team to the treasury of the winning team. The World Bank is not involved in the transaction when there is an attack. If both teams have the same number of armed weapons when there is an attack, both teams pay the World Bank $0.50 per member.

2.   If there is no attack, the set ends after 10 moves. If your team has more disarmed weapons than armed weapons, it will be awarded $0.20 per excess disarmed weapon, per member, by the World Bank. If your team has *fewer* disarmed weapons than armed weapons, your team will pay $0.20 per excess armed weapon, per member, to the World Bank.

3.   The actual dollar payoff should occur at the end of each set.

Notes to referee

1.   Try to arrange separate rooms so that the teams cannot overhear each other.

2.   In keeping the time, a timer that will ring accurately at 2-minute intervals will be helpful.

3.   Be sure to permit the teams only the specified times. You will probably need to be somewhat harsh toward the teams when directing them in order to keep them on the time schedule.

4.   You will manage the funds of the World Bank and check the accuracy of the teams' record keeping.

5.   You should not assist either team.

Step 2   Begin playing Disarmament Game, keeping track of moves on the Record of Results. Play as many sets as you can within a 1-hour time limit.
Time suggested for Steps 1 and 2: approximately 90 minutes.
Step 3   At the conclusion of the game and after all profits and losses have been calculated, get together with your competing team and discuss the following questions.
Time suggested for Step 3: 15 minutes.

1.   To make an analogy, if one of the teams was the accounting department and the other team was the production department of a manufacturing enterprise, and the World Bank was the marketplace, what types of conclusions might you make about this company and the two departments?

_____

_____

2.   What was the goal of your team? What kind of strategy to accomplish your goal did your team adopt? Did the strategy change at all during the simulation?

_____

_____

3.   Was your team aware of the need for and advantages of collaborating with the other team? If so, how did you communicate the need for collaboration to the other team?

_____

_____

The following "play money" is the $20 you will need to participate in the Disarmament Game. Cut the money out before class and in class give it to the appropriate organizations.

$5 FIVE $5	$5 FIVE $5
$5 DOLLARS $5	$5 DOLLARS $5
$5 FIVE $5	$1 ONE $1
$5 DOLLARS $5	$1 DOLLAR $1
$1 ONE $1	$1 ONE $1
$1 DOLLAR $1	$1 DOLLAR $1
$1 ONE $1	50¢ FIFTY 50¢
$1 DOLLAR $1	50¢ CENTS 50¢
20¢ TWENTY 20¢	20¢ TWENTY 20¢
20¢ CENTS 20¢	20¢ CENTS 20¢
10¢ TEN 10¢	
10¢ CENTS 10¢	

4. What part does trust play between the two teams in this simulation?

_____

_____

5. How is trust built? How does it start? Where does it come from?

_____

_____

6. Did your team trust and want to collaborate with the other team so that you could try to break the World Bank? If so, what happened as a result of your trust?

_____

_____

7. If the simulation were to run again, would you do anything differently?

_____

_____

SIMULATION 11.2   INTERGROUP BUILDING

Total time suggested: 1 hour.

A. Purpose

To provide an opportunity for group members to clarify and analyze their inter-relationships and to work on improving intergroup processes.

B. Procedures

Step 1   Form the same groups as in Simulation 11.1 and meet separately using a blackboard or newsprint to make these lists:

    1. How do we see ourselves?
    2. How we think group B sees us?
    3. How do we see group B?

The lists should not be shared or seen by the other group until Step 2.

Step 2   The groups then meet together. A representative for each group presents his or her group's lists. While group A, for example, is making its presentation, group B may not defend itself, argue, or rebut; but it does have the opportunity to ask clarifying questions (i.e., What do you mean by inflexible? Could you be more specific on autocratic?) The other group then makes its presentation.

Time suggested for Steps 1 and 2: 30 minutes.

Step 3   The groups then meet separately to discuss the discrepancies in perception.

Step 4   Subgroups of five or six are formed by mixing members of groups A and B. These cross groups have the objective of agreeing upon a diagnosis of interface problems and the development of conflict-reducing or problem-solving alternatives, with action plans and follow-up activities.

Time suggested for Steps 3 and 4: 30 minutes.

The Exley Chemical Company is a major chemical manufacturer making primarily industrial chemicals, plastics, and consumer products. Company sales and profits have grown, and its ratio of net profits to sales is about average for the industry, but in the last year or so both sales and profits have been disappointing (see Table 1).

TABLE 1

Year	Sales
5 years ago	$ 81,000,000
3 years ago	93,000,000
2 years ago	108,000,000
Last year	111,000,000

Since new products are constantly being introduced into the line and methods of use are constantly changing, the relative importance of different product groups is constantly shifting. For example, changes in percentage of total sales were experienced by the major product groups over a 5-year period (see Table 2).

TABLE 2

	PERCENT OF SALES	
	5 Years Ago	Last Year
Chemicals	61	55
Plastics	31	33
Consumer	8	12
	100	100

THE ORGANIZATION

The general structure is as shown in Exhibit 1. Production is carried on in four plants across the United States, each of which has a plant manager. The marketing manager handles sales and marketing services, including the field sales force, with 20 district managers, and industrial sales representatives, who total 25.

All research is administered and done at the corporate research laboratory, including the development section, which is responsible for the development and improvement of production processes. The engineering department handles all planning and construction and the development of new processes and pilot-plant operations.

In addition, to manage the increasing amount of new products being developed, a product development division was established about 3 years ago. Prior to this, as new products were developed by the research division, they were passed on to the engineering division from the pilot-plant operation. Unfortunately, this method was inadequate for the complex

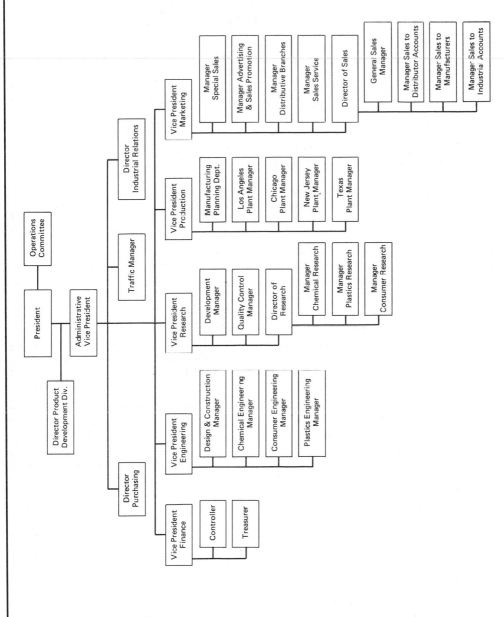

EXHIBIT 1 Organization Chart—The Exley Chemical Company

coordination of these projects, so the new division was established. The product development division was to coordinate efforts in developing new products, including recommending manufacturing capacity, sales programs, and so on. The division was to conduct surveys to analyze market potential for new products and recommend the development or production based on these surveys. During the 3-year period following the creation of the product development division, problems emerged.

THE SITUATION

Conflicts were created with several other departments. For example, the product development division started using a small force of specialty salespeople to conduct pilot marketing programs. This did not go over well with the marketing department. Also, the product division was given responsibility for market research, but the tasks of sales analysis and forecasting remained in the marketing division. Finally, a product manager was appointed for each separate group of products responsible for the coordination of all company activities for the product. This resulted in more problems.

1.   The product manager often needs to visit customers in order to get more realistic input on market conditions, but this is resented by marketing executives. They feel that all customer relations should be handled through marketing, because these visits tend to confuse the customer. "Judging from what I've seen, Product Development couldn't care less about what we are doing in terms of integrating our markets," said the marketing vice president.

2.   Sales executives tend to question the sales estimates issued by the product managers. These estimates are usually based on the total product market rather than on Exley's share, which often tends to inflate sales estimates. "The product development group is aggressive and they want to grow, but you have to grow within guidelines. The product guys are going to have to learn to work with the other divisions," said a sales manager.

3.   At a recent meeting of the Chemical Manufacturers Association, a product manager learned that a competitor was about to patent a new process for the production of polymers, which presumably will reduce costs by about one-third. Exley's research person in charge of polymers said that they had several interesting possibilities which might break in a few months. "I think corporate headquarters needs to integrate operations better. We can't be a bunch of entrepreneurs around here. We've got to have more teamwork on these projects." said the product manager.

4.   The manager of sales proposed to the consumer products group that Exley's antifreeze be promoted to retail outlets. He has forwarded a proposal to the product manager with a note: "Our customers feel this is a hot idea; can production supply the needed quantities at a competitive price?" The product manage has found that the two people in research and engineering who are most knowledgeable regarding this product are now deeply involved in a new project, so little has been done to date. "The big frustration is that you can't get help from

other departments, if it doesn't have a large return for them. Each division head works on the project that makes the most for their division, but these are not necessarily the best from a corporate standpoint," said the product manager.

CASE ANALYSIS FORM

Problems

A. Macro

  1. _____

  2. _____

B. Micro

  1. _____

  2. _____

II. Causes

  1. _____

  2. _____

  3. _____

III. Systems affected

  1. Structural

  2. Psychosocial

  3. Technical

  4. Managerial

  5.

IV. Alternatives

  1. _____

  2. _____

  3. _____

  4. _____

  5. _____

V. Recommendations

  1. _____

  2. _____

  3. _____

**V.
Summary**

Conflict is inevitable in organizations. Large organizations are divisionalized, departmentalized, and segmented to increase control and effectiveness. This creates boundaries between geographic areas or functional units, such as manufacturing, engineering, and marketing. Yet cooperation and collaboration among all of these units is essential to achieving objectives. This chapter discusses such problems of intergroup relations or interface and describes several OD interventions. The complexity and size of modern organizations often leads to competition or conflict between organization units. Large-scale organizations generate increased problems of dependence between groups, which often results in a condition of suboptimization and a resultant decrease in overall efficiency. Such problems as intergroup conflict, power imbalance, or personal conflicts inhibit coordination between groups.

To deal with intergroup problems, the OD practitioner seeks interventions that emphasize improving communication and relations between operating units. These interventions stress the involvement of the individual and the members of the group in the relation between what they do and what others are doing. The consultant uses strategies that identify areas of commonality, increase communication, and emphasize the "meta" goals. These interventions include third-party intervention, organization mirror, and intergroup team building and provide mechanisms for achieving collaboration between competing groups. The major objectives of such intergroup interventions include a better way of working together, an increased recognition of interdependence, a decrease in competition, and an increase in collaboration.

You have also had a chance in the Disarmament Game to experience a situation involving intergroup competition and conflict. Even though the conditions and opportunity for a win-win collaboration are present, many inherent factors lead to defining it as a win-lose situation. You may have experienced what happens under conditions of conflict and observed the consequences: communication between groups decreases, negative stereotypes are formed, hostility and distrust toward the other group increases while internally you may become more single minded and cohesive. The net result is usually dysfunctional in terms of overall effectiveness. The conflict between your groups may have escalated, with each group attempting to win its point by fair means or foul. Imagine what happens when such a misunderstanding arises between two departments within an organization.

You have also had a chance in the second simulation to observe how intergroup interventions might be used to reduce the dysfunctional consequences of win-lose conflict. These intergroup approaches attempt to identify the forces that restrict cooperation and open up lines of communication. The outcome should be increased understanding and insight into problem issues and how win-win opportunities can be obscured when a fixed position is held and how facts can become distorted under such conditions. The intergroup intervention provides a framework for a win-win relationship. In this simulation, therefore, you have begun to explore ways of developing more collaborative relations between interdependent groups.

Depending on how conflict is managed, negative consequences may be minimized and positive outcomes may be the result.

NOTES

1. See Dean Tjosuold, "Cooperation Theory and Organizations," *Human Relations*, 37, no. 9 (1984), pp. 743–67.

2. Richard Beckhard, *Organization Development: Strategies and Models* (Reading, Mass.: Addison-Wesley Publishing Co., Inc., 1969), p. 33.

3. Gordon Lippitt, Ronald Lippitt, and Clayton Lafferty, "Cutting Edge Trends in Organization Development," *Training and Development Journal*, July 1984, p. 60.

4. Richard C. Walton, and Robert B. McKersie, *A Behavioral Theory of Labor Negotiations—An Analysis of a Social Interaction System* (New York: McGraw-Hill Book Company, 1963).

5. Rosabeth Moss Kanter, "Dilemmas of Managing Participation," *Organizational Dynamics*, Summer 1982, p. 21.

6. Paul R. Lawrence, and Jay W. Lorsch, *Organization and Environment: Managing Differentiation and Integration* (Boston: Graduate School of Business Administration, Harvard University, 1967), p. 40.

7. William J. Hampton and Todd Mason, "GM Hasn't Bought Much Peace," *Business Week*, December 15, 1986, p. 24.

8. Ibid., p. 25.

9. Thomas J. Peters and Robert H. Waterman, Jr., *In Search of Excellence* (New York: Harper & Row, Publishers, Inc., 1982).

10. J. M. Rabbie, F. Benoist, H. Ooserbaan, and L. Visser, "Differential Power and Effects of Expected Competitive and Cooperative Intergroup Interaction on Intragroup and Outgroup Attitudes," *Journal of Personality and Social Psychology*, 39 (1974), 46–56.

11. A. Myers, "Team Competition, and the Adjustment of Group Members," *Journal of Abnormal and Social Psychology*, 65 (1962), 325–32.

12. R. Wheeler and F. Ryan, "Effects of Cooperative and Competitive Classroom Environments on the Attitudes and Achievement of Elementary Students Engaged in Social Studies Inquiry Activities," *Journal of Educational Psychology*, 65 (1973), 402–7.

13. D. W. Johnson, G. Maruyama, R. Johnson, D. Nelson, and L. Skon, "The Effects of Cooperative, Competitive, and Individualistic Goal Structures on Achievement: A Meta-Analysis," *Psychological Bulletin*, 89 (1981), 47–62.

14. P. R. Laughlin, "Ability and Group Problem Solving", *Journal of Research and Development in Education*, 1978, vol 12, pp. 114–20, Fall '78.

15. M. Okun and F. DiVesta, "Cooperation and Competition in Coacting Groups," *Journal of Personality and Social Psychology*, 31 (1975), 615–20, April '75.

16. For a comprehensive review of the research literature on competition and cooperation see Tjosuold, "Cooperation Theory and Organizations," pp. 743–67.

17. Edgar H. Schein, *Process Consultation: Its Role in Organization Development* (Reading, Mass.: Addison-Wesley Publishing Co., Inc., 1969), pp. 72–74.

18. M. Afzalur Rahim, "A Strategy for Managing Conflict in Complex Organizations," *Human Relations*, 18, no. 1 (1985), 81–86.

19. Robert R. Blake, H. Shepard, and J. Mouton, *Managing Intergroup Conflict in Industry* (Houston, Tex.: Gulf Publishing Company, 1964), K. W. Thomas, "Conflict and Conflict Management," in M. D. Dunnette, ed. *Handbook In Industrial Organizational Psychology* (Chicago: Rand McNally & Company, 1984). See also M.A. Rahim, "A Measure of Styles of Handling Interpersonal Conflict," *Academy of Management Journal*, 26 (1983), 368–76.

20. A. Downs, *Inside Bureaucracy* (Boston: Little, Brown and Company, 1968).

21. "Teaching How to Deal with Workplace Conflicts," *Business Week*, February 18, 1980, p. 136.

22. See Richard Walton, *Interpersonal Peacemaking: Confrontation and Third Party Consultation* (Reading, Mass.: Addison-Wesley Publishing Co., Inc., 1969). See also R. J. Fisher, "Third Party Consultation as a Method of Intergroup Conflict Resolution," *Journal of Conflict Resolution*, 27 (1983), 301–34.

23. To our knowledge, this technique was probably developed by Sheldon Davis and his colleagues at TRW.

24. "Team Work through Conflict," *Business Week*, March 20, 1974, p. 44.

25. See Robert R. Blake, H. Shepard, and J. Mouton, *Managing Intergroup Conflict in Industry* (Houston, Tex.: Gulf Publishing Company, 1964); Robert R. Blake and Jane S. Mouton, *Solving Costly Organizational Conflicts* (San Francisco; Jossey-Bass, Inc., Publishers, 1984).

26. Robert R. Blake and Jane S. Mouton, "Out of the Past . . . How to Use Your Organization's History to Shape a Better Future," *Training and Development Journal*, November 1983, p. 60.

27. Jack Fordyce and Raymond Weil, *Managing with People* (Reading, Mass.: Addison-Wesley Publishing Co., Inc., 1971).

28. See Blake, Shepard, and Mouton, *Managing Conflict*; and Wendell L. French and Cecil H. Bell, Jr., *Organization Development: Behavioral Science Interventions for Organization Improvement*, 3rd ed. (Englewood Cliffs, N.J.: Prentice-Hall, Inc., 1984), p. 11.

29. Warren Bennis, *Organization Development: Its Nature, Origins and Prospects* (Reading, Mass.: Addison-Wesley Publishing Co., Inc., 1969).

30. We are indebted to Norman Berkowitz of Boston College and Harvey Hornstein of Columbia University for the design of this game. Used by permission of the authors.

OD GOAL
SETTING

I. **Objectives**	Upon completing this chapter, you will be able to:
	1. Recognize how goal setting can be used as part of an OD program.
	2. Apply the major findings of research on goal setting in order to develop organizational and personal goals.
	3. Understand how management by objectives (MBO) can be applied as a management system.
	4. Experience and practice goal setting approaches.
II. **Premeeting** **Preparation**	1. Read the Background Information (Section III).
	2. Complete Step 1 of Simulation 12.1 (Section IV).
	3. Complete Step 2 of Simulation 12.2.
	4. Read and analyze Case: Western Utilities Company.

III.
Background
Information

Goals give direction to an individual's life and provide purpose; goals also give direction to an organization. Individuals are by their very nature goal seeking. Goal setting typically plays a part in an organization development program even though the goal setting process may not be formally recognized. The establishment of goals has often been found to increase the effectiveness of individuals, teams, and organizations.

There have been several approaches to goal setting used within organizations, and management by objectives (MBO) has been one of the most widely used methods. While some OD consultants would be reluctant to include MBO as an OD intervention, it is an approach that can be and has been used to improve total organization effectiveness. When used properly, MBO produces a system of mutual target setting and performance review, and enhances planning, communicating, and motivation. Unfortunately, MBO has also been misapplied. In this chapter we will first discuss goal setting concepts and then focus on management by objectives.

GOAL SETTING THEORY

Goal setting is a process intended to increase efficiency and effectiveness by specifying the desired outcomes toward which individuals, teams, and organizations should work. Goal setting may be used as an intervention strategy within an OD program. An analysis of the organization may determine that divisions are not unified in their efforts, that a division or divisions have little or no direction, or that individuals are dissatisfied with their performance and their own careers. The OD practitioner and the client may decide that, in addition to team building, intergroup development, and other intra- and interpersonal interventions, goal setting may be beneficial. The goal setting program may be implemented on the individual level to help employees improve their productivity or to help them advance their careers.

Goal setting may also be implemented on a departmental level with the intention of improving productivity and giving direction to the department's efforts. Additionally, goal setting may be used on an organization-wide basis with broad goals first set by top management and then expressed more narrowly and specifically at each successive level in the organization, until the goal setting process reaches the lowest organizational levels.[1]

The basic premise of goal setting theory discussed here, which was formulated by E.A. Locke, is that an individual's conscious intentions and values regulate his or her actions.[2] A goal is defined as what an individual is trying to accomplish and it is the object or aim of action.[3] The following paragraphs provide a summary of the major findings relevant to goal setting theory.[4]

1. More difficult goals produce better performance. Furthermore, it has been found the assignment of an easy goal results in no better performance than no goal at all. Goals must be difficult and challenging to have an effect.

2. Specific hard goals are better than "do your best" goals. In addition to goals being difficult and challenging, they should also be specific. Goals that are specific are expressed in quantitative terms or as specific events; that is, they will include time frames, standards, quotas, monetary amounts, and the like.

3. People may abandon goals if the goals become too hard. Though the goals should be difficult, people must have the ability to attain or at least approach their goals; otherwise, they tend to view the goal as impossible, become discouraged, and may abandon the goal. An individual is more likely to accept or choose a goal when there are high rather than low expectations of reaching it.[5] In several studies where goals were perceived to be impossible, performance actually decreased. The difficulty of the goals suggests the goals were not accepted in the first place.[6]

4. Feedback and goals improve performance. Feedback on an individual's performance combined with goal setting has a positive effect on performance; however, just giving feedback on a person's performance, without having previously set goals, does not lead to improved performance.[7] Also frequent, relevant, and specific feedback is important for goal setting to be a success. The feedback should occur as soon after the work activity as possible so the event and its details are remembered by the individual.

5. Goal setting improves motivation. Goal setting can improve motivation by directing attention and action, by increasing effort, by increasing persistence and time spent on the task, and by developing strategies and action plans.

6. Individual differences tend not to affect goal setting. Studies have shown goal setting programs to be successful regardless of the education and job position of the subjects. Some goal setting programs in organizations are limited to upper and middle management but research findings indicate that goal setting is just as successful for positions requiring minimum education and skills. Research also shows that the success of a goal setting program is not contingent upon number of years of service an employee has with an organization.

7. Support of management is critical. Support by all levels of management in goal setting programs is crucial to their success. Supervisors should be present to encourage the acceptance of goals by employees, to provide help in improving skills, and to give timely feedback as to how the goals are being accomplished.

A MODEL FOR GOAL SETTING

Based upon the research findings previously cited, Latham and Locke[8] have developed a useful model for goal setting (see Figure 12.1). For goal setting to be successful, goals need to be properly developed and the individuals trying to achieve the goals need to be committed to them. A goal setting program in an organization requires careful planning.

As seen in Figure 12.1, the first three factors in the goal setting process are: determining the goal, achieving goal commitment, and overcoming resistance to goal acceptance. Goals can be determined in a variety of ways. Time and motion studies can provide the basis for goals involving repetitive and standardized tasks. Another approach sometimes used to establish goals is to base standards on past performance, but this may not result in a challenging goal, especially when past performance has been poor. Goals may also be set by joint participation between the employee and the supervisor or manager. This

FIGURE 12.1 Goal Setting Model

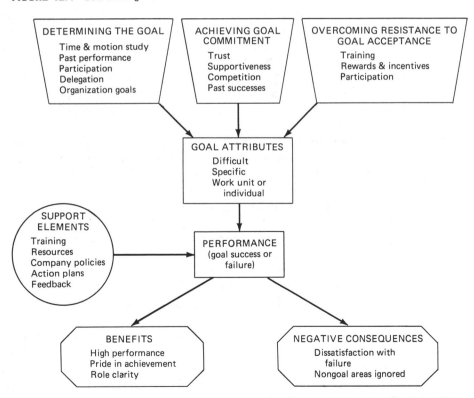

Source: Adapted, by permission of the publisher, from "Goal Setting—A Motivational Technique That Works," by Gary P. Latham and Edwin A. Locke, *Organizational Dynamics*, Autumn 1979, p. 79. © 1985 American Management Association, N.Y. All rights reserved.

method tends to lead to employee commitment, a crucial ingredient in effective goal setting. The setting of goals may be delegated to employees or based strictly on previously set organization goals.

Goal commitment can be achieved in a variety of ways. Trust in upper management as well as support by management and an effective reward and incentive system is helpful in obtaining commitment. Past successes of accomplishing goals builds excitement and a positive feeling toward future goal accomplishment. Competition between employees may be useful in some situations, but managers should avoid designing competitive situations because of the previously mentioned problem of suboptimization (see Chapter 11). There is also a danger employees may become so involved in competing with one another that they may lose sight of the goals.

Resistance to goal acceptance can be overcome by several methods and a combination of methods will likely result in a more successful goal setting program. Providing special training for employees in new techniques and procedures and providing rewards and incentives can help encourage goal acceptance.

The following goal attributes tend to work best. Goals should be difficult and challenging but not impossible to accomplish. They should be specific and measurable. Goals may be assigned to an individual, or a work unit, and should be compatible with goals formulated at higher levels of the organization.

The next step is the period of performance. Managers must be prepared to provide support. Employees may require training and additional resources, such as new equipment or information, to achieve their goals. Managers may need to work with employees in developing action plans to accomplish a goal and to provide timely and objective feedback on the accomplishment of the goal.

The results of the employees' performance can be beneficial or negative. The benefits may incur to the organization and/or the individual. Higher performance and pride in achievement of successes can be expected. Employees are more likely to have clearer roles as they more fully realize what is expected of them. Negative consequences can be expected, particularly when the goals are not achieved. This seems to particularly be a problem in situations where specific and measurable goals could not be set.

Results of Goal Setting

Research on the effects of goal setting has shown positive results on both the personal and organizational level. One study found that in 90 percent of the cases, specific and challenging goals led to higher performance than easy goals, "do your best" goals, or no goals.[9]

In a review of goal setting studies, the median improvement in performance resulting from goal setting was found to be 16 percent.[10] The same study found goal setting, when combined with the use of monetary incentives, improved performance by more than 40 percent. And another article reports that goal setting on one job saved one company $250,000 in a 9-month period.[11] The performance of the company is strongly related to the extent of goal setting and planning activities.[12]

The remainder of this chapter will look at a specific type of goal setting program: management by objectives (MBO).

MANAGEMENT BY OBJECTIVES

Management by objectives (MBO) is a specific technique used by organizations for setting goals. It is a process aimed at the integration of individual and organization goals.[13] The goals of this approach include an improved level of performance, increased communication and participation, higher morale and job satisfaction, and a better understanding of organization objectives at all levels. MBO may be defined as a system of management implemented to facilitate planning, organizing, problem solving, motivating, and other important management activities. It involves the participation of the subordinate's manager in setting and clarifying the subordinate's goals. George Odiorne (a leading MBO consultant) defines MBO as "A process whereby the superior and subordinate managers of an organization jointly identify its common goals, define each individual's major areas of responsibility in terms of results expected, and use these measures as guides for operating the unit and assessing the contribution of each of its members.[14]

Anthony Raia (a leading OD consultant and UCLA professor) suggests that management by objectives is a "philosophy of management" that reflects a "proactive" rather than a "reactive" approach to management. It is a philosophy that encourages participative management at all levels of the organization.[15]

There has been some controversy among OD practitioners as to whether or not MBO should be included as an OD intervention. Some critics feel that MBO is a manipulative approach and therefore should not be classified as an OD intervention, whereas others feel that OD and MBO are consistent approaches. Arthur Beck and Ellis Hillmar are among those who feel that OD and MBO do fit together, in fact they do not believe it is possible to have one without the other.[16] It is their contention that one of the major assumptions underlying organization development is the need to have goal setting at all levels, and consequently they feel that MBO is a legitimate OD intervention.

Among the underlying assumptions of MBO are the following:

1. People possess higher-level needs for competence and achievement.

2. People want to satisfy these higher-level needs in their work.

3. People will work harder and perform better if they set their own goals.

4. Management, then, must create a climate that encourages self-development by individuals.

The Purposes of MBO Programs

There are two underlying purposes for implementing MBO in an organization. One is to clarify organization goals and plans at all levels; the other is to gain increased motivation and participation among organization members. MBO provides a means of increasing the clarity of organization planning and of enhancing the subordinate's knowledge and understanding of his or her job. MBO may be used to identify organization goals at all levels and to encourage participation in setting the standards that will be used to evaluate subordinate performance. Participation in the goal-setting process allows managers to control and monitor their own performance by measuring performance and results against the objectives they helped to set. The late Douglas McGregor also suggested a modified approach to MBO under the concept of "management by integration and self-control."[17] According to McGregor, the MBO concept could be used to provide an opportunity for managers and subordinates to mutually define and agree upon areas of responsibility, specific performance goals, and the terms of the expected outcomes. He suggested that managers establish their own performance goals after reaching agreement with their superior regarding major job responsibilities. Then accomplishments would be appraised at the end of a short time period, usually 6 months. This self-appraisal would be in cooperation with the superior, after which another set of performance goals would be established. McGregor aimed at the commitment of organization members by the "creation of conditions such that the members of an organization can achieve their own goals best by directing their efforts toward the success of the enterprise."[18] He advocated this concept as a means for appraising performance, since it shifted the emphasis from weakness and criticism to an analysis of strength and potential. In this application of MBO the superviser's role is one of counseling, coaching, or process consultation.

For MBO to be used as an OD intervention, then, it should include (1) a team approach to setting and reviewing targets; (2) real participation by subordinates in setting goals, with an emphasis upon mutually agreed upon goals; and (3) a real concern for personal career goals as well as for organization goals. When MBO is used in this sense, it can provide individual satisfaction and motivation as well as increased organization attainment.

Among the major premises of MBO are the following:

- The first step is to identify the goals of the organization.
- Responsibility for achieving these goals is developed among individual managers.

- Managerial behavior is assumed to be more important than personality, and this should be defined in terms of results.
- Participation in goal setting and decision making is highly desirable.
- The successful manager is a manager of situations; thus there is no one best way of managing. Rather, the managerial behavior best calculated to achieve results in each situation will be most effective.[19]

The MBO Process

The MBO process usually includes the following phases:

1. The top management team studies the operating system.
2. From this study, the team sets up measures of organizational performance.
3. Goal setting sessions are then held down through the first-line supervisory level.

Although opinions vary on the specific implementation of MBO, most practitioners emphasize the need for top management's commitment to MBO. The central focus of any MBO program is the development of agreement between supervisor and subordinate about continuing objectives and targets.

Management by objectives may be described as a process consisting of a series of interrelated steps.

- *Step 1* The subordinate proposes a set of goals for the upcoming time period. This proposal sets forth specific goals and performance measures.
- *Step 2* The subordinate and the superior jointly develop specific goals and targets. These goals must be specific, measurable objectives for each area of responsibility, and they must be *mutually* agreed upon by subordinate and superior. The major responsibility, of course, should lie with the subordinate. These objectives should include both performance goals and personal development goals.
- *Step 3* A period of performance in which actual performance of the individual involved is measured against his or her individual goals.
- *Step 4* The feedback of results to the individual and appropriate rewards for performance. This individual performance review involves an appraisal of accomplishments and variances of overall performance compared with targets and is discussed by subordinate and superior.

- *Step 5* The outcome of the performance review provides
  the basis for setting new performance goals and recycling of
  the goal setting process.

Many of the guidelines for setting objectives are the same as researchers have found to be effective in other types of goal setting programs.

Every effort should be made by the superior and the subordinate to make the goals as precise and specific as possible. There must be agreement and acceptance of these objectives by both the individual and his or her superior. These interactions between a manager and a subordinate also provide a counseling and coaching opportunity and in this manner provide for management development. Although these specific steps in the MBO process may vary among organizations and practitioners, the goals are similar, including increased levels of performance and increased understanding at all levels of organization objectives.

The Results of MBO

MBO has been tried by many different types of organizations. One difficulty in appraising these approaches is that MBO has become an all-purpose term implying many different things in many different organization settings. Carroll and Tosi, in a study of 87 organizations using MBO, concluded that there are at least 10 different approaches to MBO, ranging from motivational to coercive.[20] Most research on MBO programs has reported mixed results. Some studies indicate that MBO has increased organization performance, and others indicate inefficiency and weakness in application. Although research on the effectiveness of MBO is not conclusive, the trend of findings is generally favorable. Several studies have found that goal setting results in improved performance and increased motivation and "have found that those managers working under MBO programs were more likely to have taken specific actions to improve performance than were those who continued with the traditional performance appraisal approach."[21] Other evidence indicates that MBO seems to be associated with positive attitudes toward the work situation and that participation by subordinates in decision making can improve performance level and job satisfaction. Tandem Computer has used MBO successfully (see OD Application 12.1).

Some research on MBO programs indicates that this technique can improve organization performance. In a two-part study at Purex Corporation, Anthony Raia reported that MBO reversed production rates from a 0.4 percent decline per month to an increase of 0.3 percent per month. In a second follow-up study, however, he found that participants felt that the program overemphasized production, was used as a whip, and failed to involve all levels of management.[22]

TANDEM COMPUTERS

It's 4:30 on Friday afternoon, and the weekly beer bust is in full swing at Tandem Computers' Cupertino, California headquarters. Sun shines on the basketball court beyond the corporate patio and sparkles on the company swimming pool. . . .

Five hundred cheerful souls, mostly young and casual looking, are talking animatedly, glass in hand. Every week 60 percent of the company drops in at the beer bust for an hour, joined sometimes by visiting customers or suppliers, who take away indelible memories. Says the representative of one satisfied user, a stately major bank, "When the president comes down in a cowboy hat and boots and swills beer—that's different!" . . .

Jim Treybig is a lean Texan with a BS degree in electrical engineering from Rice and an MBA degree from Stanford.

The People

Every Friday afternoon Tandem stages its weekly beer bust. This is an opportunity for all employees to gather and socialize with their bosses and subordinates. The hierarchy of work is relaxed in this setting and people have the opportunity to interact more as equals, without the hierarchical roles. Managers and subordinates are able to get to know each other as equals. This helps promote the "corporate culture" of Tandem and strengthens their team-building efforts.

Management Philosophy

Treybig's management philosophy consists of three major points: hire outstanding people, create an environment where they will be motivated to work and, perhaps most important, take an interest in every individual the company employs.

At Tandem, employees are encouraged to set their own objectives and are then rewarded with stock ownership. Therefore, every employee has a stake in the success of the company. As Jim Treybig has commented, "The culture is oriented to risk-taking. We have a pool of people willing to take risks and we have thousands of risk-oriented decisions every day."

In a survey late in fiscal 1981, 83 percent of employees said they believe advancement opportunities at Tandem are greater than at any other place they have worked. Tandem believes that promotions from within will perpetuate consistency and produce the management quality essential to the company's continued, prosperous growth.

Questions:
1. Does the risk-taking philosophy at Tandem fit with MBO?
2. What are potential strengths/weaknesses of Tandem's approach?
3. How does the MBO system relate to the corporate culture?

Source: See Myron Magnot "Managing by Mystique," *Fortune*, June 28, 1982, pp. 84–91. © 1982 Time, Inc. All rights reserved.

John Ivancevich has also described an empirically based study relating an MBO change program to improved performance variables. This study, involving 181 subordinates in production and marketing groups in two plants, found that improvements in the production units occurred earlier than in the marketing units, and that plant 2 showed significantly better performance than either plant 1 or the control plant.[23]

Criticisms of MBO

The implementation of MBO, however, usually requires large quantities of time, money, and effort for successful adaptation. Because of these limitations, MBO has traditionally been used primarily with managerial and professional employees. For employees performing more routine work at the lower levels of an organization, obtaining benefits that exceed costs has been more difficult.

Some MBO programs may also have problems because management fails to recognize that proper implementation of MBO requires new improved managerial skills and competence (see B.C. comic strip). Harry Levinson, a major critic of MBO programs, has described several of these problems. He suggests that job descriptions do not fully take into account organization interdependencies and may tend to be imposed upon the individual.[24] Steven Kerr has also criticized MBO and has pointed out several similar limitations. He questions whether joint goal setting among unequals is possible, whether the subordinates at lower levels are free to select their own objectives, whether MBO aids in evaluating and rewarding performance, whether setting objectives as expli-

Source: B.C. by permission of Johnny Hart and Creators Syndicate, Inc.

citly as possible is always functional, and finally, whether MBO is really applicable in a dynamic and changing environment.[25]

In one study of Ivancevich, Donnelly, and Lyon,[26] it was found that the MBO program's lack of top management involvement in setting up the program resulted in the program never being effectively implemented with lower-level managers. The same study found that participants in the MBO program complained of difficulty in stating goals quantitatively for all facets of the job.

MBO has been widely used in organizations and in one study of Fortune 500 companies, 86 percent report using or having used MBO.[27] However, 11 percent report not using MBO at the time of responding to the survey, mirroring somewhat of an industry trend toward discontinuing MBO programs. MBO received a good deal of publicity in the 1960s and 1970s and expectations of some managers rose to unrealistic levels.

MBO is a technique that includes a multitude of different types of programs, and many OD practitioners question whether MBO should be considered an OD intervention. Some practitioners believe that properly designed MBO programs, based upon McGregor's concepts, can have positive organization results. Others, including Levinson and Kerr, believe that MBO can be improved by placing a greater emphasis upon individual goals and examining the underlying assumptions of motivation within these programs. There should also be an emphasis on mutual goal setting and frequent feedback and interaction between superior and subordinate. Research evidence also indicates that less paperwork leads to improved effectiveness of MBO programs. In summary, MBO programs can be effective in systematically engaging individuals in target setting and performance improvement. Research on organization MBO programs indicates that this approach can improve managerial performance and organization goal setting and planning.

REVIEW QUESTIONS

1. Identify the major techniques in setting goals.

2. Compare and contrast the reasons for successful and unsuccessful MBO programs.

3. Discuss the role of participation in goal setting.

KEY WORDS AND CONCEPTS

Define and be able to use the following:

Goals   Goal setting
Goal content   Goal acceptance
Goal intensity   Participation
Management by objectives (MBO)

IV.
Simulations

SIMULATION 12.1 ORGANIZATION GOAL SETTING

Total time suggested: 1 hour, 30 minutes.

A. Purpose

This simulation is intended to allow you the opportunity to set goals within an organization setting and observe how personal and organizational goals can be in conflict. You will experience how conflicting goals can sometimes be resolved.

B. Procedure

Step 1 Prior to class form teams of seven (extras act as additional observers), select roles, and read the Vernal Corporation Background Information and your role description. Read only your role and make your individual decision. The roles are:

1. Project Manager
2. Accounting Systems Consultant
3. Information Systems Consultant
4. Technical Support Consultant
5. Government Contracts Consultant
6. OD Consultant
7. Observer(s)

Step 2 Meet with your team members and the project manager, who conducts the meeting. The OD Consultant will also be present to help with group process.
Time suggested for Step 2: 45 minutes.

Step 3 Critique your team meeting and the quality of the meeting. The observer(s) will provide feedback. Also consider the following:

1. Were individual goals made public or were they concealed? Share at this point any information not previously disclosed in the team meeting.

2. Were both individual and organization goals adequately met?

3. To what extent did the personality of an individual influence the decision?

4. Do members currently support the decision?

5. Was the OD Consultant helpful? Dysfunctional? What suggestions for improvement can you give?

Time suggested for Step 3: 15 minutes.

Step 4   Meet with the other teams to compare decisions.

1. Each team presents their decision and the factors most important in arriving at the decision.

2. To what extent was there member support for the final decision? How could support have been increased?

3. How closely did differing teams achieve goal agreement? If there were differences, to what could the differences be attributed considering all teams had the same base of information?

4. Did the OD Consultant make content suggestions or emphasize providing process interventions?

Step 5   The class should discuss the process of goal setting and conflict resolution.

Time suggested for Steps 4 and 5: 30 minutes.

VERNAL CORPORATION BACKGROUND INFORMATION

Vernal is a medium-size company offering consulting services for accounting systems and information systems, and a special unit specializing in local and federal government contracts. Until now Vernal has had only one facility for all operations and the majority of the business was conducted for clients in the metropolitan area. Because of substantial contracts recently obtained in another city in the same state, 200 miles away, Vernal has decided to open a field office there. The office will be headed by a project manager and will consist of representatives from Accounting Systems, Information Systems, Technical Support Unit, and Government Contracts Unit.

The headquarters of Vernal is a new facility located in a planned suburban community, almost a rural setting, with the most up-to-date facilities. The company has a complete health facility which is part of its "wellness" program, company-provided van pools, bicycle paths connected to the communities' extensive bicycle paths, covered and free parking lots, and a company-subsidized restaurant and cafeteria.

ROLE DESCRIPTION (READ *ONLY* YOUR ROLE)

Role 1—Project Manager   You have been selected as the Project Manager for the new facility across state. The four representatives will report directly to you and your job will be to coordinate their activities with the home office. You applied for the position and the move will mean an advancement for all those selected. The assignment is expected to last about 5 years and then you will be transferred back to company headquarters.

One of the first tasks facing you and your team before making the move is to select an office. Although you have reserved the right to make the final decision, you have called a meeting of those making the move to receive their input so that you can make a more informed decision. You are also interested in getting off to a good start with the other people as your success is largely determined by how well they do their job; therefore, you would like to have them agree upon a decision which best meets both the individual and company goals.

You have drawn up a summary of the available offices you obtained on a recent fact-finding trip (see the Office Alternative List). The four alternative offices on the summary sheet are the only choices available and the information on the sheet, though incomplete, is all that is available.

You have been informed that the maximum the company is willing to spend is $12,000 a month, though you would like to reserve $1,000 for last-minute lease changes. The offices have a monthly base lease rate and a group of options available. Most of the options have specific costs and you will have to select options that will not exceed $12,000 less the $1,000 reserve. Also, you would like to keep costs to a minimum.

You would personally like the office to be located close to the suburbs where you hope to buy a house. A private office area, such as a converted conference room, is important to you as it will lend respect to your position with the other team members. Otherwise you are not big on amenities such as a prestige office and furnishings. You are interested in bottom-line results that look good back at the home office, not a plush office.

Roles 2 through 5—All Representatives   You have been selected as the representative from your division to move to the new facility across the state. You will report directly to the project manager but you will retain close ties with your division. You applied for the position and the move will mean an advancement for all those selected. The assignment is expected to last about 5 years before you are transferred back to company headquarters.

The project manager has called a meeting of those making the move to help select an office. The project manager has reserved the right to make the final decision, but he/she would like to get your input. The manager has given you a summary of the offices with pertinent information he/she obtained on a recent fact-finding trip (See the Office Alternative List). The four alternative

OFFICE ALTERNATIVE LIST

Type	Suburban Shopping Center Office	Regional Office Building	Downtown Office Building	Downtown High Rise
Base lease	$7,000	$9,000	$8,000	$10,000
Size	Large, 4 rooms.	Adequate, 1 moderate size room.	Adequate, 1 moderate size room.	Large, 1 room.
Custodial service	$200	$300	$300	$400
Furnishings	Used carpet and furniture, fair condition, $300. New carpet and furniture, $550.	Used carpet and furniture, good condition, $400. New carpet and furniture, $550.	Used carpet and furniture, good condition, $300. New carpet and furniture, $600.	Nearly new carpet and furniture, $500. New furniture, $700.
Conference rooms including furnishings	Not available but office space has 4 rooms.	Up to 5 available, $1000 each.	Up to two available, $700 each.	Up to 4 available, $1,100 each.
Prestige of building	Little.	Moderately high.	Some	High
Windows and view	Small windows with limited view. No cost.	Large windows with view, $200. Lower 5 floors, windows with poor view, no cost.	Average windows with poor view. No cost.	Large windows with excellent view, top 5 floors, $500. Lower floors with moderate view, no cost.

324

	2 story	25 story	10 story	40 story
Size of building	2 story.	25 story.	10 story.	40 story.
Location	Suburban area. Nice housing nearby.	Large regional business center in suburban area. Various types of housing in area within 1/4 hour.	Downtown business district. Few and expensive apartments in area. Driving time to affordable housing, 3/4 hour.	Downtown business district. Apartments in building and area expensive. Driving time to affordable housing, 1/2 hour.
Parking	Street and small lot in rear. No cost.	One parking lot, $50 monthly per car. Street readily available.	One car allowed in building garage, no cost. Unlimited garage space 1 block away, $30 monthly per car. No street parking.	Unlimited in building. No cost for tenants and guests. No street parking.
Mass transportation system	None. Some bicycle paths.	None. Car pools. Some bicycle paths.	Bus. Building-sponsored van pools, $50 per office. Car pools.	Bus. Car pools.
Dining in building	Not available. Fast food next door.	Coffee shop in building. OK restaurants in area.	Coffee shop and restaurant in building. Excellent restaurants in area.	Coffee shop and excellent restaurants in building. Catering available for offices.
Coffee machine, refrigerator, stove, kitchen	Small kitchen with all appliances, $100.	Small kitchen, appliances, lunch area, $200.	No kitchen. Coffee machine, $50.	Small kitchen, appliances, and dining area, $300.
Miscellaneous services	Health club (gym and hot tub), 2 blocks away. $75 per member. Hair styling, 1 block away.	Hair styling. Complete health and recreation club next door, $100 per member.	Hair styling. No recreation facilities.	Hair styling. Hot tub, gym, pool, $200 per office. Guests allowed.

offices on the summary sheet are the only choices available and the information on the sheet, though incomplete, is all that is available.

The project manager has informed you that the maximum the company is willing to spend on the new office space is $12,000 a month. The offices have a monthly base lease rate and a group of options available. Most of the options have specific costs and you will have to select those options that will not exceed $12,000. You will also need to build support for your choices with the other representatives and most certainly try to convince the project manager of your choices. You may say anything in order to build this support.

Role 2—Accounting Systems Consultant Your goal is to select an office reasonably close to your clients, many of whom are located in the downtown area. Clients will be coming to the office so it is important to have an impressive office, at least two conference rooms, adequate parking, and proximity to restaurants. You don't like to drive so some kind of transportation other than driving is important or else you would consider an apartment within walking distance.

Role 3—Information Systems Consultant You will often entertain your clients at the office. You believe that to entertain clients in meetings, you need a prestige office with a good view, good furnishings, three conference rooms, and dining facilities. A downtown location close to your clients is desirable. You prefer to live in an apartment near your office.

Role 4—Technical Support Consultant You believe that health and recreation are the most important factor. Therefore, your goal is to select an office with full recreational and health facilities like those at the company headquarters. It would be ideal if there were amenities such as a barber/beauty shop and restaurants. As your work requires you to call on clients at their offices to work out technical problems, you see no reason to have a lavish office. You would like to be able to purchase a house reasonably close to the office.

Role 5—Government Contracts Consultant You think it is important to have functionally adequate quarters, reasonably well furnished, and with a small kitchen, because you normally eat in the office. You are normally in and out of the office a lot to call on your clients, so parking close to the office is important. You also want health facilities similar to those at the home office. Because your time is important to you, you would like to get an apartment close to your work so you can ride your bike.

Role 6—OD Consultant You hope to accomplish several things at this meeting:

1. To develop a consultant-client relationship with all committee members.

2. To help the committee members in their task by making appropriate process interventions.

3. To not become involved in the content of the problem.

Role 7—Observer You will only observe during the role play session so that you can help the team critique their meeting in Steps 3 and 4. The Observer Form may assist you in providing feedback.

OBSERVER FORM

Instructions: For each item, place a number in the blank to the right representing your reaction to how your group performed based on the following scale.

Low 1 : 2 : 3 : 4 : 5 : 6 : 7 : 8 : 9 : 10 High

1 Degree of cooperative teamwork: _____

2 Degree of team motivation: _____

3 Degree of member satisfaction: _____

4 Degree of information sharing (participation):   _____

5 Degree of consensual decision making: _____

6 Degree of team conflict or competition (i.e., conflict directly faced and resolved):   _____

7 Degree of quality of group decisions: _____

8 Degree of speed with which decision is made: _____

9 Degree of participating leadership: _____

10 Degree of clarity of goals: _____

Total ranking   _____

SIMULATION 12.2 MANAGING BY OBJECTIVES

Total time suggested: 1 hour, 15 minutes.

A. Purpose

To give participants an opportunity to practice goal setting and apply it to their own objectives, to practice MBO-type coaching and counseling relationships, and to receive feedback on their own consultant style.

B. Procedures

Step 1   Form groups of three. Each individual will have an opportunity (1) to review his or her objectives (client), (2) to act as consultant, and (3) to observe.
Step 2   The client will review his or her list of Personal Objectives for Course from Simulation 2.1, Chapter 2 and determine the progress toward the goals.

The consultant will act as a process consultant, helping the client determine specific, mutual objectives, providing feedback, and reviewing progress toward goals.

The observer is to carefully note the interaction of consultant and client (see the Observer Form), looking for actions that would facilitate or inhibit the MBO process, and indicating the consultant's style.
Step 3   Rotate roles until each person has reviewed their objectives.
Time suggested for Steps 1–3: 60 minutes.
Step 4   The total group should then discuss the process of consulting or coaching another individual in the goal-setting situation.
Time suggested for Step 4: 15 minutes.

OBSERVER FORM

Instructions: Based on the following scale, select the number that indicates your observation of the following areas. Record your choice in the blank to the right.

Very   Very

| 1 | 2 | 3 | 4 | 5 | 6 | 7 |

Little   Much

Did the consultant

1. Establish a relationship?   _____

2. Take over the problem?   _____

3. Focus on feelings?   _____

4. Encourage the client to be specific?   _____

5. Allow the client to talk?   _____

6. Lead and direct the conversation?   _____

7. Show indications of judging the client?   _____

**Case:
Western
Utilities
Company**

Western Utilities Company, a privately owned utility company, has been faced with an expansion of its facilities resulting in financial inefficiencies. Floyd Orlan, president, has requested a review of all operating standards.

He requested that John Givens and Hilda Hirsh set out a broad outline of MBO performance standards that would identify key standards with which to control performance. Three years ago, Western Utilities, under the direction of a management consulting firm, implemented a system of management by objectives (MBO) for the purpose of evaluating department managers, sales engineers, and consumer service employees.

The advantage of such a system of controls is that top management can very rapidly scan a printout and detect any trouble spots in the department. Givens and Hirsh attempted to set the standards as if the personnel were working at a normal pace. After review, Givens and Hirsh raised the performance level on several items. Their justification was that if a standard can be achieved without a challenge, it is probably too low. The president had specifically asked for goals that were not easily attainable. There was a certain amount of negative reaction, but in the end the departments agreed.

THE SITUATION

During the past year, however, a significant degree of dissatisfaction has emerged. In the first year participation was encouraged and rewards were obtained. The employees set their goals high and productivity increased.

Now, however, problems are being reported in the evaluation of performance, many managers claiming that the standards set by Hirsh were too tight or unfair. Floyd Orlan said: "Yes, we have had a few operating problems, but no system is perfect." Hirsh noted that the consumer department had exceeded their monthly labor cost standards, so she called Bill Walton and "red-lined" his performance report. Walton hit the roof. He called Givens and said: "The system is grossly unfair and inaccurate as a measure of performance. The real objective is to control total costs. My department has done this, even though we were over in labor costs. There was a heavy snowstorm last month with lots of frozen lines, and we had to get people out there on overtime. The real need is to maximize customer service and to keep costs to a minimum, which we have done."

Two other department managers complained that the system was unfair, and several engineers are threatening to resign. In their complaints to Givens, they pointed out that it appeared that Hirsh was only looking for failures to report, under the cover of the MBO system. Floyd Orlan thought: We may need to take another look at our system; maybe MBO doesn't work in a utility.

CASE ANALYSIS FORM

I. Problems

   A. Macro

      1. _____

      2. _____

B. Micro

    1. _____

    2. _____

II. Causes

    1. _____

    2. _____

    3. _____

III. Systems affected

    1. Structural

    2. Psychosocial

    3. Technical

    4. Managerial

    5.

IV. Alternatives

    1. _____

    2. _____

    3. _____

    4. _____

    5. _____

V. Recommendations

    1. _____

    2. _____

    3. _____

V. Summary

Goal setting and management by objectives have been described in this chapter. Goal setting can have highly beneficial results for both individuals and organizations as reported in the research findings. However, goal setting requires careful planning if it is to be used in an OD program. There are certain characteristics of a goal which tend to result in a more effective goal-setting program. The goal should be difficult, specific, measurable, and achievable. When implemented in an organization, feedback should be provided by management to the employee. Commitment by the individual is crucial and participation in designing the goal is one of the more effective ways to assure acceptance.

Management by objectives has been widely used in organizations but its success has been mixed. The failure of MBO programs can partially be traced to unrealistic expectations by management and to improper implementation. Despite some of the negative reports of MBO, it incorporates some very sound techniques of goal setting and should not be overlooked as an OD goal-setting technique.

In the simulations you had an opportunity to experience and practice the concept of goal setting. You set your individual goals and also acted much as a manager or OD practitioner would do in negotiating team goals. In the simulation you also experienced a situation where employees with different goals were confronted with a common problem.

NOTES

1. See F. Donaldson, "Financial Goals and Strategic Consequences," *Harvard Business Review*, May–June 1985, pp. 57–66.

2. E. A. Locke, "Toward a Theory of Task Motivation and Incentives," *Organizational Behavior and Human Performance*, 3 (1968), 157–89.

3. E. A. Locke, L. M. Saari, K. N. Shaw, and G. P. Latham, "Goal Setting and Task Performance: 1969–1980," *Psychological Bulletin*, 90, no. 1 (1981), 126.

4. For a more extensive review of the research findings see Locke, Saari, Shaw, and Latham, "Goal Setting," pp. 125–52.

5. A. J. Mento, N. D. Cartledge, and E. A. Locke, "Another Look at the Relationship of Expectancy and Goal Difficulty to Task Performance," *Organizational Behavior and Human Performance*, 25 (1980), 419–40.

6. G. P. Latham and G. A. Yukl, "A Review of Research on the Application of Goal Setting in Organizations," *Academy of Management Journal*, 18, no. 4 (December 1975), 833.

7. Locke, Saari, Shaw, and Latham, "Goal Setting," p. 135.

8. G. P. Latham and E. A. Locke, "Goal Setting—A Motivational Technique That Works," *Organizational Dynamics*, Autumn 1979, pp. 68–80.

9. Locke, Saari, Shaw, and Latham, "Goal Setting," p. 125.

10. E. A. Locke, D. B. Feren, V. M. McCaleb, K. N. Shaw, and A.T. Denny, "The Relative Effectiveness of Four Methods of Motivating Employee Performance," *Changes in Working Life*, eds. K. Duncan, M. Gruneberg, and D. Wallis (New York: John Wiley & Sons, Inc., 1980).

11. G. P. Latham and J. J. Baldes, "The 'Practical Significance' of Locke's Theory of Goal Setting," *Journal of Applied Psychology*, 60 (1975), 122–24.

12. S. Thure, "An Investigation into the Effect of Long-range Planning in Selected Industries." Unpublished MBA thesis, Bernard M. Baruch School of Business, City University of New York, 1967. Referenced in Richard M. Steers, *Organizational Effectiveness: A Behavioral View* (Santa Monica, Calif.: Goodyear Publishing Company, Inc., 1977) p. 137.

13. This description is based upon S. Carroll and W. Tosi, Jr., *Management by Objectives, Applications and Research* (New York: Macmillan, Inc., 1973); George Odiorne, *Management by Objectives* (Belmont, Calif.: Pitman Publishing Corporation, 1965); and Anthony Raia, *Managing by Objectives* (Glenview, Ill.: Scott, Foresman & Company, 1974).

14. George Odiorne, *MBO II* (Belmont, Calif.: Fearon-Pitman Publishing Inc., 1979), p. 53.

15. Raia, *Managing by Objectives*, p. 11.

16. Arthur Beck and Ellis Hillmar, "OD to MBO or MBO to OD: Does It Make a Difference?" *Personnel Journal*, November 1972, pp. 827–34.

17. Douglas M. McGregor, *The Human Side of Enterprise* (New York: McGraw-Hill Book Company, 1960), p. 61. Also Douglas M. McGregor, "An Uneasy Look at Performance Appraisal," *Harvard Business Review* May–June 1957, pp. 89–94.

18. McGregor, *Human Side*, p. 62.

19. See W. French and R. Hollman, "Management by Objectives: The Team Approach," *California Management Review*, 17 (Spring 1975), 13–22.

20. Carroll and Tosi, *Management by Objectives.*

21. See Raia, *Managing by Objectives*; and H. Meyer, E. Kay, and J. French, "Split Roles and Performance Appraisal," *Harvard Business Review*, January–February 1965, p. 123.

22. Anthony Raia, "Goal Setting and Self-control: An Empirical Study," *Journal of Management Studies*, no. 2 (1965), 34–53. See also Anthony Raia, "A Second Look at Management Goals and Controls," *California Management Review*, no. 8 (1965), 49–58.

23. John Ivancevich, "Changes in Performance in an MBO Program," *Administrative Science Quarterly*, 19: 563–74, December 1974.

24. Harry Levinson, "Management by Objectives: A Critique," *Training and Development Journal*, April 1972.

25. Steven Kerr, "Some Modifications in MBO as OD Strategy," *Academy of Management Proceedings*, 1972 National Meeting.

26. J. M. Ivancevich, J. H. Donnelly, and H. L. Lyon, "A Study of the Impact of Management by Objectives on Perceived Need Satisfaction," *Personnel Psychology*, 23 (1970), 131–51.

27. Stephen R. Michael, "Organizational Change Techniques: Their Present, Their Future," *Organizational Dynamics*, Summer 1982, p. 77.

13

OD PRODUCTIVITY INTERVENTIONS

I.
Objectives

Upon completing this chapter, you will be able to:

1. Describe the major OD productivity interventions.

2. Identify the similarities and differences in quality of work life, job design, and quality circles.

3. Diagnose job design problems as part of an OD program.

4. Experience how an OD practitioner can assist an organization in making productivity changes.

II.
Premeeting
Preparation

1. Read the Background Information (Section III).

2. Complete Step 1 of Simulation 13.1 (Section IV).

3. Read and analyze Case: The Keyboard Company.

III.
Background
Information

One of the key issues facing organizations today is the way in which they respond to an environment of "world class competition." OD interventions leading to improved productivity, efficiency, and quality have evolved to help organizations meet these challenges. In this chapter, several OD productivity interventions will be described including quality of work life, job design, and quality circles.

Changes in work design can result in increased productivity and job satisfaction. The OD practitioner can help design the jobs of line and staff employees and all levels of managers so that all of an employee's resources and capabilities are utilized.

This chapter deals with improving work processes for individuals and work teams. Much of the material applies the concepts presented in previous chapters, particularly team building and intergroup development.

Business enterprises and nonprofit organizations are increasingly confronted with problems of stable or declining productivity, worker dissatisfaction and alienation, and increased domestic and foreign competition. Many federal regulations that once tended to protect inefficient operations are being removed and companies are now confronted with increased competition. Witness the rapid changes in the services and products offered by the telecommunications industry, the rapid expansion and mergers of airline carriers, the expansion of services offered by the once conservative banking industry, and the change in the way health care is offered.

It is common to read reports in daily newspapers about the decline in U.S. productivity, another U.S. market being lost to foreign industry, or the continued deterioration in the quality of U.S. products. The United States is no longer leading the world in technological innovations. "In the 1950s, the U.S. initiated more than 80 percent of the world's major innovations; today it is close to 50 percent, and foreigners are acquiring a much larger share of U.S. patents (now over a third)."[1] But the problems are not only in the technology-based industries. Local, state, and federal governments are also trying to maintain or increase services despite budget reductions.

The OD practitioner uses work design concepts such as quality of work life, job design, and quality circles, to help organizations make productivity changes while at the same time improving the work life of employees.

QUALITY OF WORK LIFE

Quality of work life (QWL)[2] attempts to improve the quality of life for the worker. Industrialized life has traditionally placed its emphasis upon technological advancement, productivity, and growth. The worker, explicitly or implicitly, was relegated to the role of a "factor of production," together with land and capital. QWL is trying to meet the needs of an increasingly aliented worker. The traditional emphasis of QWL is upon the lower-level workers, although it is a total system program. Because of this emphasis, QWL is largely responsible for the movement of OD downward in the organization hierarchy.

What Is QWL?

QWL is a management philosophy that has been moving in and out of popularity since the early 1970s. During this time the definition of QWL has been changing and evolving. In fact, QWL may include quality circles, job enrichment, an approach to collective bargaining, employee mental health, job design, industrial democracy, participative management, and organization development. One view of QWL is that it includes all these things and more, but the lack of a generally accepted definition may spell the demise of QWL because managers may think of it as a cure-all.

The current view of QWL is that "it is a *philosophy* of managing the enterprise in general, and human resources in particular."[3] It is not a program or project. David Nadler and Edward Lawler define QWL as "a way of thinking about people, work, and organizations. Its distinctive elements are (1) a concern about the impact of work on people as well as on organizational effectiveness, and (2) the idea of participation in organizational problem solving and decision making."[4] QWL is not limited to changing the context of a job, it also includes humanizing the work environment in order to improve worker dignity and self-esteem.

QWL is a comprehensive program considering many needs and requirements. It incorporates certain legislative acts, including the Fair Labor Standards Act, equal employment opportunity acts, and workers' compensation laws. QWL recognizes unions and their concerns, including pay, job security, and due process. In companies having workers represented by a union, QWL will work closely with the union organization. For this reason QWL is perhaps the OD intervention that explicitly recognizes and works with a union. QWL incorporates the idea of psychologists of the 1950s for more humanistic management. Also included are the ideas of job enrichment originally proposed by Frederic Herzberg. Finally, QWL incorporates the ideas of social responsibility for the employer. All of these concerns are at the core of QWL and it is truly a system-wide intervention. In fact, there is some discussion as to whether QWL is a part of OD or OD is a part of QWL.

QWL is still evolving and many companies are reluctant, for proprietary reasons, to discuss the specifics. Richard E. Walton, in a paper presented to the Conference on the Quality of Working Life, has provided one of the better descriptions of an ideal QWL.[5] Walton identifies eight major categories as a framework for analyzing the quality of working life:

1. *Adequate and fair compensation.* Does the income from full-time employment meet society's standards or the worker's standard? Is the pay compatible with other types of work?

2. *Safe and healthy working conditions.* Are the work conditions physically safe? Reasonable hours of work?

3. *Immediate opportunity to use and develop human capacities.* Does the work allow the use of a wide range of skills? Does the work allow autonomy and self-control? Is relevant and meaningful information available? Is the work a complete or natural unit, or is it a small part of a unit? Does the work allow for planning?

4. *Future opportunity for continued growth and security.* Does the work permit growth of a person's capacities? Are there advancement opportunities to use newly acquired skills or knowledge? What is the employment and income security?

5. *Social integration in the work organization.* Is there freedom from prejudice? To what extent does the organization rely on status symbols and the hierarchy? Is there upward mobility? Is there interpersonal openness between members and support for each other?

6. *Constitutionalism in the work organization.* Do the members have a right to personal privacy? Can members speak out without fear of reprisal from higher authority? Is there equitable treatment of members? Is there due process for grievances and complaints?

7. *Work and the total life space.* Does the work organization allow the member to have other life roles? What are the overtime requirements, travel demands, and geographical moves?

8. *The social relevance of work life.* How does the worker perceive the social responsibility of the organization: products, waste disposal, marketing and selling techniques, employment practices, relations to underdeveloped countries, participation in political campaigns, attitude to laws, and so on?

Walton's eight categories of QWL have been placed into four managerial dimensions.[6] The first dimension is challenging and meaningful jobs, or job content, and includes utilizing the creative talents of the individual. The second dimension is job context and includes enriching jobs to build motivation and commitment. It also refers to managerial practices such as the effective use of reward systems and leadership. The third dimension is job potential which is the opportunity for learning new skills, opportunities for advancement in career paths and for security in the job. The fourth dimension of QWL is the social relevance of the work or the importance of an individual's work to the well-being of society.

The eight categories proposed by Walton can be analyzed along several lines, but it is impossible to make general conclusions as to their applicability. Some of the categories are positively correlated, such as fair compensation and socially responsible employment practices. But other categories are apparently negatively correlated; for example, to permit a person to advance in an organization, it may be necessary to require a geographical move. The general relationship of the categories to productivity cannot be made; so much depends on the perceptions of the workers. There are wide differences in the expressed needs of various employment groups and the needs change with time. A steelworker who makes more than his neighbor, who is a schoolteacher, will complain about the lack of challenge of his job while the schoolteacher complains about low pay. If one were to listen to steelworkers, the young employees might be asking for more advancement and career opportunities, while their seniors might be wanting more paid vacation time. Perhaps it is possible to resolve these problems to some extent by permitting diversity between organizations and even within an organization. An organization might specialize or tailor itself to offer a QWL program along just a few categories, and it would publically announce this and recruit along these categories. Or an organization building a QWL program along all eight categories might design work units along a particular pattern of work life and allow employees to make a selection based on individual preferences. The employee could also change from one pattern to another as life goals changed. An example of a QWL program at AT&T is described in OD application 13.1.

Results of QWL

The results of QWL efforts have been difficult to evaluate in terms of empirical research. QWL can take a variety of forms when implemented in an organization. It is also a philosophy of management. It is therefore difficult to specify what is a QWL effort in an organization in order to measure its success. Most of the reported results of QWL take the form of case studies. Though case studies are enlightening and certainly important, they are not scientific investigations. Some of the cases which have been widely reported in business journals, national television, and newspapers include efforts by General Motors at Tarrytown, New York and Brookhaven, Mississippi; General Foods at Topeka, Kansas; and Harman International Industries at Bolivar, Tennessee.

One of the largest and oldest QWL efforts is that of the United Auto Workers and General Motors where QWL dates back to 1973. Since then workers have been having a larger voice in decisions affecting their jobs. UAW is the leading union advocate of QWL, although some union officials believe it is a management strategy to dupe workers into believing they are running the plant. According to a previous GM Chairman Thomas A. Murphey, "We've had great success with [work teams] and other quality-of-work programs. We've found they improve human satisfaction and performance, and we intend to continue them."[7] This position is echoed by Irving Blueston, a UAW vice president and longtime advocate of QWL programs, who says, "Our experiments (at GM) will continue to expand." According to a *Business Week* article reporting on GM's QWL programs, "Preliminary results indicate that these programs have dramatically improved relations between workers and managers and thus reduced chances of an epidemic of local strikes." Another union official, Don Ephlin, head of UAW regional office in Hartford, Connecticut, says of GM's Tarrytown, New York plant, "The grievance load has been cut from 2,000 to 20

QUALITY OF WORK LIFE AT AT&T

Charles L. Brown, chairman of the board of AT&T, made the following comments about quality of work life activities he helped foster at AT&T:

> I have seen it as a particularly welcome thing, one that will facilitate what I think has to happen in any event in the way of management style changes. I suppose, also, I flatter myself that it is the way that I like to manage, and when I don't do it, I should. What interested me in it? I think the combination of the currentness of the matter in the literature, the experiences of other organizations, and just an inherent feeling that if we can push responsibility lower down, then we should. I was attracted to it because it would be helpful to us in facing our future.

When asked specifically what it means to be doing quality of work life activities, Brown said:

> I think one of my predecessors explained it about as well as I can. People do a superior job when they're first convinced that they have a job that's worth doing. I think that exemplifies a good deal of the thrust of the "quality of work life" idea. As soon as people understand and personally believe that they have a job worth doing, miracles occur in the way they do their job. That's certainly a major part of it—to raise the level of an individual's respect for the job that he or she is doing, as opposed to going in the other direction. Respect for one's job, after all, is one step toward respect for oneself.

> I have believed for most of my career that we have not taken enough advantage of this opportunity. We have expected too many supervisors at too many levels to do too much of the wrong thing. I'm glad to have a good reason to get on with it.

Questions:
1.   Which of the eight QWL categories defined by Walton is AT&T's program based on?
2.   How would you describe AT&T's culture and is this important in the success of a QWL program?

or so, discipline is minimal, treatment by management is better, and everybody is more of an integral part of the structure than ever before." And a Tarrytown local UAW president, Raymond Calore, reports, "There's more freedom and expression here now. What the [QWL] program has done is create an atmosphere at the workplace that is no different than it is at home. You're not turned off when you walk in the factory gate."[8]

QWL at the Topeka Pet Food Plant of General Foods began with the design and opening of the plant there in 1971.[9] The planners of the plant designed a supervisory structure, a reward system, and a social system using knowledge gained from the behavioral sciences. Supervisors were screened and received extensive managerial development training. The line workers were also screened to include characteristics such as good communication abilities, a team orientation to work, and good analytical skills. Some of the results reported after 18 months included fixed overhead reduced by 33 percent and an annual savings of $600,000 from reduced absenteeism. Another report in 1974 showed annual savings of $2 million and the plant was being labeled a success. It should be remembered that these are case studies and are therefore not scientifically conducted studies. However, they can provide some very useful information about QWL.

In research conducted by David A. Nadler, several issues were identified that need to be considered in a QWL program.[10] External consultants were used in the programs studied. A program was more likely to be successful if it had a consultant, who was active and a source of energy; however, process skills were judged to be most important. An organization should have good labor-management relations and a climate of trust. Successes early in the program are important, as are clear and specific goals.

JOB DESIGN

Job design has been a concern of managers for many years, but it was Frederick Taylor, in 1911, who proposed the scientific design of a job. The scientific management concepts that came from the industrial engineers tended to break a job down into its smallest and simplest task in order to reduce the human error, the training, and the skill required to accomplish the task. Through time-and-motion studies it was expected that productivity would increase. There was little regard for the human element other than to make sure that it was adequately controlled and supervised. More recently, organizations are discovering there is often a high price to pay in the form of absenteeism, turnover, apathy, poor work quality, or even sabotage, when the human element is not considered.

The current trend is to redesign jobs to improve worker satisfaction and productivity. There are, however, no easy solutions to redesigning jobs because there are too many variables: the worker, the nature of the work, the organization climate, and the manager's style. Some successes in job design do provide guidelines to follow and the following is a discussion of two theories of job design: job enrichment theory and job characteristics theory.

Job Enrichment Theory

Frederick Herzberg found, through interviews, that employees at all levels in the organization were interested in two basic factors relevant to their work—the quality of the work itself and the benefits or rewards of the job (money, status, etc.).[11] When the employees felt satisfied about their jobs, it was usually because something had occurred which indicated they were becoming better in their work. Employees expressed satisfaction with work situations that entailed increases in achievement, recognition, the work itself, responsibility, and advancement. Herzberg calls these factors, which are intrinsic to the job, the "motivators" or "satisfiers" because they have a positive affect on performance. When employees felt dissatisfied about their work, such things as money, status, company policy, benefits, job security, and working conditions were mentioned as a problem. This second factor, which is more extrinsic to the job, Herzberg called the "hygiene" factor because it served much the same function as hygiene does in a hospital setting (it keeps a patient from being sick but hygiene, on its own, will not make the patient well).

Job enrichment theory holds that jobs should be redesigned to improve the motivators related to a job by permitting employees to attain increased levels of responsibility and achievement. Employees can also be given appropriate recognition and advancement in their careers for a job well done. And certainly the work itself should be challenging, interesting, and meaningful. There are numerous techniques for improving these motivational factors and they will have to be tailored to fit specific situations. Several suggestions include:

1.   Give an employee or work group a natural and complete unit of work. This is in contrast to the practice of specialization of labor that has dominated the structure of most organizations in this century.

2.   Add more difficult assignments to an employee's job while providing appropriate training.

3.   Give an employee additional authority. For example, an employee could be allowed to make increasingly more important or difficult decisions.

4.   Allow a peer in a work group or team to become an expert in a specialized area. Very likely, a work team could have several specialists that other employees could go to for information and help.

5.   Make information, including company reports, directly available to an employee instead of editing or censoring the information. This is particularly important where the information is related to the employee's work.

6. Remove controls over an employee while still holding the employee accountable.

Job Characteristics Theory

Another approach to job design is the job characteristics model provided by J.R. Hackman, G.R. Oldham, R. Janson, and K. Purdy[12] and based on the work of A.N. Turner and P.R. Lawrence.[13] The model attempts to develop objective measures of job characteristics which can directly affect employee attitudes and work behaviors (see Figure 13.1).

According to the model, work motivation and satisfaction are affected by five core job dimensions: (1) skill variety; (2) task identity; (3) task significance; (4) autonomy; and (5) feedback.[14]

1. *Skill variety*—the degree to which a job requires a variety of different activities that involve the use of a number of different skills and talents. Tasks that require a person to draw upon several different skills, especially when those skills are challenged, are usually seen as meaningful by employees.

2. *Task identity*—the degree to which the job requires completion of a whole and identifiable piece of work; that is, doing a job from beginning to end

FIGURE 13.1 The Complete Job Characteristics Model

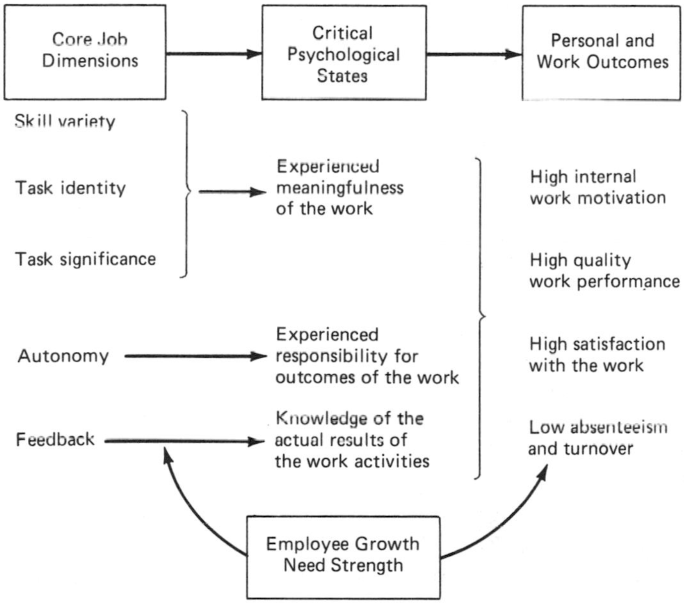

Source: Adapted from R. Hackman, G. Oldham, R. Janson, and K. Purdy, "A New Strategy for Job Enrichment," *California Management Review*, Vol. XVII, No. 4 © 1975 by the Regents of the University of California. By permission of The Regents.

with a visible outcome. An employee will probably find a task more meaningful if it entails producing the entire product rather than a small component.

3. *Task significance*—the degree to which the job has a substantial impact on the lives of other people, whether in the same organization or in the external environment. Work will likely be more meaningful when an employee perceives the results to have a substantial effect on other people.

4. *Autonomy*—the degree to which the job provides substantial freedom, independence, and discretion to the individual in scheduling the work and in determining the procedures to be used in carrying it out. Autonomy allows employees to take a larger part in planning and controlling their work. Generally, employees will have greater commitment to and ownership in their jobs when they are provided autonomy over their work.

5. *Job feedback*—the degree to which carrying out the work activities required by the job results in the individual obtaining direct and clear information about the effectiveness of his or her performance. The feedback is directly based on how well the task was performed and not on the evaluations of a peer or supervisor.

The five core job dimensions can be mathematically combined to derive a score that reflects the motivational potential of a job. As skill variety, task identity, and task significance jointly determine a job's meaningfulness, these three dimensions are treated as one dimension in the formula:

$$\text{Motivating Potential Score (MPS)} = \text{Job Meaningfulness} \times \text{Autonomy} \times \text{Job Feedback}$$

The formula can further be refined:

$$\text{Motivating Potential Score (MPS)} = \left[\frac{\text{Skill Variety} + \text{Task Identity} + \text{Task Significance}}{3}\right] \times \text{Autonomy} \times \text{Job Feedback}$$

Based on the formula, a score of near zero on the autonomy and job feedback dimensions will produce an MPS of near zero (any number multiplied by zero is always zero), whereas a number near zero on skill variety, task identity, or task significance will certainly reduce the overall MPS but will not completely undermine the motivational potential of a job.

When the core job dimensions are present in a job, the job characteristics model predicts certain positive effects in an employee's psychological state. High scores in skill variety, task identity, and task significance result in an employee experiencing meaningfulness in the job, such as believing the work to be important, valuable, and worthwhile. A high score in the autonomy dimension leads to an employee feeling personally responsible and accountable for the results of the work he or she performs. And a high score in the job feedback dimension is an indication that the employee has an understanding of how he or she is performing the job.

There are several suggestions made by the authors of the model and other authorities using research from the behavioral sciences that will enrich jobs and produce a positive impact on the five core job dimensions. One approach is to take existing, fractionalized tasks and put them back together to form a new and larger module of work. This will increase the skill variety and task identity job dimensions of the work. General Motors has used this method for several years in their successful joint venture with Toyota in Fremont, California and has just introduced it at GM's Van Nuys, California facility.[15] At these GM facilities, teams of workers are responsible for auto subassemblies, such as doors or transmissions. To implement the plan at Van Nuys, GM closed the plant for over a week and sent over 4,500 workers off site to take team concept courses. The two GM plants are the only ones of the Big Three U.S. car companies to use such extensive worker participation techniques, and the results will be closely monitored.

A second approach is to form natural work units by giving an employee a task that is an identifiable and meaningful whole. An employee will have greater ownership in and will more closely identify with the work and will understand the significance of the work. A third approach is to permit the employee to have direct contact with the people who use their product or service. This would mean directing complaints or questions from customers directly to the involved employee or employees. The result will be that an employee's interpersonal skills will improve in order to better serve the client or customer.

A fourth approach is to vertically load jobs by giving employees controlling functions such as deciding on work methods, when to take breaks, how to train new employees, formulating budgets, and managing crises. For an employee to successfully undertake these new responsibilities, which improve autonomy, it may be necessary to provide employee skill training in such areas as budgets, training techniques, and time management.

A fifth approach is to open or create feedback channels so employees can learn how well they are performing their work.

Results of Job Design Programs

The results of job design programs suggest that they can be successful if they are managed correctly and have employee involvement. In a review of the literature on work-restructuring methods, William Pasmore found that 90 percent of the reports of work-restructuring interventions cited improvements in productivity, costs, absenteeism, attitudes, or quality and that an increasing number of organizations of all kinds are considering implementing such methods.[16]

The results of job design efforts using Herzberg's job enrichment theory are not conclusive although there have been a number of studies. In a study conducted by R.N. Ford at AT&T it was shown that 18 of 19 job enrichment projects resulted in improvements in productivity, quality, and job satisfaction.[17]

Several studies have confirmed the validity of the job characteristics theory. Studies by A.N. Turner and P.R. Lawrence,[18] M.R. Blood and C.L. Hulin,[19] and J.R. Hackman and E.E. Lawler[20] provide evidence to support the general tenets of the theory.

QUALITY CIRCLES

The quality circle, first started in Japan, is a management practice relatively new to the United States. It was first brought to the United States in 1974 to be used in Lockheed's Space and Missile Unit in Sunnyvale, California. Quality circle (QC) is basically a participative management technique normally applied in production-line situations. QC uses the suggestions of small work groups with common interests as the vehicle for bringing about improvements in product quality.[21]

QCs have become the newest management fad of the 1980s with reported results of a three-to-one return on investment and a 2-year savings of $3 million. The number of QC programs is growing at a rate that may lead an organization to believe they had better implement QC programs or be left behind by their competition. According to a 1982 study by the New York Stock Exchange, 44 percent of all companies with more than 500 employees had QC programs and it is estimated that over 90 percent of the Fortune 500 companies now have QC programs.[22]

What Are Quality Circles?

Quality circles are a voluntary group of employees who meet together periodically (normally weekly or monthly) to discuss, analyze, and propose solutions to mutually shared quality problems (see CROCK comic strip). The employees have traditionally been production-line employees but increasingly QCs are being used with staff workers.

There are normally three elements in a QC: the members, a group leader, and a facilitator. Generally there are 3 to 15 volunteers who are either from the same work area or have similar jobs, thus having a common set of problems. A regularly scheduled meeting is strongly preferred to holding a meeting only when there is a problem. The meetings are held on company time and the length and number of meetings vary with organizations but it is normal to meet once a month for four hours or once a week for one hour. The members

Source: CROCK by Rechin, Parker and Wilder. © Field Enterprises, Inc. by permission of North America Syndicate Inc.

receive training in group process, communication skills, problem solving, statistical techniques, and quality control.

The leader (who may be a supervisor or an informal leader of the team) acts as a moderator and directs the activities of the QC. The leader receives special training in participative leadership techniques, motivation, communications, and group process. The facilitator is employed by the company as an expert consultant and is not a member of the QC per se. The facilitator trains QC leaders and members, helps solve internal group problems, leads the initial meetings, acts as a liaison with upper management and other QC teams, and encourages the QC program. The facilitator may also serve as a resource person by helping the team locate information within the organization and provide special skill training to the members. Middle and upper management are involved by providing their support and approving and implementing the proposals made by the QC team.

Organizations that have QC programs normally have implemented them only in selected areas. QC programs have been implemented by large corporations in product areas where there is special concern about quality control, such as aerospace; and in industries plagued by productivity and quality control problems, such as the automobile and electronics industries. The QC programs have normally been implemented on the production line, with line workers and first-line supervisors as members. Middle and upper management are not members of a QC team. Recently some QC programs have been implemented around clerical and office workers. Though there are "canned" or prepackaged QC programs available for sale from consulting companies, the actual design and operation of the QC program is normally altered to fit the particular organization.

Results of Quality Circles _____

There is concern among several writers about the real successes and future of QC.[23] Part of the problem has been the popularity of QC itself and the high expectations that managers have for QCs. The majority of the results of QCs come from the users or promoters themselves, normally in the form of anecdotal reports on the results at one plant over a short time period. Other than these results there is unfortunately a lack of published scientific investigation of QCs. QC may indeed have some very valuable contributions to make in improving the effectiveness of organizations.

At this point, QC programs seem to have some common problems. It has been estimated that of the QC programs that will be undertaken in one year, 90 percent will fail.[24] Some of the more significant problems include the following.

1.   QCs were taken from Japanese society which has a culture different than that of the U.S. If one accepts the premise of a systems approach, which this text has taken, then there is a problem in taking part of one system, placing that part in another system, and expecting similar results. Further, to identify QCs as the predominant reason for recent Japanese successes in international trade disregards many other factors unique to the Japanese economy.

2.   Expectations for the short run are higher than can realistically be expected.

3.   QC members, who normally do not share in the financial rewards of successful QC programs, may become dissatisfied with this arrangement. If the QCs are too successful, members may also fear being laid off.

4.   Unions may view QCs as a threat and as a management ploy to exploit workers.

5.   Some employers frequently rotate workers and supervisors to different shifts and different work stations within a plant. This lack of stability in workers, and especially supervisors who are serving as QC leaders, can undermine the continuity and success in a QC.

6.   In some places, the voluntary nature of the QC is violated when supervisors are pressured to start a QC and the supervisor in turn pressures subordinates.

7.   Sometimes QCs have had difficulty finding information that would help them identify and analyze problems.

8.   QC members and the leader have had inadequate training in group process skills. The supervisor may be very uncomfortable and even incompetent in this new role of a highly participative group leader.

9.   In some QC programs there has been a notable lack of support from lower and middle management. For example, Sam Clemens, a staff official for the United Steel Workers responsible for union participation in QCs (or labor-management participation teams as the USW and steel industry calls them) says ". . .there's a feeling that we (labor and industry) haven't given it the total support that the idea needs for local union and management to go ahead with it."[25] When lower and middle management, the group responsible for implementing the suggestions of the QCs, do not follow up or implement these suggestions, the result is great discouragement to QC members.

As noted, QC programs have a variety of problems but in fairness, the authors have encountered some of these same problems in other OD interventions and programs. They are not unsurmountable problems, but are certainly worthy of consideration prior to initiation of a QC program.

REVIEW QUESTIONS

1. What are the major categories that can be used for analyzing the quality of work life?

2. How does hygiene differ from motivators according to job enrichment theory?

3. Explain the job characteristics model and how it can be used to enrich jobs.

KEY WORDS AND CONCEPTS

Define and be able to use the following:

Quality of work life	Hygiene
Autonomy	Quality circles
Job design	Motivating potential score (MPS)
Job enrichment	Vertical loading
Motivators	Productivity interventions

IV.
Simulations

SIMULATION 13.1   PAPER HOUSE PRODUCTION

Total time suggested: 2 hours, 40 minutes.

A. Purpose

This simulation is designed to give you an opportunity to participate in a complex situation involving a great deal of interaction among competing teams, each striving to accomplish a specific objective. In the process of interaction, you will have an opportunity to experience:

1. Leadership patterns.
2. Evaluation of jobs using the job characteristic model.
3. Implementation of a quality circle and the redesign of jobs.
4. Group process skills in a stress situation.
5. Interaction patterns among competing teams.

In addition, you will have the opportunity to analyze your team behavior as a member of a system engaged in a complex task.

B. Procedure

Step 1   Before class, form into teams of equal size, with six to eight members. Extra class members can serve as observers. Appoint one person from each team to be a supervisor and another to be a QC facilitator. Read the Paper House Production Description and become familiar with the remaining steps in this simulation before coming to class.

Step 2   In a team meeting, plan for Production Period 1. The meeting should be formal and structured with the supervisor conducting the meeting. The supervisor should read the Note to Supervisor at the end of this simulation. The production of the houses should show a high division and specialization of labor along the tasks involved in house production. The QC facilitator is to observe only during Steps 2 through 4 and is to make no suggestions or to help in any manner. The facilitator should read the Note to Facilitator at the end of the simulation. The equipment and supply purchases will be made and recorded on the Cash Position Statement—Production Period 1.

Time suggested for Step 2: 25 minutes.

Step 3   Teams will construct houses for 20 minutes. Closely adhere to the plans made during Step 2. At the end of the production period, the FHA will purchase houses meeting the specifications. Complete the Cash Position Statement—Production Period 1, and determine the winning team. Return all equipment, supplies, and houses.

Time suggested for Step 3: 30 minutes.

Step 4   Looking at the jobs as a whole (excluding the supervisor), evaluate the jobs using the job characteristics model and determine the Motivating Potential Score (MPS) by using a ranking from 1 (low) to 7 (high).

Skill variety: _____

_____

_____

Task identity: _____

_____

_____

Task significance: _____

_____

_____

Autonomy: _____

_____

_____

Job feedback: _____

_____

_____

$$\text{Motivating Potential Score (MPS)} = \left[\frac{\text{Skill Variety} + \text{Task Identity} + \text{Task Significance}}{3} \right] \times \text{Autonomy} \times \text{Job Feedback}$$

Time suggested for Step 4: 10 minutes.

Step 5 Plan for Production Period 2. Each team forms a quality circle with the meeting closely following the suggestions for QCs listed in the text. Redesign the jobs using suggestions from the theory of job enrichment and the job characteristics model. The facilitator will assist in the meeting but should not make any production-oriented suggestions or decisions. The equipment and supply purchases will be made and recorded on lines 2 through 7 of the Cash Position Statement—Production Period 2. No cash, supplies, or equipment will be carried forward from Production Period 1.

Time suggested for Step 5: 35 minutes.

Step 6 Teams will again construct houses for 20 minutes. Closely adhere to the plans made during Step 5. At the end of the production period, the FHA will purchase houses meeting the specifications. Complete the Cash Position Statement—Production Period 2, and determine the winning team.

Time suggested for Step 6: 30 minutes.

Step 7 As you did in Step 4, look at the jobs as a whole (excluding the supervisor), evaluate the jobs using the job characteristics model, and determine the Motivating Potential Score (MPS).

Skill variety: _____

_____

_____

Task identity: _____

_____

_____

Task significance: _____

_____

_____

Autonomy: _____

_____

_____

Job feedback: _____
_____
_____

$$\text{Motivating Potential Score (MPS)} = \left[\frac{\text{Skill Variety} + \text{Task Identity} + \text{Task Significance}}{3} \right] \times \text{Autonomy} \times \text{Job Feedback}$$

Time suggested for Step 7: 10 minutes.

Step 8 In your team and then with the other teams, focus on the following questions:

    1. Was there any difference in the MPS for the two production periods?

    2. Was there any difference in the Cash Position Statements of the two production periods? How do you explain this?

    3. If there was an improvement in the Cash Position Statement in Period 2 over Period 1, to what extent could the improvement be the result of the experience of having built the houses during the first production period? And to what extent could the improvement be the result of any changes made in the job design during the QC meeting?

    4. What kinds of problems did you encounter in improving the job design?

    5. Were there compromises made between improving the quality of the jobs and improving productivity?

Time suggested for Step 8: 20 minutes.

PAPER HOUSE PRODUCTION DESCRIPTION

The members of this team have just formed a corporation. You must decide on a name for your corporation. At this point you do not have any organization structure or production plans. Take the next 25 minutes to become better acquainted with this business. You should organize your corporation and plan your strategies for the 20-minute production period which will immediately follow this planning period.

    Your corporation is, needless to say, in the paper house construction business. You produce quality paper houses, but in large quantities. Your goal is, very simply, to make the most money you can. Your corporation has $500,000 in cash available to purchase certain supplies and equipment. It may not spend more than this amount. The *only* source of supplies and equipment is your instructor (you may not use your own pen, ruler, etc.), and the supplies and equipment are available during this planning period and during the 20-minute production period (but at a higher price).

Following is a price list of supplies and equipment available.

| | PRICE WHEN PURCHASED DURING | |
Equipment	Planning Period	Production Period
Scissors	$ 7,000	$ 8,000
Cellophane tape	4,000	5,000
Ruler	5,000	6,000
Marking pen	2,000	3,000

Supplies	No. of 5″ × 8″ Cards per Package	Planning Period	Production Period
Micro pkg.	1	$ 2,000	$ 3,000
Mini pkg.	5	8,000	10,000
Poco pkg.	10	15,000	18,000
Medi pkg.	20	25,000	30,000
Maxi pkg.	40	45,000	53,000
Mogo pkg.	80	80,000	90,000

Any number or combination of packages may be purchased. Equipment and supplies unused at the end of this production period will be considered as unrecoverable salvage and will be collected. Completed houses built according to specifications will sell for $20,000 each, and you will be able to sell all you can build. Houses deviating from the specs as judged by the FHA (the FHA could be your instructor or an extra class member) are not marketable. The house plans provided are your specifications. Your house should appear as described except that your house should not have any dimensions written on it. Your company's name should be neatly printed on the roof.

House Specifications

1. The sides of the house each measure 4″ high by 7″ long. The front and back each measure 5″ wide and 4″ high (or 7⅛″ high at the top of the gable).
2. The total height of the house is 7⅛″ from the base to the highest point of the roof.
3. The roof is V-shaped and is 7″ long. It measures 4″ along the ends.
4. Your corporation's name appears in ½″-high letters on both sides of the roof. Neatly print the name with the marking pen.

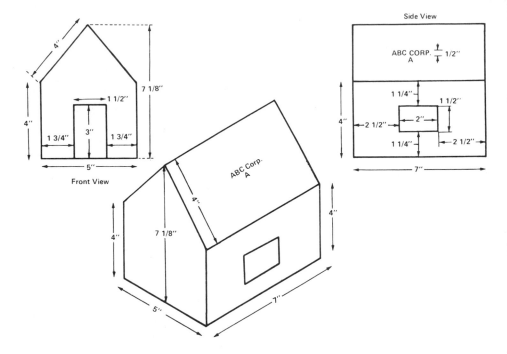

5. The two sides each have one window measuring 2" long and 1½" high, centered. Draw the windows.

6. There is a door at the front (a gable end) measuring 3" high and 1½" wide centered along the base of the wall. Draw the door.

7. There is no floor.

A Cash Position Statement for the first and second production periods is provided for you to keep a record of your financial status.

You have twenty minutes for the first production period. At the end of this time, qualifying houses will be bought and the cash position determined.

Note to Supervisor (other class members should not read)

1st Planning Meeting. Conduct the meeting in Step 2 in a highly formal and structured manner. You should have the production procedures carefully planned before coming to the meeting and during the meeting you will simply tell others of your plans and make sure your employees know what is expected of them. Suggestions from others should be discouraged and you should perform your job as a supervisor in a fairly autocratic manner.

Second Planning Meeting. Conduct the meeting in Step 5 using a participative leadership style. Do not dominate the meeting but allow suggestions and decisions to be shared among all members. The facilitator will be able to assist in the process.

Note to facilitator

As a facilitator, you are only to observe during the planning and production phases for Production Period 1. During the planning phase for Production Period 2, serve only as a facilitator for helping the team. Avoid making specific suggestions yourself but assist the team to work more effectively by making process interventions. In the production periods, you do not take part in fabrication of houses nor in making suggestions.

CASH POSITION STATEMENT—PRODUCTION PERIOD 1
_____ CORPORATION

1. Beginning cash $500,000
2. Cost of purchases during planning period:
3.   Scissors   _____
4.   Cellophane tape   _____
5.   Ruler   _____
6.   Marking pen and pencil   _____
7.   Supplies (cards)   _____
8. Total cost of purchases during planning period:
   (add lines 3 through 7)   _____
9. Cost of purchases during production period:
10.   Scissors   _____
11.   Cellophane tape   _____
12.   Ruler   _____
13.   Marking pen and pencil   _____
14.   Supplies (cards)   _____
15. Total cost of purchases during production period:
    (add lines 10 through 14)   _____
16. Total cost of purchases:
    (add lines 8 and 15)   _____
17. Adjusted cash balance after purchases:
    (subtract line 16 from 1)   _____
18. Cash inflow from sale of houses:

Number of houses sold	times	Selling price	equals	Sales receipts
_____	×	$20,000	=	$_____

19. Ending cash balance:
    (add lines 17 and 18)   _____

CASH POSITION STATEMENT—PRODUCTION PERIOD 2

_____ CORPORATION

1. Beginning cash $500,000
2. Cost of purchases during
   planning period:
3.   Scissors   _____
4.   Cellophane tape   _____
5.   Ruler   _____
6.   Marking pen and pencil   _____
7.   Supplies (cards)   _____
8. Total cost of purchases during
   planning period:
   (add lines 3 through 7)   _____
9. Cost of purchases during
   production period:
10.   Scissors   _____
11.   Cellophane tape   _____
12.   Ruler   _____
13.   Marking pen and pencil   _____
14.   Supplies (cards)   _____
15. Total cost of purchases during
    production period:
    (add lines 10 through 14)   _____
16. Total cost of purchases:
    (add lines 8 and 15)   _____
17. Adjusted cash balance after
    purchases:
    (subtract line 16 from 1)   _____
18. Cash inflow from sale of houses:

Number of houses sold	times	Selling price	equals	Sales receipts
_____	×	$20,000	=	$_____

19. Ending cash balance:
    (add lines 17 and 18)   _____

**Case:
The Keyboard
Company**

The Keyboard Company is a medium-sized manufacturing firm supplying computer keyboards to many national computer manufacturers. The company has experienced rapid growth since its beginning by president John Zoltan and is now moving into advanced electronics from the electromechanical assembly of the past. John Zoltan had recently attended a university executive seminar, and was so impressed that he brought in the professor as a consultant. At one of their meetings, it was decided that to achieve the "organizational excellence" that Zoltan desired for his company, he should start an internal OD consulting group. The president ran an ad in the WSJ and he and the consultant selected four young M.B.A.'s. These four, and one young internal prospect from personnel, were formed into what was called the *OD group*. (See Exhibit 1).

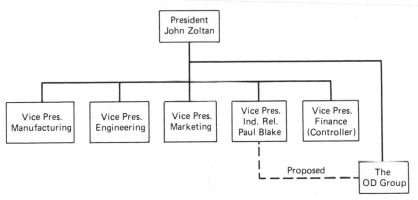

EXHIBIT 1 Partial Organization of the Keyboard Company.

THE OD GROUP

The OD group was housed in an old conference room and began with a high level of enthusiasm and energy. The members of the group ranged in age from 23 to 34. The members were Pete Loomis, 25, M.B.A., a behavioral specialist, who had done training in industry; Kay Hughes, 27, M.B.A., who had been a sales representative prior to graduate school; Bill Heller, 26, M.B.A., specializing in group dynamics with no industry experience; Don Morgan, 34, M.B.A., with OD experience in the military; and George Kessler, 23, three years of experience in the personnel department.

The group spent their first month getting to know the various members of the organization, and held weekly conferences with John Zoltan, who was very interested and active in the planning stages of the OD program.

At that point the group (the "hot-shots" as they were known in the plant) started a company-wide training program focusing on managerial style. The program involved 3-day training sessions at an off-site location, a resort motel with good meals and so on. This was called the "country club" by disparaging employees.

The group itself was a highly cohesive work team. Because of their open office they spent long hours tossing ideas around and providing support and enthusiasm for each other's ideas. They were all involved in the design of the program (as was Zoltan) and worked hard to make it a success. Often the group would sit around until nine, ten, or even midnight, critiquing the sessions and planning new approaches for change.

Within the group there was a diversity of dress and so on, but with individuality and openness being a norm. Pete, George, and Bill usually dressed informally, in Levis and sport shirts, while Don and Kay dressed in more of an executive style, wearing sport jackets and the like. This difference in dress also reflected a division of thought within the group. Pete, George, and Bill wanted to be more confrontational and aggressive in approach. They wanted innovative changes and wanted to overhaul the production operations . . . The others felt that they needed to be accepted first and favored more gradual changes. They felt that the group needed to start "where the system was" if they were to be effective. About this time, Zoltan left for a visit to the Orient to inspect new marketing opportunities.

THE ACTIVITIES

As the training continued through all levels of the organization, they were also collecting organization survey data to be used in planning the next phase of the OD program. Here the controversy began to emerge. Some wanted to hold feedback sessions and to confront the members with the data, then begin a job design program leading to quality control circles. The second group, including Don and Kay, suggested a slower and more gradual approach. They thought that given their low level of acceptance in the organization, they should start with something less threatening, such as data gathering and feedback.

A second rift occurred when they began to see less and less of Zoltan as the training progressed. However, Kay could call the president's office and get an appointment anytime, which she often did. Don Morgan also held a weekly briefing session with Zoltan when he was in town.

The other members, particularly Pete, made a lot of jokes about this fact, but there was often an edge of seriousness under the humor. For example, Pete and Bill had been trying for 2 weeks to see Zoltan to explain their ideas, but he was unavailable. Yet his secretary called for Kay Hughes to join him for coffee. When this was discussed by the group, Don and Kay simply stated that they were trying to maintain and develop the group's relationship with the client. Peter replied, "I thought the whole organization was our client."

Unfortunately, the evaluation of the training program was mixed. Some managers and departments were full of praise for the program, whereas others were highly negative, calling it "a waste of time and money."

In a meeting with John Zoltan, the controller expressed the idea that, in view of the disappointing results, it would be a good idea to move the OD group to the industrial relations section (I/R) for budgeting purposes. The group was currently charging over $200,000 per year into overhead, and this was highly unpopular among the line managers since overhead costs were allocated. Zoltan said he would give the matter some thought and discuss this possibility with the executive committee.

THE MEETING

Shortly after this (approximately 1 year after the group had been formed) they were invited into the executive committee meeting, where the performance of the OD program was discussed and evaluated. John Zoltan and others expressed high praise for the work of the group. However, the executive committee suggested some ideas for improving the group in the future. First, Zoltan suggested a need for more coordination and integration of training activities and for improved budgetary control. Consequently, they were recommending that the group be placed within the I/R department for budgeting purposes, reporting to Paul Blake. They were assured that this would not affect the way the group operated. Second, they suggested that one person be designated central contact person. Don Morgan was the one person that they all felt would be acceptable to a majority of the company managers, and they recommended him but left the decision up to the group.

As the group walked back to the office, several angry suggestions were made along the line that Zoltan "could take this job and shove it!" Both Kay and Pete said they were considering resigning from the company.

CASE ANALYSIS FORM

I. Problems

   A. Macro

      1. _____

      2. _____

   B. Micro

      1. _____

      2. _____

II. Causes

      1. _____

      2. _____

      3. _____

III. Systems affected

      1. Structural

      2. Psychosocial

      3. Technical

      4. Managerial

      5.

IV. Alternatives

      1. _____

      2. _____

      3. _____

      4. _____

      5. _____

V. Recommendations

1. _____

2. _____

3. _____

V.
Summary

In this chapter we have examined some of the productivity interventions in work design that could be part of an OD program. Some interventions have been used over a period of several years with varying degrees of success, while other methods are relatively new.

Two views of job design include job enrichment and job characteristics. The results of both theories are mixed, but both can be useful to the practicing manager and the OD practitioner.

Quality circles represent a relatively new participative management technique that has normally been applied to production line situations, although it has potentially broader applications for all types of organizations. Although there is a lack of conclusive research on QC programs, there is some information available that can help managers and OD practitioners implement more successful programs.

Quality of work life (QWL) is more of a management philosophy than a program; it is a way of viewing the organization life of workers. QWL is seen by some as incorporating work design, collective bargaining, industrial democracy, and organization development.

In the last several years, productivity interventions have received much more attention and seem to be having some positive impact in improving organizations. There are a number of methods which will help managers and practitioners in improving productivity, but there is a definite need for additional research into work design programs.

NOTES

1. Rosabeth Moss Kanter, "SMR Forum: Innovation—The Only Hope for Times Ahead?" *Sloan Management Review*, Summer 1984, p. 51.

2. For additional information on QWL, see: Annette Hartenstein and Kenneth F. Huddleston, "Values: The Cornerstone of QWL," *Training and Development Journal*, October 1984, pp. 65–66; David Lewin, "Collective Bargaining and the Quality of Work Life," *Organizational Dynamics*, Autumn 1981, pp. 37–53; David A. Nadler, "Consulting with Labor and Management: Some Learnings from Quality-of-Work-Life Projects," in *The Cutting Edge: Current Theory and Practice in Organization Development*, ed. W. Warner Burke (La Jolla, Calif.: University Associates, Inc., 1978), pp. 262–77; David A. Nadler and Edward E. Lawler III, "Quality of Work Life: Perspectives and Directions," *Organizational Dynamics*, Winter 1983, pp. 20–30; Barry A. Macy, "A Progress Report on the Bolivar

Quality of Work Life Project," *Personnel Journal*, August 1979, pp. 527–30; Leonard A. Schlesinger and Barry Oshry, "Quality of Work Life and the Manager: Muddle in the Middle," *Organizational Dynamics*, Summer 1984, pp. 5–19; Richard E. Walton, "From Control to Commitment in the Workplace," *Harvard Business Review*, March–April 1985, pp. 76–84; Richard E. Walton, "Quality of Working Life: What Is It?," *Sloan Management Review*, Fall 1973, pp. 11–21; Marvin R. Weisbord, "Participative Work Design: A Personal Odyssey," *Organizational Dynamics*, Spring 1985, pp. 5–20; David A. Whitsett and Lyle Yorks, "Looking Back at Topeka: General Foods and the Quality-of-Work-Life Experiment," *California Management Review*, 25, no. 4 (Summer 1983), 93–109; and Shaker A. Zahra, "Building a Wholesome Quality of Working Life," *Management Quarterly*, Summer 1983, pp. 10–14.

3. Zahra, "Building a Wholesome Quality of Working Life," p. 12.

4. Nadler and Lawler, "Quality of Work Life," p. 26.

5. Walton, "Quality of Working Life," pp. 11–21.

6. Zahra, "Building a Wholesome Quality of Working Life," pp. 11–12.

7. "Hot UAW Issue: 'Quality of Work Life,' " *Business Week*, September 17, 1979, p. 120.

8. Ibid.

9. Whitsett and Yorks, "Looking Back at Topeka," pp. 93–109.

10. Nadler, "Consulting with Labor and Management," pp. 262–77.

11. For additional information see: Frederick Herzberg, Bernard Mausner, and B. Snyderman, *The Motivation to Work* (New York: John Wiley & Sons, Inc.) 1959; Frederick Herzberg, "One More Time: How Do You Motivate Employees?" *Harvard Business Review*, January–February 1968, pp. 53–62; and M. Scott Meyers, "Conditions for Manager Motivation," *Harvard Business Review*, January–February 1966, pp. 58–71.

12. J.R. Hackman, G.R. Oldham, R. Janson, and K. Purdy, "A New Strategy for Job Enrichment," *California Management Review*, Summer 1975, pp. 57–71.

13. A.N. Turner and P.R. Lawrence, *Industrial Jobs and the Worker* (Boston: Harvard Graduate School of Business Administration, 1965).

14. Hackman, Oldham, Janson, and Purdy, "A New Strategy," pp. 57–71; and Hackman and Suttle, *Improving Life at Work* (Santa Monica, Calif.: Goodyear Publishing Co., Inc., 1977), pp. 130–31.

15. Harry Bernstein, "GM 'Team Concept' Car Making Shifts Into High Gear," *Los Angeles Times*, April 22, 1987, Part IV, p. 1.

16. William A. Pasmore, "Overcoming the Roadblocks in Work-Restructuring Efforts," *Organizational Dynamics*, Spring 1982, p. 55.

17. R.N. Ford, *Motivation Through the Work Itself* (New York: American Management Association, 1969).

18. Turner and Lawrence, *Industrial Jobs and the Worker*.

19. M.R. Blood and C.L. Hulin, "Alienation, Environmental Characteristics, and Worker Responses," *Journal of Applied Psychology*, 51 (1967), 284–90.

20. J.R. Hackman and E.E. Lawler, "Employee Reactions to Job Characteristics," *Journal of Applied Psychology Monograph*, 55 (1971), 259–86.

21. For additional information on Quality Circles, see: David A. Garvin, "Quality on the Line," *Harvard Business Review*, September–October 1983, pp. 64–75;

Edward E. Lawler III and Susan A. Mohrman, "Quality Circles After the Fad," *Harvard Business Review*, January–February 1985, pp. 64–71; Gordon W. Meyer and Randall G. Stott, "Quality Circles: Panacea or Pandora's Box?" *Organizational Dynamics*, Spring 1985, pp. 34–50; Herbert S. Parker, "Do Productivity-Enhancing Strategies Deal with Cultural Differences? Can Japanese Theories Work in America?," *The Collegiate Forum*, Spring 1982; Robert C. Wood, "Squaring off on Quality Circles," *Inc.*, August 1982, pp. 98–100; Robert Wood, Frank Hull, and Koya Azumi, "Evaluating Quality Circles: The American Application," *California Management Review*, XXVI, no. 1 (Fall 1983), 37–53; Ed Yager, "Examining the Quality Control Circle," *Personnel Journal*, October 1979, pp. 682–84; and Edward E. Lawler III and Susan A. Mohrman, "Quality Circles: After the Honeymoon," *Organizational Dynamics*, Spring 1987, pp. 42–54.

22. Lawler and Mohrman, "Quality Circles After the Fad," p. 66.

23. Meyer and Stott, "Quality Circles: Panacea or Pandora's Box?"; Parker, "Do Productivity-Enhancing Strategies Deal with Cultural Differences?"; Howard S. Schwartz, "A Theory of Deontic Work Motivation," *The Journal of Applied Behavioral Science*, 19, no. 2 (1983), 204; Wood, "Squaring off on Quality Circles"; and Wood, Hull, and Azumi, "Evaluating Quality Circles: The American Application."

24. Schwartz, "A Theory of Deontic Work Motivation," p. 204.

25. Aaron Bernstein and Matt Rothman, "Steelmakers Want to Make Teamwork an Institution," *Business Week*, May 11, 1987, p. 84.

OD SYSTEM-WIDE INTERVENTIONS

I. **Objectives**	Upon completing this chapter, you will be able to:

1. Recognize how system approaches are used in organization development change programs.
2. Identify several basic OD intervention techniques.
3. Experience and practice these system approaches.

II. **Premeeting** **Preparation**	

1. Read the Background Information (Section III).
2. Complete Step 1 of Simulation 14.1 (Section IV).
3. Read and Analyze Case: Grayson Chemical Company.

**III.
Background
Information**

All OD interventions are aimed at improving organization effectiveness, but certain interventions are aimed at the successful implementation of change within the total system. As noted, OD is essentially a systems approach to the complex set of group, functional, and interpersonal relationships that are found in organizations. The system-level intervention may be described as a structural design framework for viewing the organization which examines (1) the way the organization is designed; (2) the flow patterns of the organization; and (3) the interaction of individuals and groups within the flows and structures of the system. The major system-level interventions include Likert's system 4 approach, survey feedback, and Grid® organization development.

Organizations inevitably change because they are open systems in constant interaction with their environment. Although the impetus for change may arise from internal or external forces, the underlying factor is the degree of openness of the organization to the changing demands, technologies, and values that influence the system.[1]

In earlier chapters it was noted that the organization may be viewed as a sociotechnical system. The relationships between individuals, work units, and organization subsystems determine the output of the system. Certain OD interventions may be applied to selected individuals or groups, whereas others are more comprehensive and are designed to improve the effectiveness of the total organization.

Richard Beckhard described a change model applicable to large and complex systems, suggesting that large system interventions focus on system diagnosis, determining change strategies, understanding the relationship to external environments, and understanding such organizational processes as power, reward systems, decision making, interaction, and planning.[2] In this chapter, we examine several system-wide approaches to change.

One of the most widely used approaches to system-wide planned change is *Grid organization development*, a change model designed by Robert R. Blake and Jane S. Mouton and marketed by Scientific Methods, Inc.

A second approach is termed *survey feedback* and involves gathering data and then feeding these data back to a management group for action. Although many OD practitioners use this approach, the Institute for Social Research at the University of Michigan is perhaps the organization most associated with this method. The institute has a copyrighted questionnaire covering 18 items which it uses to analyze organization functioning.

Rensis Likert has also developed a theory of management called *system 4 management*, which provides a framework and a set of structural dimensions that may be used to differentiate between ineffective and effective organizations.

In this chapter an overview of many of the most widely used total system intervention techniques is presented. It should be noted that the system may be an organization or a reasonably well isolated unit such as a large segment or subsystem within the total organization.

THE GRID® OD PROGRAM

One of the most widely used approaches to system-wide planned change is *Grid organization development*, a change model designed by Robert R. Blake and Jane S. Mouton and marketed by Scientific Methods, Inc.[3] This program is a systematic approach aimed at achieving corporate excellence. Blake and Mouton feel that in order to increase the effectiveness of managers and the organization, change must take place in the basic culture of the system.

Grid organization development starts with a focus on individual behavior, specifically on the managerial styles of executives using what Blake and Mouton call The Managerial Grid. The program then moves through a series of sequential phases involving the work team, the relationships between groups or subunits, and finally to the culture of the organization itself. The Managerial Grid and Grid OD represent one of the most extensively applied approaches to organization improvement and, administered by Scientific Methods Inc., have been used by such major U.S. corporations as Procter & Gamble, Conoco, Westinghouse, and Whirlpool, as well as by a number of foreign organizations. Texas Instruments, for example, has run over 2,200 managers through the Grid, including its president and top executives. Blake estimates that perhaps 750,000 managers have been involved with the Grid in one way or another and that perhaps 5,000 companies have engaged in Grid development activities. These are necessarily estimates, as there is no realistic basis for a head count. It is known that the 1964 *Managerial Grid* book has sold approximately 500,000 copies in English and more than 100,000 copies in Japanese. The book has also been translated into a number of other languages and has enjoyed wide popularity.[4]

The Managerial Grid seminars are used as a starting point for a planned change program called Grid OD. Grid OD has as its objectives the maximizing its managers' concerns for both their subordinates and the organization. In order to increase the effectiveness of an individual manager dealing with his or her subordinates, change must take place in the organization culture itself. The Grid OD program consists of the following six phases.

Phase 1: Grid Seminars

Organizations get involved in a Grid OD program in various ways, but involvement usually begins with someone in a responsible management position reading an article or book on the Managerial Grid. He or she may decide to become more familiar with the Grid by attending a public seminar to gain firsthand knowledge. These seminars last a week, are held both day and evening, and are conducted at various locations around the country and the world. There are about 30 to 40 hours of prework in addition to the work at the seminar. The learning objectives of the week include:

1. Learning the Grid as a way to analyze thinking.
2. Increasing personal objectivity in appraising oneself.
3. Achieving clear and candid communication.
4. Learning and working effectively in a team.
5. Learning to manage intergroup conflict.
6. Analyzing one's corporate work culture by applying the Grid framework.
7. Gaining understanding of the phases of Grid OD.

The seminar is highly structured, with most of the activities devoted to short lectures and team projects. It is highly intensive and emotionally demanding, since it encourages competition between teams and confrontation between team members. Participants who leave the seminar committed to the precepts of the Grid will probably encourage other key members of their organization to attend a similar seminar.

The sessions include investigation by each person of his or her own managerial approach and alternative ways of managing which can be learned about, experimented with, and applied. Participants study methods of team action. They measure and evaluate team effectiveness in solving problems with others. A high point of seminar learning is reached when each participant receives a critique of his or her style of managerial performance from other members of the team. Another is when managers critique the dominant style of their organization's culture, its traditions, precedents, and past practices. A third is when participants consider steps for increasing the effectiveness of the whole organization.

Phase 2: Teamwork Development _____

An organization is composed of many subgroups or teams whose members range from top management to assembly-line workers. Phase 2 is concerned with improving teamwork and includes a boss and his or her immediate subordinates meeting together for a 1-week session. *Teamwork development* begins with the top manager in the organization and the employees who report directly to him or her. These people later attend another team meeting with their own subordinates. This continues down through the entire organization.

Teamwork development is a planned activity that begins with each team member completing various Grid instruments. The teams deal with subjects directly relevant to their daily operations and behaviors. The team members are also getting feedback from participants on their Grid styles in real situations. Before the conclusion of the week, the team sets group and individual goals.

Phase 3: Intergroup Development _____

The Phase 2 teamwork development meetings have cut vertically through the organization encompassing natural work teams, but people also relate with others along a horizontal dimension: people interact with others in different teams, departments, divisions, and sections. Unintended competition between departments may develop into a win-lose contest resulting in a loss of organization effectiveness. Coordination, cooperation, and collaboration between elements are necessary for an effective organization, and to accomplish this *intergroup development* meetings are held and attended by the key members of two segments or divisions where barriers exist. Intergroup development involves group-to-group relationships where members of interfacing teams meet for 3 or 4 days to identify those things that would be present in an ideal relationship between their two segments. The objective is for the two segments to agree on the elements for an ideal relationship and then develop specific actions to attain the ideal. As in Phase 2, participants leave the meetings with actual goals and objectives plus an increased understanding of communication with one another.

Phase 4: Development of an Ideal Strategic Model _____

The development of an *ideal strategic model* provides an organization with the knowledge and skills to move from a reactionary approach to one of systematic development. This phase is concerned with the overall norms, policies, and structure of the organization. The responsibility for these matters is with the top manager and those reporting to him or her. During a week of study, the key people in the organization define what the organization would be like if it were truly excellent. It is not unusual for a moderate-sized organization to spend 6 months to a year perfecting the ideal strategic model. During this time other people at various levels have the opportunity to contribute to the model. This helps build commitment to the model needed for implementation.

Phase 5: Implementing the Ideal Strategic Model _____

The manner in which the ideal strategic model is implemented determines the success of Grid OD in the organization. An edict coming from above will probably fall on deaf ears and be doomed to failure from the beginning. The Grid OD program has an implementation model that can be adapted to any organization. An organization can be divided into identifiable segments such as products, profit centers, or geographical areas. Once the segments are identified, the top management team assigns one planning team to each segment, one team to the corporate headquarters, and a coordinator of Phase 5. The coordinator recommends tactics of implementation to the top-line executive. The task of each planning team is to analyze all aspects of its section's operations and determine how that section would act ideally. The design is based on the ideal strategic model determined in Phase 4 but is interpreted and implemented for each section by the planning team. The task is aided by the skills attained during Phases 1, 2, and 3. The studies to convert the ideal model into reality for each section may take 3 months to a year, and the actual conversion may take 6 months to 5 years or even longer.

Phase 6: Systematic Critique

The final phase in Grid OD is a systematic examination of progress toward change goals. The *systematic critique* determines the degree of organization excellence after Phase 5 compared with measurements taken *before* Phase 1. The basic instrument is a 100-question survey investigating managerial behavior, teamwork, intergroup relations, and corporate strategy. Through the use of instruments administered at each phase, it is possible to observe the degree of change and gain insight into the total process of change. It is gratifying for people to see the movement they have made toward their goals, as success may not be readily apparent considering that the entire Grid OD program may have been implemented over a period of 5 to 10 years. Because change never ceases, this discovery sets the stage for a new beginning.

The Results of Grid OD Programs

As with many OD intervention techniques, there is a great deal of anecdotal evidence regarding Grid OD programs but little empirical evidence. The results of one Grid OD program have been reported in an article by Blake, Mouton, Barnes, and Greiner.[5] Their findings can be summarized as follows:

1. The analysis of data showed within a 3-year period an increase in productivity of 30 percent and a decrease in costs of 14 percent.

2. Subordinates reported a 12 percent improvement in ratings of their managers' style and ability to manage.

3. The study suggests that managerial and team effectiveness can be improved and that Grid OD can make significant contributions to organization effectiveness.

Two other studies present some results from two different organizational settings on the application of this intervention. H. John Bernardin and Kenneth M. Alvares question the Grid's effectiveness, while Howard Hart presents findings which suggest that the Grid can be an effective development tool.[6] Another study of the Grid at Union Mutual Life Insurance Company also reported positive results.[7] Suffice it to say that there is at least some evidence which supports the contention that organizations which have applied Grid OD have become more efficient. But there are other studies, however, which report mixed or unfavorable results.[8]

SURVEY RESEARCH AND FEEDBACK

Survey research and feedback is a process in which outside OD practitioners and members of the organization collaboratively collect data and use the data as a basis for changing organization relationships.[9] The survey feedback method, as developed by the Survey Research Center at the Institute for Social Research, University of Michigan, consists of collecting data by questionnaire on a number of organization dimensions and then feeding these data back to work groups at successively lower levels. The work group then uses these data to diagnose problems and to generate action plans altering organization structure and work relationships. The questionnaire probes into such dimensions as leadership, communication, decision making, superior-subordinate relations, and job satisfaction. The data generated by the questionnaire are then used as a basis for further change efforts.

Therefore, this method provides techniques for changing work relationships and also a means for measuring the effects of such changes within organizations. The client system is usually involved in the data collection activities, and members of management and other organization members are usually asked to submit questions for the survey and to plan the data collection itself. The data are usually fed back to the organization through family groups, that is, the superior and those immediately reporting to him or her in a work-related group. These feedback conferences then provide the client system with data about problems, leading to specific action plans and programs to improve work team effectiveness.

The Steps in Survey Feedback

The survey feedback approach as developed by the Survey Research Center usually includes the following steps:

Step 1. The involvement of top management in preliminary planning of the survey questionnaire. Other organization members may be involved if appropriate.

Step 2. The survey questionnaire is administered by the outside staff to all organization members.

Step 3. The data are summarized by the outside staff and then fed back to work teams or family groups throughout the hierarchy of the organization, usually beginning with the top management group and flowing down to successive levels of the organization, a so-called waterfall effect.

Step 4. Each manager then has a meeting of his or her own work group to diagnose problems from the data presentation and to develop action plans and programs for improvement. An outside consultant involved in the survey usually attends each work-group meeting acting as a process consultant or resource person.

Floyd Mann has described this process as "a series of interlocking conferences or meetings structured in terms of organizational family units—the superior and immediate subordinates—considering the survey data together. The data presented to each group were those pertaining to their own group or for those subunits for which members of the organizational unit were responsible."[10] The purposes of survey feedback include the following: (1) to develop an understanding of the problems, (2) to improve working relationships, and (3) to identify factors and opportunities for change or to determine areas where more research is required.

Mann has reported on one such company-wide study of employee and management attitudes and opinions. Over a period of 2 years, three different sets of data were fed back: (1) information on the attitudes and perceptions of 8,000 nonsupervisory employees toward their work, promotions opportunities, supervision, fellow employees, and so on; (2) first- and second-line supervisors' feelings about various aspects of their job and supervisory beliefs; and (3) information from intermediate and top levels of management about their supervisory philosophies, roles, policy formation, problems of organizational integration, and so on.[11]

The Results of Survey Research and Feedback _____

Most of the evidence regarding the results of survey research and feedback methods has been obtained by the Survey Research Center and indicates positive changes in employee attitudes and perceptions.[12] The observations of the Survey Research Center indicate that these methods are a powerful process for creating and reporting changes within an organization. It also found that the greater the involvement of all members of the organization, the greater the change. Other conclusions are more ambiguous but suggest that a process of change did begin as a result of survey feedback, although quantitative measures did not show more than chance fluctuations.[13] When survey feedback interventions are the only type of intervention used, the success is usually short-range; but when feedback is combined with other interventions, the effects are usually more substantial and long-range. Survey feedback techniques have been widely used in organization change. John C. Aplin and Duane E. Thompson describe this process and they suggest that the returns from increased efficiency offset the costs of the survey activities.[14]

The survey research and feedback process is therefore based upon three elements: (1) the collection of data from all organization members, (2) the feedback of data to work teams in group meetings with member diagnosis and action planning, and (3) the process analysis of group meetings so that the group learns to better understand its own behavior during the survey feedback sessions. Although relatively little empirical evidence has been generated, the results seem to indicate that survey research and feedback can be an effective intervention approach to organization change.

LIKERT'S SYSTEM 4 MANAGEMENT

Another system-wide intervention has been developed by Rensis Likert and is called *system 4 management.*[15] Likert found through extensive research that organizations can be described on a continuum with traditional bureaucratic organizations (ineffective) at one end and participative (effective) organizations at the other. (See CROCK comic strip.) Likert then identified four systems as follows:

- System 1—exploitive-authoritative
- System 2—benevolent-authoritative
- System 3—consultative
- System 4—participative

To determine the degree to which an organization approximates the system 4 parameters, Likert devised a measurement device. This is a 51-item questionnaire on which employees indicate their perception of the organiza-

Source: CROCK by Rechin, Parker and Wilder. © Field Enterprises, Inc. by permission of North America Syndicate, Inc.

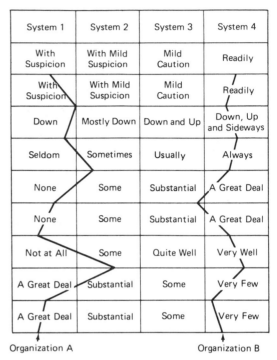

	System 1	System 2	System 3	System 4
Communication:				
1. How is downward communication accepted?	With Suspicion	With Mild Suspicion	Mild Caution	Readily
2. How is upward communication accepted?	With Suspicion	With Mild Suspicion	Mild Caution	Readily
3. What is direction of communication?	Down	Mostly Down	Down and Up	Down, Up and Sideways
Leadership:				
4. Are ideas of subordinates sought and used?	Seldom	Sometimes	Usually	Always
5. What is the degree of warmth and support between subordinates and their leaders?	None	Some	Substantial	A Great Deal
6. To what extent are the rewards and encouragements given to subordinates?	None	Some	Substantial	A Great Deal
Policies:				
7. Are the policies clearly understood?	Not at All	Some	Quite Well	Very Well
8. Are there a lot of rules, policies, and procedures a person has to know to get his job done?	A Great Deal	Substantial	Some	Very Few
9. Are there unnecessary procedures?	A Great Deal	Substantial	Some	Very Few

Organization A   Organization B

Source: Adapted from Rensis Likert and Jane Gibson Likert, *New Ways of Managing Conflict* (New York: McGraw-Hill Book Company, 1976).

FIGURE 14.1 Profile of Organization Characteristics

tion. The results are then plotted on a profile, as shown in Figure 14.1. The profile illustrates the differences that can occur in organizational functioning.

According to Likert's model, the profile indicated by Organization A tends toward system 1 design; Organization B tends toward system 4 functioning. Likert has found that system 1 organizations tend to be least effective, whereas system 4 organizations tend to be highly effective. Consequently, to improve organizations, the OD practitioner tries to move the pattern of functioning closer to the right, toward the system 4 operation. For an example of an organization, Digital Equipment Corporation, operating more from a system 4 perspective, see O.D. Application 14.1.

OD programs in utilizing system 4 approaches, then, measure the present state of the system and design training interventions emphasizing participative goal setting and decision making. In this way, one attempts to shift the key organizational factors toward the system 4 framework.

Several organizations have used system 4 theory as an approach to change. William Dowling has reported on one OD program using system 4 methods. At General Motors, he reported that grievances were reduced, waste costs were cut, and operating efficiency was improved.[16]

A NEW STRATEGY AT DEC—OVERHAULING THE SYSTEM

Kenneth H. Olsen, founder, president, and CEO of Digital Equipment Corporation (DEC), rode the data processing trend to become the second largest computer maker in the world, with annual revenues of $7.6 billion. In 1986, *Fortune* proclaimed him as America's most successful entrepreneur.

Changes in Direction

Olsen has found that drastic changes in total system performance were necessary to retain competitive vitality. Now revolution is sweeping the computer industry again. Personal computers and office automation systems are putting computer power directly onto the desks of managers and executives. "DEC for a period of time seemed to lose strategic direction—which markets it would go after and what its targets were," says Aaron C. Goldberg, a researcher at International Data Corp. in Framingham, Massachusetts.

System Changes

To get the company back on track, the 57-year-old Olsen has again moved into the company's day-to-day operations and launched a massive—and risky—corporate overhaul. Olsen's goal: a radical transformation of his engineering-oriented company into a tough, market-driven competitor. "The issues [that led to this overhaul] are not technical but have to do with products and marketing," Olsen says. "The key strategy of the corporation," he adds, is to make the new low-end desk top products work together with DEC's bread-and-butter minicomputer line, then to sell them together.

Three Key Systems

Three key pieces of this restructuring are only now falling into place.

1. *Products.* Olsen's new product strategy calls for a broad range of computers, from small desk-top machines to large office minicomputers, that can communicate easily with one another. Due to a strategy Olsen adopted 15 years ago, DEC now enjoys a wide technological lead in linking computers into networks.

2. *Marketing.* DEC is adopting aggressive new marketing tactics for office automation, personal computers, and small-business users. It is working hard to develop closer ties with customers, organize new distribution channels, and launch more innovative promotions. In an effort to impress upon his managers the importance of the customer, Olsen ordered 24 senior executives to a warehouse where they spent a day uncrating and hooking up computers and learned just what customers had to contend with.

3. *Management.* Olsen is streamlining an overgrown corporate bureaucracy and decentralizing decision making. Olsen has long been an advocate of delegating responsibility and he makes extensive use of committees. Olsen generally leaves the decisions up to the participants. He says of his role, "The most important decision I make is when to break for lunch."

In the late 1970s and early 1980s, critics of Olsen questioned his ability to move DEC from a growth company to a mature, large corporation. There were some who thought he suffered from "founder's disease." In order to ensure DEC's future, Olsen led the company to a new computer line, a VAX superminicomputer. But the plan required DEC to perform new functions, such as engineering and manufacturing its own microprocessors and writing software to run networks.

In order to accommodate the new product line, DEC also underwent a major reorganization and created a unified marketing organization. The corporate overhaul, which took five years, amounted to "a vast transformation that ranks as one of the most critical periods in the company's history," says Frederic G. Withington, industry analyst at Arthur D. Little Inc., a Cambridge, Massachusetts consulting company.

The work has paid off for DEC though not all of Olsen's lieutenants, including his brother, survived the changes. Olsen thinks that although he avoided founder's disease, many of his vice presidents fell victim to it by becoming complacent and ignoring changes in the market place. The new computers and networks have taken their competition by surprise and DEC is considered to be IBM's most serious competition in 20 years. Net profits were up 38 percent, sales up 14 percent, and stock prices rose 97 percent in one year (1986).

Questions:
1. Why do companies find themselves in transition?
2. What steps might be taken to make changes go smoothly?
3. How might Likert's system 4 management and Grid OD be used at DEC?

Sources: Peter Petre, "America's Most Successful Entrepreneur," *Fortune*, October 27, 1986, pp. 24–32; and "A New Strategy for Minicomputers," *Business Week*, May 2, 1983, pp. 66–75.

In this chapter we have presented several of the major system-wide approaches to OD. Several of these models present contradictory approaches to change, and perhaps emphasize that there is no one best way for all systems or organizations to manage change. Among the more popular approaches are Grid OD and survey feedback; however, the research evidence supporting any one approach or models make it difficult to make meaningful comparisons. Our knowledge of system-wide approaches to change is incomplete. Our purpose here is to make you aware of the differing methods and models. Given a certain situation or set of conditions, you may decide that one approach may be more effective than others for that particular application.

REVIEW QUESTIONS

1. Identify and give examples of the major system-wide OD intervention techniques.

2. Compare and contrast the reasons for successful and unsuccessful change programs.

KEY WORDS AND CONCEPTS

Define and be able to use the following:

Grid OD	Ideal strategic model
Managerial Grid	Survey research and feedback
Grid phases	System 4 model

**IV.
Simulations**

SIMULATION 14.1 THE CONTINENTAL MANUFACTURING COMPANY

Total time suggested: 2 hours, 25 minutes.

A. Purpose

The purpose of this simulation is to provide a situation in which you will need to influence others. During and after the simulation you are encouraged to become aware of the processes you use in your attempts to influence and relate with others. You will also be provided the opportunity to design an OD program.

B. Procedures

Step 1 All participants read Continental Manufacturing Background Information. Form groups of seven to act out the executive committee role play. (Roles should be selected prior to the class meeting.) Additional class members will serve as observers. Each player should read only their role.

Step 2 Each consultant and the executive committee meet in an executive meeting. The meeting is scheduled to last 45 minutes.
Time suggested for Step 2: 45 minutes.

Step 3 After the executive meeting, each consultant completes the diagnosis and formulates an OD program to present to the executive committee for their consideration. While the consultant is designing the OD program, the executive committee of Brentwood should discuss questions for the consultant.
Time suggested for Step 3: 15 minutes.

Step 4 The consultant presents diagnosis and OD program to their respective companies. Then each company with their consultant jointly develop an OD program.
Time suggested for Step 4: 30 minutes.

Step 5 At the conclusion of the role play, the observer will feed back observations.
Time suggested for Step 5: 10 minutes.

Step 6 As a class, each consultant should present their company's OD program for class discussion and critique.

Time suggested for Step 6: 30 minutes.

Step 7 As a class, discuss the seven questions in the Observer Role Description.

Time suggested for Step 7: 15 minutes.

CONTINENTAL MANUFACTURING BACKGROUND INFORMATION

The Continental Manufacturing Company is a leading manufacturer of fabricated metal products. The company is divided into several major functional groups, each headed by a vice president. One of these groups is the Products Group which is divided into a number of product divisions, each headed by a division general manager (see Figure 14.2).

The Brentwood Division's General Manager oversees the directors for Engineering, Marketing, Production, and Human Resource Development. Brentwood's performance has been excellent, especially over the past 10 years, but with the exception of the most recent 2 years. In fact, Brentwood has a record of being one of the most profitable divisions of Continental in terms of amount of profit and return on investment. However, 2 years ago profits dropped by 4 percent and last year they dropped by 11 percent reflecting a decline in sales of 6 percent and 13 percent respectively. Continental uses cost centers with each division relatively autonomous in its operations; however, each division is expected to be self-supporting.

FIGURE 14.2 Continental Manufacturing Company

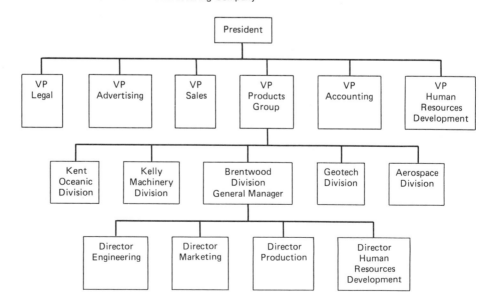

Brentwood employs about 1,200 people and operates from one plant location. The increase in employees has been rapid within the past 10 years but the increase leveled off this year because of the sales decline. So far there have been no layoffs but if the current sales trend continues, layoffs may have to be considered as a possibility to reduce costs. The employees are unionized as is common in this industry, but both Brentwood and Continental have exceptionally positive relationships with the unions. This is due largely to the diligent work at corporate headquarter's Human Resource Development Department where the contracts are formulated.

The major problem with sales has been attributed to two new major competitors who have entered the field. To date, the product line has faced little competition, probably because of the expensive and technologically advanced processes used in the fabrication. Because of the technological orientation of the products, it is important that Brentwood be able quickly to respond to the changing demands of their customers. Also, for Brentwood to be really competitive it is increasingly necessary for it to outguess the needs of its customers and bring in technologically superior products before its competitors. Most recently, Brentwood's ability to effectively respond to its competitors has been diminished because several dynamic middle managers and other key employees were lost to its competitors.

Brentwood products are used as components in a variety of industrial and military products. The military contracts have been declining but at no greater rate than the civilian sales. The products themselves are fabricated metal and plastic parts that are components of larger items; so Brentwood does not actually make or market finished products. Many of the materials used in the manufacturing process are exotic metals and plastics that are very difficult to fabricate. In many cases the products must be extremely lightweight and have high strength. In some cases the composition of the products and the processes used in manufacturing are the result of inventions developed at Brentwood to which it owns the patent rights.

Corporate headquarters has recently formed a new OD division. It has been suggested by the vice president of the Products Group that Brentwood Division consider using the services of OD group. As Continental believes it is important to allow its divisions to be fairly autonomous, Brentwood has the authority to choose to participate and help design an OD program that best fits its own culture and needs.

ROLE DESCRIPTIONS (READ *ONLY* YOUR ROLE)

Role 1—Brentwood General Manager   You are 46 years old and have been with the company for 8 years, 5 in your current job. Although you started fast, things have slowed down for the past 2 years. Your goal is to be promoted to group vice president, and to do this you need to turn things around right now and show a good profit profile. To accomplish this, you want to cut labor costs by 10 percent, cut expenses to the bone, and get rid of any fat or deadwood that exists. You operate best in a directive, structured, and centralized situation and feel that the current problems stem from a lack of control and coordination among departments. Your goal now is to increase short-run profits at any cost.

During the meeting you want to convince the directors to voluntarily cut labor costs by 10 percent, which will directly affect the bottom line. You also hope to sell them on a more centralized and controlled operation: a "taut ship." You feel that the basic causes of the current problems are the operating relations between departments and the lack of proper controls on spending.

You see the OD consultant as a possible ally in achieving your goal of promotion. A good word back at corporate headquarters would undoubtedly increase your chances. Consequently, you want to appear to be highly competent, dynamic, a "mover and a shaker," and an integrative manager.

Role 2—Director of Marketing   You are 28, an M.B.A., with the company for 4 years. You feel that a decentralized organization is most effective and believe that dividing Brentwood into major product groups instead of the current functional form would be best suited for the company. You are very concerned with good relationships as well as goal accomplishment and are known as a "super salesman." You feel strongly that what the organization needs to solve its problems is an increased marketing and promotional effort. You recognize that the established market is important, but also that a firm must be innovative and adapt to changing markets with new products and promotions. A decentralized, product-oriented organization will best allow Brentwood to respond quickly to changing markets.

In the meeting, you wish to push strongly for an aggressive marketing campaign aimed at increasing market share as a way to solve current problems. This requires increasing the sales force by 10 percent, and a 15 to 20 percent increase in advertising. The only way to halt a sales decline is to increase the marketing effort. You feel strongly that a decentralized, product-oriented organization is the way to go, with a product manager responsible for each major product line. The past problems were largely due to high manufacturing costs and poor product quality and an inability to respond to the customers' demands. You hope to convince the OD consultant to support the major product group structure.

Role 3—Director of Production   You are 55 years old and have been with the company for over 20 years. You worked your way up through the ranks and have found that a structured, decisive leadership style works best. You see increased efficiency as the major goal, since excessive spending in marketing and engineering is needlessly raising costs. You are convinced that costs can be reduced drastically by limiting engineering changes, limiting the number of products, and by slowing down the introduction of new products (which marketing always wants). This will allow a more stable and efficient production-line operation, rather than the hectic, constantly changing situation you have now.

In the meeting, you are going to push for some "no nonsense" cost controls on overhead, particularly in marketing and engineering. You strongly oppose any layoffs in production, because skilled workers are hard to get and you are forced to pay overtime now. You also need a more automated assembly line, which in the long run will cut production costs and reduce the need for overtime. You suggest a more centralized operation with tighter financial controls. For example, you feel that salespeople pad their expense reports beyond reason. You hope to get support from the consultant for a more efficient and centralized form of operation.

Role 4—Director of Human Resource Development You are 35, with a master's degree in psychology, and have been with the company for 5 years. You favor a more decentralized organization and a type of leadership that is concerned with human needs and have been working toward this goal. You feel strongly that the most important resource in the organization is people. Morale and the satisfaction of individuals are the primary goals as you see it. You have already initiated several OD-type programs (communication and leadership training) and would like to see more innovative OD programs to improve the organization's long-term effectiveness.

In the meeting, you strongly oppose any form of layoffs. The negative effects on morale would be almost irreversible. What is needed, you feel, is a raise in pay and improved coordination between departments instead of the constant bickering and fighting which prevails. You urge implementation of an MBO program, which will solve these problems, as it would improve the communication and coordination between groups. Naturally, you would be designing the MBO program. If it is successful, this could lead to the application of MBO in the whole company. You see the OD consultant as an ally in gaining support for the MBO program, and you hope to make a favorable impression as a dynamic manager who could head up a company-wide MBO program.

Role 5—Director of Engineering You are 33, with an M.S.E.E. and have been with the company for 3 years. You feel that a highly decentralized structure with a participative leadership is most effective. You see long-term effectiveness as the most important goal. Both profit and market share depend on the ability to remain innovative in R&D. You feel that the company must become more innovative and improve product marketability to survive.

In the meeting you wish to propose increased expenditures in R&D for the next 2 years. You also need two new engineers (in stress analysis and thermal dynamics) for these advanced projects. You feel that a reduction in manufacturing costs, less overtime, and reducing advertising budgets will allow for this. You feel that the current problems are due to stagnant management, low-risk strategies, front-office interference, and a lack of R&D in emerging fields. The production department is old and obsolete, both in its methods and equipment. You have suggested new methods, but your advice has been rejected. You hope to gain the consultant's support in creating a more innovative, R&D-oriented organizational climate. Recently you have lost several of your key researchers to other companies. You think Brentwood's lack of an incentive system tends to stifle any innovation. You would like to see the company use some of the techniques you used when you were at TRW, such as quality circles and team building.

Role 6—OD Consultant Guidelines You are the consultant from the company's newly formed OD consulting group. You hope to accomplish several things at this meeting:

1. To develop a consultant-client relationship with all the committee members.
2. To make a preliminary diagnosis of possible problems.
3. To assist the committee by doing process consultation during the meeting.

Role 7—Observer Use Likert's system 4 scale to analyze group style.

	System 1	System 2	System 3	System 4
Communication:				
1. How is downward communication accepted?	With Suspicion	With Mild Suspicion	Mild Caution	Readily
2. How is upward communication accepted?	With Suspicion	With Mild Suspicion	Mild Caution	Readily
3. What is direction of communication?	Down	Mostly Down	Down and Up	Down, Up and Sideways
Leadership:				
4. Are ideas of subordinates sought and used?	Seldom	Sometimes	Usually	Always
5. What is the degree of warmth and support between subordinates and their leaders?	None	Some	Substantial	A Great Deal
6. To what extent are the rewards and encouragements given to subordinates?	None	Some	Substantial	A Great Deal
Policies:				
7. Are the policies clearly understood?	Not at All	Some	Quite Well	Very Well
8. Are there a lot of rules, policies, and procedures a person has to know to get his job done?	A Great Deal	Substantial	Some	Very Few
9. Are there unnecessary procedures?	A Great Deal	Substantial	Some	Very Few

Did the consultant

1. Establish a relationship?
2. Take over the problem?
3. Focus on feelings?
4. Encourage the client to be specific?
5. Allow the client to talk?
6. Lead and direct the conversation?
7. Show indications of judging the client?

**Case:
The Grayson
Chemical
Company**

THE COMPANY

The Grayson Chemical Co. manufactured industrial chemicals for sale to other industrial companies. The company was about 40 years old and had been run by a stable management under only two presidents. Within the past few years, however, declining earnings and sales had brought pressure from the board of directors, investment bankers, and stockholder groups to name a new president. The company had grown increasingly stagnant—although at Grayson they refer to it as conservative—and had steadily lost market standing and profitability. Finally, the Board decided to go outside the company to find a new CEO and was able to recruit a dynamic manager from another major corporation, Tom Baker. Baker is 47, an M.B.A. and had helped build his prior company into a leadership position. However, when another executive was chosen for the top job, Baker decided to accept the position with Grayson.

Baker was clear about what he needed to do. He knew that he needed to develop a top management team that could provide the leadership to turn the company around. Unfortunately, the situation at Grayson was not very favorable.

Decisions were made by the book, or taken to the next higher level. Things were done because "they have always been done this way," and incompetent managers were often promoted to high-level jobs.

THE MEETING

In a meeting with three members of the Board, Robert Temple (chairman), James Allen, and Hartley Ashford each had a different bit of advice to offer.

Robert Temple said: "Look, Tom, you can't just get rid of the old organization if you want to maintain any semblance of morale. Your existing people are all fairly competent technically, but it's up to you to develop performance goals and motivate them to achieve these standards. Make it clear that achievement will be rewarded and that those who can't hack it will have to go."

James Allen, puffing on his pipe, noted: "Let's face it, Tom, you need to bring in a new top management team. Probably only six or so, but people who know what top performance means, people who are using innovative methods of managing and, above all, people you trust. That means people whom you've worked with closely, from ABC or other companies, but people you know. You can't retread the old people and you don't have time to develop young M.B.A.'s, so you need to bring in your own team even though it might upset some of the old timers."

Hartley Ashford smiled and said: "Sure, you're going to have to bring in a new team from the outside, but rather than bring in people you've worked with before, bring in only managers with proven track records. People who have proven their ability to lead, motivate and perform, from different industries. This way you will get a synergistic effect from a number of successful organizations. And the old people will see that favoritism is not the way to get ahead. So get a top performance team, and if you lose a few old timers, so much the better."

CASE ANALYSIS FORM

I. Problems

  A. Macro

    1. _____

    2. _____

  B. Micro

    1. _____

    2. _____

II. Causes

    1. _____

    2. _____

    3. _____

III. Systems affected

    1. Structural

    2. Psychosocial

    3. Technical

    4. Managerial

    5.

IV. Alternatives

    1. _____

    2. _____

    3. _____

    4. _____

    5. _____

V. Recommendations

    1. _____

    2. _____

    3. _____

V.
Summary

This chapter has examined system-wide approaches to organization development: (1) Grid OD; (2) survey research and feedback; and (3) Likert's system 4 model. All these approaches use methodologies similar to those of the action research model. They involve the collection of data, the feeding back of these data to appropriate individuals, and the generation of action plans by system members. Although the research evidence on the results of these system-wide approaches is incomplete, it does indicate positive results in certain organization settings. More research evidence is needed to determine under what conditions one approach is more effective than another and why certain approaches are more appropriate within certain organization settings or on certain organization problems.

In the simulations you have had an opportunity to experience and practice the concepts of system-wide change approaches. You also had a chance to experience an organizational meeting, which provides a method for rapidly generating information, identifying problems, and designing action solutions. You had an opportunity to apply Likert's system 4 model as a means of diagnosing system problems, and as a framework for recommending action plans.

NOTES

1. Robert R. Blake and Jane S. Mouton "Out of the Past: How to Use Your Organization's History to Shape a Better Future," *Training and Development Journal*, 37, no. 11 (November 1983), 58–65.

2. Richard Beckhard, "Conversation with Richard Beckhard," *Organizational Dynamics*, 12, no. 1 (Summer 1983), 29–38.

3. This material is based on Robert R. Blake and Jane S. Mouton, *Corporate Excellence through Grid Organization Development: A Systems Approach* (Houston, Tex.: Gulf Publishing Company, 1968).

4. Robert R. Blake and Jane Srygley Mouton, *The Managerial Grid III* (Houston: Gulf Publishing Company, 1985), p. 182.

5. Robert S. Blake, Jane S. Mouton, L. Barnes, and L. Greiner, "Breakthrough in Organization Development," *Harvard Business Review*, November–December 1964, pp. 133–55.

6. H. John Bernardin and Kenneth M. Alvares, "The Managerial Grid as a Prediction of Conflict Resolutions and Managerial Effectiveness", *Administrative Science Quarterly*, March 1976; and Howard Hart, "Grid Appraisals—Phases 1 and 2," *Personnel*, September 1976.

7. Using the Managerial Grid to Ensure MBO," *Organizational Dynamics*, 2, no. 4 (Spring 1974), 54–65.

8. See for example, M. Beer and S. Kleisath, "The Effects of Managerial Grid on Organizational and Leadership Dimensions," in *Research on the Input of Using Different Laboratory Methods for Interpersonal and Organizational Change*, ed. S. S. Zalkand, symposium presented at American Psychological Association, Washington, D.C., September 1976.

9. See Tony Condeni, "The Survey Solution," *Management World*, 12, no. 4a (May 1983), 30–31, which describes the use of an "OES" Survey.

10. Floyd Mann, "Studying and Creating Change: A Means to Understanding Social Organization," in *The Planning of Change*, ed. W. Bennis, K. Benne, and R. Chin (New York: Holt, Rinehart & Winston, 1957), p. 613.

11. Ibid., p. 612.

12. Ibid., p. 611.

13. M. Miles and others, "The Consequences of Survey Feedback: Theory and Evaluation," in *The Planning of Change*, 2nd ed., ed. W. Bennis, K. Benne, and R. Chin (New York: Holt, Rinehart & Winston, 1969), p. 466.

14. J. Aplin, and D. Thompson, "Feedback: Key to Survey-based Change," *Personnel Management*, November 1974. See also Edward J. Conlon and Lawrence O. Short, "Survey Feedback as a Large Scale Change Device: An Empirical Examination," *Group and Organization Studies*, 9, no. 3 (September 1984), 399–416.

15. Rensis Likert and Jane Gibson Likert, *New Ways of Managing Conflict* (New York: McGraw-Hill Book Company, 1976).

16. William Dowling, "System 4 Builds Performance and Profits," *Organizational Dynamics*, 3, no. 3 (Winter 1975), 23–38.

OD STRATEGY INTERVENTIONS

I.
Objectives

Upon completing this chapter, you will be able to:

1. Identify the strategy-culture gap in relation to the change process.

2. Understand the basic strategy-culture matrix and other approaches to changing the culture to fit the strategy.

3. Recognize the importance of corporate culture and its relation to strategy.

4. Experience these concepts in a management simulation.

II.
Premeeting
Preparation

1. Read the Background Information (Section III).

2. Complete Step 1 of Simulation 15.1 (Section IV).

3. Read and analyze Case: The Space Electronics Corporation.

III.
Background
Information

What makes one organization a winner, while another fails to make use of the same opportunities? How do some smaller companies move forward and seize new market and product opportunities, while other larger companies fail to take advantage of their size and situation? How did CEO John Young and others lead Hewlett-Packard from virtual obscurity to the Fortune Top 500, while at the same time Gulf Oil, once the ninth largest U.S. corporation, was taken over by another company? The answer lies in the firm's strategy: the action plan for achieving future objectives.

In a recent survey, Hewlett-Packard was rated better than any other company in attracting and keeping talented people, and among the top five in quality of management.[1] Good management does not mean trying harder by using old, out-of-date methods. It involves developing techniques for coming up with new products, making sure they are what the customer wants, and getting the new products to market in time to gain a competitive advantage.

Accelerating changes in technology, shorter product life cycles, and new unexpected competition contribute to make succeeding in business harder than ever. The evidence indicates that managers play a major role in whether or not an organization performs. Managers make strategy and strategy determines business success or failure.[2]

A very revealing study of 43 of America's best-managed corporations, conducted by Tom Peters and Robert Waterman, provides some insight into developing a strategically effective organization.[3] These excellent companies recognize the importance of corporate culture in devising and executing new strategies. In fact, they suggest that the biggest stumbling block in the path of strategic change is usually an old and inflexible corporate culture.

A culture that prevents a company from meeting competitive threats, or from adapting to changing economic or social environments, can lead to the company's stagnation and ultimate failure unless it makes a conscious effort to change. These cultural change efforts include activities which are designed to improve the skills, abilities, structure, or motivational levels of organization members. The goals are improved technical skills or improved interpersonal competence. Such implementation efforts may also be directed toward improved leadership, decision making, or problem solving among organization members. The assumption underlying such efforts is that by developing an improved culture, a more effective organization will result.

The strategy-culture matrix provides one model that can be used to assess the readiness of a corporate culture for strategic changes. A growing body of research has indicated that the culture does indeed affect strategy formulation and implementation, as well as the organization's ability to achieve a high level of corporate excellence. *Strategic change management*, another type of intervention, involves integrating the organization's strategy with its structure and people and aligning these factors to the larger environment. In this chapter, several of the major strategic interventions will be described.

THE CORPORATE CULTURE

Each organization forms its own culture. As noted in Chapter 3, an organization's culture includes the shared values, beliefs, and behaviors formed by the members of an organization over time. The leadership style of top management and the norms, values, and beliefs of the organization's members combine to form the corporate culture. Organization effectiveness can be increased by creating a culture that achieves organizational goals and at the same time satisfies member needs. The CEO's words alone do not produce culture; rather the actions of managers do, as noted by *Business Week*:

> A corporation's culture can be its major strength when it is
> consistent with its strategies. Some of the most successful
> companies have clearly demonstrated that fact, including:
> International Business Machines Corp., where marketing
> drives a service philosophy that is almost unparalleled. The
> company keeps a hot line open 24 hours a day, seven days a
> week, to service IBM products.[1]

The corporate culture influences how managers approach problems, react to competition, and implement new strategies.

The Strategy-Culture Fit

Strategy refers to a course of action used to achieve major objectives. This includes all the activities leading to the identification of the objectives and plans of the organization and is concerned with relating the resources of the organization to opportunities in the larger environment.

Culture provides a set of values for setting priorities on what is important, and "the way things are done around here." Because of this, culture is a critical factor in the implementation of a new strategy. An organization's culture can be a major strength when there is a fit with the strategy and can be a driving force in implementing a successful change.

Each organization evolves a unique culture. But this culture must change to meet changing conditions. A number of studies have indicated that corporate strategy alone cannot produce winning results. Management consultants have suggested that only one company in ten can successfully carry out a complex change in strategy. But the need for devising and executing strategic changes is rapidly increasing.

Culture: A Definition

There is widespread agreement that organizational culture refers to a system of shared values held by members that distinguishes one organizaton from another. Five characteristics that describe an organization's culture include:

1. *Individual autonomy*—the degree of responsibility, independence, and the opportunities for exercising initiative for members of the organization.

2. *Structure*—the degree of rules and regulations, and amount of direct supervision used to control member behavior.

3. *Support*—the degree of assistance and warmth provided by managers.

4. *Performance incentives*—the degree to which incentives in the organization (i.e., salary increases, promotions) are based on member performance.

5. *Risk Behavior*—the degree to which members are encouraged to be aggressive, innovative, and risk seeking.[5]

By combining each of these characteristics, then, a composite picture of the organization's culture is formed. The culture becomes the basis for the shared understanding that members have about the organization, how things are done and the way members are supposed to behave.

A company's success rests on its ability to change strategy in order to meet rapidly changing market conditions. Under these conditions the culture must be adjusted so the firm can confront and deal with factors that may contribute to its failure, stagnation, or success. The culture influences each member's adjustment to these changes. Productive corporate changes increase the company's capacity to meet new challenges. To be effective, managers must be able to motivate their employees and help them adapt to changing conditions. Success depends on management's skills and strategy, and on the acceptance of change by the organization members.

CULTURAL STRENGTH

Every organization has a culture, but some cultures are stronger than others. IBM, for instance, has a more tightly held culture than does a conglomerate of newly acquired companies, or a very young firm. Harvard University has a more cohesive culture than many newer state universities. AT&T has a more solid corporate identity than many of its newer competitors. In strong cultures, the behavior of members is constrained by mutual accord rather than by command or rule.

It has become increasingly popular to differentiate between strong and weak cultures. The evidence suggests that strong cultures have a greater impact on employee behavior and are more directly related to reduced turnover.[6]

A strong culture is characterized by the organization's basic values being both intensely held and widely shared, as shown in Figure 15.1. Each dimension can be envisioned as existing along a continuum from low to high. The more members sharing these basic values and the greater their commitment to those values, the stronger the culture.

By this definition, IBM and AT&T would be assigned as having strong

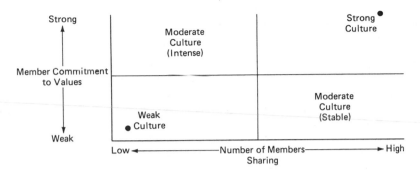

FIGURE 15.1 Relative Strength of Corporate Cultures

cultures, whereas relatively young companies or ones which have had a high turnover of executives and employees would be considered to have weaker cultures. It should also be noted that once an organization develops a "strong" culture, there is a high resistance to changes which affect the culture. The organization can survive high turnover at lower ranks because new members can be strongly socialized into the organization.[7]

It is important to recognize that cultural strength does not necessarily guarantee corporate effectiveness. Though many current writers argue that strength is desirable, the fact remains that the relationship between culture and effectiveness is not simple. The definition of the culture and the degree to which its solutions fit the problems posed by the environment seem to be the critical variables here, not strength alone.

Managers often have a difficult time in recognizing the relationship between culture and the critical performance factors on which excellence depends. There are several key components of the organization—structure, systems, people, style—that influence the way key managerial tasks are performed. Culture is the product of these components. Strategic change is largely concerned with adjustments in these components to accommodate the perceived needs of a new strategy. So, managing the strategy-culture relationship requires sensitivity to the interaction between the changes necessary to implement strategy and the compatibility or "fit" between those changes and the organization's culture. This is described in OD Application 15.1.

THE STRATEGY-CULTURE MATRIX

Strategic changes can more effectively be implemented when the culture of the organization is considered. In an effort to minimize the risks inherent in a proposed change, the extent of the need for change and the degree to which the change is compatible with the culture should be viewed together as each impacts upon the other. Four basic alternatives in determining strategy changes are:

OD
Application
15.1

JOHNSON & JOHNSON: CHANGING A CORPORATE CULTURE

JOHNSON & JOHNSON is a leading manufacturer of health-care products and has been rated as a well-managed company under chief executive officer James E. Burke, a Harvard MBA. Burke is now attempting to change the strategy and move from a consumer goods firm into an advanced technology leader—"from band-aids to high tech."

The company has been known for its unique decentralized operating structure, with each of its 170 businesses operated as autonomous profit-center units. However, the number of old, maturing products were slowing future growth. Therefore Burke has focused more resources in high-growth, high-margin businesses (such as pharmaceuticals) by consistently increasing Research and Development expenditures in these areas to well over the industry average. Burke has also used an acquisition strategy to move into new high-tech areas, including biotechnology, nuclear magnetic resonance (NMR) and surgical lasers.

Changing the Culture

But J&J failed to adapt to these changes. The type of cooperation and communication between units needed by the new strategy has not been completely accepted by the old culture. In the old culture managers operated as independent profit centers, and were evaluated by their own results. Under the new plan, managers need to share marketing and R&D resources which requires collaborative teamwork versus the old independent operation.

Culture Shock

Many managers failed to adapt to these changes. Managing high-tech products required different managerial skills and styles than the older consumer product lines. The kind of communication and sharing of resources was in direct conflict with existing cultural values.

J&J is trying to regain share in its traditional markets, and to exploit new strategies in biotechnology and magnetic resonance. The change in strategy and culture has caused many problems and poses big risks for an old line company.

Questions:
1.   Corporate executives have been quoted as saying that the greatest challenge J&J faces is to change its culture. Do you agree?
2.   Summarize the characteristics of the old and new cultures at J&J.
3.   Suggest some ways that Burke might use to change the culture.

Sources: "Changing A Corporate Culture," *Business Week*, May 14, 1984, p. 130; J. R. Wiese, "The Delivery of Facility Planning Assistance in a Decentralized Corporate Structure," *Industrial Development*, July-August 1986, pp. 3–4; "Loyalty and Pride at J&J," *Sand MM*, Dec. 3, 1984, p. 40. "Picture of Health," *Barron's* Weekly, March 30, 1987:15.

1. Manage the change (manageable risk).
2. Reinforce the culture (negligible risk).
3. Manage around the culture (manageable risk).
4. Change the strategy to fit the culture (unacceptable risk).[8]

The need for strategic change and the compatibility of the change, viewed together as a strategy-culture matrix, will largely influence the method used to manage the strategic change (see Figure 15.2).

Manage the change (manageable risk). An organization in quadrant 1 (Figure 15.2) is implementing a strategy change that is important to the firm, where the changes are compatible with existing corporate culture. Therefore, the company can pursue a strategy requiring major changes and should manage the change by using the power of cultural acceptance and reinforcement. The change strategies should emphasize these basic elements:

1. The changes must be related to the overall goals and mission of the organization. This builds on existing strengths and makes any changes legitimate to members.

2. Reshuffle power to raise key people to positions important in implementing the new strategy. Key people make visible the shared values and norms that lead to cultural compatibility.

3. Reinforce the new value system. If the new strategic direction requires changes in marketing, production, and so forth, the changes should be reinforced by the organization's reward structure.

Reinforce the culture (negligible risk). An organization in quadrant 2 needs relatively little strategic change, and the changes needed are highly compatible with the existing culture. Here the consultant should emphasize two factors:

1. Forge a vision of the new strategy that emphasizes the shared values, to make it work.

2. Reinforce and solidify the existing culture.

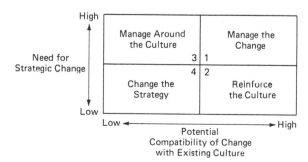

FIGURE 15.2 The Strategy-Culture Matrix

At Apple Computer, CEO John Sculley made changes to the firm's competitive position, but he was also determined to reinforce the existing culture in carrying out the new strategy.

Manage around the culture (manageable risk). Organizations in quadrant 3 need to make some strategic changes, but these changes are potentially incompatible with the corporate culture. Here the critical point is whether these changes can be implemented with a reasonable probability of success. The key element is to manage around the culture, without confronting direct cultural resistance (see B.C. comic strip). The approaches include:

1. Reinforce the value system.
2. Reshuffle power to raise key people.
3. Use any available levers of change such as the budgeting process and reorganization.

Change the strategy (unacceptable risk). An organization in quadrant 4 faces a different challenge because the strategic change is important to the company, but the changes are incompatible with the entrenched corporate culture.

First Chicago Bank, for example, illustrates the dilemma faced by an organization under these conditions. The company faced the challenge of attempting to change its culture from an "aversion for risk," to an "aggressive

B.C. by permission of Johnny Hart and Creators Syndicate, Inc.

risk-taking style." The challenge of changing the culture is an expensive long-term undertaking that is practically impossible to achieve.

When an organization is in this situation, facing large-scale change with a high probability of cultural resistance, the OD consultant and management must determine whether strategic change is really a viable alternative. The key question is: Can the strategic change be made with any possibility of success? If the answer is no, the organization should modify its strategy to fit more closely with the existing culture.

STRATEGIC CHANGE MANAGEMENT

Noel Tichy proposed the strategic change management model which provides an important integration of the strategic interventions discussed earlier.[9] Tichy's model seeks an alignment among an organization's strategy, structure, and human resource systems, and a fit between them and the organization's environment. Strategic change is a function of how well an organization manages these alignments.

Tichy proposes that organizations are composed of three systems: technical, political, and cultural. Three basic management tools, including organizational strategy and structure, and human resource management, may be used to align the three systems with each other and with the larger environment (see Figure 15.3).

FIGURE 15.3 Environmental Forces and Organizational Systems

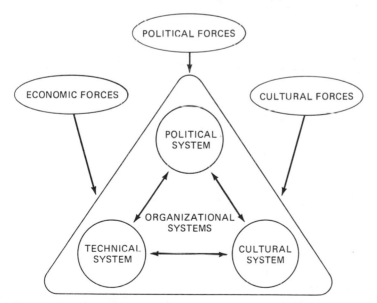

Source: Reproduced by permission. From N. Tichy, "Strategic Change Management" (Working paper, GSBA, The University of Michigan, April 1982), p. 17.

Organizations are perpetually experiencing increasing amounts of environmental change and uncertainty. This turbulence often causes existing structures and strategies to become obsolete, requiring major strategic changes. For example, the banking industry, long regarded as a stable and unchanging industry has faced monumental changes because of deregulation and electronic banking.

Tichy describes the three organizational systems as follows:

1. *The technical system* is designed to solve the organization's production problems. It includes the mission, strategy, and organizational structure necessary to become effective.

2. *The political system* resolves the allocation problem: how to distribute resources and power, including reward systems, career succession, budgets and power structure.

3. *The cultural system* is designed to solve the value/belief problem—what values members share, what objectives should be pursued, and so forth.

The technical, political, and cultural systems are interrelated and form an organizational system, as discussed in Chapter 2. Strategic change management, then, involves the alignment of these systems to meet environmental pressures.

Tichy's approach to change suggests the following steps:

1. Develop an image of desired organization with the technical, political, and cultural systems aligned. Change must start with a strategic vision of a desired organizational state. This vision should include a futuristic view of each of the three systems, as well as what the organization will look like when the systems are aligned.

2. Separate the three systems and intervene separately in each one. Because each of the systems tends to be mutually reinforcing, it is necessary to unlock the systems from each other before strategic change can occur.

3. Plan for reconnecting the three systems. After strategy interventions have been made in the three systems separately, it is necessary to determine how they will be reconnected. This reconnecting plan determines how the three systems will achieve the desired state or strategic vision in step 1.

CHANGING THE CULTURE

The organization culture may inhibit the implementation of a strategy and prevent a firm from meeting competitive threats or from adapting to changing economic conditions. This can lead to the firm's decline, stagnation or even ultimate demise unless the culture is changed. One company that has systematically changed its cultural emphasis is PepsiCo., Inc. under chairman Donald M. Kendell.

At one time, the company was content in its number two position, offering Pepsi as a cheaper alternative to Coca-Cola. But today, a new employee at PepsiCo quickly learns that beating the competition, whether outside or inside the company, is the surest path to success. In its soft-drink operation, for example, Pepsi's marketers now take on Coke directly, asking consumers to compare the taste of the two colas. That direct confrontation is reflected inside the company as well. Managers are pitted against each other to grab more market share, to work harder, and to wring more profits out of their businesses. Because winning is the key value at Pepsi, losing has its penalties. Consistent runners-up find their jobs gone. Employees know they must win merely to stay in place—and must devastate the competition to get ahead.[10]

Terrence Deal and Allan Kennedy suggest that there are only five reasons to justify large-scale cultural changes.[11]

1. When the company has strong values that do not fit a changing environment.
2. When the industry is very competitive and changes with lightning speed.
3. When the company is mediocre or worse.
4. When the firm is about to join the ranks of the very largest.
5. When the firm is small but growing rapidly.

For many businesses, changing the culture is not in the best long-term interests of the firm. For example, Apple Computer management recognizes that its most important challenge will be to retain its small-company culture even though it has grown into a top Fortune 500 firm.

REVIEW QUESTIONS

1. Compare and contrast individual values and corporate culture. How are they similar or dissimilar?

2. What forces might contribute to making a culture strong?

3. How does the culture affect an organization's ability to change?

4. Can you identify the characteristics that describe your organization's culture?

KEY WORDS AND CONCEPTS

Define and be able to use the following:

OD strategy interventions
Organization culture
Corporate culture
The strategy-culture matrix
Strength of cultures

Culture characteristics
Changing cultures
Strategic change management
Technical, political, and culture
   systems

**IV.
Simulations**

SIMULATION 15.1   THE GENTECH COMPANY

Total time suggested: 2 hours, 10 minutes.

A. Purpose

In this simulation you will be able to develop cultural change strategies in an organization. You will also critique and receive feedback on the effectiveness of your strategies. The goals include:

1. Determine appropriate intervention strategy.
2. Diagnose the corporate culture.
3. Provide feedback on consulting approaches.

B. Procedures

Step 1   Form GenTech Company teams of six. Additional class members may serve as observers. All participants and observers read the Company Background. Each participant select one role and read only their role description. The roles should be selected and read prior to the class meeting. The roles are:

1. Executive Vice President
2. Vice President of Personnel
3. Vice President of Manufacturing
4. Vice President of Marketing
5. Vice President of Finance
6. OD Consultant

Step 2   The vice presidents meet in a separate and an informal meeting with their counterpart(s) from the original company (either GenTech or Byte). The Executive vice president and the OD consultant will meet together. The purpose of this meeting is to determine the shared interests and the strategy you will pursue in the larger company-wide meeting of all the vice presidents. *Time suggested for Step 2: 20 minutes.*

Step 3 Meet with the other vice presidents and the OD consultant to form a new corporate strategy. During this task, assume that it is desirable to be self-assertive and to let others know what you want to happen. Your team's planning will be improved by answering the following questions:

1. What are the self-interests and cultural values of the vice presidents?
2. What do you see as becoming the new culture of the combined company?
3. What are the strengths and weaknesses of the company's departments?
4. What are the company goals?
5. What strategy options are available?

There are at least three possible strategies that your team can follow:

1. High risk, high growth.
2. Low risk, low growth, cost control.
3. Some trade-off between the first two strategies.

Develop a corporate strategy for the new GenTech.
Time suggested for Step 3: 60 minutes.

Step 4 Critique your team meeting by discussing the following:

1. What did the OD consultant do that was helpful? Dysfunctional?
2. Share with other team members their behavior that was helpful or a hindrance.
3. Using Figure 15.2, evaluate GenTech on the matrix as you have defined the strategy.
4. What types of strategies were actually used (long-term vs. short-term, etc)?
5. A major barrier to change involves cultural values; how did your team deal with the differences?
6. How did the team resolve the problems (vote, consensus, authority)?
7. How well did your team use total information in arriving at the solution?
8. What managerial styles were used and how effective was each?

Time suggested for Step 4: 20 minutes.

Step 5 In a meeting with the entire class, address the following:

1. Report the strategy your team developed.
2. Were there any similarities and/or differences between the teams' strategies?
3. To what extent could the differences be attributed to the personality of the individual who was playing the role?
4. Does any team's strategy seem more likely to be successful?
5. Using the stretegy-culture matrix, explain what quadrant your team has decided to follow and why.
6. What was the role of the OD consultant? And was the consultant helpful in your team?

Time suggested for Step 5: 30 minutes.

THE GENTECH COMPANY BACKGROUND

The GenTech Company is a medium-sized company manufacturing a wide variety of power equipment such as electric motors, solenoids, and gear boxes. Until the past 5 years, GenTech has had a strong and steady growth record and its products have traditionally been highly rated by customers. GenTech has a sound financial position but during the last 5 years it has been losing its market share because of new competitors entering the field with more advanced products and at lower prices.

GenTech has been particularly noted for its stability—an organization structured along classical functional lines, and closely adhering to formal lines of authority. People always know where they stand around GenTech. However, recently several of the newer and more promising managers and engineers have quit to join competitors.

In order to improve both technologically and financially, GenTech recently acquired Byte Electronics. Byte is a high-tech firm selling computers, computer components, software, and information systems. As a relative newcomer to the computer industry (it was founded 11 years ago), Byte is still a small to medium-size company in its industry, but it has been modestly successful competing with DEC and IBM. Byte is a fast-moving company and somewhat unorthodox in its organization structure and employee behavior in that both are highly flexible. Byte has operated on the concept of "Let's get it done now and we'll worry about rules and regulations tomorrow."

The executive vice president has called a meeting of two key members from both companies to form a new corporate strategy based upon the strengths of each of the original companies. An OD consultant has just been retained and will also be present at the meeting. One key factor is how to merge the two cultures into one company.

The people present at the meeting and their original company affiliations are:

1. Executive Vice President—GenTech
2. Vice President of Personnel—Byte
3. Vice President of Manufacturing—GenTech
4. Vice President of Marketing—Byte
5. Vice President of Finance—GenTech
6. OD Consultant

ROLE DESCRIPTIONS (READ *ONLY* YOUR ROLE)

Executive Vice President   You have been with GenTech for the past 7 years with 4 years in your present position. A large part of Gentech's growth and success has been due to your own ability to select and motivate others. You are 36 and a college graduate. You have attended many executive training seminars and you have tried to apply these concepts to GenTech.

You still maintain close contact with day-to-day operations since you believe in hands-on management. Over the past few years, growth at GenTech has slowed, sales and earnings have declined, and turnover problems have emerged. You see the infusion of new blood from Byte may be just what GenTech needs.

You are convinced that the lack of coordination between operating groups is the major problem and that a more decentralized operation will help resolve this. You are concerned with trying to integrate Byte's fast moving organization into GenTech's rather deliberate method of responding to changing conditions. You believe that the new organization needs better morale and improved bottom-line results.

You feel that the environment is becoming more dynamic and the company must become more adaptive to change and more innovative. Either some new products should be developed or new markets for the existing product line are needed. You see your managerial style as a team player, but able to be directive if a crisis emerges. You feel that the company must achieve at least a ten percent rate of growth and average profits, if you are to be promoted.

Your strategy is to use calculated risks, and to increase some areas and cut costs in others. Your goal is to keep your managers happy, yet get new managers to supply the necessary profits and growth.

Vice President of Personnel   You are 29, have a degree in Human Resources Management, and were with Byte for 4 years in your present position. You had some initial reservations about GenTech's acquisition of Byte, but since you were selected as the VP of Personnel over your counterpart at GenTech, you figure things can't be too bad in that company. So now you must become part of the corporate team.

You see several problems facing the newly merged organization. After looking over GenTech's operations, you believe it has a poor organization structure, a lack of coordination among departments, and weak managerial competence and training at all levels. It looks to you that some of the people have been in their positions so long that they have become complacent.

You think the answer to the problem is a decentralized operation with increased integration and coordination between departments. There is a need to get conflicts into the open where they can be resolved rather than each unit seeking its own best interest. You are a believer in the necessity of a unified team effort.

You have attempted to initiate several training and change programs since the acquisition. Though these programs were generally successful at Byte before the acquisition, they have been undercut by GenTech managers, even though the executive vice president has been strongly supportive. You believe an aggressive growth strategy is needed to improve GenTech's original product line and to enable the company to remain on the leading edge of the fast-moving computer industry.

You feel that the company needs change, but not too rapidly until the merger aligns the old culture (slow, traditional, low-risk) to the new (dynamic, innovative, high-risk) and developing new markets for the existing products. You are easy going, empathic, using a people-oriented style versus numbers, leading to a stress on human relationships and open communications.

Your strategy is aimed at the 20 percent growth rate in the computer market to increase market share with a high-risk strategy. Your goal is to develop open communications and teamwork, and convince the managers that a new strategy and culture is the most effective in the long run.

Vice President of Manufacturing You are 42 and have been with the company for 22 years, working your way up through GenTech. You got your degree in electrical engineering while working on the production line at GenTech. In fact, if it were not for GenTech helping out with the tuition, you probably would still be working on the line. You worked hard for your current position and have been in charge of manufacturing for the past 11 years.

You believe you are competent in your position and that the main reason for past successes at GenTech is due to your efforts. The acquisition of Byte is a little disturbing to you. You feel they have grown too fast, as evidenced by a loose structure and a lack of control. You believe that any new products and changes should be sent through the proper channels for thorough review. So far it looks like Byte has too many meddling staff managers (particularly in marketing and personnel) who do not contribute to profits and only cause problems for the line managers like yourself.

You feel that the competition is increasing, and your firm must react to these changes by becoming more cost efficient by cutting back 15 percent on all staff, and by selling existing products to our old, tried, and true customers. This would allow for cuts in advertising and R&D. You use a strong, directive management style based upon confrontation of differences and driving your team to accomplish its goals.

Your strategy is to use a low-risk, cost-cutting approach to increase profits by 10 percent in the solid base market, and cut out the frills in the computer business, which everyone knows is not tightly managed.

You believe the company should pursue a strategy of a highly centralized structure and run a tight ship as you do. In an effort to cut costs and make a lean organization, you believe GenTech should appoint a vice president (like yourself, for example) to centralize cost control. You think the company should follow a low-risk and deliberate policy of change while constantly watching costs.

Vice President of Marketing   You came to Byte 3 years ago as the vice president of marketing and you are now 28 years old. You have a college degree with majors in marketing and journalism and previous experience in sales with a large competitor. You think that marketing is the major factor in the company's growth and if your product managers were given greater authority, they could turn the profit picture around at GenTech. These efforts really paid off at Byte.

You were originally concerned about losing your job when Byte was acquired by GenTech, but their head of marketing decided to retire. You have concerns about GenTech's ability to move forward in an increasingly competitive market. You see the major problem at GenTech as the lack of communication among departments and the failure to utilize talented managers. You think a reduction in manufacturing costs will result in improved selling ability and increased sales volume.

Despite these problems, you believe that with several changes the new GenTech will prosper. You believe it is important to decentralize the firm into major independent groups and bring in more fast-track product managers and give them more authority over product operations. This is similar to the structure at the original Byte. You would like to see yourself as a vice president over the product managers.

You feel the firm must seek long-term effectiveness and anticipate market changes, not the usual reactive, fire-fighting focusing on short-term goals. You feel your management style is a team style, assertive, aggressive and people oriented, with an emphasis on fast decisions and taking risks even though some mistakes will be made.

Your strategy is to use an aggressive, high-risk strategy in the high-growth computer markets which are growing at 20 percent per year, by increasing expenses and market share, by developing new products and new markets in a fast-moving, high-tech culture.

Vice President of Finance   You are 38 and have a degree in accounting from a major school. You have had 10 successful years at GenTech. You instituted all financial systems and made it a smooth operation.

You were a strong advocate of GenTech's acquisition of Byte so as to take advantage of what you think could be Byte's future growth in the computer industry. But you also see some problems at Byte. Now that you have reviewed Byte's operations more closely after the acquisition, you think they have been making too many changes in too short a time. The company has too many bright young kids that don't seem to report to any department, and too many wasteful practices. It seems they do not have an adequate structure to account for and control costs. You have found situations where a group of people from engineering, production, and marketing have undertaken new projects without formal new organization structures being formed.

You think it is important to go back to the basics by instituting a tighter centralized system of financial control and cutting costs by about 10 percent. You think that you would be a natural to be put in charge of cost control. You would set up some basic company rules and then force the department heads to enforce them. You believe that all new projects should come before you for a thorough financial and marketing review. You are a strong believer in a clean functional organization structure with no overlapping departments and each area (such as marketing and production) staying out of the other department's business.

Your goal is to develop a more centralized, tightly controlled operation, with a solid, no-nonsense culture, with yourself as executive vice president in charge of this more profitable operation. You believe GenTech should follow a stable, low-risk strategy to protect profits.

OD Consultant   This will be your first meeting with the vice presidents of GenTech. You hope to accomplish several things at this meeting:

1. To develop a consultant-client relationship with all of the committee members.
2. To help the vice presidents in their meeting by making appropriate process interventions during the meeting.
3. To make a preliminary diagnosis of possible strategy and culture problems.

**Case:
The Space
Electronics
Corporation**

The Space Electronics Corporation is a subsidiary of a major firm with sales in excess of $200 million. The company held substantial positions in commercial and military electronic system markets; however, profitability and market position have been declining. About a year ago it became apparent that two R&D projects were coming up: the stealth bomber and the Star Wars proposals. These appeared to be the only two major projects coming up in the next few years. The executive committee was to decide whether or not they should pursue these two projects. This would involve taking a radically new course of action, going after the prime contract, whereas in the past they had operated as a subcontractor to other primes.

THE EXECUTIVE COMMITTEE MEETING

In mid-September, Reade Exton, the president, opened the meeting. "As you all know, our profitability and market position have been declining. We have landed only one new proposal during this period, and there is great pressure from headquarters to go after these major projects. We have all had an opportunity to review a copy of the proposals, and I'll let Glenn start the discussion."

Glenn Overton, Vice President, Engineering. "About a year ago it became obvious that our engineering activity was going to decline. The decision was made that a joint effort with marketing would be undertaken and after a series of meetings, it was decided that our best course of action was to aggressively pursue these two large contracts."

Oliver Whittier, Vice President, Finance. "Frankly, Glenn, I have reservations about such a major departure from our past policies and by the magnitude of these projects. I'm worried about the increased overhead and the drain on our current profits. And I have a gut feeling that our probabilities of getting those contracts is less than you seem to think."

Ted Byron, Vice President, Marketing. "Although you may estimate that the probability of gaining these projects is low, the payoff is enough to turn our whole picture around. These contracts will put us on the map. My best 'guesstimate' is that our chances are closer to 75 percent than 60 percent. Don't forget, I have a lot of personal contacts back in Washington, and while that is no guarantee, it sure doesn't hurt."

Paul Brown, Vice President, Industrial Relations. "I agree with Oliver: I have my doubts as to our chances of getting such a large-scale project, and I am worried about our people. If we should fail to get these contracts, people could get hurt. We may have to have layoffs and that is a bad business. I think we have a certain responsibility to the people here."

Mort Jensen, Vice President, Manufacturing. "Let's face it, if we pull these two proposals out of the hat, they will love us at headquarters. We'll be superstars! But on the other hand, we could take a real beating if these projects fizzle out. I think we have to consider the risk factor and what might happen to the company if we fail. And, like Paul says, a number of our line employees could take a beating if things don't work out."

Glenn Overton. "Listen, fellows, there are no lead-pipe cinches in this business. But don't you think Ted and I have a better feel for our probabilities than people in personnel? If a downturn were to occur, our company will be hard pressed anyway. Frankly, I'm not quite as optimistic as Ted here, but I still think our chances are in the 60 percent range. Even at that it seems like a good risk, because even if we only get one of the projects, our company will benefit greatly. Plus our R&D will stand to gain a heck of a lot by being involved in the state of the art. We'll be able to attract new talent."

Mort Jensen. "One of our past problems was the isolation of R&D from the rest of the organization. I feel that we should seek to achieve more interdepartmental cooperation. So I think it is important to get all the differing viewpoints out on the table."

Reade Exton. "I think we have had a good discussion, but now what is our decision? As you know, there is a lot of pressure from headquarters to go after these projects, but it has to be a group decision. Frankly, we are between a rock and a hard place. There will have to be a significant expenditure just to pursue these major contracts, and our R&D activity will be almost exclusively devoted to the proposals for about 3 months, and that will include 10-hour days and 7-day work weeks. There definitely is a degree of risk involved, although the exact odds are hard to predict. One thing is sure: if we don't go after the projects, we won't get them."

CASE ANALYSIS FORM

I. Problems

   A. Macro

      1. _____

      2. _____

   B. Micro

      1. _____

      2. _____

II. Causes

      1. _____

      2. _____

      3. _____

III. Systems affected

      1. Structural

      2. Psychosocial

      3. Technical

      4. Managerial

      5.

IV. Alternatives

      1. _____

      2. _____

      3. _____

      4. _____

      5. _____

V. Recommendations

      1. _____

      2. _____

      3. _____

V.
Summary

In the chapter, several strategy interventions were discussed. These strategy programs are aimed at relating the organization to its broader environment, and achieving a higher level of corporate excellence.

The strategy-culture matrix provides one tool that the OD practitioner can use in implementing strategic changes. Changing the corporate culture can be an extremely challenging task. Such change requires clear strategic vision, reinforcement of new values, and reshuffling the power-reward systems to fit the new strategy. Strategic change management presents another systems view of the organization as technical, political, and cultural systems, and involves aligning these systems with the environment. In the simulation you had the chance to experience the meshing of two different cultures in forming a strategy. One important point is the difficulty and complexity of strategic change programs, and the need for OD practitioner skills in implementing change programs in organizations.

NOTES

1. Patricia Sellers, "America's Most Admired Corporations," *Fortune*, January 7, 1985, p. 18.

2. See Andrew D. Szilagyi, Jr., and David M. Schweiger, "Matching Managers to Strategy," *Academy of Management Review*, 9, no. 4 (1984), 626–37; and LaRue T. Hosmer, "The Importance of Strategic Leadership," *The Journal of Business Strategy*, 3, no. 2 (Fall 1982), 58.

3. Thomas J. Peters and Robert H. Waterman, Jr., *In Search of Excellence: Lessons from America's Best-Run Companies* (New York: Harper & Row, Publishers, Inc., 1982).

4. "Corporate Culture," *Business Week*, October 27, 1980, p. 148.

5. Adapted and modified from J. P. Campbell, M. D. Dunnette, E. E. Lawler III, and K. E. Weick, *Managerial Behavior, Performance, and Effectiveness* (New York: McGraw-Hill Book Company, 1970), p. 303.

6. E. H. Schein, "The Role of the Founder in Creating Organizational Culture," *Organizational Dynamics*, Summer 1983, pp. 13–28.

7. Ibid.

8. Howard Schwartz and Stanley M. Davis, "Matching Corporate Culture and Business Strategy," *Organizational Dynamics*, Summer 1981, p. 43.

9. Noel Tichy, *Managing Strategic Change* (New York: John Wiley & Sons, Inc., 1983).

10. "Corporate Culture," *Business Week*.

11. T. E. Deal and A. A. Kennedy, *Corporate Cultures: The Rites and Rituals of Corporate Life* (Reading, Mass.: Addison-Wesley Publishing Co., Inc., 1982), pp. 65–66.

16

ORGANIZATION DEVELOPMENT:
The Challenge and The Future

I.	Upon completing this chapter, you will be able to:
Objectives	1. Understand the basic issues in using organization development as an approach to planned change.
	2. Recognize ways of maintaining and stabilizing a change program.
	3. Identify some of the future trends and problems facing the OD practitioner.
	4. Understand the process of terminating the consultant-client relationship.

II.	1. Read the Background Information (Section III).
Premeeting Preparation	2. Complete Step 1 of Simulation 16.1 (Section IV).
	3. Complete Steps 1 and 2 of Simulation 16.2.

**III.
Background
Information**

Change is happening in all organizations, but with differing degrees of rapidity and significance. Some organizations operate under highly volatile conditions causing rapid system-wide realignment and adaptation. Other organizations exist in relatively placid environments, with subsequently slower rates of change and less impact on the whole system.

However, there is always a need for long-range strategies to improve organizational decision making and work relationships to meet these changing conditions. From these needs, organization development, the newest discipline in planned change techniques, has emerged. Clearly, OD is being viewed by organizations of all types—industrial, governmental, and health care—as a field of expertise that can provide results. Still, there are issues and challenges facing this discipline if it is to continue to provide a viable option for planned change.

Change is a continuing process. Every organization exists in a continuous state of adapting to change. Some changes are caused by external competitive forces, whereas others emerge as a result of shifting forces within the organization. Many management theorists feel that authoritarian or bureaucratic systems are too rigid to adapt to this increasing rate of change and therefore become reactive organizations—reacting drastically after problems emerge.

More and more organizations are finding that employees are no longer satisfied with simply filling a slot in the organization chart. In a survey of American workers conducted for the U.S. Labor Department, the University of Michigan's Survey Research Center found that 41.5 percent responded "very true" when asked if they had interesting work with the freedom to decide how to do the job. This is 9.8 percent lower than the results in a similar earlier survey. Also, when asked about having enough information and authority to accomplish their job, workers responded 52.4 percent "very true." This was down 10.9 percent from the earlier survey. It is not likely that jobs are getting worse. Rather, employees are probably getting better; that is, people are achieving higher educational levels, with a resulting increase in the level of motivational needs.

Because organizations are in a continuous state of change, OD is a continuing process. As one set of change objectives is achieved, new standards of excellence and new challenges arise. As a result, the OD practitioner has two primary criteria of effectiveness. One criterion is the stability of the OD effort after the practitioner stops working with the client system; the other is the ability of the client system to maintain innovation within the system or the development of a self-renewal capability.

Since an OD program is an approach to improving effectiveness, there is a need for an evaluation of the results. The organization members involved in the change process need feedback on the results of their efforts in order to determine whether to modify, continue, or discontinue these activities. At this point there is also usually a disengagement between the OD practitioner or consultant and the client—a termination of the change program relationship.

Organization development is an ongoing process because an organization cannot remain static and be effective. In today's changing environment, organizations must develop adaptive mechanisms and anticipative management systems. To cope with these changing conditions, an OD practitioner needs to be able to monitor and assess progress toward change goals and to recognize when these efforts may be phased out. The participants and teams involved in an OD program need feedback to measure their progress toward goals and to stabilize change efforts. This continuing assessment also acts to prevent deterioration or degradation to prior behavior, attitudes, or values. An organization might implement a management-by-objectives program and initially feel that the program is successful. A year later, however, most managers may have discarded MBO and returned to prior management methods unless there is some stabilization of the MBO program.

Because OD is an ongoing, continuing process, the completion of one change cycle leads into another cycle in the process of development. In this chapter, we examine the evaluation and termination process, discuss several emerging issues, and examine the future of the OD field.

MONITOR AND STABILIZE ACTION PROGRAMS

In Chapter 2, an eight-stage model of the organization development process was presented. Stage seven of OD involves three factors: (1) generating and communicating data to participating members so they can measure their progress; (2) stabilizing or "freezing" the change or desired behavior so that it will be continued; and (3) evaluating the OD program results.

The Feedback of Information

The organization members involved in an OD program need feedback on the results of the change in order to determine whether to modify, continue, or discontinue their activities. If the client system obtains no feedback on the consequence of a change program, it may be perceived as a failure and be discontinued. Therefore, part of the OD consultant's job is to see that necessary information is made available to participating members and groups. In research conducted on quality-of-work-life programs (QWL), it was found that more successful programs had early payoffs that the participants could see and be encouraged by.

One criterion for determining the effectiveness of a change program is whether or not system problems have been corrected. In certain instances data will be readily available, particularly around operational indices of performance or productivity. In other instances the consultant may gather after-the-fact interview or questionnaire data to verify the degree of change in less tangible factors, such as morale, leadership style, or job satisfaction.

Work teams may also use such techniques as the "organization mirror" to gain information on how other organization groups view their changed status. Some systematic and periodic appraisal of results should be designed into the change effort to determine when desired levels have been achieved. This requires the setting of some type of "benchmark" to measure the extent or degree of change over time.

The OD practitioner and the managers also need to provide reinforcement and support for change by giving recognition, encouragement, and approval for positive change. Receiving information or performance data is important, but a major factor in the deterioration of performance is lack of recognition or reinforcement.

The Stabilization of Change

When a state of disequilibrium has been corrected and the change objectives have been achieved, some means must be devised to ensure that the new equilibrium is stabilized. If this is not done, the tendency is for the individual or the system to deteriorate and revert to previous ineffective behaviors. As an example, an individual may desire to discontinue some habit, such as smoking, and actually change for a short period of time. However, the change objective is not accomplished if the person begins smoking again 6 months later. One criticism of laboratory learning is called "fade-out," where, for example, a manager develops new behaviors while at the seminar, but the change erodes away back on the job because the work environment has not changed and is not supportive. Fade-out, or deterioration of change, may occur in an OD program when the change is not stabilized into the system and behavior gradually slips back into previous ineffective modes. Obviously, one measure of success is whether or not the change is permanently accepted by the client system.

The change program itself may have a stabilizing effect because of its advantages and support. At TRW Systems, team development has become so widely accepted that many project managers request a team building session every time a new project is assembled. There is also a sort of Hawthorne effect surrounding many change methods, such as team building or Managerial Grid techniques, so participating managers feel they are an elite group and sell the benefits of the OD program to other managers, thus stabilizing the acceptance of change.

Sometimes an OD program is initiated in one division or subsystem of an organization, and the performance results may be used to demonstrate the effectiveness of the new techniques to another division. Where results are obtainable, such as those relating to decreased turnover or costs, this recognition may act as a stabilizing force. The proof is in the pudding, so to speak.

Once a change effort is fully accepted, the change may become institutionalized or internalized by group members. The acceptance and adoption of a change effort depend upon practice and familiarity, so that the innovation becomes a routine part of organization activity. At Xerox, the Managerial Grid is a continuing innovation. Managers continue to level with one another over on-the-job behavior, and they are constantly critiquing one another in Grid terms. "Your decision today seemed like a country club style, Bill." In other words, the change has been integrated into the organization structure, norms, and culture.

Finally, some form of continuing assessment of the change effort during later periods should be included to guard against degradation over time. The greater the investment in the OD program, the more detailed the reappraisal mechanisms should be.

The Evaluation of OD Programs

One major problem in OD lies in the need for the development of better research designs and methods. As Frank Friedlander and L. Dave Brown have pointed out, if the practice and theory of OD is to merge into a broader field of planning change, research will play a crucial role.[1] The primary purpose of OD research programs is to measure what happens to operating variables when interventions are made to change the system. Unfortunately, there are usually many uncontrollable variables, such as economic conditions and technological changes, which influence the state of the organization over time.[2]

Many OD practitioners feel that the evaluation method should be designed into the change process itself. Achilles A. Armenakis and others surveyed OD practitioners to see what evaluation practices were being used and from these data, developed a set of guidelines. They suggest that OD evaluations will be important in the future for three groups: (1) the key organizational decision makers: to show them that OD expenditures are providing the desired results; (2) the OD participants: to provide feedback about their change efforts; and (3) the OD specialists: to develop their expertise and reputations based upon their experiences.

The authors point out that the evaluative practice will be determined by three factors: "(1) the training of the OD specialist, (2) the cooperation of the organizational members involved in the effort, and (3) the willingness of organizational decision makers to pay for a rigorous evaluation."[3]

TERMINATION OF THE CONSULTANT-CLIENT RELATIONSHIP

Stage eight of the OD process occurs at the place in an OD program when the basic change objectives have been accomplished and either the consultant or the client or both feel that members of the system can continue the change effort. Perhaps that place has been reached when there is a diminishing rate of return for efforts expended. The practitioner may feel that little more can be accomplished; the evaluation indicates that desired change levels have been achieved, and the client system feels able to continue renewal processes on their own.

The change program should have as part of its strategy some provision for a gradual disengagement of the consultant's help and a transition to internal resources as the primary focus of change (see B.C. comic strip). One problem here is to ensure that the changes are not short term or temporary, followed by a regression to former operating patterns. A second is to prepare for a continuity of change efforts with periodic follow-ups and a gradual phasing in of new change objectives.

Developing a Self-Renewal Capacity _____

One of the basic objectives of the OD consultant is to develop the ability to innovate within the client system. The client system needs a self-sustaining capability to devise and implement change programs without outside support. Watson and Glaser have noted that

> . . . following any important change comes a period during which the new equilibrium is being stabilized. Yet that condition, too, is only temporary. The organization that has

B.C. by permission of Johnny Hart and Creators Syndicate, Inc.

accepted an innovation may need a breathing spell in which
to consolidate what it has learned. But if the organization is
geared to continued growth, its members will value forward-
moving change as a recurrent and desirable phenomenon.
From the plateau on which equilibrium is regained, the
cycle of change can be launched again.[4]

As an example, Herb Shepard (then of Case Western Reserve University)
helped Sheldon Davis and James Dunlap of TRW Systems initiate an OD program, but the continuing responsibility for innovation shifted to Shel Davis and
his internal consulting team. Here, one of Shepard's objectives was to give the
client system a problem-solving and innovating capability. TRW demonstrated
that it could carry on innovation by extending its team development and
intergroup team building on a system-wide basis.[5] Usually, the mechanism for
this self-renewal capacity is some internal OD practitioner or group. Such internal consultants can continue with new data collection, diagnosis, and evaluation to determine the need for further change strategies and programs.

Termination and Disengagement from the Client System

As the client system develops a self-renewal capability, the need for a
consultant should decrease. If the consultant has successfully developed within
the client system a self-renewal capacity, a gradual termination of the consultant-client relationship should be a smooth transition; however, if the client
system has become overdependent upon the OD practitioner, termination of
the relationship may be difficult.

The OD consultant considers disengagement when the benchmarks used
to evaluate change have been achieved and the client system appears capable of
continuing innovation; that is, the client system has the resources and competence necessary to continue change efforts. The consultant-client relationship
may also be discontinued or terminated by the client if the change program
objectives have not been achieved. Although we hear mainly about the successes, there are also many failures. Such reasons for termination may include
the failure to accomplish objectives, dissatisfaction with the consultant, or simply an economic downturn.

According to Edgar Schein, the process of disengagement is usually characterized by the following features:

1. Reduced involvement is a mutually agreed upon decision rather than a unilat-
eral decision by consultant or client

2. Involvement does not generally drop to zero but may continue at a very low
level.

3. The door is always open from the consultant's point of view for further work
with the client if the client desires it.[6]

It should be emphasized that continued involvement and a gradual termination is usually advisable. The consultant is available for emergency help or special consultation. Continued formal or informal contacts are always possible, and the consultant may become involved again in some new change effort.

Some Conditions for Success of OD Efforts

Several OD practitioners have attempted to identify conditions leading to possible success of OD efforts, as follows:

1. The organization is generally under considerable external or internal pressure to improve. Top management has been aroused to action and is searching for solutions.

2. Intervention takes place at the top of the organization in the form of a catalyst, who is either a new member of or a consultant to the top team. This generally induces reorientation and reassessment of past practices and current problems.

3. Top management assumes a direct and responsible role in the process. Several levels of management generally participate in the collection of data and the analysis of specific problems.

4. New ideas and methods for developing solutions are generated at a number of levels in the organization. This results in some level of commitment to change by organization members.

5. Some degree of experimentation with innovation takes place. The proposed solutions are generally developed, tested, and found acceptable before the scope of the change is expanded to include larger problems or the entire system.

6. The organization development program is generally reinforced by positive results. The change effort spreads with each successful experience and, as management support grows, is gradually accepted as a way of life.[7]

Organization development, then, involves long-term, system-wide application of behavioral science techniques to increase organization effectiveness. OD works on the idea that improving the way people work together and the way work groups cooperate increase performance. The management style needed to work in an innovative manner differs from traditional concepts, and OD programs are designed to focus upon the manager's attitudes and upon a managerial style that encourages action in the presence of risk. OD strategies try to increase the manager's tolerance for ambiguity and uncertainty and the ability to communicate with and motivate others.

The field of OD has grown rapidly. Many innovative techniques have been developed, and many more are still being developed. Because of this rate of growth, there are also many problems and disagreements among practitioners over what is and what is not an OD technique and what interventions or strategies are most used. Although initially OD strategies emphasized the behavioral aspects of change, OD practitioners are increasingly using an integrated, eclectic, or systems approach which includes structural and technical strategies.

One thing, is clear—the field of OD is itself developing and changing. You must decide for yourself what rings true in terms of your own experience and what does not. Organization development has been described as a process designed to increase organization effectiveness by integrating the needs of the individual members for growth and development with organization goals. In a changing environment, OD provides strategies to alter beliefs, attitudes, values, and structures of organizations, making them more anticipative and adaptive to deal with problems of "future shock."

Organization development represents a major change from more traditional methods of management development and training. OD is a means for changing organization systems and revitalizing them in line with the needs of the individuals within the system and environmental constraints. Because of the changing environment, it is important that individual managers be aware of and understand the advantages and disadvantages of the techniques and strategies available for managing in this changing context. OD is not a panacea; however, it does provide a dynamic and powerful methodology for helping people and organizations collaboratively work together and become a winning team.

EMERGING ISSUES

OD is a growing, developing and changing field of study. Consequently, there are a number of evolving theories and concepts which have contributed to the field, and a number of approaches which have emerged from OD. At this stage, the field is still in transition, which makes it difficult to define exact boundaries of what is or is not an OD intervention. As a result, there are three key issues which will be examined in the following sections: (1) OD: fad or discipline? (2) the field of OD; and (3) the role of values.

OD: Fad or Discipline?

A number of writers have presented arguments concerning whether OD will emerge as a long-term *contribution* to management and organization theory, or will soon fade away into the dusty archives together with scientific management and other short-lived trends. This is a little like asking the question: "Is air travel a fad?" After all, it has only been around for 60 years or so. Similarly, OD now has some 30 years of background history and if anything has, at this point, not yet reached its apex either in quantity or quality of effort.

OD has already developed and experimented with a variety of new approaches to organization innovation and renewal and the state of the art is still evolving. OD is an exciting new field. As with any new discipline, there are unsolved issues, problems, and controversy. Edgar F. Huse commented on this:

> Rather than being a fad, OD appears to be one of the
> primary methods for helping organizations adjust to
> accelerated change. As a result, OD is not a fad, but an
> emerging discipline. Bennis points out that OD rests on
> three basic propositions. The first is the hypothesis that each
> age adopts an organizational form which is most appropriate
> to that particular age and that changes taking place in that
> age make it necessary to "revitalize and rebuild our
> organizations." The second basic proposition is that the only
> real way to change organizations lies in changing the
> "climate" of the organization—the "way of life," a system of
> beliefs and values, an accepted form of interaction and
> relating. It is more important to change the climate of the
> organization than the individual if organizations are to
> develop. The third basic proposition is that "a new *social*
> awareness is required by people in organizations," since
> social awareness is essential in our current world. In short,
> the basic thrust behind OD is that the world is rapidly
> changing and that our organizations must follow suit.[8]

As noted in *Business Week*, a lot of executives these days would like to latch on to almost any new concept that promises a quick fix for their problems:

- Having trouble developing new products? Try "Entrepre
  neurship" the process for getting entrepreneurial juices
  flowing in a big company.
- Having a tough time competing against foreign competition? Try "Quality Circles," a way to involve workers in
  finding ways to increase productivity and ensure quality.[9]

There is nothing inherently wrong with any of these theories, but too often managers use them as gimmicks or quick fixes, rather than facing the basic problems. Unless such solutions are systematically thought out and supported by the commitment of top management, they may become mere fads. A similar situation has occurred with the management concepts advocated in the bestselling book *In Search of Excellence* (see OD Application 16.1).

George Strauss, however, takes a more pessimistic view of OD's future:

> There is a real chance that the term itself will become
> as anchronistic as "scientific management" and "human
> relations" are today. Yet, like these earlier movements,
> which were also controversial in their time, OD will have
> left its mark on managerial practice.[10]

**OD
Application
16.1**

WHAT WENT WRONG IN THE SEARCH FOR EXCELLENCE?

At least 15 of the 43 excellent companies highlighted by Thomas Peters and Robert Waterman in their book, *In Search of Excellence*, lost their luster soon after the book's publication. And one, People Express, which had been considered an example of what to do right in an organization, just escaped bankruptcy by being purchased by its rival, Texas Air.

Companies such as Eastman Kodak and Texas Instruments, if judged on their performance during the last decade, would not pass the financial tests for excellence laid down in the book. Others, including Atari, Avon, and Levi Strauss, have suffered significant earnings declines stemming from serious business or management problems.

Failure of U.S. businesses is at its all-time high since the Great Depression. Though the entrepreneurial drive is strong—there were 250,456 new businesses started in 1986—57,067 businesses went bankrupt and more than half of them were less than 5 years old.

In Search of Excellence suggested that U.S. firms needed to regain their competitive edge by placing more emphasis on the people side of business—customers and employees—and by sticking to what they do best. Then why have so many excellent companies had problems? One criticism has been that companies have ignored such fundamental factors as technology, fundamental changes in markets, and broad economic and business trends.

Companies such as Lockheed learned their lessons the hard way. In the initial stages of the L-1011 Tristar production with high costs coupled with losses in defense contracts, Lockheed was saved from bankruptcy by federal loan guarantees. Yet when the crisis was passed and it was clear to analysts that there was not a large enough market to support the Tristar, Boeing's 747, and McDonnell Douglas DC-10, Lockheed continued with production. To Lockheed the Tristar was a symbol of getting back in the commercial aircraft business and they hung on despite the lack of enough firm orders to see the project to the break-even point. Eventually Lockheed gave up and took a $400 million write-off.

The excellent companies of today do not have a guarantee on remaining excellent. Companies that have followed one set of rules such as those espoused in *In Search of Excellence* have tended to get into trouble just as companies did when they followed the strict rules of the financial number crunchers.

Questions:
1. Were the companies illustrated in the book excellent in the first place?
2. Are there universal rules of excellence or are they specific to an organization?
3. For organizations having problems, what can be done to pull them out of their problems?

Sources: "Failure: Spotlight on a Neglected Side of Business," *Wall Street Journal*, December 15, 1986, p. 29; and "Who's Excellent Now?" *Business Week*, November 5, 1984, pp. 76–86.

It is our contention that organization development is not a passing fad. OD is contributing a technology that will be required even more as the rate of change increases. It is our view that OD emerged as a response to the needs of organizations and individuals for innovative ways to adapt to change. OD presents the technology for creating and seeking *organizational excellence*, which is the underlying goal of the modern manager and organization. The successful managerial organizations are seeing the need to practice "anticipative" management styles rather than using "reactive" styles, that is, waiting until after the fact to react to change.

THE FIELD OF OD

As the rate of change has increased, so has the range of interventions used in OD. Organization Development has moved far beyond its historical antecedents and is continually adding new approaches and techniques as new problem areas emerge. As noted earlier, new system-wide approaches are needed to tie together the basic OD approaches. Each OD intervention is aimed at solving technical or human problems, but what is needed are comprehensive, long-term approaches which integrate these systems into long-term solutions.

The Role of Values

There is also a diversity among OD practitioners over how OD techniques should be applied to improve organizational functioning. In the application of OD, practitioners face several complex dilemmas, including the following:

The professionalism of OD. Many theorists question OD on the grounds that it is ill-defined and that it presents "a moving target." They point to the lack of a common body of knowledge, research, and techniques. It is generally recognized that because of its rapid emergence, there is not enough empirical evidence to provide scientific validation of all, or perhaps any, of the major OD intervention techniques. OD's basic thrust arises from its face validity: it seems to work in the organization environment.

Another issue addresses the question of the certification of OD practitioners. There are currently a number of organizations with an OD orientation or an OD division but no single organization that accredits or certifies OD practitioners. Some theorists feel that the rapid growth of the OD field leads to the possibility that unqualified persons (or charlatans) may represent themselves as professionals and that a certifying agency might prevent this. Others feel that many certifying bodies are less than effective and suggest: "let the free enterprise system operate."

An overemphasis upon human and social intervention. A second issue is that OD approaches seem to overemphasize changing the behavioral patterns of members, with a consequent lack of recognition of other significant factors, such as structural and technological elements. Many practitioners suggest a broadening trend in OD practices to a more systematic, comprehensive, or integrated approach to change.

The reality of organization dynamics is a subject Jerry Harvey, an OD consultant, explores. Basically, Harvey is concerned that the area of OD has been reduced to a series of "mythical theoretical propositions." He confronts some basic OD propositions, stating that (1) *there is no such thing as resistance to change*; (2) *time is irrelevant*—if the consultant handles situations competently as they arise, significant changes can occur almost simultaneously; and (3) *OD should not exist as a noun*—it should be a verb or adjective describing an approach to change.[11] This last statement ascribes the same factors (emphasis of social responsibility, self-control, and democratic ideals) to the OD approach to change as it does to the goals sought by OD programs.

Whether or not Harvey's purported myths of OD are indeed myths or just "hair splitting" arguments aimed at phrases and definitions composed for convenience is not to be decided here. What is important is that we proceed with our study of OD with a questioning, inquiring, and irreverent attitude. Many practitioners join with Jerry Harvey in suggesting that new vitality, potency, and creativity are needed if OD is to continue its own growth and evolution.

The use of limited models. Another criticism of OD is its reliance upon the use of collaboration models, which frequently increase cohesion within units but fail to deal with organization power issues or with relations to external systems. OD efforts seem to be successful under conditions of trust and collaboration but less able to deal with conditions of distrust, power, and conflict.

As D.D. Warwick suggests, the rapid growth of OD in the public sector has brought out some important issues as to the applicability of OD and presents many difficult obstacles for the OD practitioner.[12] He points out some of the special considerations that evolve when dealing with differing organizational conditions.

The limitations of time and terminality. Jerry B. Harvey has emphasized this point by suggesting that time is an irrelevant variable, or as George Allen, former coach of the Washington Redskins, states: "The future is now!" OD interventions are generally regarded as a long-term, 2- to 5-year process. What about a system that requires immediate change? OD, at this point, offers few short-term improvement techniques that allow rapid change to occur.

OD is usually undertaken in relatively healthy organizations that desire to become more effective. What does OD offer for the self-destructing system? What does it offer organizations in crisis which may be fighting for survival? Is there a need for short-term, crisis OD interventions which can help introduce change under conditions where urgency and survival may be the immediate concern?

FUTURE TRENDS IN ORGANIZATION DEVELOPMENT ⎯⎯⎯⎯⎯⎯⎯⎯

The application of OD technology is growing rapidly. New models, techniques, and approaches are being constantly developed and old techniques discarded. OD itself is facing future shock.

An awareness of the complex environment in which organizations exist is evidenced by the popularity of new trend books in management, such as *In Search of Excellence, Entrepreneurship*, and *Corporate Cultures*. As shapers of change, OD practitioners will play a critical role in helping organizations adjust to the changing forces and trends that affect them.

Because of the rapid changes, predicting the future trends in OD is difficult if not impossible. However, there are a number of "cutting edge" trends which appear to be affecting the future directions of OD[13]:

Macrosystem Trends ⎯⎯⎯⎯⎯⎯⎯⎯⎯⎯⎯⎯⎯⎯⎯⎯⎯

These trends focus on the organizational system, including:

1. *The impact of culture change.* It will become increasingly important to understand the impact of culture on morale, productivity, competence, organizational health, and especially the relationship of culture to strategy.

2. *Total resource utilization.* Another trend which has emerged during this decade is the need for a systems approach to ensure efficient use of the organization's resources. OD practitioners will increasingly be required to work with complex client systems.

3. *Centralization vs. decentralization.* In organizations of the future, it will be necessary to both centralize and decentralize functions, structure, and governance.

4. *Conflict resolution.* Conflict management has become an important element in today's complex organizations, and value and goal differences are continuing problems. Future OD activities should include helping managers to diagnose conflict and to resolve disputes.

5. *Interorganization collaboration.* As limited resources and increased complexity confront the manager of the future, increased sharing, collaboration, and cooperation among organizations will be necessary. Networking offers alternative routes for organizational action.

Human Resource System Trends ⎯⎯⎯⎯⎯⎯⎯⎯⎯⎯⎯⎯⎯

These trends focus on group dynamics including:

1. *Merging line and staff functions.* There is a trend toward reducing layers of management, increasing participation, and developing temporary systems for problem solving. OD specialists may be facilitating teamwork, as-

sisting in "downsizing," and managing the transition to "do more with less" systems.

2. *Resource linking.* As problems become more complex, it becomes important to develop ad hoc problem solving groups.

3. *Integrating QWL and productivity.* An increasing emphasis on productivity and quality suggest future trends for OD practitioners to develop links between the goals of management and improving productivity systems.

4. *Pluralism.* There are increasing trends toward greater heterogeneity of the work force, including multinational corporations and a need for and integration of values and skills.

5. *Networking.* In order for organizations to benefit from knowledge and innovation, efficient systems for identifying and accessing information will be needed.

The Individual Trends

These trends focus on the individual:

1. *Intrinsic worth.* Evidence suggests that intrinsic, not extrinsic, motivation is a factor in stress and its symptoms. The OD practitioner can assist in shared understanding and training to deal with these problems.

2. *Change in individuals.* With an increased emphasis on corporate training and development efforts, the OD practitioner will need to make this process easier and more effective.

3. *The effects of thinking.* The concept of the thinking individual raises the question of corporate values and cultures as belief systems, and offers the OD specialist a vehicle for creating a positive, research-based value system in the organization.

4. *Health and fitness.* Currently, "fitness" models focus on organizational and individual health, and such models will provide an increase in self-selected excellence and fitness approaches for the OD practitioner in the future.

5. *Interdependence.* Finally, the increasing complexity emphasizes the interdependent relationship between the individual and the organization. The OD practitioner attempts to develop synergy among organizational elements.

THE FUTURE OF OD

As a result of the accelerating rate of change in the modern environment, organization development is increasingly viewed and applied as a technique for making organizations more creative, efficient, and competent. OD is the leading edge in the state of the art of planned change. However, there have been numerous critics, including some practitioners, who have expressed dissatisfaction with or questioned the direction and state of OD. Will OD return to its original potency, creativity, and prominence, or will it deteriorate into an unused technology, unable to adapt its own discipline to new challenges?

William E. Halal suggests that due to the steady increase in the size of organizations and their dispersion over wider geographic areas, executives are becoming more in need of a system to obtain information about their organization. He feels that a formalized information system is becoming essential for all organizational operations and that communication barriers, intergroup rivalry, and conflicts are becoming more prevalent. Thus, technology is becoming more complex, and therefore organizations are facing more social trauma.

Halal indicates that there will be an increasing need for OD in the future and for the expansion of OD to include more methods for modifying the behavior of organizations. He also feels that OD will have to become a more comprehensive system, so that models of complete organizations can be constructed and with continued development the OD practitioner will approach greater accuracy in predicting the performance variance in organizations.[14]

Organization development is an expanding and vital technology. A great deal has been accomplished in the past three decades of growth and certainly much more needs to be done in the future. OD is being applied in a multinational framework and in a variety of organizational settings, including industrial, governmental, and health-care institutions. It is agreed by most theorists that there is a need for more empirical studies on the relationship of various intervention processes to other organizational variables. It is widely acknowledged that techniques to deal effectively with external systems and power-coercive problems are yet to emerge.

Yet, the very controversy and questioning of the myths and rituals of OD are themselves an indication of a healthy discipline. When OD practitioners become complacent, when controversy over various approaches and techniques subsides, and when the discipline becomes stagnant, then perhaps there will be an even deeper need to worry about the future of OD.

REVIEW QUESTIONS

1. Identify some of the conditions for success of an OD program.

2. Is OD an emerging discipline or only a passing fad?

3. Do you agree or disagree with the criticisms of OD?

KEY WORDS AND CONCEPTS

Define and be able to use the following:

Monitoring
Stabilizing
Self-renewal capacity
Disengagement

Organizational excellence
Professionalism of OD
Entrepreneurship
In search of excellence

IV.
Simulations

SIMULATION 16.1 CONSULTANT BEHAVIOR PROFILE II[15]

Total time suggested: 1 hour.

A. Purpose

The purpose of this profile is to help you gauge for yourself some aspects of your behavior. During this course you have gained additional opportunities to obtain information about yourself on how you behave in organization situations. This feedback may provide the impetus for you to change, but the ultimate responsibility for that change is with you.

B. Procedures

Part A   Profile Survey

Step 1   Based on the following scale, select the number to indicate the degree to which you feel each description is characteristic of you. Record your choice in the blank to the right.

1	2	3	4	5	6	7
Not at All Characteristic			Somewhat Characteristic			Very Characteristic

1   Having the ability to communicate in a clear, concise, and persuasive manner: _____

2   Being spontaneaous—saying and doing things that seem natural on the spur of the moment: _____

3   Doing things "by the book"—noticing appropriate rules and procedures and following them: _____

4   Being creative—having a lot of unusual, original ideas; thinking of new approaches to problems others do not often come up with: _____

5   Being competitive—wanting to win and be the best: _____

6   Being able to listen to and understand others: _____

7   Being aware of other people's moods and feelings: _____

8 Being careful in your work—taking pains to make sure everything is "just right": _____

9 Being resourceful in coming up with possible ways of dealing with problems: _____

10 Being a leader—having other people look to you for direction; taking over when things are confused: _____

11 Having the ability to accept feedback without reacting defensively, becoming hostile, or withdrawing: _____

12 Having the ability to deal with conflict and anger: _____

13 Having written work neat and organized; making plans before starting on a difficult task; organizing details of work: _____

14 Thinking clearly and logically; attempting to deal with ambiguity, complexity, and confusion in a situation by thoughtful, logical analysis: _____

15 Having self-confidence when faced with a challenging situation: _____

16 Having the ability to level with others, to give feedback to others: _____

17 Doing new and different things; meeting new people; experimenting and trying out new ideas or activities: _____

18 Having a high level of aspiration, setting difficult goals: _____

19 Analyzing a situation carefully before acting; working out a course of action in detail before embarking on it: _____

20 Being effective at initiating projects and innovative ideas: _____

21 Seeking ideas from others; drawing others into discussion: _____

22 Having a tendency to seek close personal relationships, participating in social activities with friends; giving affection and receiving it from others: _____

23 Being dependable—staying on the job; doing what is expected: _____

24 Having the ability to work as a catalyst, to stimulate and encourage others to develop their own resources for solving their own problems: _____

25 Taking responsibility; relying on your own abilities and judgment rather than those of others: _____

26 Selling your own ideas effectively: _____

27 Being the dominant person; having a strong need for control or recognition: _____

28 Getting deeply involved in your work; being extremely committed to ideas or work you are doing: _____

29   Having the ability to evaluate possible solutions critically: _____

30   Having the ability to work in unstructured situations, with little or no support and to continue to work effectively even if faced with lack of cooperation, resistance, or hostility: _____

Step 2   Get together with two other people with whom you have worked. Share the information from your Profile and obtain feedback and perceptions from your partners.

Step 3   In Chapter 2, Simulation 2.1, you first filled in the OD Consultant Behavior Profile I. Transfer your responses to Table 2.1 (Profile Form) by placing a check mark in the appropriate box. Compare the changes in your answers and, with your two partners, discuss whether or not the changes reflected on the Profile seem accurate.

Time suggested for Steps 2 and 3: 30 minutes.

Part B

Working with your consulting partners, develop a set of self-renewal objectives, setting forth how you plan to continue your growth and development.

A.   Objectives   B.   Growth

1. _____   1. _____
2. _____   2. _____
3. _____   3. _____
4. _____   4. _____
5. _____   5. _____
6. _____   6. _____
7. _____   7. _____
8. _____   8. _____
9. _____   9. _____
10. _____   10. _____

Time suggested for Part B: 30 minutes.

SIMULATION 16.2   THE OD CONSULTANT

Total time suggested: 1 hour, 35 minutes.

A.   Purpose

To provide an opportunity to apply the skills you have learned in this course.

B. Procedure

Step 1   Before class, read the Bob Knowlton case and complete individually the questions following the case. Record your answers on the Bob Knowlton Record Form.

Step 2   Using the steps in an OD program, develop a preliminary diagnosis and an OD intervention strategy and how you would suggest solving the problem if you were an OD consultant. Use the Diagnostic/Strategy Form at the end of the case as a guide.

Step 3   Form groups of five or six members each and come up with a team consensus on questions and OD strategies and techniques. Place your answers on the Bob Knowlton Record Form. Each team writes its solution on newsprint or blackboard and discusses differences.

Time suggested for Step 3: 30 minutes.

Step 4   Individually complete the Team Process Profile (Individual Form) and tabulate the individual results on the Team Process Profile (Group Form). Discuss the results.

Time suggested for Step 4: 15 minutes.

Step 5   Using the answers given by the instructor, score your individual and team answers. Where the actual and correct answers match, put +10 in columns (2) and (4) on the Record Form. If the actual and correct answers do not match, put 0 points in columns (2) and (4). By totaling the points, an individual and a team score can be calculated.

Individuals and teams can be compared based on these scores. However, the score may not reflect how effectively decisions were made by the team.

Step 6   Compare and discuss group answers. How many different problems were identified? What different interventions might have been used? Can you come to a class consensus on an OD intervention strategy? Compare team solutions.

Time suggested for Step 6: 30 minutes.

Step 7   As a class, discuss your group and individual self-renewal capability, what it means, how to measure it and so on.

Time suggested for Step 7: 15 minutes.

THE BOB KNOWLTON CASE[16]

Bob Knowlton was sitting alone in the conference room of the laboratory. The rest of the group had gone. One of the secretaries had stopped and talked for a while about her husband's coming induction into the Army, and had finally left. Bob, alone in the laboratory, slid a little further down in his chair, looking with satisfaction at the results of the first test run of the new photon unit.

He liked to stay after the others had gone. His appointment as project head was still new enough to give him a deep sense of pleasure. His eyes were on the graphs before him but in his mind he could hear Dr. Jerrold, the project head, saying again, "There's one thing about this place that you can bank on. The sky is the limit for a man who can produce!" Knowlton felt again the tingle of happiness and embarrassment. Well, dammit, he said to himself, he had produced. He wasn't kidding anybody. He had come to the Simmons Laboratories two years ago. During a routine testing of some rejected Clanson components he had stumbled on the idea of the photon correlator, and the rest just happened. Jerrold had been enthusiastic; a separate project had been set up for further research and development of the device, and he had gotten the job of running it. The whole sequence of events still seemed a little miraculous to Knowlton.

He shrugged out of the reverie and bent determinedly over the sheets when he heard someone come into the room behind him. He looked up expectantly; Jerrold often stayed late himself, and now and then dropped in for a chat. This always made the day's end especially pleasant for Bob. It wasn't Jerrold. The man who had come in was a stranger. He was tall, thin, and rather dark. He wore steel-rimmed glasses and had on a very wide leather belt with a large brass buckle. Lucy remarked later that it was the kind of belt the Pilgrims must have worn.

The stranger smiled and introduced himself, "I'm Simon Fester. Are you Bob Knowlton?" Bob said yes, and they shook hands. "Doctor Jerrold said I might find you in. We were talking about your work, and I'm very much interested in what you are doing." Bob waved to a chair.

Fester didn't seem to belong in any of the standard categories of visitors: customer, visiting fireman, stockholder. Bob pointed to the sheets on the table. "There are the preliminary results of a test we're running. We've got a new gadget by the tail and we're trying to understand it. It's not finished, but I can show you the section that we're testing."

He stood up, but Fester was deep in the graphs. After a moment, he looked up with an odd grin. "These look like plots of a Jennings surface. I've been playing around with some autocorrelation functions of surfaces—you know that stuff." Bob, who had no idea what he was referring to, grinned back and nodded, and immediately felt uncomfortable. "Let me show you the monster," he said, and led the way to the work room.

After Fester left, Knowlton slowly put the graphs away, feeling vaguely annoyed. Then, as if he had made a decision, he quickly locked up and took the long way out so that he would pass Jerrold's office. But the office was locked. Knowlton wondered whether Jerrold and Fester had left together.

The next morning, Knowlton dropped into Jerrold's office, mentioned that he had talked with Fester, and asked who he was. "Sit down for a minute," Jerrold said. "I want to talk to you about him. What do you think of him?" Knowlton replied truthfully that he thought Fester was very bright and probably very competent. Jerrold looked pleased. "We're taking him on," he said. "He's had a very good background in a number of laboratories, and he seems to have ideas about the problems we're tackling here." Knowlton nodded in agreement, instantly wishing that Fester would not be placed with him. "I don't know yet where he will finally land," Jerrold continued, "but he seems interested in what you are doing. I thought he might spend a little time with you by way of getting started." Knowlton nodded thoughtfully. "If his interest in your work continues, you can add him to your group." "Well, he seemed to have some good ideas even without knowing exactly what we are doing," Knowlton answered. "I hope he stays; we'd be glad to have him."

Knowlton walked back to the lab with mixed feelings. He told himself that Fester would be good for the group. He was no dunce, he'd produce. Knowlton thought again of Jerrold's promise when he had promoted him—"the man who produces gets ahead in this outfit." The words seemed to carry the overtones of a threat now.

That day Fester didn't appear until mid-afternoon. He explained that he had had a long lunch with Jerrold, discussing his place in the lab. "Yes," said Knowlton, "I talked with Jerry this morning about it, and we both thought you might work with us for awhile." Fester smiled in the same knowing way that he had smiled when he mentioned the Jennings surfaces. "I'd like to," he said. Knowlton introduced Fester to the other members of the lab. Fester and Link, the mathematician of the group, hit it off well together, and spent the rest of the afternoon discussing a method of analysis of patterns that Link had been worrying over for the last month.

It was 6:30 when Knowlton finally left the lab that night. He had waited almost eagerly for the end of the day to come—when they would all be gone and he could sit in the quiet rooms, relax, and think it over. "Think what over?" he asked himself. He didn't know. Shortly after 5:00 P.M. they had all gone except Fester, and what followed was almost a duel. Knowlton was annoyed that he was being cheated out of his quiet period, and finally resentfully determined that Fester should leave first.

Fester was sitting at the conference table reading, and Knowlton was sitting at the desk in the little glass-enclosed cubby that he used during the day when he needed to be undisturbed. Fester had gotten the last year's progress reports out and was studying them carefully. The time dragged. Knowlton doodled on a pad, the tension growing inside him. What the hell did Fester think he was going to find in the reports?

Knowlton finally gave up and they left the lab together. Fester took several of the reports with him to study in the evening. Knowlton asked him if he thought the reports gave a clear picture of the lab's activities. "They're excellent," Fester answered with obvious sincerity. "They're not only good reports; what they report is damn good, too!" Knowlton was surprised at the relief he felt, and grew almost jovial as he said goodnight.

Driving home, Knowlton felt more optimistic about Fester's presence in the lab. He had never fully understood the analysis that Link was attempting. If there was anything wrong with Link's approach, Fester would probably spot it, "And if I'm any judge," he murmured, "he won't be especially diplomatic about it."

He described Fester to his wife, who was amused by the broad leather belt and the brass buckle. "It's the kind of belt that Pilgrims must have worn," she laughed. "I'm not worried about how he holds his pants up," he laughed with her. "I'm afraid that he's the kind that just has to make like a genius twice each day. And that can be pretty rough on the group."

Knowlton had been asleep for several hours when he was jerked awake by the telephone. He realized it had rung several times. He swung off the bed muttering about damn fools and telephones. It was Fester. Without any excuses, apparently oblivious of the time, he plunged into an excited recital of how Link's patterning problem could be solved. Knowlton covered the mouthpiece to answer his wife's stage-whispered "Who is it?" "It's the genius," replied Knowlton.

Fester, completely ignoring the fact that it was 2:00 in the morning, proceeded in a very excited way to start in the middle of an explanation of a completely new approach to certain of the photon lab problems that he had stumbled on while analyzing past experiments. Knowlton managed to put some enthusiasm in his own voice and stood there, half-dazed and very uncomfortable, listening to Fester talk endlessly about what he had discovered. It was probably not only a new approach, but also an analysis which showed the inherent weakness of the previous experiment and how experimentation along that line would certainly have been inconclusive. The following day Knowlton spent the entire morning with Fester and Link, the mathematician, the customary morning meeting of Bob's group having been called off so that Fester's work of the previous night could be gone over intensively. Fester was very anxious that this be done and Knowlton was not too unhappy to call the meeting off for reasons of his own.

For the next several days Fester sat in the back office that had been turned over to him and did nothing but read the progress reports of the work that had been done in the last six months. Knowlton caught himself feeling apprehensive about the reaction that Fester might have to some of his work. He was a little surprised at his own feelings. He had always been proud—although he had put on a convincingly modest face—of the way in which new ground in the study of photon measuring devices had been broken in his group. Now he wasn't sure, and it seemed to him that Fester might easily show that the line of research they had been following was unsound or even unimaginative.

The next morning, as was the custom, the members of the lab, including the girls, sat around a conference table. Bob always prided himself on the fact that the work of the lab was guided and evaluated by the group as a whole and he was fond of repeating that it was not a waste of time to include secretaries in such meetings. Often, what started out as a boring recital of fundamental assumptions, to a naive listener, uncovered new ways of regarding these assumptions that would not have occurred to the researcher who had long ago accepted them as a necessary basis for his work.

These group meetings also served Bob in another sense. He admitted to himself that he would have felt far less secure if he had had to direct the work out of his own mind, so to speak. With the group-meeting as the principle of leadership, it was always possible to justify the exploration of blind alleys because of the general educative effect on the team. Fester was there; Lucy and Martha were there; Link was sitting next to Fester, their conversation concerning Link's mathematical study apparently continuing from yesterday. The other members, Bob Davenport, George Thurlow and Arthur Oliver, were waiting quietly.

Knowlton, for reasons that he didn't quite understand, proposed for discussion this morning a problem that all of them had spent a great deal of time on previously, with the conclusion that a solution was impossible, that there was no feasible way of treating it in an experimental fashion. When Knowlton proposed the problem, Davenport remarked that there was hardly any use of going over it again, that he was satisfied that there was no way of approaching the problem with the equipment and the physical capacities of the lab.

This statement had the effect of a shot of adrenalin on Fester. He said he would like to know what the problem was in detail and, walking to the blackboard, began setting down the "factors" as various members of the group began discussing the problem and simultaneously listing the reasons why it had been abandoned.

Very early in the description of the problem it was evident that Fester was going to disagree about the impossibility of attacking it. The group realized this and finally the descriptive materials and their recounting of the reasoning that had led to its abandonment dwindled away. Fester began his statement which, as it proceeded, might well have been prepared the previous night although Knowlton knew this was impossible. He couldn't help being impressed with the organized and logical way that Fester was presenting ideas that must have occurred to him only a few minutes before.

Fester had some things to say, however, which left Knowlton with a mixture of annoyance, irritation and, at the same time, a rather smug feeling of superiority over Fester in at least one area. Fester was of the opinion that the way that the problem had been analyzed was really typical of group-thinking and, with an air of sophistication which made it difficult for a listener to dissent, he proceeded to comment on the American emphasis on team ideas, satirically describing the ways in which they led to a "high level of mediocrity."

During this time, Knowlton observed that Link stared studiously at the floor, and he was very conscious of George Thurlow's and Bob Davenport's glances toward him at several points of Fester's little speech. Inwardly, Knowlton couldn't help feeling that this was one point at least in which Fester was off on the wrong foot. The whole lab, following Jerry's lead, talked if not practiced the theory of small research teams as the basic organization for effective research. Fester insisted that the problem could be approached and that he would like to study it for a while himself.

Knowlton ended the morning session by remarking that the meetings would continue and that the very fact that a supposedly insoluble experimental problem was now going to get another chance was another indication of the value of such meetings. Fester immediately remarked that he was not at all averse to meetings for the purpose of informing the group of the progress of its members—that the point he wanted to make was that creative advances were seldom accomplished in such meetings, that they were made by the individual "living with" the problem closely and continuously, a sort of personal relationship to it.

Knowlton went on to say to Fester that he was very glad Fester had raised these points and that he was sure the group would profit by re-examining the basis on which they had been operating. Knowlton agreed that individual effort was probably the basis for making the major advances, but that he considered the group meetings useful primarily because of the effect they had on keeping the group together and on helping the weaker members of the group keep up with the ones who were able to advance more easily and quickly in the analysis of problems.

It was clear as days went by and meetings continued that Fester came to enjoy them because of the pattern which the meetings assumed. It became typical for Fester to hold forth and it was unquestionably clear that he was more brilliant, better prepared on the various subjects which were germane to the problems being studied, and that he was more capable of going ahead than anyone there. Knowlton grew increasingly disturbed as he realized that his leadership of the group had been, in fact, taken over.

Whenever the subject of Fester was mentioned, in occasional meetings with Dr. Jerrold, Knowlton would comment only on the ability and obvious capacity for work that Fester had. Somehow he never felt that he could mention his own discomforts, not only because they revealed a weakness on his own part, but also because it was quite clear that Jerrold himself was considerably impressed with Fester's work and with the contacts he had with him outside the photon laboratory.

Knowlton now began to feel that perhaps the intellectual advantages that Fester had brought to the group did not quite compensate for what he felt were evidences of a breakdown in the cooperative spirit he had seen in the group before Fester's coming. More and more of the morning meetings were skipped. Fester's opinion concerning the abilities of others of the group, with the exception of Link, was obviously low. At times, during morning meetings or in smaller discussions, he had been on the point of rudeness, refusing to pursue an argument when he claimed it was based on the other person's ignorance of the facts involved. His impatience of others led him to also make similar remarks to Dr. Jerrold. Knowlton inferred this from a conversation with Jerrold in which Jerrold asked whether Davenport and Oliver were going to be continued on; and his failure to mention Link, the mathematician, led Knowlton to feel that this was the result of private conversations between Fester and Jerrold.

It was not difficult for Knowlton to make a quite convincing case on whether the brilliance of Fester was sufficient recompense for the beginning of this breaking up of the group. He took the opportunity to speak privately with Davenport and with Oliver and it was quite clear that both of them were uncomfortable because of Fester. Knowlton didn't press the discussion beyond the point of hearing them in one way or another say that they did feel awkward and that it was sometimes difficult for them to understand the arguments he advanced, but often embarrassing to ask him to fill in the background on which his arguments were based. Knowlton did not interview Link in this manner.

About six months after Fester's coming into the photon lab, a meeting was scheduled in which the sponsors of the research were coming in to get some idea of the work and its progress. It was customary at these meetings for project heads to present the research being conducted in their groups. The members of each group were invited to other meetings which were held later in the day and open to all, but the special meetings were usually made up only of project heads, the head of the laboratory, and the sponsors.

As the time for the special meeting approached, it seemed to Knowlton that he must avoid the presentation at all cost. His reasons for this were that he could not trust himself to present the ideas and work that Fester had advanced, because of his apprehension as to whether he could present them in sufficient detail and answer such questions about them as might be asked. On the other hand, he did not feel he could ignore these newer lines of work and present only the material that he had done or that had been started before Fester's arrival. He felt also that it would not be beyond Fester at all, in his blunt and undiplomatic way—if he were present at the meeting, that is—to make comments on his [Knowlton's] presentation and reveal Knowlton's inadequacy. It also seemed quite clear that it would not be easy to keep Fester from attending the meeting, even though he was not on the administrative level of those invited.

Knowlton found an opportunity to speak to Jerrold and raised the question. He remarked to Jerrold that, with the meetings coming up and with the interest in the work and with the contributions that Fester had been making, he would probably like to come to these meetings, but there was a question of the feelings of the others in the group if Fester alone were invited. Jerrold passed this over very lightly by saying that he didn't think the group would fail to understand Fester's rather different position and that he thought that Fester by all means should be invited. Knowlton then immediately said he had thought so, too; that Fester should present the work because much of it was work he had done; and, as Knowlton put it, that this would be a nice way to recognize Fester's contributions and to reward him, as he was eager to be recognized as a productive member of the lab. Jerrold agreed, and so the matter was decided.

Fester's presentation was very successful and in some ways dominated the meeting. He attracted the interest and attention of many of those who had come, and a long discussion followed his presentation. Later in the evening—with the entire laboratory staff present—in the cocktail period before the dinner, a little circle of people formed about Fester. One of them was Jerrold himself, and a lively discussion took place concerning the application of Fester's theory. All of this disturbed Knowlton, and his reaction and behavior were characteristic. He joined the circle, praised Fester to Jerrold and to others, and remarked on the brilliance of the work.

Knowlton, without consulting anyone, began at this time to take some interest in the possibility of a job elsewhere. After a few weeks he found that a new laboratory of considerable size was being organized in a nearby city, and that the kind of training he had would enable him to get a project head job equivalent to the one he had at the lab, with slightly more money.

He immediately accepted it and notified Jerrold by a letter, which he mailed on a Friday night to Jerrold's home. The letter was quite brief, and Jerrold was stunned. The letter merely said that he had found a better position; that there were personal reasons why he didn't want to appear at the lab any more; that he would be glad to come back at a later time from where he would be, some forty miles away, to assist if there was any mixup at all in the past work; that he felt sure that Fester could, however, supply any leadership that was required for the group; and that his decision to leave so suddenly was based on some personal problems—he hinted at problems of health in his family, his mother and father. All of this was fictitious, of course. Jerrold took it at face value but still felt that this was very strange behavior and quite unaccountable, for he had always felt his relationship with Knowlton had been warm and that Knowlton was satisfied and, as a matter of fact, quite happy and productive.

Jerrold was considerably disturbed, because he had already decided to place Fester in charge of another project that was going to be set up very soon. He had been wondering how to explain this to Knowlton, in view of the obvious help Knowlton was getting from Fester and the high regard in which he held him. Jerrold had, as a matter of fact, considered the possibility that Knowlton could add to his staff another person with the kind of background and training that had been unique in Fester and had proved so valuable.

Jerrold did not make any attempt to meet Knowlton. In a way, he felt aggrieved about the whole thing. Fester, too, was surprised at the suddenness of Knowlton's departure and when Jerrold, in talking to him, asked him whether he had reasons to prefer to stay with the photon group instead of the project for the Air Force which was being organized, he chose the Air Force project and went on to that job the following week. The photon lab was hard hit. The leadership of the lab was given to Link with the understanding that this would be temporary until someone could come in to take over.

THE BOB KNOWLTON CASE: QUESTIONS

1. The matrix organization structure violates which of the following principles:

    a. Importance of decentralization.
    b. Unity of command.
    c. Keeping the chain of command limited.
    d. Mixing types of departmentation.

2. Fester's role in the organization was determined by:

    a. A set of expectations.
    b. The formal organization structure.
    c. Based on the authority of the position.
    d. Largely his personality.

3. Jerrold's approach to leadership included:

    a. Providing direction and performing management functions.
    b. Influencing others and setting goals.
    c. Providing direction and influence.
    d. Influencing and pressuring to produce.

4. Jerrold's decision to promote Fester was based upon:

    a. Leadership traits.
    b. Leadership behavior.
    c. Situational factors.
    d. Contingency factors.

5. In Bob's group, which is most correct:

    a. Conflict was successfully managed.
    b. Conflict indicates that problems exist in the organization.
    c. Conflict is something to be avoided.
    d. Conflict is only damaging when it is unresolved.

6. In this organization one problem was:

    a. Getting too many people with conflicting opinions involved in the decisions.

    b. Collecting "yes" men who did not encourage diversity of opinion.

    c. Considering how others would react to decisions.

    d. Delegating too many decisions for others.

7. Jerrold's managerial style (see Chapter 4) is predominately:

    a. Craftsman

    b. Jungle fighter

    c. Company Man

    d. Gamesman

8. Bob's managerial style is predominately:

    a. Craftsman

    b. Jungle fighter

    c. Company Man

    d. Gamesman

9. Fester's style is predominately:

    a. Craftsman

    b. Jungle Fighter

    c. Company Man

    d. Gamesman

10. The main cause of the problem is:

    a. Jerrold

    b. Knowlton

    c. Fester

    d. The organization

DIAGNOSTIC/STRATEGY FORM

Individual	A. Problem	B. Target System	C. Intervention
1.	_____	_____	_____
2.	_____	_____	_____
3.	_____	_____	_____
4.	_____	_____	_____
5.	_____	_____	_____

Team
Consensus   6. _____   _____   _____

7. _____   _____   _____

8. _____   _____   _____

9. _____   _____   _____

10. _____   _____   _____

BOB KNOWLTON RECORD FORM

Question	(1) Individual Answer	(2) Individual Score	(3) Correct Answer	(4) Team Score	(5) Team Answer
1					
2					
3					
4					
5					
6					
7					
8					
9					
10					
	Individual Score		Team Score		

TEAM PROCESS PROFILE
(INDIVIDUAL FORM)

Instructions: For each item, place a number in the blank to the right representing your reaction to how your group performed based on the following scale.

Low 1 : 2 : 3 : 4 : 5 : 6 : 7 : 8 : 9 : 10 High

1 Degree of cooperative teamwork: _____

2 Degree of team motivation: _____

3 Degree of member satisfaction: _____

4 Degree of information sharing (participation): _____

5 Degree of consensual decision making: _____

6 Degree of team conflict or competition (i.e., conflict directly faced and resolved): _____

7 Degree of quality of group decisions: _____

8 Degree of speed with which decision is made: _____

9 Degree of participating leadership: _____

10 Degree of clarity of goals: _____

Total ranking _____

TEAM PROCESS PROFILE (GROUP FORM)

INDIVIDUAL RATINGS

Item	Names of Individuals								Total	Average
1										
2										
3										
4										
5										
6										
7										
8										
9										
10										
Totals										

SIMULATION 16.3   UNFINISHED BUSINESS

A. Purpose

You will soon be leaving this organization, and this simulation is intended to provide you an opportunity to bring the class to a close. More specifically, it will allow you to clear up any questions you may have about the content of the subject matter.

B. Procedure

You are encouraged to share any thoughts, feelings, opinions, and so forth, that you may have relative to the class and its members. There is no format to this simulation. It is suggested that it be conducted as an informal discussion.

V.
Summary

In this book we have examined the practice and application of organization development as an approach to planned change. It seems fair to say that despite criticism and controversy, OD is a growing, developing, and workable discipline. OD has come a long way in the past three decades, since its inception by Douglas McGregor, Richard Beckhard, Robert Blake, and Herbert Shepard in their early work with organizational systems. Since that time, an array of new intervention techniques, methodologies, and applications have evolved. Still, many practitioners feel OD has become too ritualized, that the field lacks rigorous empirical foundations, and that it fails to deal with critical issues.

As you have probably noted, there is a wide divergence of opinion over what are or should be called OD interventions and also whether or not certain interventions lead to successful outcomes.

One problem is that much of the research supporting various OD activities has either been biased or failed to be replicated with similar results. Consequently, one study may suggest that a certain intervention has been very effective within an organization, whereas a second similar study finds just the opposite: a complete lack of positive impact. Given much conflicting data, how is one to evaluate the various methodologies, strategies, and interventions that may be utilized in an OD program?

A second problem is that of overgeneralization on limited or short-term data. In a number of instances, very positive initial reports have initiated a "halo effect," so that everyone tries to duplicate an apparent success only to discover later that the final outcome is not as positive as initial reports appeared.

One example of this at a food plant involved an OD program based upon the team concept, in which self-managed work teams were assigned areas of responsibility. The program had some very positive results, but other pressures emerged and analysts reported later that the program seemed to be deteriorating. The OD program resulted in lower unit costs, decreased turnover, and lower accident rates, but external pressures from the power system seemed to be posing new problems, which may have affected long-term results.

In conclusion, it is not believed that OD is merely a passing fad. We are optimistic about the future of OD and believe that it will continue to grow and be more widely used. This growth will not result from more practitioners moving into the OD field or because more techniques become available, but because the problems of adapting to a more rapidly changing world create the need for expanded use of OD. As more organizations seek to achieve organizational excellence, there will be a parallel growth in the need for new OD models, new OD strategies, new OD interventions, and new OD practitioner roles in the future.

NOTES

1. F. Friedlander and L. Brown, "Organization Development," *Annual Review of Psychology*, 25 (1974), 336.

2. See John B. Miner "The Validity and Usefulness of Theories in an Emerging Organizational Science," *Academy of Management Review*, 9, no. 2 (April 1984), 535–41; and R.J. Bullock and Patti F. Bullock, "Pure Science Versus Science-Action Models of Data Feedback," *Group and Organization Studies*, 9, no. 1 (March 1984); 22–27.

3. A. Armenakis, H. Field, and D. Mosley, "Evaluation Guidelines for the OD Practitioner," *Personnel Journal*, February 1975.

4. G. Watson and E. Glaser, "What Have We Learned about Planning for Change?" *Management Review*, November 1965, p. 45.

5. "TRW: Digging Deeper," *Business Week*, July 1, 1985, p. 80.

6. E. Schein, *Process Consultation: Its Role in Organization Development* (Reading, Mass.: Addison-Wesley Publishing Co., Inc., 1969), p. 129.

7. Larry Greiner, "Patterns of Organizational Change," *Harvard Business Review*, May–June 1967, pp. 119–230.

8. E. Huse, *Organization Development* (New York: West Publishing Co., 1975), p. 8.

9. "Business Fads—What's In and Out," *Business Week*, January 20, 1986, pp. 52–61.

10. G. Strauss, "Organization Development: Credits and Debits," in *The Management Process*, 2nd ed., S. Carrol, F. Pline, and J. Mower, eds. (New York: Macmillan Inc., 1977). p. 404.

11. J. Harvey, "Eight Myths OD Consultants Believe In—and Die By," *OD Practitioner*, February 1975.

12. D. D. Warwick, "Applying OD to the Public System," *Personnel Management*, May 1976.

13. Gordon Lippitt, Ronald Lippitt, and Clayton Lafferty, "Cutting Edge Trends in Organization Development," *Training and Development Journal*, 38, no. 7 (July 1984), 59–62.

14. W. Halal, "Organizational Development in the Future," *California Management Review*, Spring 1974.

15. For information on a computerized management survey for use in organizations, please contact the authors.

16. We are indebted to Professor Alex Bavelas, of Stanford University, for the use of this case and it is used with his permission.

INDEX

Action research, 44, 207
Active listening, 177, 182–83
Adaptive organization, 8, 27, 34,
    37–40, 65, 67, 68
Analysis of data, 137–38
Analytical model, 128–29
Anticipative management, 27, 38, 40,
    63, 69, 406, 415

Behavioral intervention, 123, 197–205
Biofeedback, 207, 232

Career, 227
Career counseling, 233

Career life planning, 207, 221, 226–28
Career planning. (*see* Career life
    planning)
Change:
    acceptance, 158–60, 405
    model, 157–58
    resistance, 66, 102, 152–53, 160–67,
      205
    resisting forces, 160–67
    stabilization, 407–8
    strategies, 125, 163–67, 198–97
Client contact, 96
Client motivation, 102, 158–60
Client sponsor, 96
Client system, 41, 96, 123, 133–40,
    158, 200, 367

Client. (*see* Consultant-client relationship)
Climate, 41, 63, 101–4, 136, 139, 205, 232, 340, 413
Climate survey, 42
Clique, 135
Closed questions, 136–37
Closed system, 29–30
Cohesiveness, 255–59
Collaboration, 4, 67, 86, 91, 102, 105–6, 125, 161, 251, 292, 365, 412, 416
Collage, 136
Communication, 45, 90, 100, 133, 163–64, 177, 178, 180, 182–83, 223–26, 250, 258, 281, 287, 289–90, 292, 314, 339, 345, 365, 367, 406
Communication networks, 124
Competition, 90, 282, 284–85, 286–88, 313, 364, 365
Conflict, 259, 281–83, 285–86, 288–89
Confrontation, 290–91
Confrontation meeting, 200, 291–93, 364
Consensus, 179
Conservative management, 38, 39
Consultant, 40–41, 156, 163–67, 201 (*see also* Consultant-client relationship)
  agreeable style, 88–91
  analytical style, 88–91
  characteristics, 55–56
  client relationship, 96–101
  communication process, 100
  definition, 4–5
  external, 44–45, 84–87, 93–94, 104–5, 156, 163, 339
  external-internal team, 86–87
  initial intervention, 95–101
  integrative style, 89–92, 94–95
  internal, 44–45, 84–87, 93, 156, 410
  persuasive style, 89–91
  process, 94–95, 177–82, 207, 315, 368
  supportive style, 89–91
  types, 87–91
Consultant-client relationship, 45, 96–105, 141, 160, 177

contract, 104–5
dependency, 99–100
ground rules, 104
modes, 102–4
power, 103–4, 105
red flags, 105–6
termination, 48, 408–12
trust, 100–102
Content, 41–42, 178, 183
Contingency approach, 33, 201
Contingency theory, 34
Cooperation, 90, 128, 286–88, 289, 365
Creative individualism, 13
Culture, 7–9, 11–13, 33, 62–73, 91, 126, 138–39, 154, 157–58, 162–63, 346, 363, 364, 384–93, 408, 417, 418
  definition, 11, 64

Data collection, 91, 124, 131–39, 197, 260–61, 367–69
  analysis of data, 124, 137–38
  evaluation of effectiveness, 138–39
  implementation, 137
  methods, 133–37
  red flags, 139–41
Decentralization, 126, 207
Decision making, 90, 124, 178–79
Dependency, 99–100
Diagnosis, 46–47, 92, 122–41, 160, 197, 293
  definition, 123–24
Diagnostic models, 128–31
Differentiation-integration model, 128
Dilemma interactions, 99
Directed interview, 136
Direct observation, 136–37
Disequilibrium, 44, 46, 47, 84, 123, 407
Driving forces, 130–31
Dynamic equilibrium, 30

Effectiveness, 2–4, 41, 42, 43, 47, 69, 154, 157, 197, 201, 281, 282, 284, 288, 335, 365, 369–70, 385, 387, 412

Efficiency, 68, 84, 89
Emergent-group behavior model, 129
Empathy, 182–83
Entrepreneur, 67–68
Equilibrium, 130, 407
Ethics, 69–73 (*see also* Organization
    Development, goals and values)
Excellence, 65–66, 154, 363, 366, 415
Experiential learning, 14–16
External consultant. (*see* Consultant,
    external)

Family groups, 367
Feedback, 30, 124–25, 129, 134, 177,
    180, 182–83, 225–26, 230, 282,
    291, 293, 311, 316, 341–43, 364,
    367–69, 405, 406–7
Force-field analysis, 129–31
Future shock, 2, 27, 28, 33–34, 154,
    412, 417

Gap analysis, 127
Goal, 30, 31–32, 42, 64, 69, 128–29,
    133, 198, 207, 227, 230, 251,
    254, 261, 281, 283, 284, 289,
    310–20, 339, 364, 385, 406, 412,
    416, 417
Goal setting, 124, 207, 227, 310–20,
    370
Goals and values of OD. (*see*
    Organization Development,
    goals and values)
Grid OD, 207
Group, 135, 254, 255, 281
Group effectiveness, 41, 182
Group problem solving, 124
Group process. (*see* Process)
Groupthink, 256–57

Hawthorne effect, 139, 293, 407
Hygiene, 340

Ideal strategic model, 365
Information, 35, 131–32

Information collection, 46
Interdependence, 28, 30, 281
Interface, 281, 292, 365
Intergroup collaboration, 281–83, 292
Intergroup competition, 284–85
Intergroup conflict, 281–83, 285–86,
    288–89, 292
Intergroup cooperation, 286–88, 289
Intergroup development, 47, 207, 365
Intergroup development interventions,
    206–7, 281–93, 365
Intergroup operating problems, 283–86
Intergroup relations, 281
Intergroup team-building, 46, 291–93,
    366
Intergroup techniques, 206–7, 289–93
Internal consultant. (*see* Consultant,
    internal)
Interpersonal interventions, 206–7,
    221–33
Interpersonal skills, 221–33, 253
Intervention, 87, 91–101, 125, 415, 419
    definition, 93
    strategies, 197–202
    techniques, 47, 97, 197, 200, 205–7
Interview, 46, 136–38, 291, 406–7
Isolates, 135

Job burnout, 230–32, 233
Job characteristics theory, 341–44
Job content, 336
Job context, 336
Job design, 207, 334, 335, 339–44
Job enrichment, 207, 335, 336, 340–41,
    343–44
Johari Window, 21, 223–26

Laboratory learning, 9, 47, 207,
    221–23, 227, 407
Laboratory training. (*see* Laboratory
    learning)
Leadership, 41, 90, 101–2, 124, 178,
    179–80, 221, 255, 287, 345, 367,
    407
Likert's system 4. (*see* System 4)

Maintenance functions, 178–80
Management by objectives, 47, 207, 228, 310, 314–20, 406
Managerial Grid, 9, 47, 200, 207, 221, 363–64, 407–8
Matrix organization, 46, 82, 285, 289
Meta goals, 289–90
Motivating forces, 158–60, 163–67
Motivational climate, 68
Motivators, 340–41
Mutual choice, 135

Natural work team, 251
Nondirected interview, 137
Nonverbal communication, 177
Norms, 11–12, 41, 129, 136, 138–39, 162–63, 178, 179, 205, 254, 255, 257, 263, 281, 286, 365, 385, 389, 408
  peripheral, 12–13
  pivotal, 12–13

One-way choice, 135
Open-ended questions, 136–37
Open loop, 282
Open system, 29–31, 362
Organization climate. (see Climate)
Organization development:
  diagnostic process, 2–5, 122–41, 406, 411
  evaluation of program, 408–9
  future, 412–19
  goals and values, 68–73, 91, 102
  history, 9–10
  intergroup interventions, 280–93
  interpersonal interventions, 220–33
  intervention strategies, 196–207
  process skills, 176–83
  productivity interventions, 333–47
  stages, 42–48
  strategy interventions, 383–93
  system-wide interventions, 361–72
  team development interventions, 247–64
  termination, 410–12

Organization effectiveness. (see Effectiveness)
Organization excellence. (see Excellence)
Organization mirror, 47, 207, 291, 407

Parkinson's laws, 205
Participant observer, 42
Participation, 164–66, 230, 252–53, 312, 314, 344, 369
Perceptions, 96–97, 102, 368, 369
Performance gap, 125, 127–28, 130, 197
Personal interventions. (see Interpersonal interventions)
Personality conflict, 285–86
Planned change, 40–42
Power, 48, 97, 99, 103, 105–6, 133, 157, 162, 166–67, 178, 285, 290, 292, 362, 392, 416, 419
Power tools, 67–68
Problem identification, 124–25
Problem, symptoms. (see Symptoms)
Process, 41–42, 178–80, 257, 258, 334, 346
Process consultant. (see Consultant, process)
Process interventions, 180–81
Process observation, 41
Productivity intervention, 333–47
Psychological contract, 13–14
Psychosocial system, 31–32, 221

Quality circles, 47, 203, 207, 334, 335, 344–47
Quality of work life, 207, 334–39, 406, 418
Quasi-stationary equilibrium, 130
Questionnaire, 46, 128, 134, 137, 291, 367, 369, 407

Reactive management, 38, 39, 63, 314, 415
Resistance to change. (see Change, resistance)

Resisting forces, 160–67
Restraining forces, 130
Role, 263
Role ambiguity, 263–64, 285
Role analysis, 207, 248, 263–64
Role conception, 263–64
Role conflict, 263–64, 285
Role expectation, 263–64
Role negotiation, 207, 248, 262–63
Role playing, 292

Satisficing management, 38, 39–40
Satisfiers, 340–41
Secondary sources, 133–34
Selective perception, 98–100, 140, 161
Self-renewal, 405, 409–10
Socialization, 12–13, 226–27
Social responsibility, 8, 35, 70, 335–36
    (see also Ethics)
Sociogram, 135, 178
Sociometric approach, 134–35
Sociotechnical system, 31–33, 129, 362
Star, 135
Strategic change management, 384,
    391–92
Strategy, 197
Strategy-culture matrix, 384, 387–91
Strategy intervention, 384–93, 417
Stream analysis, 203–4
Stress management, 207, 221, 228–33
Structural intervention, 123, 128,
    197–205
Structure, 8, 31–32, 43, 126, 128, 154,
    157, 180, 198, 205, 384
Suboptimization, 284
Subsystem, 30–33, 128, 129, 198, 281,
    282, 285, 362, 407
Survey, 134, 136, 138, 367–69
Survey feedback, 9–10, 200, 207, 362,
    367–69
Survey research, 9–10, 367–69
Symptoms, 124, 141

System, 22–29, 43, 128, 129, 154, 335,
    362, 370, 391–92, 405, 410
System 4, 207, 362, 369–70
System approach, 27, 28–31, 43, 232,
    346, 362–72, 412, 415, 417
System intervention, 362–72

Task activities, 41, 178–80, 283
Team, 32, 251, 257
Team building, 46, 47, 200, 207, 221,
    248, 250, 259, 407, 410 (see also
    Team development)
Team development, 248–64, 364, 407
    (see also Team building)
  cohesiveness, 255–57
  need for, 251–54
  problems, 254–55
  role analysis, 207, 248, 263–64
  role negotiation, 207, 248, 262–63
  steps in, 259–62
Team interventions, 206–7, 248
Teamwork, 48, 248, 281, 366
Technical intervention, 123, 162,
    197–205
Temporary task team, 251
Termination, 408–12
Thematic apperception test, 135–36
Third-party consultation, 290–91
Third-party intervention. (see Third-
    party consultation)
Transcendental meditation, 232–33

Values, 64, 134, 136, 159, 167, 197,
    201, 205, 258, 282, 385, 389,
    392, 406, 412, 413, 415, 417,
    418 (see also Organization
    Development, goals and values)
  conflicts, 70–73, 101–2

Wellness program, 233